Science and Engineering Mathematics with the HP 49 G

VOLUME II
Uni- and Multi-Variate Calculus, Ordinary and Partial Differential Equations, Statistics

ISBN 1-58898-044-8

Science and Engineering Mathematics with the HP 49 G

VOLUME II
Uni- and Multi-Variate Calculus, Ordinary
and Partial Differential Equations, Statistics

Gilberto E. Urroz, Ph.D., P.E.
greatunpublished.com
No. 44

Science and Engineering Mathematics with the HP 49 G

VOLUME II
Uni- and Multi-Variate Calculus, Ordinary and Partial Differential Equations, Statistics

To my professors at the Iowa Institute of Hydraulic Research and Department of Civil and Environmental Engineering, University of Iowa, (1981-1988):

- Dr. Robert Ettema
- Dr. John F. Kennedy
- Dr. Enzo O. Macagno
- Dr. Forrest Holly
- Dr. Peter Kitanidis
- Dr. Subhash C. Jain
- Dr. Virendra C. Patel
- Dr. Belagavadhi Ramaprian
- Dr. Allen T. Chwang
- Dr. Tatsuaki Nakato
- Dr. C. J. Chen

Their courses and research projects opened up for me a whole universe of applications of advanced mathematics.

Table of contents

14 Multivariate and vector calculus 77

15
Differential equations 167

16 Partial Differential Equations and Fourier transforms 268

17 Statistical applications 302

Preface

This book covers a variety of Analysis-based mathematics utilizing the amazing algebraic, numerical, and graphical capabilities of the HP 49 G calculator. The book emphasizes the practical applications of mathematics to engineering and the physical sciences. Each chapter includes a review of the mathematical concepts used, a description of the appropriate calculator features, and examples showing their application.

This book is the result of many years of experience in teaching courses on:

- Engineering Mechanics II (Dynamics),
- Uncertainty in Engineering Analysis (i.e., probability and statistics applied to engineering),
- Hydraulics,
- Fluid Mechanics, and
- Numerical Methods in Engineering

in which the use of the programmable calculators HP 48 G/G+/GX and HP 49 G has been emphasized. Many of the examples presented throughout the book had been published previously as class handouts and class notes. In the preparation of my courses, and even in some research activities, I have developed many User RPL programs for the HP 48 G/G+/GX and the HP 49 G, a good number of which are also included in this book.

The book, in its present form, developed from a set of class notes I prepared in the Spring of the year 2000 for a colleague's Engineering Freshmen Seminar class. The HP 48 series calculator has been required from our engineering students since the HP 48 SX was introduced back in the early 1990's. This year, the HP 49 G made its debut among the Freshmen class, therefore, there was a need to produce some training material using this calculator. The task fell on me, given my extensive experience with the HP 48 G series calculator, and my familiarity with the HP 49 G calculator since it first came out in August of 1999. The 23-page-long handout I produced for my colleague's class, together with the class notes I have prepared for the HP 48 G series calculator through the last six years, plus long hours of typing away in my computer, have developed into the book you now have in your hands.

The reader should think of this book as a mathematics handbook that emphasizes the extraordinary capabilities of the HP 49 G calculator in demonstrating different mathematical concepts. While I have made the effort of introducing those concepts before using them in each chapter, detailed explanation of mathematical concepts and proofs of theorems used in this book is to be found in more traditional mathematical textbooks. A list of references is provided in the book for that purpose.

Although the calculator includes features useful in number theory and in operations with number bases other than decimal, the book does not expand on these subjects beyond some basic description of the appropriate functions. The reason for this omission is the lack of experience of the author in those subjects. Please keep in mind that the author's training is in Civil and Environmental Engineering, where the emphasis is in Analysis-based mathematics.

Get yourself a notebook: I recommend that you go through the book armed with your calculator and a notebook. You want to have a notebook handy because sometimes the calculator display is not large enough to hold all the information you want to see when solving a given problem. Also, you may want to keep your own notes on particular types of operations with the calculator that are of interest to you.

1

A note about RPN: While the calculator uses the algebraic mode by default, I make it clear from the start that the book emphasizes the Reverse Polish Notation (RPN) mode. The emphasis on RPN mode is not only because it is the mode that most HP 48 G series users are familiar with, but because it is more efficient than the algebraic mode in using the calculator display. I should also point out that the HP 49 G converts function calls and programs into RPN mode when performing operations. Therefore, it is useful that the user learn the RPN mode to better understand the workings of the calculator, and to be able to communicate with the wide community of HP 48/49 calculator users around the world.

Preferred calculator settings: When you take the calculator out of the box, or when it recovers after a system crash, the original calculator settings are such that the calculator's Operating Mode is set to Algebraic, the beep option is selected, the calculator's display is set to Textbook mode, and system flag 117 is cleared (i.e., CHOOSE boxes, rather than Soft MENU keys are selected), among other default settings. For the applications in this book I prefer that you change your settings as follows:

⬥ Press [MODE][+/-] to change to RPN mode. Change other settings so that the CALCULATOR MODES screen should looks like this:

```
░░░░░░░░░CALCULATOR MODES░░░░░░░░░
Operating Mode..[RPN          ]
Number Format....Std              _FM,
Angle Measure....Radians
Coord System......Rectangular
_Beep   _Key Click  ✓Last Stack

Choose calculator operating mode
[FLAGS][CHOOS][ CAS ][ DISP ][CANCL][ OK ]
```

⬥ Press [CAS] (i.e, the F3 key). [CAS stands for *Computer Algebraic System*, a generic name given to programs that lets you produce algebraic and calculus operations in a computer or, in this case, a calculator]. Change settings, if needed, so that the CAS MODES screen looks like this:

```
░░░░░░░░░░CAS MODES░░░░░░░░░░
Indep var:'X'
Modulo:  [3          ]
_Numeric  _Approx     _Complex
_Verbose  _Step/Step  _Incr Pow
✓Rigorous✓Simp Non-Rational
Enter modulo value
[EDIT][    ][    ][    ][CANCL][ OK ]
```

2

⬇ Press [OK] to return to the CALCULATOR MODES screen. Within that screen press [FLAGS] (i.e., the F1 key). Next, press [▲] to access the last flags in the list. Press [▲][▲] to highlight system flag 117, then press [✓CHK] (i.e., the F3 key) to change the setting to Soft MENU. The SYSTEM FLAGS screen should look like this:

⬇ Press [OK][OK] to return to normal (that is, RPN mode) calculator display.

A note on CAS modes: One of the greatest features of the HP 49 G calculator is its CAS (Computer Algebraic System). The CAS is used in almost every operation in the calculator that involves algebraic or calculus manipulations. The CAS prefers that you use the Exact mode for most operations in order to provide the most accurate result. You will know that the Exact mode is selected if you see that the Approx mode is *not* selected in the CAS MODES screen (see above). Make sure that your calculator is set to Exact mode all the time. While in the stack, in RPN mode, this can be quickly accomplished by clearing system flag 105:

[1][0][5][+/-][ALPHA][ALPHA][C][F][ENTER].

Many errors produced when operating the calculator can be traced to not having it set to Exact mode. On the other hand, whenever the calculator, set to Exact mode, tries to evaluate expressions involving floating point numbers (i.e., numbers with decimals), it will request that the CAS mode be changed to Approx. Accept the request for changing the CAS mode, but, when done, make sure that you return the calculator to Exact mode.

Many other operations will request you to change the mode to Complex. Accept the changes when requested to obtain complex results. Within the stack, in RPN mode, if you want to return to Real (i.e., not Complex) mode, clear system flag 103:

[1][0][3][+/-][ALPHA][ALPHA][C][F][ENTER].

In normal calculator display you can check what the current CAS settings, and other calculator settings, are by checking the characters in the upper left corner of the display. The settings I prefer, unless otherwise noticed, will look like this:

```
RAD XYZ HEX R= 'X'
<HOME>
5:
4:
3:
2:
1:
EDIT VIEW STACK RCL PURGE CLEAR
```

1

The items in the upper left corner are interpreted as follows:

- RAD stands for radians for angular measure
- XYZ stands for rectangular (i.e., Cartesian) coordinates
- HEX stands for hexadecimal numbers as the default for binary operations
- R means Real, as opposite to Complex, CAS mode
- The equal sign (=) stands for CAS Exact mode, as opposite to ~, which means Approx mode
- 'X' means that the default CAS independent variable (stored in VX, is the upper case X)

Thus, before starting any operation involving algebraic or calculus manipulations (i.e., most operations in the calculator) make sure that the icon R= is present in the upper part of the display.

Preface to Volume II

Volume I (Introduction, programming, pre-calculus mathematics, graphics, linear algebra) of this series includes subjects corresponding to mathematics at the pre-calculus level. This second volume includes subjects on differential and integral calculus, multi-variate and vector calculus, some differential geometry, ordinary differential equations (analytical and numerical solutions), Fourier analysis and its applications to partial differential equations, and statistical applications. This volume starts with Chapter 13, to continue the chapter numbering of Volume I.

Calculus. Chapter 13, the first chapter in this volume, includes HP 49 G operations related to limits of functions, derivatives, the Chain Rule, applications of derivatives, and other important subjects of differential calculus. The chapter includes applications of integration through limits of summations, anti-derivatives, integration techniques, improper integrals, and other relevant subjects of integral calculus of one variable. A third subject covered in this Chapter is the issue of infinite series, and approximation of functions through Taylor and Maclaurin's series. Applications of differential and integral calculus, taken from science and engineering disciplines, conclude this chapter.

Multivariate and vector calculus. This Chapter starts with the concepts of partial derivatives and total differentials and their applications to functions of two or more variables, as well as to functions of a complex variable. Applications of multi-variate calculus to potential flow concludes this first part of the Chapter. The subject of multiple integrals is presented next including practical applications in the physical sciences. The Chapter continues with coverage of vector calculus concepts and their application to differential geometry. The subject of vector analysis is covered extensively with applications of the *del* operator to scalar and vector fields. Vector differential operations in generalized orthogonal coordinates and the calculus of surfaces concludes this chapter.

Ordinary differential equations. This Chapter includes an extensive catalog of solution techniques for first-order ODEs, the use of Laplace transform in the solution of linear ODEs, Fourier series and their applications, solution to classical second-order equations, and numerical and graphical solutions to linear ODEs.

Fourier transforms and parabolic PDEs. This Chapter includes a number or analytical solutions to parabolic PDEs using separation of variable techniques and Fourier analysis applications. The chapter covers concepts and applications of Fourier transforms and their application to discrete signals through the Fast Fourier Transform (FFT) algorithm.

Statistical applications. This chapter covers a variety of applications of the HP 49 G calculator to the analysis and reduction of data: e.g., analysis of single data sets to obtain sample statistics, analysis of frequency distribution and plotting of histograms, and fitting of data through a number of pre-programmed functions. The Chapter includes practical applications of statistical inference such as the generation of confidence intervals, and the test of hypotheses. The Chapter concludes with a presentation of the method of least-squares for linear regression and inference procedures applied to such data fitting.

The subjects covered in Chapter 13 (Calculus) include subjects that are typically covered in two to three Calculus courses at the Freshmen and Sophomore level in College. The elementary subjects of Chapter 13 can be easily covered in an AP preparation class at the High-School level. The material covered in Chapter 14 (Multivariate and vector calculus) is typically included in two courses in Advanced Calculus at the junior to senior levels. The subject of Chapter 15 (Ordinary differential equations) can be covered in one course on general ODEs and part of one course on advanced engineering mathematics or mathematical physics, typically at the junior and senior level.   Chapter 16 (Fourier transforms and parabolic PDEs) includes subjects that are taught in specialized courses in physics and engineering, typically at the senior undergraduate or elementary graduate level.   The subjects presented in Chapter 17 (Statistical applications) can be presented in any statistics course.   It should be pointed out that some of the subjects covered throughout the first two volumes of this book include probability applications (e.g., see Chapters 4, 5, 10, 11 and 12 in Volume I, and Chapter 13 in Volume 2) can be included in a calculus-based probability and statistics course. This course will typically be taught at the junior or senior level, or even as an introductory graduate level class for students that have not taken statistics in their undergraduate studies (if there still are some of them around).

2

13 Calculus

In this chapter we discuss applications of the HP 49 G calculator to differential and integral calculus, multi-variate calculus, power series, and vector calculus.

Limits and derivatives

Differential calculus deals with derivatives, or rates of change, of functions. The derivative of a function is defined as a limit of the difference of a function as the increment in the independent variable tends to zero. Limits are used also to check the continuity of functions.

The function LIMIT

The HP 49 G calculator provides the function LIMIT to calculate limits of functions. This function uses as input an expression representing a function and the value where the limit is to be calculated. The function LIMIT is available through the keystroke sequence [↰][CALC][LIMIT][LIMIT]. (Change CAS setting to Exact.) Some examples are shown below:

'X^2+2*X-1' [ENTER] 'X = 3' [ENTER] [↰][CALC][LIMIT][LIMIT], Result: '14', i.e.,

$$\lim_{X \to 3} (X^2 + 2 \cdot X - 1) = 14.$$

'(t^2-1)/(t+1)'[ENTER] 't = -1' [ENTER] [↰][CALC][LIMIT][LIMIT], Result: '-2', i.e.,

$$\lim_{t \to -1} \frac{t^2 - 1}{t + 1} = -2$$

'SIN(θ)/θ' [ENTER] 'θ=0' [ENTER] [↰][CALC][LIMIT][LIMIT], Result: '1', i.e.,

$$\lim_{\theta \to 0} \frac{\sin \theta}{\theta} = 1.$$

'(m+1)/(m^2+1)' [ENTER] 'm=+∞' [ENTER] [↰][CALC][LIMIT][LIMIT], Result: '0', i.e.,

$$\lim_{m \to 0} \frac{m + 1}{m^2 + 1} = 0.$$

'((x+h)^2-x^2)/h' [ENTER] 'h = 0' [ENTER] [↵][CALC][LIMIT][LIMIT], Result: '2*x', i.e.,

$$\lim_{h\to 0} \frac{(x+h)^2 - x^2}{h} = 2 \cdot x.$$

'm*v/ √ (1 - (v/c)^2)'[ENTER] 'v = c' [ENTER] [↵][CALC][LIMIT][LIMIT], Result: '∞', i.e.,

$$\lim_{v\to c} \frac{m \cdot v}{\sqrt{1 - \left(\dfrac{v}{c}\right)^2}} = \infty.$$

Derivatives

The derivative of a function f(x) at x = a is defined as

$$\frac{df}{dx} = f'(x) = \lim_{h\to 0} \frac{f(x+h) - f(x)}{h}.$$

One of the examples on limits in the previous section shows how to calculate the derivative of f(x) = x^2 using this definition. Other examples follow:

'(EXP(x+h)-EXP(x))/h' [ENTER] 'h = 0' [ENTER] [↵][CALC][LIMIT][LIMIT], Result: 'EXP(x)', i.e.,

$$\frac{d}{dx}(e^x) = \lim_{h\to 0} \frac{e^{x+h} - e^x}{h} = e^x.$$

'(SIN(x+h)-SIN(x))/h' [ENTER] 'h = 0' [ENTER] [↵][CALC][LIMIT][LIMIT], Result: 'COS(x)', i.e.,

$$\frac{d}{dx}\sin x = \lim_{h\to 0} \frac{\sin(x+h) - \sin x}{h} = \cos x.$$

'(1/(x+h)-1/x)/h' [ENTER] 'h = 0' [ENTER] [↵][CALC][LIMIT][LIMIT], Result: '-1/x^2', i.e.,

$$\frac{d}{dx}\left(\frac{1}{x}\right) = \lim_{h\to 0} \frac{1/(x+h) - 1/x}{h} = -\frac{1}{x^2}.$$

'(ABS(x+h)-ABS(x))/h' [ENTER] 'h = 0' [ENTER] [↵][CALC][LIMIT][LIMIT], Result: 'x/ABS(x)', i.e.,

$$\lim_{h\to 0} \frac{|x+h| - |x|}{h} = \frac{x}{|x|}.$$

3

The functions DERIV and DERVX

Of course, calculating derivatives using the formal definition given above turns into a pretty tedious endeavor. Instead, we use formulas for derivatives, which in the HP 49 G calculator are available through the functions DERIV or DERVX. The function DERIV is used to take derivatives in terms of any independent variable, while the function DERVX takes derivatives with respect to the CAS default variable VX (typically X). These functions are available in the DERIV menu: [↰][CALC][DERIV]. Some examples follow:

'x^2 - 5*x + 2'[ENTER] 'x' [ENTER] [↰][CALC][DERIV][DERIV], result = 'x*2-5', i.e.,

$$\frac{d}{dx}(x^2 - 5 \cdot x + 2) = 2 \cdot x - 5.$$

'SIN(R) + ATAN(R)' [ENTER] 'R' [ENTER] [↰][CALC][DERIV] [DERIV], result = 'COS(R)+1/(SQ(R)+1)', i.e.,

$$\frac{d}{dx}(\sin R + \tan^{-1} R) = \cos R + \frac{1}{1 + R^2}.$$

Check that your VX variable in the HOME directory contains the variable 'X', then try the following:

'(X^2+COS(X))/EXP(X)' [ENTER] [↰][CALC][DERIV][DERVX], result = '(EXP(X)*(X*2-SIN(X))-(X^2+COS(X))*EXP(X))/SQ(EXP(X))', i.e.,

$$\frac{d}{dx}(\frac{X^2 + \cos X}{e^X}) = \frac{e^X \cdot (2X - \sin X) - (X^2 + \cos X) \cdot e^X}{e^{2X}}.$$

Calculating derivatives with ∂

The symbol is available as [↱][∂] (the COS key). It implements the DERIV function directly in the keyboard. For example,

'SIN(t) -LN(t)' [ENTER] 't' [↱][∂], result: 'COS(t) - 1/t', i.e.,

$$\frac{d}{dx}(\sin t + \ln t) = \cos t - 1/t.$$

Note: The symbol ∂ is used formally in mathematics to indicate a partial derivative, i.e., the derivative of a function with more than one variable. However, the HP 49 G calculator does not distinguish between ordinary and partial derivatives, utilizing the same symbol for both. The user must keep this distinction in mind when translating results from the calculator to paper.

4

Formulas for derivatives

You can use the function DERIV or the symbol ∂ to recall formulas for derivatives by using as argument a generic function f(x). For example,

'x^n' [ENTER] 'x' [↦][∂], result: 'x^(n-1)*n', i.e., $d(x^n)/dx = n \cdot x^{n-1}$.

'(f(x))^n'[ENTER] 'x' [↦][∂], result: 'f(x)^(n-1)*n*d1f(x)', i.e., $d[f(x)]^n/dx = n \cdot [f(x)]^{n-1} \cdot df/dx$. Here, the symbol d1f(x) stands for "the first derivative of f(x) with respect to x".

'u(x)*v(x)' [ENTER] 'x' [↦][∂], result: 'd1u(x)*v(x)+u(x)*d1v(x)', i.e.,

$$\frac{d}{dx}(u(x) \cdot v(x)) = \frac{du(x)}{dx} \cdot v(x) + u(x) \cdot \frac{dv(x)}{dx}.$$

The chain-rule

The chain rule for derivatives applies to derivatives of composite functions. A general expression for the chain-rule is

$$d\{f[g(x)]\}/dx = (df/dg) \cdot (dg/dx).$$

Using the calculator, this formula results in:

'f(g(x))' [ENTER] 'x' [↦][∂], result: 'd1g(x)*d1f(g(x))'.

Other examples would be:

'LN(f(x))' [ENTER] 'x' [↦][∂], result: 'f(x)/d1f(x)', i.e., $d/dx[\ln(f(x))] = f(x)/[df(x)/dx] = f(x)/f'(x)$.

'√SIN(X^2)' [ENTER] [↤][CALC][DERVX], result = 'COS(X^2)*(X*2)/(2*√SIN(X^2))', i.e.,

$$\frac{d}{dx}[\sin(x^2)]^{1/2} = \frac{2x\cos x^2}{2\sqrt{\sin x^2}} = \frac{x\cos x^2}{\sqrt{\sin x^2}}.$$

Derivatives in formulas

Derivatives can be written explicitly in the equation writer or between quotes by using the symbol ∂. For example, the derivative $d/dx[\exp(-x^2)]$ can be written as:

[EQW][↦][∂] [ALPHA][↤][X] [▶][↤][e^x] [ALPHA][↤][X] [y^x] [▶] [+/-] [ENTER], and will be entered in the stack as: '∂x(EXP(-x^2))', or as

5

$$\frac{\partial}{\partial x}\left(EXP\left(-x^2\right)\right)$$

if using textbook display format.

To evaluate this expression use: [→][EVAL]. The result is `EXP(-x^2)*-(x*2)`, i.e., -$2 \cdot x \cdot exp(-x^2)$.

To type a derivative in stack level 1 use:

[→]['] [→][∂] [ALPHA][↰][X] [↰][( )] [SIN] [ALPHA][↰][X] [ENTER], produces `∂x(SIN(x))`. Press [→][EVAL] to get `COS(x)`.

Higher-order derivatives

You can calculate second order derivatives by applying the function [→][∂] twice to an expression. For example,

'SIN(x)'[ENTER] 'x' [ENTER] [→][∂] 'x' [ENTER] [→][∂], result: '−SIN(x)'

You can write a second-order derivative by using the symbol [→][∂] twice in the equation writer. For example:

[EQW] [→][∂] [ALPHA][↰][X] [▶][→][∂] [ALPHA][↰][X] [▶] [↰][e^x] [ALPHA][↰][X] [y^x] [▶] [+/-] [ENTER], and will be entered in the stack as: `∂x(∂x(EXP(-x^2)))`, or as

$$\frac{\partial}{\partial x}\left(\frac{\partial}{\partial x}\left(EXP\left(-x^2\right)\right)\right)$$

if using textbook display format.

To evaluate this expression use: [→][EVAL]. The result is

`EXP(-x^2)*-(x*2)*-(x*2)+EXP(-X^2)*-2`,

Press [→][ALG][EXPAN], resulting in `(4*x^2-2)/EXP(x^2)`, i.e., $(4x^2-2)/exp(x^2)$.

Derivatives of equations

You can use the HP49G calculator to take derivatives of equation, i.e., derivatives will exist in both sides of the equal sign. For example, to take the derivative of the equation: x(t) = 2 r cos θ(t), use:

[→]['] [ALPHA][↰][X] [↰][( )] [ALPHA][↰][T] [▶] [→][=] [2][×] [ALPHA][↰][R] [×][COS] [ALPHA][→][T] [↰][( )] [ALPHA][↰][T] [ENTER]

['] [ALPHA][↰][T] [ENTER] [→][∂]

6

The result is `'d1x(t) = 2*r*-(SIN(θ(t))* d1θ(t))'`, i.e., $x'(t) = -2\,r\theta'(t)\sin\theta(t)$.

Take a second derivative, as follows: [↱]['] [ALPHA][↰][T] [ENTER] [↱][∂][↱][ALG][EXPAN]
The result is now:

`'d1d1(t)=-(2*r*SIN(θ(t))*d1d1θ(t)+2*r*d1θ(t)^2*COS(θ(t)))'`, or

$$x''(t) = -\,(2\,r\,[\theta'(t)]2\cos\theta(t) + 2\,r\theta''(t)\sin\theta(t))\,.$$

Implicit derivatives

Try taking the derivative with respect to t of the equation: $[r(t)]^2 = 2\cdot[\theta(t)]^3$. Use the following keystrokes:

[↱]['][↰][( )] [ALPHA][↰][R] [↰][( )] [ALPHA][↰][T] [▶] [▶] [yˣ] [2]
[↱][=] [2][×] [↰][( )] [ALPHA][↱][T] [↰][( )] [ALPHA][↰][T] [▶] [▶] [yˣ] [3] [ENTER]
[↱] ['] [ALPHA][↰][T] [ENTER] [↱][∂]

The result is: `'d1r(t)=2*(θ(t)^2*3*d1θ(t))'`, i.e., $r'(t) = 2\,\theta'(t)\,[\theta(t)]^2$.

Application of derivatives

Analyzing graphics of functions

In Chapter 11 we presented some functions that are available in the graphics screen for analyzing graphics of functions of the form y = f(x). These functions include [(X,Y)] and [TRACE] for determining points on the graph, as well as functions in the ZOOM and FCN menu. The functions in the ZOOM menu allow the user to zoom in into a graph to analyze it in more detail. These functions are described in detail in Chapter 11. Within the functions of the FCN menu, we can use the functions SLOPE, EXTR, F', and TANL to determine the slope of a tangent to the graph, the extrema (minima and maxima) of the function, to plot the derivative, and to find the equation of the tangent line.

Try the following example for the function y = tan(x).

⬥ Press [↰][2D/3D], simultaneously to access to the PLOT SETUP window.

⬥ Change TYPE to FUNCTION, if needed, by using [CHOOS].

⬥ Press [▼] and type in the equation 'TAN(X)'.

⬥ Make sure the independent variable is set to 'X'.

⬥ Press [NXT][OK] to return to normal calculator display.

⬥ Press [↰][WIN], simultaneously, to access the PLOT window (in this case it will be called PLOT -POLAR window).

⬥ Change the H-VIEW range to -2 to 2, and the V-VIEW range to -5 to 5.

7

🔸 Press [ERASE][DRAW] to plot the function in polar coordinates.

The resulting plot looks as follows:

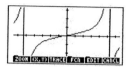

🔸 Notice that there are vertical lines that represent asymptotes. These are not part of the graph, but show points where TAN(X) goes to $\pm \infty$ at certain values of X.

🔸 Press [TRACE] [(X,Y)], and move the cursor to the point X: 1.08E0, Y: 1.86E0. Next, press [NXT][FCN][SLOPE]. The result is Slope: 4.45010547846.

🔸 Press [NXT][NXT][TANL]. This operation produces the equation of the tangent line, and plots its graph in the same figure. The result is shown in the figure below:

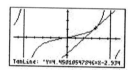

🔸 Press [NXT][PICT][CANCL][ON] to return to normal calculator display. Notice that the slope and tangent line that you requested are listed in the stack.

The function TABVAR

This function is accessed through the catalog only. It uses as input the function f(VX), where VX is the default CAS variable. The function returns the following:

🔸 Level 3: the function f(VX)

🔸 Two lists, the first one indicates the variation of the function (i.e., where it increases or decreases) in terms of the independent variable VX, the second one indicates the variation of the function in terms of the dependent variable.

🔸 A graphic object showing how the variation table was computed.

Example: Analyze the function Y = $X^3-4X^2-11X+30$, using the function TABVAR. Use the following keystrokes:

'X^3-4*X^2-11*X+30' [ENTER][CAT][ALPHA][T](select TABVAR)[OK].

8

This is what the calculator shows in stack level 1:

```
RAD XYZ HEX R= 'X'
{HOME}              02:55,MAY:30
1: Graphic 161 × 95
      F=:(x³-4·x²-11·X+30)
      F'=:(x²·3-4·X·2-11)
EXPAN FACTO LACOL  LIN SOLVE SUBST
```

This is a graphic object. To be able to see it in its entirety, press [▼]. The top of the GROB shows the following:

```
F=:  (X³-4·X²-
11·X+30)
F'=:  (X²·3-4·X·2 -
11)
→  ((3X-11)·(X+1))
Variation table:
```

Use the down-arrow key, [▼], and the right-arrow key, [▶], to see the rest of the screen. The bottom of the screen shows the variation table of the function as follows:

Variation table

$$\begin{bmatrix} -\infty & + & -1 & - & 11/3 & + & +\infty & X \\ -\infty & \text{``↑''} & 36 & \text{``↓''} & -400/2 & \text{``↑''} & +\infty & F \end{bmatrix}$$

Press [ON] to recover normal calculator display. Press [⇦] to drop this last result from the stack.

Two lists, corresponding to the top and bottom rows of the graphics matrix shown earlier, now occupy level 1. These lists are useful for programming purposes. Press [⇦] to drop this last result from the stack.

Level 1 is now occupied by the original function.

The interpretation of the variation table shown above is as follows: the function F(X) increases for X in the interval $(-\infty, -1)$, reaching a maximum equal to 36 at X = -1. Then, F(X) decreases until X = 11/3, reaching a minimum of -400/27. After that F(X) increases until reaching $+\infty$. Also, at X = $\pm\infty$, F(X) = $\pm\infty$.

9

Using derivatives to calculate extreme points

"Extreme points," or extrema, is the general designation for maximum and minimum values of a function in a given interval. Since the derivative of a function at a given point represents the slope of a line tangent to the curve at that point, then values of x for which f'(x) =0 represent points where the graph of the function reaches a maximum or minimum. Furthermore, the value of the second derivative of the function, f"(x), at those points determines whether the point is a *relative or local maximum* [f"(x)<0] or *minimum* [f"(x)>0]. These ideas are illustrated in the figure below.

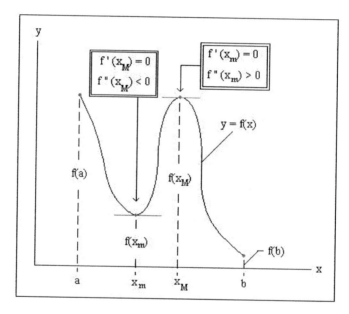

In this figure we limit ourselves to determining extreme points of the function y = f(x) in the x-interval [a,b]. Within this interval we find two points, x = x_m and x = x_M, where f'(x)=0. The point x = x_m, where f"(x)>0, represents a local minimum, while the point x = x_M, where f"(x)<0, represents a local maximum. From the graph of y = f(x) it follows that the absolute maximum (maximum maximorum) in the interval [a,b] occurs at x = a, while the absolute minimum (minimum minimorum) occurs at x = b.

10

Suppose that you want to determine the radius of a cylinder so that the volume of the cylinder is optimized while keeping the total area of the cylinder constant. This could be a problem to be tackled by an industrial engineer in charge of designing a cylindrical container for a liquid or granular material.

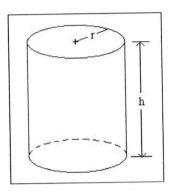

The external area of the cylinder is given by $A = \pi r^2 + 2\pi r h$ = constant, while the volume is $V = \pi r^2 h$. By isolating h from the equation for the area and replacing the resulting expression into the volume equation we will get at function or the radius, V(r), which we can optimize. To use the calculator to help us in the solution follow these steps:

🔹 Type in the equation 'π*r^2*h'[ENTER][ENTER] (2 copies), followed by 'A = π*r^2+2*π*r*h' [ENTER].

🔹 Then, isolate h by using: 'h'[ENTER][↵][S.SLV][ISOL]. The result is: 'h = (A-r^2*π)/(2*r* π)'.

🔹 Now, replace this expression for h into the expression for V by using: [→][ALG][SUBST], resulting in 'π *r^2*((A-r^2* π)/(2*r*π)'.

🔹 To simplify the expression use [→][ALG][EXPAN]. This results in '-((r^3*π-r*A)/2)'.]

🔹 To convert it into a function use: 'V(r)' [ENTER][▶][→][=], which produces 'V(r)= -((r^3*π-r*A)/2)'.

🔹 Use [↵][DEF] to create the function V(r).

🔹 Press [VAR] [→] [V] to see the contents of the function, i.e., << →r '-((r^3*π-r*A)/2)'>>. Press [⇦] to drop this result from the stack.

🔹 To obtain the derivatives of the function V(r), use:

[EQW][→][∂][ALPHA][↵][R][▶][ALPHA][V][↵] [( )] [ALPHA][↵][R] [▲][▲][▲] [EVAL]

The result is '-2*(π*3*r^2-A)/4', i.e., V'(r) = -2·(3πr^2-A)/4.

🔹 Press [ENTER][ENTER] to keep an additional copy of the derivative in the stack.

🔹 Press [▼] to activate the equation writer again. The expression for V'(r) must be selected now. Enter:

[→][∂][ALPHA][↵][R] [▲][▲] [EVAL] [→][ALG][EXPAN].

11

The result is '-(3*r*π)', which corresponds to V"(r) = -3·π·r.

♦ Press [ENTER] to get back to stack, and [▶] to swap levels 1 and 2.

♦ Turn the expression for V'(x) into the equation V'(r) = 0, by entering [0][ENTER] [→][=], and use

[→]['][ALPHA][←][R][ENTER] [←][S.SLV][ISOL] to solve for r. The result is the list

$$\{ \ 'r = -(\sqrt{\ (3*(\pi*A))/(3*\pi))}' \ 'r = (\sqrt{\ (3*(\pi*A))/(3*\pi))}' \ \}.$$

♦ Out of this list we want to keep only the positive result by using: [→][EVAL] [▶] [⇐].

♦ Press [ENTER] to get a new copy of the expression for r, and save it into variable *rc*, i.e.,

[→]['][ALPHA][←][R][ALPHA][←][C][STO▶].

♦ Now, use [→][ALG][SUBST] to replace the value of r into the expression for V"(r), to get '-(3*(√ (3*(A*π))/(3*π))*π)'. Press [→][ALG][EXPAN] to simplify the expression. The result is now '-√ (3*(A* π))', i.e., V"(rc) < 0.

♦ Because V"(r)<0 at r = rc, the value of V(r) at rc = √ (3*(π*A))/(3*π) is a maximum. This maximum can be calculated by using:

[VAR]	Recover variables menu
[rc]	Places contents of [rc] on stack
[←][PRG][TYPE][OBJ→]	Decompose equation
[⇐][⇐][▶][⇐]	Drop eq. elements so that only value of r
remains	
[VAR][V]	Evaluate V(r) with the value of rc
[→][ALG][EXPAN]	Simplify result

The result is '√3*A*√ (A*π)/(9* π)', or $V_{max} = A \cdot (3 \cdot \pi \cdot A)^{1/2}/(9 \cdot \pi)$, at $rc = (3 \cdot \pi \cdot A)^{1/2}/(3 \cdot \pi)$.

Note: The keystroke sequence used above to solve this problem shows a very efficient use of the calculator's stack. In most problems, such efficient use follows only after you have outlined the steps of the solution in paper. Since I expect that you will have a notebook handy to keep track of the calculations, you don't need to worry about optimizing stack operations. Keep track of your results by hand, and re-enter any result you may need. Alternatively, you can store intermediate results from your calculations in global variables, which you can easily recall to the stack when needed.

Integrals calculated through summations

The integral of a function f(x) in an interval (a,b), is defined as the limit of the sum

$$S_n = \sum_{i=1}^{n} f(\xi_i)\Delta x_i,$$

as $\Delta x_i \to 0$, or $n \to \infty$. The values Δx_i represent the length of n sub-intervals in (a,b), so that the values ξ_i are contained within the i-th sub-interval. The sub-intervals are limited by the values $x_1, x_2, ..., x_n, x_{n+1}$, therefore,

$\Delta x_i = x_{i+1} - x_i$,

and

$$x_i < \xi_i < x_{i+1}.$$

The figure below illustrates the meaning of the terms in the summation. The terms $f(\xi_i)\Delta x_i$ represent increments of area, ΔA_i, under the curve y = f(x) in the interval (a,b).

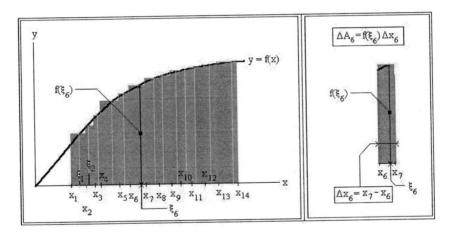

While there are no restrictions in the way we may divide the interval (a,b) to generate n sub-intervals, or where to select ξ_i within a sub-interval, dividing it into n equally-spaced sub-intervals, and selecting the values of ξ_i in a regular fashion, facilitates the calculation of the summation, as well as of its limit when n grows unbounded.

To divide the interval (a,b) into n sub-intervals we take,

$$\Delta x = (b-a)/n,$$

therefore,

$x_1 = a$, $x_2 = x_1 + \Delta x$, $x_3 = x_1 + 2 \cdot \Delta x$, ..., $x_i = x_1 + (i-1)\cdot \Delta x$, ..., $x_n = x_1 + (n-1)\cdot \Delta x = b$.

The value of can be selected to be the leftmost value in the sub-interval (x_i, x_{i+1}), i.e., $\xi_i = x_i$, the center of the sub-interval, i.e., $\xi_i = (x_i + x_{i+1})/2$, or the right-most value of the sub-interval, i.e., $= x_{i+1}$. Suppose that we call SL_n the summation when $\xi_i = x_i$, then we can write:

13

$$SL_n = \left(\frac{b-a}{n}\right) \cdot \sum_{i=1}^{n} f(x_i).$$

If we call SM_n the summation when $\xi = (x_i + x_{i+1})/2$, then we have

$$SM_n = \left(\frac{b-a}{n}\right) \cdot \sum_{i=1}^{n} f\left(\frac{x_i + x_{i+1}}{2}\right)$$

Finally, for the summation when , we have

$$SU_n = \left(\frac{b-a}{n}\right) \cdot \sum_{i=1}^{n} f(x_{i+1}).$$

A program for summations approximating integrals for finite values of *n*

Using lists it would be really easy to program the calculation of SL_n, SM_n, and Su_n, in User RPL. In this section we develop programs for calculating the sums SL_n, SM_n, and SU_n, given an expression of X to integrate between values *a* and *b* using *n* equally-spaced sub-intervals.

First of all, let's create a sub-directory called SUMINT (SUMmation approximating INTegrals) within the HOME directory, using:

[↱]['][ALPHA][ALPHA][S][U][M][I][N][T][ENTER]   Enter sub-directory name 'SUMINT'
[↰][PRG][MEM][DIR][CRDIR]   Create sub-directory SUMINT
[VAR][SUMIN]   Access sub-directory

The next step is to create three main programs (SLn, SMn, and SUn) and the required sub-programs within the sub-directory. Here is the listing of the main programs:

Main program SLn:

<<	Start main program SLn
INDAT DUP	Call program INDAT, duplicate output (a list)
1 + MKLST	Add a 1 to the list, invoke sub-program MKLST
1 GTLIST	Use 1 as input, invoke sub-program GTLIST
"SLn" →TAG	Tag result of summation as "SLn"
→ R	Pass tagged result as R
<<	Start first sub-program within SLn
DRAWRECT	Call sub-program DRAWRECT
{ } PVIEW	Bring contents of PICT to screen
R	Place tagged result for summation in stack
>>	End first sub-program within SLn
>>	End main program SLn

14

The main programs corresponding to SMn and SUn are exactly the same as SLn , but using 2 and 3 for SMn and SUn, respectively, instead of 1, and changing the tagging string to "SMn" and "SUn," respectively. The listings of the programs SMn and SUn are as follows:

Main program SMn:

<< INDAT DUP 2 + MKLST 2 GTLIST "SMn" →TAG →R << DRAWRECT {} PVIEW R >> >>

Main program SUn:

<< INDAT DUP 3 + MKLST 3 GTLIST "SUn" →TAG →R << DRAWRECT {} PVIEW R >> >>

The listing of the sub-programs used by SLn, SMn, and SUn, follows:

Sub-program INDAT: gets input data, uses an input string with the INPUT function

<<	Start sub-program INDAT (Input DATa)
"Enter a, b, n, EQ(X):"	Prompt title for inputting data
{ "↵ : EQ: ↵ : a: ↵ : b: ↵ : n :" {1 0 } V }	Input string
INPUT	INPUT function using two previous lines
OBJ→	Decomposes input string into three tagged
values	
1 4 FOR j	Start FOR loop to de-tag values, j = 1,2,3,4
DTAG	De-tag last value in stack
4 ROLLD	Roll-down three elements in stack
NEXT	End of FOR loop
4 →LIST	Create list with the three de-tagged values
>>	End of sub-program INDAT

Sub-program MKLIST:

<<	Start sub-program MKLST (MaKe a LiST)
EVAL	Decomposes input list
→ EXPR a b n IS	Input values EXPR, a, b, n, IS
<<	Start first sub-program within MKLST
'(b-a)/n' →NUM { }	Calculate x-increment and place an empty list
→ Δ xL	Pass increment and empty list as Δ and xL
<<	Start second sub-program within MKLST
1 n 1 + FOR j	Start FOR loop with j = 1, 2, ..., n+1
'a+(j-1)*Δ' →NUM DUP	Calculate x_j = a+(j-1)*Δ, duplicate result
xL SWAP + 'xL' STO	Add x_j to xL and save the new list
'X' SWAP 2 →LIST	Create list {X x_j}
EXPR SWAP	→NUM	Evaluate EXPR at X = x_j, i.e., $f(x_j)$
NEXT	End FOR loop
n 1 + →LIST	Create list of values {$f(x_j)$...}
Δ xL 3 ROLLD	Place Δ and xL in stack, roll list {f(xj)...} to level 1
>>	End second sub-program within MKLST
>>	End first sub-program within MKLST
>>	End sub-program MKLST

15

Sub-program *GTLIST*:

```
<<
→ xL Δ IS                          Start sub-program GTLIST (GeT LIST)
  <<                               Get input values
  xL TAIL DUP                      Start first sub-program within GTLIST
                                   Place list xL, remove element 1 with TAIL,
duplicate
  xL REVLIST TAIL REVLIST  DUP     Place list xL, reverse, get TAIL, reverse, duplicate
  3 ROLLD ADD 2 /                  Calculate a list averaging the last two lists
  3 ROLL                           Roll three levels of stack
  3 →LIST                          Create list of lists
  IS GET DUP                       Get list number IS, duplicate it
  ΣLIST Δ *                        Sum list, multiply by Δ
  Δ SWAP                           Place Δ in stack, swap with early summation
  >>                               End first sub-program within GTLIST
>>                                 End sub-program GTLIST
```

Sub-program *DRAWRECT* (DRAW RECTangles):

```
<<
→ xL yL Δ                          Start sub-program DRAWRECT
  <<                               Input data: lists xL, yL, and Δ
  EVAL                             Start first sub-program within DRAWRECT
  → EXPR a b n                     Decompose third of input lists
    <<                             Pass values as EXPR, a, b, and n
    a b EXPR  PPLT                 Start second sub-program within DRAWRECT
                                   Using input: a, b, and EXPR, call sub-program
PPLT
    xL yL n DRBOXS                 Using input xL, yL, n, call sub-program DRBOXS
    >>                             Close second sub-program within DRAWRECT
  >>                               Close first sub-program within DRAWRECT
>>                                 Close sub-program DRAWRECT
```

Sub-program DRAWRECT uses sub-programs PPLT and DRBOXS. Their listings are shown following:

Sub-program *PPLT*:

```
<<
→ a b EXPR                         Start sub-program PPLT (Prepare PLoT)
  <<                               Input data: a, b, EXPR
  FUNCTION                         Start first sub-program within PPLT
  EXPR STEQ                        Select FUNCTION type of graph
  a b XRNG                         Store contents of EXPR in EQ to be plotted
  AUTO                             Set up x-axis range
  ERASE DRAX DRAW                  Let y-axis range be selected automatically
  'X' PURGE                        Erase PICT, draw axes, draw graph
                                   Purge variable X, which was used for the plot
  >>                               End first sub-program within PPLT
>>                                 End sub-program PPLT
```

16

Sub-program DRBOXS:

```
<<
→ xL yL n
  <<
  1 n FOR j
     xL j GET yL j GET
     R→C
     XL j 1 + GET 0 R→C
     BOX
0)
  NEXT
  >>
>>
```

Start sub-program DRBOXS (Draw BOXeS)
Input data: lists xL, yL, and value n
Start first sub-program within DRBOXS
Start FOR loop with j = 1,2, ..., n
Get element j out of lists xL and yL
Create point (xL_j, yL_j)
            Create point $(xL_{j+1}, 0)$
Draw a box between points (xL_j, yL_j) and $(xL_{j+1},$

End FOR loop
End first sub-program within DRBOXS
End sub-program DRBOXS

Using the program

Find the soft menu key [SLn] in your variables menu. Use [VAR] to recover that menu if necessary. To run a first example use this:

[SLn]
[↵]['][ALPHA][X][▼]
[0][▼] [1][▼] [1][0] [ENTER]

Starts program SLn
Enter 'X' as the function to integrate
Use a = 0, b = 1, n = 10

Wait for the program to produce the graph. The result will be the following graph:

To recover normal calculator display, press [ON]. You will get the result of the summation, SLn: .45. There will be new variables PPAR and EQ in your menu.

Before continuing, it will be a good idea to order the variables in the sub-directory so that the programs SLn, SMn, and SUn are the first three variables in your menu. You can re-order the variables by using:

[←][{}][VAR] [SLn][SMn][SUn][ENTER]
[←][PRG][MEM][DIR][NXT][ORDER]
first

Creates list {SLn SMn SUn}
Order the variables placing those in the list

Now, let's try calculating the values of SMn and SUn for the conditions used earlier:

[SMn]
[↵]['][ALPHA][X][▼]
[0][▼] [1][▼] [1][0] [ENTER]

Starts program SLn
Enter 'X' as the function to integrate
Use a = 0, b = 1, n = 10

17

Wait for the program to produce the graph. The result will be the following graph:

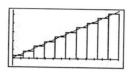

Press [ON] to obtain the summation value, SMn = 0.5.   Next, try using the function SUn as follows:

[SUn]   Starts program SLn
[↦]['][ALPHA][X][▼]   Enter 'X' as the function to integrate
[0][▼] [1][▼] [1][0] [ENTER]   Use a = 0, b = 1, n = 10

Wait for the program to produce the graph. The result will be the following graph:

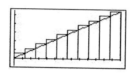

Press [ON] to produce the following result: SUn: .55.

Here is another example:

[SLn]   Starts program SLn
[↦]['][↤][e^x][+/-][X][y^x][2][÷][2][▼]   Enter 'EXP(-X^2/2)' as the function to integrate
[4][+/-][▼] [4][▼] [4][0] [ENTER]   Use a = 0, b = 1, n = 40

Be patient with the result. Since we are using 40 rectangles, it takes the calculator about a minute to finish the plot:

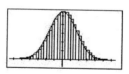

Press [ON] to obtain, SLn: 2.5064606298.

Now try:

[SMn]   Starts program SLn
[↦]['][↤][e^x][+/-][X][y^x][2][÷][2][▼]   Enter 'EXP(-X^2/2)' as the function to integrate
[4][+/-][▼] [4][▼] [4][0] [ENTER]   Use a = 0, b = 1, n = 40

18

After about a minute, the calculator produces the graph:

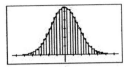

Press [ON] to obtain, SMn: 2.50646062976.

Next try:

[SUn]   Starts program SLn
[↵]['][↵][eˣ][+/-][X][yˣ][2][÷][2][▼]   Enter 'EXP(-X^2/2)' as the function to integrate
[4][+/-][▼] [4][▼] [4][0] [ENTER]   Use a = 0, b = 1, n = 40

The new graph is:

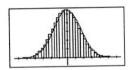

Press [ON] to obtain, SUn: .

You can use any expression involving X in EQ for input to the programs SLn, SMn, and SUn.

Summations in the HP 49 G calculator

Although the definitions of SLn, SMn, and SUn, in the previous section involve summations, we avoided using the summation function by operating with lists. In the next section we will use the summation function to evaluate some integrals. We introduced summations and integrals back in Chapter 6. (Review the section entitled "Applications of function definitions - probability distributions" in Chapter 6 to get the basic idea on the use of the summation function.) Use of integrals will be presented in more detail in a later section.

To calculate a summation directly in the stack you need to enter the following elements, in the order indicated: (1) Name of the index; (2) Initial value of the index; (3) Final value of the index; and, (4) Expression to be summed that involves the index name. For example, to calculate

$$\sum_{j=3}^{10}(j^2+1),$$

directly in the stack, use the following:

19

[↱]['][ALPHA][↰][J] [ENTER]   Enter index name, j
[3] [ENTER]   Enter initial value of j
[1][0] [ENTER]   Enter final value of j
[↱]['] [↰][( )] [ALPHA][↰][J] [y^x][2][+][1][ENTER]   Enter expression (j^2+1)
[↱][Σ]   Calculate the summation

The result is 388, i.e.,

$$\sum_{j=3}^{10}(j^2+1)=388.$$

Calculating summations in which n goes to infinity

Given a function $y = f(x)$ to be integrated between $x = a$ and $x = b$, we indicated earlier that the integral can be approximated by the summations SLn, SMn, and SUn, using equally spaced sub-intervals in the interval (a,b). Suppose that we estimate the integral using SMn, i.e.,

$$SM_n=\left(\frac{b-a}{n}\right)\cdot\sum_{i=1}^{n}f\left(\frac{x_i+x_{i+1}}{2}\right)$$

Since $x_i = a + (i-1)\cdot(b-a)/n$, and $x_{i+1} = a+i\cdot(b-a)/n$, then $\eta_i = (x_i + x_{i+1})/2 = a + (i-1/2)\cdot(b-a)/n$, and SMn can be written as

$$SM_n=\left(\frac{b-a}{n}\right)\cdot\sum_{i=1}^{n}f(\eta_i)=\left(\frac{b-a}{n}\right)\cdot\sum_{i=1}^{n}f\left(a+\frac{(i-1/2)\cdot(b-a)}{n}\right)$$

Given values of a and b and the function f(x), it is possible to find an expression SMn = F(n), using the formula shown above, for which we can take the limit when n→ ∞. The result will be the value of the integral

$$I=\int_a^b f(x)dx.$$

This approach works well when the function f(x) is an algebraic function of x, because the summation can be expressed as a polynomial in n. For example, if $f(x) = x^2$, a = 1, b = 2, we can write

$$\eta_i = a + (i-1/2)\cdot(b-a)/n = 1+(i-1/2)\cdot(2-1)/n= (i+n-0.5)/n,$$

and

$$SM_n=\left(\frac{2-1}{n}\right)\cdot\sum_{i=1}^{n}\left(\frac{i+n-0.5}{n}\right)^2=\frac{1}{n^3}\cdot\sum_{i=1}^{n}(i+n-0.5)^2.$$

20

To evaluate the summation in this equation in the HP 49 G calculator use (using *j* instead of *i*):

[EQW] [→][Σ] [ALPHA][↰][J] [▶] [1] [▶] [ALPHA][↰][N] [▶]
[↰][( )] [ALPHA][↰][J] [+] [ALPHA][↰][N] [–] [.][5] [▶][▶][▶][▶] [y^x][2]
[ENTER]

Resulting in **Σ** (j=1,n,(j+n-.5)^2)ʼ. Before evaluating this expression we need to make sure that the calculator's CAS is in the Exact mode, using:

[MODE][CAS][▼][▼][✓CHK].

Make sure that the check is off the **_Approx** option in the CAS MODES screen. Press [OK][OK] to return to normal calculator display. Now, press

[→][EVAL].

Interestingly enough, the calculator will ask if you want to use Approximate mode. Select YES, and press [OK]. The calculator will try to expand the expression in the summation, giving as a result:

`2.33333333333*n^3+-.0000000000001*n^2+-0.08333333333*n+0.`

Press [→] **[EVAL]** once more to see if you can simplify the expression further. The only simplification in this case is to eliminate the last zero in the expression. Producing:

'2.33333333333*n^3+-.0000000000001*n^2+-0.08333333333*n'

On the other hand, the coefficient of the term in n^2 is practically zero. To eliminate this term you can use the function [EPSX0] (Find it through the catalog: [CAT][ALPHA][E], then use arrow keys to select EPSX0, then press [OK].) The result is now:

'2.33333333333*n^3+0*n^2+-0.08333333333*n+0.'

Press [?][EVAL] once more to calculate the product . The final result is

'2.33333333333*n^3+-0.08333333333*n+0.'

In other words,

$$\sum_{i=1}^{n}(i+n-0.5)^2 = 2.33333333333 \cdot n^3 - 0.08333333333 \cdot n.$$

From which it follows that,

$$SM_n = \frac{1}{n^3} \cdot \sum_{i=1}^{n}(i+n-0.5)^2 = 2.33333333333 - \frac{0.08333333333}{n^2}.$$

The latter result can be obtained in the calculator by using:

[⊢]['][ALPHA][↰][N][y^x][3][ENTER][÷].

To calculate the limit when n grows without bound, use:

[⊢]['][ALPHA][↰][N] [⊢][=] [↰][∞][ENTER]
[↰][CALC][LIMIT][LIMIT]

At this point you get asked if you want the **Approximate** mode off, select YES and press [OK]. Then, you get asked if you want the **Approximate** mode on. Again, select YES and press [OK]. The result is '2.33333333333'. This result represents

$$\int_1^2 x^2 \, dx = \lim_{n \to \infty} SM_n = \lim_{n \to \infty} [\frac{1}{n^3} \cdot \sum_{i=1}^{n} (i + n - 0.5)^2] =$$

$$\lim_{n \to \infty} [2.33333333333 - \frac{0.08333333333}{n^2}] = 2.333333333.$$

Notes:

(1) Because the final result of the summation expansion is given in terms of n (a symbolic result), you need to set your CAS to **Exact** before attempting to expand the summation - as shown in the example above. If the **Approximate** mode is selected when attempting to expand a summation in terms of a symbolic variable (e.g., n in this case), the calculator simply responds by reproducing the original summation expression, or, perhaps, re-arranging some of the terms.

(2) In the evaluation of the limit to infinity the calculator seems indecisive to whether use **Exact** mode or not, just humor it, and it'll give you back the right result.

A program to calculate integrals through infinite summations

The program described below makes the process shown above automatic. To type it in, I suggest you first create a sub-directory, say SMnLIM (SMn calculated through a LIMit as n → ∞), within which you will create the program and its associated sub-programs. The listing of the main program, called 'INTGRL', is shown below:

22

© **2000 Gilberto E. Urroz**
All rights reserved

Main program *INTGRL*:

```
<<                                         Start main program INTGRL
INDAT                                      Call sub-program INDAT, result {EXPR a b}
EVAL → EXPR a b                            Decompose list, pass values as input to sub-
program
  <<                                       Start first sub-program within INTGRL
  EXPR                                     Place EXPR (a function of X) in stack
  'a+(j-1/2)*((b-a)/n)' EVAL               Evaluate η_j = a + (j-1/2)·(b-a)/n
  'X' SWAP 2 →LIST |                       Create list {X η_j} and evaluate EXPR for X = η_j
  { j 1 n } SWAP +                         Create a list {j 1 n}, then add previous result to
list
  EVAL  Σ                                  to obtain {j 1 n EXPR|_x}. Decompose list, set up
Σ.
  '(b-a)/n' EVAL *                         Multiply summation by Δx = (b-a)/n.
  EXPAND DUP                               Expand result and duplicate it
  -105 CF                                  Change mode to Exact
  EVAL → R                                 Evaluate second copy of SMn, pass it as R
    <<                                     Start second sub-program within INTGRL
    R                                      Place value of R
    IF SAME THEN                           If stack levels 1 and 2 are the same, then
indicate that
      "Cannot evaluate limit " R →STR MSGBOX          the limit cannot be evaluated directly
    ELSE                                   If stack levels 1 and 2 are different, then obtain limit
      R 'n= ∞' LIMIT                       by placing result R in stack & taking limit as
n→ ∞
    END                                    End IF statement
    >>                                     End second sub-program within INTGRL
  >>                                       End first sub-program within INTGRL
>>                                         End main program INTGRL
```

The only sub-program used is INDAT, which is the same used in the calculations of SLn, SMn, and SUn in the previous section, but not using the input for n. The listing for sub-program INDAT follows:

Sub-program *INDAT*:

```
<<                                         Start sub-program INDAT (Input DATa)
"Enter EQ(X),a, b:"                        Prompt title for inputting data
{ ": EQ: ↵  : a: ↵  : b: " { 1 0 } V }     string
INPUT                                      INPUT function using two previous lines
OBJ→                                       Decomposes input string into three tagged
values
1 3 FOR j                                  Start FOR loop to de-tag values, j = 1,2,3,4
    DTAG                                   De-tag last value in stack
    3 ROLLD                                Roll-down three elements in stack
NEXT                                       End of FOR loop
3 →LIST                                    Create list with the three de-tagged values
>>                                         End of sub-program INDAT
```

This program takes as input and expression in terms of X, and values of a and b. It returns a list consisting of { EXPR a b}.

23

As an example, run the program using the data from the previous example, as follows:

[INTGR]   Start program
[↵]['][X][y^x][2][▼]   Enter 'X^2' as the function to integrate
[1][▼] [2][▼] [ENTER]   Use a = 1, b = 2
Because we placed the command -105 CF (Clear system flag 105 to produce Exact mode), you will be asked whether you want Approx mode on. Select YES and press [OK]. Then, when trying to calculate the limit, if possible, you will be asked to select Exact mode first (Approx mode off), then Approx mode. Just press [OK] to answer YES to both questions. (These are the same questions we faced when doing the example step by step in the last section). As in the example above, the result is '2.33333333333'.

Let's use the program INTGRL again to calculate the limit as n→∞ for f(x) = 1/x, a = 1, b = 5. Use the following keystrokes:

[INTGR]   Start program
[↵]['][1][÷][X][▼]   Enter 'X^2' as the function to integrate
[1][▼] [2][▼] [ENTER]   Use a = 1, b = 2
[OK]   Turn Approx mode on when asked

You get as a result the message:

```
Cannot evaluate Limit 'Σ(j=1.,n,1./((j+(n-.5))/ n))/n'
```

Press [OK] to return to normal calculator display.

The result of the second example of the program INTGRL is an expression whose limit, as indicated in the message box, cannot be evaluated. However, you may be able to evaluate this limit if you manipulate the expression around.   A different version of INTGRL, call it GETΣn, is shown below. The program generates the expression for the summation in SMn, but does not calculate the limit, leaving it up to the user whether to proceed with the limit calculation, or manipulate the expression further.   The program GETΣn can be obtained from INTGRL by eliminating the entire ELSE option of the IF statement contained in INTGRL. The listing of the program GETΣn follows:

Main program GETΣn:

<<	Start main program GETΣn
INDAT	Call sub-program INDAT, result {EXPR a b}
EVAL → EXPR a b	Decompose list, pass values as input to sub-
program	
<<	Start first sub-program within GETΣn
EXPR	Place EXPR (a function of X) in stack
'a+(j-1/2)*((b-a)/n)' EVAL	Evaluate $\eta_j = a + (j-1/2)\cdot(b-a)/n$
'X' SWAP 2 →LIST |	Create list {X η_j} and evaluate EXPR for X = η_j
{ j 1 n } SWAP +	Create a list {j 1 n}, then add previous result to
list	
EVAL Σ	to obtain {j 1 n EXPR|$_X$}. Decompose list, set up
Σ.	
'(b-a)/n' EVAL *	Multiply summation by $\Delta x = (b-a)/n$.
EXPAND DUP	Expand result and duplicate it
-105 CF	Change mode to Exact
EVAL → R	Evaluate second copy of SMn, pass it as R
<<	Start second sub-program within GETΣn
R	Place value of R
IF SAME THEN	If stack levels 1 and 2 are the same, then
indicate that	
"Cannot evaluate limit " R →STR MSGBOX	the limit cannot be evaluated directly
END	End IF statement
R	Place R in stack
>>	End second sub-program within GETΣn
>>	End first sub-program within GETΣn
>>	End main program GETΣn

The result from this program is, therefore, the expression for SMn after replacing the value η_i in it.

Running the program GETΣn

As an example, try:

[GETΣn]	Start program
[→]['][1][÷][X][▼]	Enter 'X^2' as the function to integrate
[1][▼] [2][▼] [ENTER]	Use a = 1, b = 2
[OK]	Turn Approx mode on when asked

You get as a result the message:

```
Cannot evaluate Limit 'Σ(j=1.,n,1./((j+(n-.5))/n))/n'
```

Press [OK] to return to normal calculator display. Unlike the previous example, now the expression whose limit the calculator couldn't evaluate, is available to the user for manipulation.

25

We will perform some editing or manipulating of the expression in the stack using the summation obtained in the previous example. First, press [ENTER], to make sure that you have an extra copy of the expression. Then, press [▼] to invoke the equation editor. The screen will look like this:

Then, use the following to highlight only the expression affected by the summation: **[▼][▼][►][►][►]**. Once the screen looks like the following, press **[→][ALG][EXPAN]**.

After the expansion, the expression will look like this:

The *n* in the numerator of the summation expression is a constant value (i.e., it does not depend on the value of *j*) and can be taken out of the summation, thus canceling *n* out of the expression. To help eliminate the *n*'s from the expression, use [▼] to highlight the n in the numerator. Then, use [⇦][⇦] to erase the *n*, and [1] to replace it with a 1. Press [▼] to highlight the 1 in the numerator, then press [►], four times, to highlight the *n* in the denominator of the entire expression. Use [⇦][⇦][1] to replace the *n* in the denominator with a 1. Then press [►], to highlight the entire expression, and press [EXPAN] to expand and simplify terms. The result is the following screen:

Now, press [ENTER] to make this expression available in the stack. Press [ENTER] once more to keep an additional copy of the expression available.

Obtaining the limit of the summation as n → ∞

Type [→]['][ALPHA][←][N][→][=][←][∞] to place the expression 'n=∞' in stack level 1.

Then, use [←][CALC][LIMIT][LIMIT] to try to evaluate the limit of the summation.

Press [OK] when asked for Approx mode off, and [OK] again when asked for Approx mode on. The limit of the expression, as given by the calculator, is '0.' This is, however, wrong. The way that this value is obtained is by evaluating every term in the summation as zero, since $1/(j+n-.5) \to 0$ as n→ ∞. However, the correct approach is to first evaluate the summation, as function of n, and then try to obtain the limit.

Since we kept an additional copy of the simplified expression for the summation, let's try to evaluate the summation before attempting the limit. Press [⇦] to drop the result '0.' from the stack. Press [ENTER] to keep an additional copy of the summation expression, just in case. Next, type:

$$[1][0][5][+/-][ALPHA][ALPHA][C][F]$$

to ensure that system flag 105 is cleared (Exact mode), and press [→][EVAL]. Press [OK] when asked if you want Approx mode on. The result is exactly the same as the original expression, meaning that the calculator cannot find a closed-form expression to replace the summation. (An attempt to use [←][ALG][EXPAN], after clearing system flag 105, also fails to produce a closed-form expression).

Let's try some numerical evaluation of the expression by using a relatively large value for n, say n = 1000. Type [→]['][ALPHA][←][N][→][=][←][1][0][0][0][ENTER] to place the expression 'n=1000' in stack level 1. Then, enter [→][ALG][SUBST]. This command will not only substitute the value n = 1000 in the expression, but also will evaluate the expression, producing as a result the value '.694147149309'.

Let's drop this result by pressing [⇦], and evaluate at n = 2000, by using:

$$[→]['] \ [ALPHA][←][N] \ [→][=] \ [←][2][0][0][0][0] \ [ENTER] \ [→][ALG][SUBST]$$

The calculator will take longer to produce this result, as we are asking it to evaluate a series twice as long as the previous one, so you have to be a bit patient here. After about one minute or two, the calculator returns the value '.6931471727521'.

These two values, '.694147149309' and '.6931471727521', indicate that there is some finite value for the summation as n→ ∞. Whatever that value is, these results indicate the number's two first decimals are 0.69. The rest of the decimals will change as n increases. Of course, the larger the value of n, the better the approximation to the actual limit. However, as we increase n in the calculator, the time required for the series to converge to a value increases too. Thus, for an example like this, using the series to approximate the integral, even after simplifying it with the equation editor, is not the most efficient way to evaluate an integral.

The _anti-derivative_ of a function f(x) is a function F(x) such that f(x) = dF/dx. For example, we know that $d(x^n)/dx = n \cdot x^{n-1}$, thus, an anti-derivative of $f(x) = n \cdot x^{n-1}$ is $F(x) = x^n$. The functions $F(x) = x^n + 5$, or $F(x) = x^n - 10$, or, in general, $F(x) = x^n + C$, where C is any constant, are anti-derivatives of $f(x) = nx^{n-1}$. One way to represent anti-derivatives is through an _indefinite integral_, i.e.,

$$\int f(x)dx = F(x) + C,$$

where C is a constant, if and only if, dF/dx = f(x).

Indefinite integrals in the HP 49 G

There are three functions that can be used to obtain indefinite integrals in the HP 49 G, these are the functions INTVX, RISCH, and INT. They are described following.

The function INTVX

Indefinite integrals in the HP 49 G can be obtained through the function INTVX if the function to be integrated, f(x) in the formula above, is given in terms of the current CAS default variable (typically X). For example, with VX = 'X' (default value), you can obtain the following indefinite integral $\int x^2 dx$, as follows

[→]['][X][yˣ][2] [ENTER]
[↵][CALC][DERIV][NXT][INTVX]

The result returned by the calculator is

'.333333333333*X^3'.

This corresponds to $\int x^2 dx = x^3/3$.

What would INTVX return for 'n*X^(n-1)'? Try it:

[→]['][ALPHA][↵][N] [×] [X] [yˣ] [↵][( )] [ALPHA][↵][N][-][1] [ENTER]
[↵][CALC][DERIV][NXT][INTVX]

The result returned by the calculator is

'EXP(n*LN(X))'.

Using the properties of logarithms and the fact that LN and EXP are inverse functions, by hand, we can prove that $exp(n \ln x) = exp(\ln x^n) = x^n$, which is the result we prefer. The moral of this example is: _do not expect the calculator to simplify every result for you - you need to know your mathematics to be able to manipulate your solutions to your taste._ The calculator, of course, can help you simplify the solution as much as possible, but, remember, unlike you, the calculator does not have a fully functional, 3-lb brain.

Other examples of indefinite integrals are:

'EXP(X)'	[↰][CALC][DERIV][NXT][INTVX]	Result:	'EXP(X)'
'1/X'	[↰][CALC][DERIV][NXT][INTVX]	Result:	'LN(X)'
'1/(1+X^2)'	[↰][CALC][DERIV][NXT][INTVX]	Result:	'ATAN(X)'
'LN(X)'	[↰][CALC][DERIV][NXT][INTVX]	Result:	'X*LN(X)-X'
'X+1/X'	[↰][CALC][DERIV][NXT][INTVX]	Result:	'SQ(X)+LN(X)'

Some results depend on the CAS mode settings. For example, with `Complex` mode selected, if you try

'SIN(X)' [↰][CALC][DERIV][NXT][INTVX]

The result is   '-1/2*EXP(i*X)+-1/2*EXP(-(i*X))'

Try the same integration, but setting the CAS mode to Real:

[MODE][CAS][▼][▼][▶] (remove check from _ `Complex`) [OK][OK]
[↱]['][SIN][X][ENTER] [↰][CALC][DERIV][NXT][INTVX]

The result is now: '-COS(X)'.

The integral can include complex variables, for example (CAS mode changed to `Complex`):

'EXP(I*X)'   [↰][CALC][DERIV][NXT][INTVX] Result: '-(i*EXP(i*X))'
'1/(i*X)'   [↰][CALC][DERIV][NXT][INTVX] Result: '-(i*(LN(i)+LN(X))'
'1/(1-X^2)'   [↰][CALC][DERIV][NXT][INTVX] Result: '1/2*LN(X+1)+-1/2*LN(X-1)'

The function RISCH

Using the function INTVX we are restricted to use as independent variable that contained in VX. If you want to obtain an indefinite integral using any integration variable, use the function RISCH. For example,

'SIN(s) + EXP(-s)' [ENTER] 's'[ENTER]   [↰][CALC][DERIV][NXT][RISCH]

The result is   '-COS(s)+-1*EXP(-s)'

Other examples are:

'ABS(k)' [ENTER] 'k' [ENTER] [↰][CALC][DERIV][NXT][RISCH]

Result: 'SIGN(k)/2*k^2'

'SINH(u)' [ENTER] 'u' [ENTER] [↰][CALC][DERIV][NXT][RISCH]

Result: '1/2*EXP(u) — 1/2/EXP(u)'

There are, of course, expressions for which a closed-form anti-derivative does not exist, such as exp($-t^2/2$). Try using the function RISCH with this expression:

'EXP(-t^2/2)'[ENTER] 't' [ENTER] [↰][CALC][DERIV][NXT][RISCH]

29

The result is the symbolic formula 'INT(1/EXP(tt^2/2), tt, t)', which uses the function INT (see next sub-section). The variable tt in the previous expression is a dummy variable selected by the calculator.

The function INT

Indefinite integrals can also be obtained by using the function INT. This function requires you to specify no only the integration variable, but also a value or expressing where the integral will be evaluated. The function INT is only accessible through the catalog. For example:

't^2-3*t' [ENTER] 't' [ENTER] 't' [CAT] [ALPHA][I] (find INT with arrow keys) [OK]

The result is   '1/3*t^3-3/2*t^2'

If you want to evaluate this integral at a given value, say t =10, you can use:

[↰][UNDO] [⇦] [1][0] [ENTER] [CAT] (INT should be selected) [OK]

The result is '550/3'. Or, using [↰][→NUM], 183.333333333.

When using INT, the second input parameter (stack level 2) is a dummy integration variable. The expression to be integrated (the *integrand*) should be a function of the dummy variable. The integrand belongs in stack level 3. The last parameter (stack level 3) is the value or expression at which the anti-derivative, of indefinite integral, will be evaluated. Some possible applications follow (assuming INT is readily available through [CAT]):

'm^2'[ENTER] 'm' [ENTER] 'a+1' [ENTER] [CAT] (find INT) [OK] Result: '(a^3+3*a^2+3*a+1)/3'.

This can be interpreted as

$$\int m^2 dm \Big|_{m=a+1} = \frac{a^3 + 3a^2 + 3a + 1}{3}.$$

Other examples using INT are:

'1/r' [ENTER] 'r' [ENTER] '1/X' [ENTER] [CAT] (find INT) [OK] Result: 'LN(1/ABS(X))'

'(y^2+2)/y' [ENTER] 'y' [ENTER] 'x' [ENTER] [CAT] (find INT) [OK] Result: '(4*LN(ABS(x))+x^2)/2'

Note: The indefinite integrals produced by the calculator ignore the integration constant. In your solutions, however, do not forget that an integration constant must be included.

30

Definite integrals and the fundamental theorem of calculus

Definite integrals are those that contain limits of integration. Such were the integrals we were trying to approximate using summations in an earlier section. The fundamental theorem of calculus link definite integrals to anti-derivatives by stipulating that

$$\int_a^b f(x)\,dx = F(x)\big|_a^b = F(b) - F(a),$$

where F(x) is an anti-derivative of f(x), i.e., f(x) = dF/dx.

The HP 49 G calculator offers at least two ways to calculate definite integrals, by using the function PREVAL, or by using the integral sign ([→][∫] – the right-shift function corresponding to the [TAN] key).

The function PREVAL

The function takes three inputs: an expression in terms of the current CAS variable VX (typically X), the lower limit and the upper limit of integration (stack levels 3, 2, and 1, respectively). It returns the definite integral of the expression with respect to VX. In the following examples we assume that VX = 'X'.

'X^3' [ENTER] 1 [ENTER] 0 [ENTER] [←][CALC][DERIV][NXT][PREVA]

Using the integral sign in the equation writer

Using the integral sign in the equation writer one can write definite integrals the same way you would do in paper. For example, try this exercise:

[EQW][→][∫] [1][▶] [5][▶] [1][÷][ALPHA][←][X] [▶][ALPHA][←][X]

The result, as shown in the equation writer is:

You could evaluate this result directly in the equation writer by selecting the integral (press [▲][▲]) and pressing the soft-menu key [EVAL]. The result is LN(5). Press [ENTER] to return to normal calculator display.

Try another example, using the equation writer:

[EQW][→][∫] [0][▶] [←][π][▶] [SIN][ALPHA][→][T] [▶][ALPHA][→][T]

31

The definite integral will be written as follows in the equation writer:

$$\int_{0}^{\pi} SIN(\theta)d\theta$$

`EDIT CURS BIG ▪ EVAL FACTO TEXPR`

This time, however, we will evaluate the integral in the stack. Press [ENTER] to return to normal calculator display. Stack level 1 will show the algebraic expression ' ∫ (0,π,SIN(θ),θ)'. To evaluate the integral, simple use [→][EVAL]. The result is the number 2, i.e.,

$$\int_{0}^{\pi} \sin\theta \ d\theta = 2.$$

You can type an integral directly into the stack by creating an algebraic expression that uses the integral sign. The general form of the algebraic expression is

'∫(lower limit, upper limits, integrand expression, variable of integration)'

For example, type the following integral directly into the stack:

[→]['] [→][∫] [ALPHA][←][A] [→][,] [5] [→][,] [√x] [ALPHA][←][T] [→][,] [ALPHA][←][T]
[ENTER]

The result is the algebraic expression ' ∫ (a,5, √t, t)'. If you have selected the Textbook display option ([MODE][DISP] [▼][▼][▶][✓CHK][OK][OK]), the integral will look like this in your display:

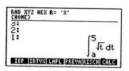

To evaluate press [→][EVAL]. The result, with textbook mode off is: '-((-(10*√5)+2*a*√a)/3)'. In textbook mode the result is:

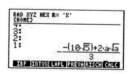

32

This example illustrates the fact that you can have one, or both, of the integral limits be an algebraic expression. The following example shows a case in which both limits of integration are algebraic expressions. The integrand also contains an unevaluated variable (g):

[EQW][→][∫] [ALPHA][↩][T][0][▶] [ALPHA][↩][T][ALPHA][↩][F][▶]
[ALPHA][↩][G] [×] [ALPHA][↩][T] [▶][ALPHA][↩][T]
[ENTER]

The resulting expression in the stack is ' ∫ (t0,tf,g*t, t)'. Press [→][EVAL] to obtain the following result: '-((g*t0^2-g*tf^2)/2) '. This can be written as

$$\int_{t0}^{tf} g \cdot t \; dt = \frac{g \cdot tf^2 - g \cdot t0^2}{2}.$$

Another way to calculate an integral will be to list the different elements of the algebraic expression for the integral in stack levels 4 through 1 in the order they appear in the expression, i.e.,

- Stack level 4: Lower limit of integration
- Stack level 3: Upper limit of integration
- Stack level 2: Integrand expression
- Stack level 1: Variable of integration

Once these four values are entered, to calculate the definite integral, simply press [→][∫]. For example:

[1][ENTER]	Enter lower limit of integration
[2][.][5][ENTER]	Enter upper limit of integration
[→]['][ALPHA][↩][Y] [y^x] [↩][( )][1][÷][3][ENTER]	Enter integrand expression
[ALPHA][↩][Y][ENTER]	Enter variable of integration
[→][∫]	Calculate integral

If your CAS is set to Exact mode you will be asked to change to Approx mode, press [OK] to accept the change. The result is 1.79476651555, i.e.,

$$\int_{1}^{2.5} y^{1/3} dy = 1.79476651555.$$

In the sub-section on indefinite integrals (see above) we indicated that some integrals do not have a closed-form solution. In this case, the fundamental theorem of calculus can not be used to directly evaluate the definite integral. For example, to evaluate

$$\int_{0}^{1.5} \exp(-\frac{t^2}{2}) dt,$$

---

use:

[0][ENTER] [1][.][5][ENTER] [→]['][↩][e^x] [+/-][ALPHA][↩][T][y^x][2][÷][2][ENTER]
[ALPHA][↩][T][ENTER] [→][∫]

If you start from your CAS in Exact mode, you will be asked whether to change to Approx mode, press [OK] to accept the option YES. The result is the expression:

33

$$`\int (0., 1.5, \text{EXP(tt\^2)/EXP(tt\^2)}, tt)',$$

which is the expression for the integral put together into a single algebraic expression. The dummy integration variable selected by the calculator is tt. To evaluate this integral numerically, you can use [↦][EVAL] or [↦][→NUM]. The result is the value 1.08585331767.

Integrating an equation

Suppose that you want to evaluate the following equation involving integrals

$$\int_{v0}^{v} \frac{dv}{\sqrt{v}} = \int_{0}^{t} (\alpha + \beta\, t)dt.$$

You can type the equation in the equation writer by using:

[EQW][↦][∫] [ALPHA][←][V] [0][▶] [ALPHA][←][V] [▶][1][÷] [√x] [ALPHA][←][V]
[▶] [ALPHA][←][V] [▶] [↦][=]
[EQW][↦][∫] [0][▶] [ALPHA][←][T] [▶] [↦][( )][ALPHA][↦][A][+]
[ALPHA][↦][B][×][ALPHA][←][t][▶] [ALPHA][←][T]

The result is

Press [▲][▲][EVAL] to evaluate the integrals. The result is now:

34

Techniques of integration

While the calculator will provide integrals for many functions, some quite complicated, it is still useful to review some of the integration techniques traditionally used to calculate some types of integrals. The techniques presented here include:

- Integration by substitution or change of variable
- Integration by parts
- Integration by partial fractions

Integration by substitution or change of variable

Suppose that you want to calculate the integral

$$\int_0^2 \frac{x}{\sqrt{1-x^2}} dx$$

Let's type the integral in the equation writer:

[EQW][→][∫] [0][▶] [2][▶][ALPHA][↤][X] [÷] [√x] [1][-][ALPHA][↤][X][y^x][2]
[▶][ALPHA][↤][X][ENTER]

We suggest using the change of variable u = 1-x². We need find out how to replace x in terms of u, so enter the expression 'u =1-x^2' in the stack:

[→]['][ALPHA][↤][U] [→][=] [1][-][ALPHA][↤][X][yx][2][ENTER],

and isolate x by using:

[→]['][ALPHA][↤][U] [→][ALG][SOLVE].

The result is the list   { 'x=– √ – (u–1)' 'x=√ – (u–1)' }.

Press [→][EVAL] [▶][⇦] to keep only the result 'x=√ – (u–1)'. Next, press [→][ALG][SUBST] to replace the latter result in the integral. The resulting integral is:

'∫ (–(0^2–1),–(2^2–1),–(√u/(2*u)), u)'.

The best way to simplify this expression is to simplify term by term in the equation writer. To access the equation writer press [▼].

The screen will look like this:

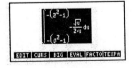

35

To simplify the limits and integrand use the following:

[▼][EVAL]
[▶][EVAL]   Simplifies the lower limit to 1
[▶][EVAL]   Simplifies the upper limit to -3
                                             Provides no simplification of the integrand

At this point the screen will look like this:

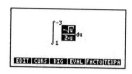

The integrand cannot be simplified by using [EVAL] (or [FACTO]), however, we can edit this expression by pressing [EDIT]. This triggers the stack editor which provides for us the line '-√u/(2*u)'. To edit this line to read '-1/(2*√u)', use: [▶][▶][▶][▶][⇔][⇔][1] [▶][▶][▶][▶][√x]. When done, press [ENTER]. Now, we're ready to integrate the simplified expression. Press [▲][EVAL]. The result is:

i.e.,

$$\int_0^2 \frac{x}{\sqrt{1-x^2}}dx = \int_1^{-3} -\frac{du}{\sqrt{u}} = 1 - i \cdot \sqrt{3}.$$

Note: if your calculator's CAS is set to Real before evaluating the integral, you will be asked to switch to the Complex mode. Press [OK] to accept the option YES.

The integral we just calculated can also be solved by using the substitution x = sin θ, or θ = sin⁻¹x. Let's try this exercise with this new substitution, as follows:

First, enter the integral as you did earlier:

[EQW][→][∫] [0][▶] [2][▶][ALPHA][↩][X] [÷] [√x] [1][-][ALPHA][↩][X][yˣ][2]
[▶][ALPHA][↩][X][ENTER]

Next, type: [→]['] [ALPHA][↩][X] [→][=] [SIN] [ALPHA][→][T][ENTER]

Next, press [→][ALG][SUBST] to replace the latter result in the integral. The resulting integral is:

'∫(ASIN(0),ASIN(2),-(COS(θ)*SIN(θ)*√-(SIN(θ)^2-1)/(SIN(θ)^2-1)),θ)'.

Let's simplify the different terms using the equation writer:

36

[▼]	Launch equation writer
[▼][EVAL]	Simplify lower limit to 0
[▶][EVAL]	Attempt to simplify upper limit fails

Here you could try to force a numerical value by using [↱][→NUM] while the upper integration limit is highlighted. The result is a complex number (1.507079632679,-1.31695789692).

[▶][↱][TRIG][NXT][TRIG]   Simplify integrand to SIN(θ)

> Thus, the integral has become now:

$$\int_0^{(1.51,-1.32)} \sin\theta \, d\theta.$$

To evaluate the integral, press [▶][▶] [↱][EVAL]. You will be asked if you want the Approx mode on, select YES, and press [OK]. The result is (0.9999999999,-1.73205080756), which is basically the same as the result $1-i\cdot\sqrt{3}$ found earlier.

Differentials

A differential is a representation of an infinitely small increment in a variable or function.

Using the notation, y'(x) = dy/dx, for the derivative, we can write a differential of y as dy = y'(x)·dx, where dx is a differential of x. Differentials of variables and functions can be operated upon as with any number.

Differentiation formulas can be written in terms of differentials, for example,

$$d(u(x)\cdot v(x)) = u(x)\cdot dv(x)+du(x)\cdot v(x).$$

This generic formula for differentials can be converted into a formula for derivatives if we divide by dx, thus:

$$d(u\cdot v)/dx = u\cdot(dv/dx)+(du/dx)\cdot v(x).$$

From the definition of anti-derivatives, it follows that

$$\int (dF/dx)\cdot dx = \int dF = F(x).$$

Integration by parts

Integration by parts is a technique that can be used if the integrand can be expressed as u(x)dv(x). From the definition of the differential of a product shown above, we can write:

$$d(u(x)\cdot v(x))-du(x)\cdot v(x). = u(x)\cdot dv(x)$$

and,

$$\int [d(u(x)\cdot v(x))-du(x)\cdot v(x)] = \int u(x)\cdot dv(x)$$

37

or

$$\int d(u(x) \cdot v(x)) - \int du(x) \cdot v(x) = \int u(x) \cdot dv(x).$$

Thus, we can write

$$\int u \cdot dv = u \cdot v - \int v \cdot du.$$

The function IBP

The function IBP takes as input the integrand of interest expressed as the product of two functions u(X)·v'(X), and the anti-derivative of v'(X). These two input items must occupy levels 2 and 1, respectively. The function is available through [←][CALC][DERIV][NXT][IBP]. The output consists of the terms u(X)·v(X) in stack level 2, and -u'(X)·v(X) in stack level 1. As an example, to obtain the components of integration by parts of the integral

$$\int X \cdot \exp(X) \cdot dX,$$

we first identify u(X) = X, v'(X) = exp(X), with v(X) = exp(X), and enter the following expressions in the calculator:

[→]['] [X] [×] [←][e^x] [X] [ENTER]
[→]['] [←][e^x] [X] [ENTER]

To calculate the elements of the integration by parts use:

[←][CALC][DERIV][NXT][IBP]

The result is:

This relationships are interpreted as follows:

⬇ The expression in stack level 2 is u(x)·v(x) ='EXP(X)*(X*EXP(X)/EXP(X)' which simplifies to 'X*EXP(X)'.
⬇ The expression in stack level 1 is -v(x) ·u'(x) = '-(EXP(X)^3./EXP(X)^2.)' which simplifies to '-EXP(X)'.

Translating this to paper we can write:

$$\int xe^x dx = xe^x + \int -e^x dx = xe^x - e^x = e^x(x-1).$$

38

Let's try another example: u(X) = ln X, v'(X) = X, with v(X) = X^2/2. Use:

$$[\rightarrow][\,'\,] [X] [\times] [\rightarrow][LN] [X] [ENTER]$$
$$[\rightarrow][\,'\,] [X][y^x][2][\div][2] [ENTER]$$

To calculate the elements of the integration by parts use:

$$[\leftarrow][CALC][DERIV][NXT][\,IBP\,]$$

The result is:

```
RAD XYZ HEX C~ 'X'
{HOME}
4:
3:
2:  'X^2./2.*(X*LN(X)/X
    )'
1:     '-(.5*X^4./X^3.)'
IBP INTVX LAPL PREVX RISCH CALC
```

This result is interpreted as:

✦ The expression in stack level 2 is u(x)·v(x) ='X^2/2*(X*LN(X)/X)' which simplifies to 'X^2*LN(X)/2'.
✦ The expression in stack level 1 is -v(x) ·u'(x) = '-(.5*X^4./X^3.)' which simplifies to '-.5*X'.

Translating this to paper we can write:

$$\int x \cdot \ln x\, dx = \frac{x^2}{2}\ln x + \int -\frac{x}{2}dx = \frac{x^2}{2} \cdot \ln x - \frac{x^2}{4} = \frac{x^2}{2}(\ln x - \frac{1}{2}).$$

Integration by partial fractions

Integrands that contain fractions can be simplified by re-writing the fraction as a sum of partial fractions. The function PARTFRAC, introduced in Chapter 8, decomposes a fractional expression in terms of the CAS default variable, VX (typically X), into a sum of partial fractions. After decomposing the expression into partial fractions integration can be performed in each of the partial fractions. For example, to obtain the integral

$$\int \frac{X^5 + 5}{X^4 + 2X^3 + X^2}dX,$$

Type in the integrand as follows:

[EQW] [X] [y^x][5][▶] [+][5][▶] [÷] [X] [y^x][4][▶] [+] [2][×][X] [y^x][3] [▶][▶][▶] [+][X] [y^x][2][ENTER]

First of all, because the order of the polynomial in the numerator is larger than that in the denominator, we need to convert this into a proper fraction by using the function PROPFRACT. Find this function using the catalog: [CAT][ALPHA][P], then use the up- and down-arrow keys to find PROPFRACT. Press [OK]. This decomposes the fraction into:

39

'X-2+(3*X^3+2*X^2+5)/(X^4+2*X^3+X^2)'

To form the partial fractions of this result, use the catalog again [CAT], and find the function PARTFRAC. Press [OK] to obtain the following:

'X-2+(5/X^2-10/X+(4/(X+1)^2+13/(X+1)))',

i.e.,

$$\frac{X^5+5}{X^4+2X^3+X^2} = X-2+\frac{5}{X^2}-\frac{10}{X}+\frac{4}{(X+1)^2}+\frac{13}{(X+1)}.$$

To proceed with the integration use:

[←][CALC][DERIV][NXT][INTVX]

The result is:

'SQ(X)/2-2*X+(-5/X)-10*LN(X)+(-(4/(X+1))+13*LN(X+1)))', i.e.,

$$\int \frac{X^5+5}{X^4+2X^3+X^2}dX = \frac{X^2}{2}-2X-10\ln X -\frac{4}{X+1}+13\ln(X+1).$$

You may want to try checking what result you get by directly integrating the original expression, i.e.,

[EQW] [X] [y^x][5][▶] [+][5][▶] [÷] [X] [y^x][4][▶] [+] [2][×][X] [y^x][3] [▶][▶][▶] [+][X] [y^x][2][ENTER]

[←][CALC][DERIV][NXT][INTVX].

Improper integrals

Improper integrals are those with infinite limits of integration. The general approach for evaluating these integrals is to replace the infinite limit with a variable, say ε, and then take the limit when ε → ∞. This can be written, for one particular case, as

$$\int_{-\infty}^{\infty} f(x)dx = \lim_{\varepsilon \to \infty}\int_{-\varepsilon}^{\varepsilon} f(x)dx = \lim_{\varepsilon \to \infty}[F(\varepsilon)-F(-\varepsilon)],$$

where f(x) = dF/dx.

As an example, to evaluate the integral

$$\int_1^{\infty} \frac{dx}{x^2} = \lim_{\varepsilon \to \infty}\int_1^{\varepsilon} \frac{dx}{x^2},$$

40

use

[EQW][→][∫] [1][▶] [ALPHA][→][E] [▶][1][÷] [ALPHA][¬][X] [yˣ][2] [▶] [ALPHA][¬][X]
[▲] [▲][EVAL][ENTER]

The result is '(ε-1)/ε'. To evaluate the limit when ε → ∞, use:

[→]['][ALPHA][→][E] [→][=][¬][∞][ENTER]
[¬][CALC][LIMIT][LIMIT]

The result is '1.'

The HP 49 G calculator allows you to enter the integral with one or two infinite limits. When you request evaluation of the integral, the limit, if it exist, will be calculated. Thus, for the present example you could write:

[EQW][→][∫] [1][▶] [¬][∞] [▶][1][÷] [ALPHA][¬][X] [yˣ][2] [▶] [ALPHA][¬][X]
[▲] [▲][EVAL]

The result is 1, as expected.

Series

A *sequence* or progression of numbers consists of numbers ordered so that knowing a given number in the sequence the preceding and subsequent numbers are completely specified. Typically, a *general term* of the sequence defines the rule by which the sequence is created. For example, the following is the sequence of even positive numbers: 2, 4, 6, ..., 2k, 2(k+1), ...

A *series* is the sum of the terms of a sequence. For example, $S_n = 2 + 4 + 6 + ... + 2k + ... + 2n$, defines the series consisting of the sum of the first n positive even integers. S_n represents a *finite series*, i.e., one that has initial and ending terms. If n→ ∞, the resulting series, $S_∞$, becomes an *infinite series*.

Series can be represented by summations, for example, the following is a finite series:

$$S_{10} = \sum_{j=1}^{10} \frac{1}{j^2+1} = \frac{1}{2} + \frac{1}{5} + \frac{1}{10} + ... + \frac{1}{j^2+1} + ... + \frac{1}{101}$$

This is an infinite series:

$$S_\infty = \sum_{r=1}^{\infty} |e^{-r}| = |e^{-1}| + |e^{-2}| + ... + |e^{-r}| + ...$$

The last two series are *series of positive terms*. The following is an *alternating series* (signs alternate from term to term)

$$S_\infty = \sum_{l=0}^{\infty} \frac{(-1)^n}{1+e^l} = \frac{1}{2} - \frac{1}{1+e} + ... + \frac{(-1)^n}{1+e^l} + ...$$

A *convergent series* is an infinite series whose sum converges to a finite value. If the sum of an infinite series does not converge to a finite value, we have a *divergent series*.

Using the summation sign in the equation writer makes handling finite and infinite series very easy in the HP 49 G calculator. Try the following exercises (assuming Exact mode is selected):

Examples of series obtained in the calculator

 A finite series

To calculate the series

$$\sum_{k=1}^{100} k^2,$$

Use:

[EQW][→][Σ] [ALPHA][↰][K] [▶] [1][▶] [1][0][0] [▶][ALPHA][↰][K] [yˣ][2] [▲][▲][▲] [EVAL]

The result is 338350.

A convergent infinite series

To calculate the series

$$\sum_{n=1}^{\infty} \frac{1}{n^2},$$

Use:

[EQW][→][Σ] [ALPHA][↰][N] [▶] [1][▶] [↰][∞]
[▶][1][÷][ALPHA][↰][N] [yˣ][2] [▲][▲][▲][▲] [EVAL]

The result is $\pi^2/6$. Using [→][→NUM], the result is 1.64498406685.

A divergent infinite series

To calculate the series

$$\sum_{j=1}^{\infty} \frac{1}{j},$$

Use:

[EQW][→][Σ] [ALPHA][↰][J] [▶] [1][▶] [↰][∞] [▶][1][÷][ALPHA][↰][J] [▲][▲][▲][EVAL]

The result is $+\infty$.

An alternating infinite series

To calculate the series

$$\sum_{m=1}^{\infty} \frac{(-1)^{m+1} \cdot \pi^{2m-1}}{(2m-1)!},$$

Use:

[EQW][↱][Σ] [ALPHA][↰][M] [▶] [1][▶] [↰][∞] [▶] [↰][( )] [1][+/-] [▶][▶] [y^x]
[ALPHA][↰][M] [+][1] [▶][▶] [×] [↰][π][÷][2] [▶] [y^x] [2][×][ALPHA][↰][M][-][1]
[▶][▶][▶][▶] [÷][2][×][ALPHA][↰][M][-][1] [▶][▶] [↰][MTH][NXT][PROB][!]

The series will look as follows in the equation writer:

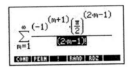

Press [▶][▶] to select the entire expression in the equation writer, then press [↱][EVAL].
After about 10 seconds you get as a result a question mark '?'. This indicates that the exact
result that the calculator is trying to find for the series is inconclusive.

Press [↱][UNDO] to recover the series in the equation writer. As an approximation, let's
replace the value of infinity by a relatively large number, say 100, using:
[▼][▶][▶][⇦][⇦][1][0][0]. Press [▲][▲] to highlight the series again, and press [↱][EVAL].
The result, obtained after about 10 seconds, is 1.00000000001.

Press [↱][UNDO] to recover the series in the equation writer. Now, change the value of 100 to
200, to see if there is any major change in the value of the series, use:
[▼][▶][▶][⇦][⇦][⇦][⇦] [2][0][0]. Press [▲][▲] once more to highlight the series, followed
by [↱][EVAL]. Wait another 10 or 15 seconds to get as a result the same value:
1.00000000001.

These results tell us that the series converges to 1.0 with 100 elements or less, with an error of
1×10^{-11}. Because the series is an alternating series, the calculator has difficulties figuring out
what the value of the sum is. However, we trick it by replacing the upper limit of the index
(∞) with a relatively large number (100). The second attempt to obtain a numerical value,
using 200 as the upper limit, was used to verify any major changes in the value of the series by
duplicating the upper limit. Since no changes were observed by doubling the upper limit of the
summation index, we have the feeling that the series does converge to the value of 1.0.
"Having the feeling" that the series converge is as accurate as we can get here unless we use
some of the convergence criteria listed below.

43

Convergence criteria for infinite series

There are a number of tests that you can perform to determine whether an infinite series converges to a finite value or not. For series of positive terms you can use the comparison test of the d'Alembert's ratio test. These tests are described following.

Comparison test for positive-term series

Suppose that we know that the infinite series

$$\sum_{k=1}^{\infty} a_k,$$

where a_k is the general term of the series, and $a_k > 0$ for all values of k, converges. Convergence of a series can be expressed by writing

$$\sum_{k=1}^{\infty} a_k < \infty.$$

Let b_k be the general term of another infinite positive-term series,

$$\sum_{k=1}^{\infty} b_k.$$

If for all values of k you can prove that $b_k < a_k$, then the second series also converges.

For example, we found earlier that the series

$$\sum_{n=1}^{\infty} \frac{1}{n^2},$$

converges to the value $\pi^2/6$. Because for $n > 1$, $n^3 > n^2$, then $1/n^2 > 1/n^3$, or $1/n^3 < 1/n^2$, then the series

$$\sum_{n=1}^{\infty} \frac{1}{n^3}$$

also converges.

44

The infinite series

$$\sum_{k=1}^{\infty} a_k,$$

where a_k is the general term of the series, and $a_k > 0$ for all values of k, is convergent if

$$\lim_{k \to \infty} \frac{a_{k+1}}{a_k} < 1.$$

Otherwise, the series diverge.

For example, to check whether the series

$$\sum_{n=1}^{\infty} \frac{1}{n!}$$

converges, we can take $a_n = 1/n!$, and $a_{n+1} = 1/(n+1)!$, and calculate the limit

$$\lim_{n \to \infty} \frac{a_{n+1}}{a_n} = \lim_{n \to \infty} \frac{(n+1)!}{n!} = \lim_{n \to \infty} \frac{(n+1) \cdot n!}{n!} = \lim_{n \to \infty} (n+1) = \infty$$

The series diverges.

The alternating series

$$\sum_{k=1}^{\infty} (-1)^{n-1} a_k,$$

converges if

$$a_{k+1} \leq a_k \text{ for all } k,$$

and

$$\lim_{k \to \infty} a_k = 0.$$

For example, consider the series

$$\sum_{k=1}^{\infty} \frac{(-1)^{n+1}}{n},$$

45

with $a_n = 1/n$. Obviously, $a_{n+1} < a_n$, since $1/(n+1) < 1/n$, for $n > 1$. Also,

$$\lim_{n \to \infty} a_n = \lim_{n \to \infty} \frac{1}{n} = 0.$$

Therefore, the series converges.

To determine the value of this series using the calculator, try the following (use Exact mode):

[EQW][→][Σ] [ALPHA][⌐][N] [▶] [1][▶] [⌐][∞] [▶] [⌐][( )] [1][+/-] [▶][▶]
[y^x] [ALPHA][⌐][N] [+][1] [▶][▶] [÷] [ALPHA][⌐][N]
[▲] [▲][▲][EVAL]

As in the previous example with an alternating series, the calculator is at a lost on the value of this series (The result is '?'). Let's calculate the series using the first 100 and 200 elements, as follows:

Press [→][UNDO] to recover the series.
Use [▼][▶][▶][⇦][⇦][1][0][0] to replace the upper limit with the value 100.
Press [▲][▲] to highlight the series again, and press [→][EVAL].

The result, obtained after about 5 seconds, is 0.688172179304.

Press [→][UNDO] again to recover the series.
Use [▼][▶][▶][⇦][⇦][⇦][⇦] [2][0][0] to replace the upper limit with the value 200.
Press [▲][▲] to highlight the series again, and press [→][EVAL].

The new result is 0.690653430437.

Although the result seems to converge to a number close to 0.69, increasing the upper limit from 100 to 200 still produces an error of the order of 0.01. So, let's try re-calculating the series with an upper limit of 500, to see what it does to its value.

Press [→][UNDO] again to recover the series.
Use [▼][▶][▶][⇦][⇦][⇦][⇦] [5][0][0] to replace the upper limit with the value 500.
Press [▲][▲] to highlight the series again, and press [→][EVAL]. (Give the calculator some time here).

The updated result is 0.692148180548.

Still, the last two result differ in the third decimal. We will have to try an upper limit larger than 500 to see if we are getting closer to the value of the series. For example, for an upper limit of 600:

Press [→][UNDO] again to recover the series.
Use [▼][▶][▶][⇦][⇦][⇦][⇦] [6][0][0] to replace the upper limit with the value 600.
Press [▲][▲] to highlight the series again, and press [→][EVAL]. (Be patient here while the calculator calculates the series).

The updated result is 0.69231454166.

The difference is now in the fourth decimal, so we can say, that the series converges to 0.692 with an error of 0.0001. If you feel adventuresome, and have lots of time, try using an upper limit of 1000. The result is 0.692647430554.

Absolute and conditional convergence

An alternating series, Σa_n, is said to be _absolutely convergent_ if the series $\Sigma|a_n|$ converges. If the original series, Σa_n, converges but the absolute-value series, $\Sigma|a_n|$, diverges, then the series is said to be conditionally _convergent_.

The criteria used for positive-term series can be used to check absolute-value series for convergence. If a series is absolutely convergent then it is convergent.

Power Series

A power series is a series that involves a power of a certain (independent) variable in its general term. Power series can be used to represent functions of that independent variable, for example:

$$f(x) = \sum_{k=1}^{\infty} (-1)^{n+1} \frac{(x-2)^n}{(2n+1)!}.$$

In general, when the function f(x) can be written as

$$f(x) = \sum_{k=1}^{\infty} a_k (x-c)^n,$$

we say that this expression represents an _expansion of the function into a power series about the point x = c._

Taylor's and Maclaurin's series expansions

Let $f^{(k)}(x)$ represent the k-th order derivative of a function $f(x)$ with respect to x, i.e., $f^{(k)}(x) = d^k f/dx^k$, with $f^{(0)}(x) = f(x)$, then the Taylor series expansion of the function $f(x)$ about the point $x = x_0$ can be written as

$$f(x) = \sum_{n=0}^{\infty} \frac{f^{(n)}(x_0)}{n!} \cdot (x-x_0)^n.$$

47

If the expansion is calculated about the point x = 0, then the resulting series is called a Maclaurin's series expansion, i.e.,

$$f(x) = \sum_{n=0}^{\infty} \frac{f^{(n)}(0)}{n!} \cdot x^n.$$

Taylor polynomial and remainder

The purpose of expanding a function into its Taylor's or Maclaurin's series is to be able to evaluate certain transcendental functions, e.g., sine, cosine, exponential, etc., numerically. These series are then implemented in calculators or computers to produce values for those functions. The numerical results thus obtained necessarily involve only a finite number of terms in the series, thus we could write a function f(x) as

$$f(x) = P_k(x) + R_k(x) = \sum_{n=0}^{k} \frac{f^{(n)}(x_0)}{n!} \cdot (x - x_0)^n + R(x).$$

The function $P_k(x)$, representing a finite polynomial of order k, is known as the _Taylor's polynomial_ of the function f(x). The function R(x) is known as the _remainder_ of the series. The remainder can be written as

$$R_k(x) = f(x) - P_k(x) = \frac{f^{(n+1)}(\xi)}{n!} \cdot (x - x_0)^{n+1},$$

where $|\xi-x| \leq |x_0-x|$, i.e., and the number x lies between x_0 and x!.

If we let $x = x_0+h$, where h is a small quantity, we can re-write the Taylor's series expansion of the function f(x) as follows:

$$f(x) = \sum_{n=0}^{k} \frac{f^{(n)}(x_0)}{n!} \cdot h^n + R(x),$$

with

$$R_k(x) = \frac{f^{(n+1)}(\xi)}{n!} \cdot h^{n+1}.$$

Typically, the value of ξ is not known, however, we can give an estimate of the order of the error involved in using the Taylor polynomial, as opposite to using the full series, by writing

$$R_k(x) = K \cdot h^{n+1} = O(h^{n+1}).$$

Here K is a constant (typically unknown) and the symbol O(r) is interpreted as "is of the order of r." Thus, the last equation indicates that the error (remainder) in estimating a function by using its Taylor polynomial is of the order h^{n+1}.

48

While, in most cases, this result will not let us estimate the error exactly, it does provide information on the relative magnitude of the error. For example, knowing that the error is of the order h^{n+1}, and letting $h<1.0$, means that the more terms we add to the polynomial (i.e., the larger the value of n) the smaller the error involved in the estimate using the Taylor polynomial. Also, when using the Taylor polynomial for numerical estimation, the smaller the value of h, the better the approximation.

The HP 49 G calculator provides the functions TAYLOR0, TAYLR, and SERIES to automatically calculate Taylor's (or Maclaurin's) series expansions.

The function TAYLOR0

The function TAYLOR0 performs a fourth-order Taylor's series expansion (Taylor polynomial) of an expression given in terms of the CAS default variable VX (typically X) about the point X = 0. In other words, the function TAYLOR0 performs a Maclaurin's series expansion. The only input this function needs is the expression that you want to expand as a Maclaurin's series. This function is useful to obtain the first few terms in a Maclaurin's series.

For example, to obtain the fourth-order Taylor polynomial the function f(X) = sin X, about X = 0, use:

[↱]['][SIN][X][ENTER]	Enter 'SIN(X)'
[↰][CALC][LIMIT][TAYLO]	Invoke function TAYLOR0

The result is: '1/120*X^5+ –1/6*X^3+X'.

Other examples:

'EXP(X)' [ENTER] [↰][CALC][LIMIT][TAYLO] Result:
'1/24*X^4+1/6*X^3+1/2(X^2+X+1'
'LN(X+1)'[ENTER] [↰][CALC][LIMIT][TAYLO] Result:
'–1/4*X^4+1/3*X^3+–1/2*X^2+X'
'1/(X+2)'[ENTER] [↰][CALC][LIMIT][TAYLO] Result:
'1/32*X^4+–1/16*X^3+1/8*X^2+–1/4*X+1/2'

The function TAYLR

The function TAYLR takes as input three elements:

- A symbolic expression in terms of a certain global variable (stack level 3).
- The global variable (stack level 2), and
- The relative order, i.e., the difference in order between the largest and smallest powers desired in the resulting polynomial (stack level 1),

The function returns the Maclaurin's series expansion of the expression based on the global variable.

For example:

'SIN(y-π/2)' [ENTER] 'y' [ENTER] 6 [ENTER]   [↰][CALC][LIMIT][TAYLO]
Result: '1/720*y^6+-1.24*y^4+1/2*y^2-1'

'COSH(S)' [ENTER] 'S' [ENTER] 8 [ENTER]   [↰][CALC][LIMIT][TAYLO]
Result: '1/40320*S^8+1/720*S^6+1/24*S^4+1/2*s^2+1'

'ATAN(R)' [ENTER] 'R' [ENTER] 6 [ENTER]   [↰][CALC][LIMIT][TAYLO]
Result: '-1/7*R^7+1/5*R^5+-1/3*R^3+R'

The function SERIES

The function SERIES calculates a Taylor's or Maclaurin's series expansion of a function f(x). The input of the function requires the following three elements:

  ⬥ The function f(x), in stack level 3
  ⬥ The variable name alone for a Maclaurin's series, or the variable name and the point about which the Taylor's series is expanded in the form 'x=a', and
  ⬥ The order of the series to be obtained.

The function returns as a result two output items:

  ⬥ A list containing the bi-directional limit of the function at the point where the series is developed, an equivalent value of the function near the point of expansion of the series, an expression approximating the function near the limit point, and the order of the remainder. All the terms in the list are expressed in terms of a small parameter h representing (x-a).

  ⬥ An expression for the small parameter h in terms of the original variable.

For example:

'SIN(X)' [ENTER] 'X=π/2' [ENTER] 6 [ENTER] [↰][CALC][LIMIT][SERIE]

Result:

The result is interpreted as follows:

  ⬥ Stack level 1: $h=X-\pi/2$, is the increment in the independent variable used in the Taylor series expansion.
  ⬥ Stack level 2: a list containing the following information:
  Limit: 1, i.e., the limit of the function when $X \rightarrow \pi/2$ is 1.0.
  Equiv: 1, i.e., the function is equivalent to 1.0 near the point $X = \pi/2$.
  Expans: '-1/720*h^6+1/24*h^4+-1/2*h^2+1', i.e., the Taylor polynomial of order 6 is:

$$'-1/720 \, (X-\pi/2)^6+1/24*(X-\pi/2)^4+-1/2*(X-\pi/2)^2+1'$$

50

Remain: 'h^7', i.e., the remainder of the polynomial expansion in Expans is

$$R_6(x) = O(h^7) = O[(X - \pi/2)^7]$$

A second example:

'LN(t)' [ENTER] 't =e' [ENTER] 6 [ENTER] [↰][CALC][LIMIT][SERIE]

Result:

The result is interpreted as follows:

⬇ Stack level 1: h=t-e, is the increment in the independent variable used in the Taylor series expansion.

⬇ Stack level 2: a list containing the following information:

⬇ Limit: 1, i.e., the limit of the function when t→ e is 1.0.

⬇ Equiv: 1, i.e., the function is equivalent to 1.0 near the point t=e.

⬇ Expans:'-1/(6*e^6)*h^6+1/(5*e^5)*h^5+-1/(4*e^4)*h^4+1/(3*e^3)*h^3+-1/(2*e^2)*h^2+1/e*h+1'

i.e., the Taylor polynomial of order   6 is: '(t-e)^6/(6e^6)+(t-e)^5/(5e^5)+(t-e)^4/(4e^4)+(t-e)^3/(3e^3)+(t-e)^2/(2e^2)+(t-e)/e+1'

⬇ Remain: 'h^7', i.e., the remainder of the polynomial expansion in Expans is
$$R_6(x) = O(h^7)=O[(t-e)^7].$$

51

Univariate calculus applications

In this section we present some examples of applications of derivatives and integrals of one variable in selected physical and engineering sciences.

Dynamics: rectilinear motion applications

Let s(t) represent the position along a straight-line path of a particle as a function of time t. By definition the velocity of the particle is v(t) = ds/dt, and its acceleration is a(t) = dv/dt = d^2s/dt^2. Another relationship that is commonly used results from eliminating dt from the equations for v(t) and a(t), which results in dv/a = ds/v or v·dv = a·ds. The latter result is useful when you are given a = a(s).

Example 1 - Given *s(t)* = *t*-sin *t*, plot the displacement, velocity, and acceleration of the particle as a function of t in the interval [0, 5].

⚓ First, enter the expression for s(t):

[EQW] [ALPHA][↵][S] [↵][( )] [ALPHA][↵][T] [▶] [→][=] [ALPHA][↵][T] [▶] [-] [SIN][ALPHA][↵][T] [ENTER] [↵][DEF]

This creates variable [s].

⚓ Next, calculate the velocity v(t):

[EQW] [ALPHA][↵][V] [↵][( )] [ALPHA][↵][T] [▶] [→][=] [→][∂][ALPHA][↵][T] [▶][ALPHA][↵][S] [↵][( )] [ALPHA][↵][T] [ENTER] [→][EVAL] [↵][DEF]

This creates variable [v].

⚓ The next step is to calculate the acceleration a(t):

[EQW] [ALPHA][↵][A] [↵][( )] [ALPHA][↵][T] [▶] [→][=] [→][∂][ALPHA][↵][T] [▶][ALPHA][↵][V] [↵][( )] [ALPHA][↵][T] [ENTER] [→][EVAL] [↵][DEF]

This creates variable [a].

⚓ To plot these functions you need to load the list {'s(t)' 'v(t)' 'a(t)'} into EQ, change the independent variable to t, change the range of values of t from 0 to 5, use AUTO to generate the range of values for the y-axis, and proceed to create the plot. For details in creating FUNCTION type plots see the examples in Chapter 11. The result is the following plot:

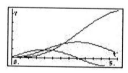

52

Example 2 - Given the speed of a particle as function of time t, v(t) = exp(-t/5), obtain an expression for the position of the particle s(t) if the particle started at s = -5 when t = 2. Also, find the acceleration of the particle at t = 1.

🔸 First, we define the velocity function:

[EQW] [ALPHA][↵][V] [↵][( )] [ALPHA][↵][T] [▶] [→][=] [↵][eˣ] [+/-] [ALPHA][↵][T] [÷][5] [ENTER] [↵][DEF]

This creates the variable [v   ]

🔸 From the definition of velocity, v(t) = ds/dt, we can write ds = v(t)dt, and integrate

$$\int_{-5}^{s} ds = \int_{2}^{t} v(t)dt$$

by using:

[EQW] [→][∫] [5][+/-][▶] [ALPHA][↵][S] [↵][( )] [ALPHA][↵][T][▶] [1][▶]
[ALPHA][↵][S][▶] [→][=] [→][∫] [2][▶] [ALPHA][↵][T][▶] [ALPHA][↵][V] [↵][( )]
[ALPHA][↵][T][▶] [ALPHA][↵][T] [▲][▲][▲] [EVAL]

This is the result shown in the equation writer screen (small font):

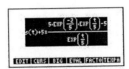

🔸 Press [ENTER] [→]['][5] [→][=][5][ENTER][–] [→][ALG][EXPAN] to eliminate the 5 from the left-hand side of the equation (using ISOL does not work here). The result is:

's(t)=((5*EXP(-2/5)-5)*EXP(t/5)-5)/EXP(t/5)'.

🔸 To find the acceleration of the particle can be found by using:

[EQW] [ALPHA][↵][A] [↵][( )] [ALPHA][↵][T] [▶] [→][=] [→][∂][ALPHA][↵][T]
[▶][ALPHA][↵][V] [↵][( )] [ALPHA][↵][T] [ENTER] [→][EVAL] [↵][DEF]

The result is 'a(t)=-1/(5*EXP(t/5))'.

🔸 To find the value of the acceleration at t = 1, use:

[→]['][ALPHA][↵][T] [→][=] [1] [ENTER] [→][ALG][SUBST]

The result is: 'a(1) = -1/(5*EXP(1/5))'.

🔸 To get a numerical value out of this expression, we need to separate the expression as follows:

53

[↤][PRG][TYPE][OBJ→][⇦][⇦] [↦][→NUM]

The result is -0.163746150616.

Example 3 - A particle is moving with an acceleration $a = -1.5\ v^{1/2}$, with $v = 4$, when $t = 0$. Determine and expression for the velocity, $v(t)$, and evaluate the velocity at $t = 2$.

⬇ From the definition of acceleration, $a = dv/dt$, and using the initial conditions indicated above, we can write the following integral equation:

$$\int_4^v \frac{dv}{\sqrt{v}} = -1.5 \int_0^t dt$$

⬇ Enter the integral in a similar fashion as done in Example 2. The equation should look like this in the equation writer:

$$\int_4^v \frac{1}{\sqrt{v}} dv = \int_0^t -1.5\, dt \blacktriangleleft$$

EDIT CURS BIG ■ EVAL FACTO TEXPR

⬇ Make sure your CAS mode is set to Exact (-105 CF). Press [ENTER][↦][EVAL] to calculate the integrals in the equation. When asked for Approx mode on, choose YES, and press [OK]. The result is '-4.+2.* √v=-(1.5*t)'

⬇ Then, use [↦]['][ALPHA][↤][V] [↤][S.SLV][ISOL] to obtain: 'v=.5625*t^2+ –3*t+4.'

⬇ To evaluate this expression at t = 2, use:

[↦]['] [ALPHA][↤][T] [↦][=] [2][ENTER] [↦][ALG][SUBST] [↦][EVAL]

The result is 'v=0.25'.

Dynamics: motion in polar coordinates

Example 1 - Finding velocity and acceleration in the radial direction given $r = f(\theta(t))$.

When describing the trajectory of a particle in polar coordinates, $r = f(\theta)$, we are usually required to find the derivatives,
$$v_r = r' = dr/dt, \text{ and } a_r = r'' = dv_r/dt = d^2r/dt^2.$$

If $\theta(t)$ is given, then, we can just replace it into $f(\theta)$, to get $r = g(t) = f(\theta(t))$. For example, if r = 2.5 sinθ, and, $\theta = 3.5t^2$ - 2t, we can simply write r = 2.5 sin($3.5t^2$ - 2t).

To obtain the derivatives using the HP48G or GX calculator, we enter the expression for r(t) in the display and use the [↦][∂] keystroke sequence. For example, enter the expression,

    '2.5*SIN(3.5*t^2 - 2*t)'

in stack level 1 of the calculator, and store it into the variable r by using

54

$$[\rightarrow][\,'\,][ALPHA][\leftharpoondown][R][STO\blacktriangleright].$$

Then, calculate the derivative by using:

$$[VAR][\;\;r\;\;][\rightarrow][\,'\,]\;[ALPHA][\leftharpoondown][T][ENTER]\;[\rightarrow][\partial]$$

Simplify the expression by using the function COLCT (COLleCT), available through the command catalog: [CAT][ALPHA][C] (find COLCT)[OK], to get an expression for r'(t) as

$$'(17.5*t-5.)*COS(3.5*t^2 - 2*t)'$$

Save this expression into variable *rt*, by using:

$$[\rightarrow][\,'\,][ALPHA][\leftharpoondown][R]\;[ALPHA][\leftharpoondown][T]\;[STO\blacktriangleright].$$

To obtain the second derivative of r with respect to t, use:

$$[VAR][\;\;rt\;\;][\rightarrow][\,'\,]\;[ALPHA][\leftharpoondown][T][ENTER]\;[\rightarrow][\partial][CAT][OK]$$
(Note: the function COLCT should be readily available)

The result is:

$$'-((122.5*t^2.+-70.*t+10.)*SIN(3.5*t^2.-2.*t)-17.5*COS(3.5*t^2-2.*t))'$$
or,
$$r'' = -((122.5t^2-70t+10)sin(3.5t^2-2t)-17.5\,cos(3.5t^2-2t)).$$

Example 2 -- Finding velocity and acceleration in the radial direction given r = f(θ).

If you want to find the derivatives r' and r'' for r = f(θ), where θ is not given explicitly as a function of time, you can still use the HP 49 G calculator to obtain expressions in terms of θ' =dθ/dt, and θ'' = $d^2\theta/dt^2$. We will need to write the expression for r as f(θ(t)) and take derivatives with respect to t.

For example, given r = 2.5 sinθ, evaluate r' and r'' when θ = 0.5 rad, θ' = -3.5 rad/s, and θ'' = 2 rad/s².
We will write in the calculator the following expression:

$$'2.5*SIN(\theta(t))'$$

and save it into r:

$$[VAR][\leftharpoondown][\;\;r\;\;].$$

Then, calculate the derivative dr/dt by using:

$$[VAR][\;\;r\;\;]\;[\rightarrow][\,'\,]\;[ALPHA][\leftharpoondown][T][ENTER]\;[\rightarrow][\partial]$$

We get the result:

$$'2.5*(COS(\theta(t)))*\,d1\theta(t))',$$

where *d1θ(t)* represents θ' = dθ/dt. In other words, our result is

$$r' = 2.5 \cdot cos\,\theta \cdot \theta'.$$

Save the expression in stack level 1 into variable *rt*, by using:

[VAR][↤][rt].

To obtain the second derivative of r with respect to t, use:

[VAR][rt] [↦]['] [ALPHA][↤][T][ENTER] [↦][∂][CAT][OK]

(Note: the function COLCT should be readily available)

The resulting expression is   `'2.5*COS(θ(t))*d1d1θ(t)-2.5*d1θ(t)^2.*sin(θ(t))'`.

With the understanding that `d1d1θ` represents the second derivative of θ with respect to t, i.e., θ", we can write:

$$r" = -2.5 \cdot [\theta']^2 \cdot \sin\theta + 2.5 \cos\theta \cdot \theta".$$

At this point we can replace the values given earlier for θ'and θ". Keeping the last expression in stack level 1 create the following list:

`{ 'θ(t)=.5' 'd1θ(t)=-3.5' 'd1d1θ(t)=2'}` [ENTER]

and use the keystroke sequence:

[↤][DEF]

to define the three "functions" (actually constant values) to be able to evaluate the expressions for the derivatives. Now, enter

[↦][EVAL]

to get the value -10.2944943103.

To evaluate the first derivative r'(t) and the position r(t) use:

[VAR] [**rt**] [↦][EVAL]	Result:	-7.67884741655
[**r**] [↦][EVAL]	Result:	1.19856384651

When done, you may want to purge all the variables defined here by creating the list:

`{'θ' 'd1θ' 'd1d1θ' 'rt' 'r'}` [ENTER]

and using

[TOOL][PURGE].

The function COLCT

The function COLCT belongs in the old HP 48 G/G+/GX SYMBOLIC menu, but it is still available in the HP 49 G calculator through the command catalog as shown in the examples above.

Probability: Calculations with continuous random variables

For probability distributions of continuous random variables, probabilities are calculated using the *cumulative distribution function* (CDF), F(x) = P(X ≤x). The definition of the CDF for continuous variables utilizes definite integrals. We can use the HP48G series calculator to evaluate such integrals either symbolically or numerically. Following we present some examples within a new subdirectory HOME\STATS\INTS :

1) Suppose that the pdf of a continuous random variable is given by f(x) = K/(1+x²), for - ∞ < x < ∞. We are asked to find the value of K. By definition,

$$\int_{-\infty}^{+\infty} f(x)dx = 1$$

$$K \cdot \int_{-\infty}^{+\infty} \frac{dx}{1+x^2} = 1.$$

for this particular case, we can write

It should be straightforward to type this equation in the equation writer to produce:

Press [ENTER][→][EVAL], to get the result: 'K*π=1'. Of course, you can easily figure out that K = 1/π, and find this value by using: [←][π][1/x][→][→NUM], i.e., K = 0.318309886184.

2) Consider the expression for the Standardized Normal distribution,

$$f(x) = \frac{1}{\sqrt{2 \cdot \pi}} \exp(-\frac{x^2}{2}).$$

Prove that, for this distribution, $_{-\infty}\int^{+\infty} f(x)dx=1$. First, type in the expression

$$\int_{-\infty}^{\infty} \frac{1}{\sqrt{2 \cdot \pi}} \exp(-\frac{x^2}{2})dx$$

in the equation writer, to produce:

57

$$\int_{-\infty}^{\infty} \frac{1}{\sqrt{2 \cdot \pi}} \cdot EXP\left(-\frac{x^2}{2}\right) dx$$

| EDIT | CURS | BIG ■ | EVAL | FACTO | TEXPA |

A direct evaluation, by using [ENTER][⊢][EVAL] produces no numerical result. One possibility is to use the substitution *x = tan y*. Thus, having the integral listed in stack level 1, enter:

'x=TAN(y)' [ENTER][⊢][ALG][SUBST].

Next, press [▼] to activate the equation writer, and enter [▼][▶][▶][▶][⇐]. Your equation writer screen should now look like the figure below:

$$\int_{ATAN(-\infty)}^{ATAN(\infty)} \frac{\sqrt{2} \cdot TAN(y)^2 + \sqrt{2}}{2 \cdot \sqrt{\pi} \cdot EXP\left(\frac{TAN(y)^2}{2}\right)} dy$$

| EDIT | CURS | BIG ■ | EVAL | FACTO | TEXPA |

Let's evaluate the limits of integration by using: [▶][▼][EVAL] [▶][EVAL]. The limits of integration now become $-\pi/2$ and $\pi/2$. Press [ENTER] to exit the equation writer, change CAS mode to Approx, by using [1][0][5][+/-][ALPHA][ALPHA][S][F][ENTER], and use [⊢][→NUM] to obtain a numerical value. Be aware that it takes the calculator up to five minutes to obtain the numerical result: 0.999999999996, which is as close to 1.0 as we can get.

Note: The integral calculated above is an improper integral (i.e., one or both limits are $\pm\infty$). You can use the transformation *x= tan(y)* to convert the improper integral into a proper integral . The transformation is expressed by the following formula:

$$\int_a^b f(x)dx = \int_{\arctan(a)}^{\arctan(b)} f(\tan y)(1 + \tan^2 y)dy$$

If $a = -\infty$, then $\arctan(a) = -\pi/2$. Also, if $b = \infty$, then $\arctan(b) = \pi/2$. Also, $\arctan(0) = 0$.

Note: Some integrals, for example,

$$\int_1^\infty \frac{dx}{x} = \int_{\pi/4}^{\pi/2} \frac{(1 + \tan^2 y)}{\tan y} dy$$

do not converge to a value. And, in most cases, there is no way to tell from just looking at the integral that such is the case. (The case above is simple, since we know that $\int_1^x dx/x = \ln(x)$, therefore, $\int_1^\infty dx/x = \ln(\infty) = \infty$.)

58

3) On to a simpler example: If $f(x) = \cos x$, for $0 < x < \pi/2$, and $f(x) = 0$, *elsewhere*, find $P(0<X< \pi/4)$. We need to calculate the following integral:

$$P(0 < X < \frac{\pi}{4}) = \int_0^{\pi/4} \cos(x)dx$$

Use the following:

[→]['] [→][∫] [0] [→][,] [→][π][÷][4] [→][,] [COS] [X] [▶] [→][,] [X] [ENTER] [→][EVAL].
The result is '√2/2'. If you use [→][→NUM], this result is shown as 0.707106781185.

4) To calculate the mean [$\mu = \int x \cdot f(x)dx$] of the pdf in case 3, enter the following integral:

Press [▲][▲][EVAL] to get the result $\mu = (\pi-2)/2$.

Store this value in a variable called μ by using:

[ENTER][⌐][PRG][TYPE][OBJ→][⇔][⇔] [▶] [STO▶]

5) To calculate the variance [$\sigma^2 = \int (x-\mu)^2 f(x)dx$] of the pdf defined in 2, whose mean was calculated in 4, type in the following integral:

The display now shows: 0.141592....(i.e., $\sigma^2 = 0.141592...$).

59

Statics: properties of areas

Consider the region R in the x-y plane limited by the x-axis (y = 0), the curve y = f(x), and the vertical lines x = a and x = b as sketched in the figure below.

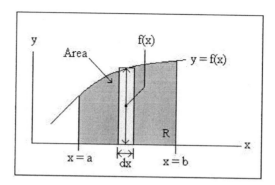

The small rectangle of width dx and height f(x) is a representative *differential of area* dA = f(x) dx for the region of interest. The area of the region will be calculated by adding the infinitesimal area elements between the values of x = a and x = b, i.e., by calculating the integral

$$A = \int_R dA = \int_a^b f(x)dx$$

The product x·dA = dM$_y$ is the infinitesimal first moment of the differential of area dA with respect to the y-axis. Here, x represents the location of the *centroid* (center of mass, center of gravity) of the infinitesimal rectangle dA. Integrating dM$_y$ over the values of x =a and x = b, we obtain the first moment of the area with respect to the y-axis, i.e.,

$$M_y = \int_R dM_y = \int_a^b x \cdot f(x)dx$$

Using the element of area shown above, it is possible to define a differential first moment of dA with respect to the x-axis as dM$_x$ = (y/2)·dA, since y/2 represents the location of the centroid of dA with respect to the x-axis. Thus, the first moment of the region R with respect to the x-axis is given by

$$M_x = \int_R dM_x = \frac{1}{2} \cdot \int_a^b [f(x)]^2 dx$$

The first moments of the area, My and Mx, are used to calculate the coordinates of the centroid,

$$\bar{x} = My/A, \text{ and } \bar{y} = Mx/A.$$

60

The quantity $dI_y = x^2 \cdot dA$ is referred to as the moment of inertia of the infinitesimal area dA with respect to the y-axis. The moment of inertia of the region R with respect to the y-axis is given by

$$I_y = \int_R dI_y = \int_a^b x^2 \cdot f(x)dx$$

The moment of inertia of the differential of area dA with respect to the x-axis, dI_x, is not as simple to write as that with respect to the y-axis, dI_y. The expression for dIx follows from the expression for the moment of inertia of a rectangle. Consider the rectangle shown in the figure below.

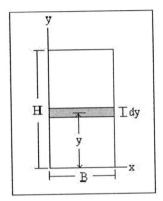

If we use the horizontal strip of the rectangle as a differential of area, $dA_H = B \, dy$, we can write $(dI_x)_R = y^2 dA^H = By^2 dy$, where the sub-index R stands for "rectangle." The moment of inertia of the rectangle with respect to the x axis can be calculated as the integral $\int_R By^2 dy$, between y = 0 and y = H. Using the HP 49 G calculator, the integral should look like this:

```
 ⌠H
 ⌡0  B·y² dy◄

EDIT CURS BIG■ EVAL FACTO TEXPR
```

Press [ENTER][↦][EVAL] to get the result $(I_x)_R = B \cdot H^3/3$. Thus, the moment of inertia of dA, the vertical infinitesimal rectangle of width dx and height f(x), is given by $dI_x = (1/3)(dx)[f(x)]^3 = (1/3)[f(x)]^3 dx$, and the moment of inertia of the region R with respect to the x-axis is calculated as

$$I_x = \int_R dI_x = \frac{1}{3}\int_a^b [f(x)]^3 \, dx.$$

61

The moment of inertia of the region R with respect to the origin (or, more properly, with respect to the z-axis, perpendicular to the x-y plane) is defined as

$$I_o = I_x + I_y = \int_a^b x^2 f(x) \cdot dx + \frac{1}{3} \int_a^b [f(x)]^3 \, dx.$$

Associated with the concept of moment of inertia is the idea of a radius of gyration. The radius of gyration about the y-axis is given by $k_y = (I_y/A)^{1/2}$, the radius of gyration about the x-axis is $k_x = (I_x/A)^{1/2}$, and that about the origin (or z-axis) is $k_o = (I_o/A)^{1/2}$.

Example: The figure below shows the region R defined by 0 < y < ln(x+1), 2<x<4. Use your HP 49 G calculator to obtain the area of the region , the coordinates of the centroid, the moments of inertia and radii of gyration about the x- and y-axis, and about the origin.

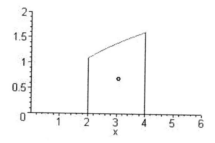

The solution requires you to use a = 2, b = 4, and f(x) = ln(x+1). Thus, the area would be calculated by

which produces the value ' -(3*LN(3)-(5*LN(5)-2))', or A = 2.75135269614. Store this value in a variable called A.

The following screens shown the integrals corresponding to the first moments My, Mx, and the moments of inertia Iy, and Ix:

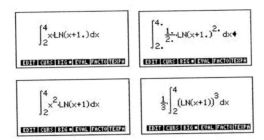

Once evaluated, the following results are obtained: My = 8.42286591025, Mx = 1.91394984757, Iy = 26.6864290145, and Ix = 1.7943172852. From these values we get, x = My/A = 3.06135448282, $\overline{y}$ = Mx/A = 0.695639584934, k_y = $(I_y/A)^{1/2}$ = 3.11438356332, and k_x = $(I_x/A)^{1/2}$ = 0.807563138712. Also, Io = Ix + Iy = 28.4807462997, and k_o = $(I_o/A)^{1/2}$ = 3.21738142011.

Dynamics: properties of solids of revolution - disk method

Consider the solid of revolution resulting from the rotation of the region R = {0 < y < f(x), a<x<b} about the x-axis, as illustrated in the figure below.

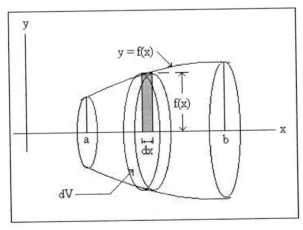

As the region rotates about the x-axis, the element of area - the shaded rectangle of width dx and height f(x) - generates a cylinder, or disk, of radius f(x) and height dx. The volume of this elementary cylinder (differential of volume) is

$$dV = \pi \cdot [f(x)]^2 \cdot dx.$$

The volume of the entire solid of revolution, contained in a<x<b, is, therefore,

63

$$V = \int_R dV = \int_a^b \pi \cdot [f(x)]^2 \cdot dx.$$

The external area of this elementary cylinder (differential of external area) is

$$dA_s = 2 \cdot \pi \cdot f(x) \cdot dx.$$

The total external area of the solid of revolution is, therefore,

$$A_s = \int_R dA_s = \int_a^b 2 \cdot \pi \cdot f(x) \cdot dx.$$

Let ρ represent the density (mass/volume) of the material composing the solid of revolution. By definition, $\rho = dm/dV$, where m represents mass. Therefore, the mass of the element of volume (differential of mass) is

$$dm = \rho \cdot dV = \pi \cdot \rho \cdot [f(x)]^2 \cdot dx.$$

This expression for dm applies if ρ is a constant. We can let the density vary with x, r(x), in which case the differential of mass is given by

$$dm = \rho \cdot dV = \pi \cdot \rho(x) \cdot [f(x)]^2 \cdot dx.$$

For constant ρ, the mass of the solid of revolution is simply

$$m = \rho \cdot V,$$

with V as calculated earlier.

For $\rho = \rho(x)$, the mass of the solid of revolution is to be calculated with the integral

$$m = \int_a^b \pi \cdot \rho(x) \cdot [f(x)]^2 \cdot dx.$$

The x-axis is an axis of symmetry for the solid of revolution, therefore, the y-coordinate of its center of mass is $\bar{y} = 0$. Assuming, in general, that $\rho = \rho(x)$, the first moment of the differential of mass with respect to the y-axis is given by

$$dM_y = x \cdot dm = x \cdot \rho \cdot dV = \pi x \cdot \rho(x) \cdot [f(x)]^2 \cdot dx.$$

The first moment of the solid of revolution with respect to the y-axis is, therefore,

$$M_y = \int_a^b \pi \cdot x \cdot \rho(x) \cdot [f(x)]^2 \cdot dx.$$

The x-coordinate of the solid body's center of mass is given by

$$\bar{x} = M_y / m.$$

The moment of inertia of the differential of mass with respect to the y-axis is given by

$$dI_y = x^2 \cdot dm = x^2 \cdot \rho \cdot dV = \pi \cdot x^2 \cdot \rho(x) \cdot [f(x)]^2 \cdot dx.$$

This expression results from the conditions of symmetry of the differential of mass about the y-axis that allows us to consider the inertial effect of the mass differential as that of a particle

64

of mass dm located at a distance x from the y-axis. The moment of inertia with respect to the y-axis is calculated using the following integral

$$I_y = \int_R dI_y = \int_R x^2 \cdot dm = \int_R x^2 \cdot \rho \cdot dV = \int_a^b \pi \cdot x^2 \cdot \rho(x) \cdot [f(x)]^2 \cdot dx.$$

To calculate the moment of inertia of the cylindrical differential of mass from the solid of revolution we need to use the expression for the moment of inertia of a cylinder of radius R and height H about its axis. This result, which is proved later in the book by using double integrals in polar coordinates, is given by

$$(I_y)_R = \frac{1}{2} \cdot \pi \cdot \rho \cdot H \cdot R^4.$$

Using this result with the elementary disk in the solid of revolution provides an expression for the differential of moment of inertia with respect to the x-axis:

$$dI_y = \frac{1}{2} \cdot \pi \cdot \rho(x) \cdot [f(x)]^4 \cdot dx.$$

Thus, the moment of inertia of the solid of revolution with respect to the x-axis will be given by the integral

$$I_x = \int_a^b \frac{1}{2} \cdot \pi \cdot \rho(x) \cdot [f(x)]^4 \cdot dx.$$

Radii of gyration of the solid of revolution with respect to the y- and x-axes, respectively, are given by

$$k_y = (I_y/m)^{1/2}, \text{ and } k_x = (I_x/m)^{1/2}.$$

Example - Consider the region R = { 0 < y < ln(x+1), 2<x<4} shown in the figure below. The region rotates about the x-axis generating the solid of revolution sketched in the figure below. Assuming that the density of the solid is given by $\rho(x) = \exp(-x/4)$, calculate the solid's volume, exterior area, mass, x-coordinate of its center of mass, moments of inertia and radii of gyration with respect to the y- and x-axes.

The approach I suggest for calculating the required properties for the solid of revolution is to define the functions f(x) = ln(x+1) and $\rho(x) = \exp(-x/4)$ in the HP 49 G calculator. You can also store the values of a=2 and b=4 in the calculator, and then simply type in the formulas shown earlier to obtain the different properties. Here is how to define the functions:

[EQW] [ALPHA][↰][F] [↰][( )] [ALPHA][↰][X] [▶] [↱][=] [↱][LN] [ALPHA][↰][X] [+][1] [ENTER] [↰][DEF]

This operation creates the variable [f].

To create the density function use:

[EQW] [→][CHARS] (find the character ρ) [ECHO1] [←][( )] [ALPHA][←][X] [▶] [→][=] [←][eˣ]
[ALPHA][←][X] [+/-] [÷][4] [ENTER] [←][DEF]

This operation creates the variable [ρ].

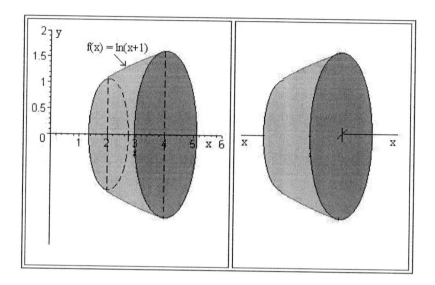

The next step is to store the values of a and b:

[2] [→]['][ALPHA][←][A][STO▶]   [4] [→]['][ALPHA][←][B][STO▶]

To calculate the mass, for example, type the integral

$$\int_a^b \pi \cdot \rho(x) \cdot (f(x))^2 \, dx$$

EDIT CURS BIG ■ EVAL FACTO TEXPA

Then, press [ENTER][→][→NUM] to obtain a numerical value for the integral. The mass is m =
5.56740083556.

The following screens show the integrals you need to type to produce the first moment M_y, and
moments of inertia I_y and I_x, respectively:

$$\int_a^b \pi \cdot x \cdot \rho(x) \cdot f(x)^2 \, dx$$

EDIT CURS BIG ■ EVAL FACTO TEXPA

$$\int_a^b \pi \cdot x^2 \cdot \rho(x) \cdot f(x)^2 \, dx$$

EDIT CURS BIG ■ EVAL FACTO TEXPA

$$\int_a^b \frac{1}{2} \cdot \pi \cdot \rho(x) \cdot f(x)^4 \, dx$$

EDIT CURS BIG ■ EVAL FACTO TEXPA

66

The corresponding values are M_y = 16.9252199715, I_y = 53.2640598494, and I_x = . Also, $\bar{x}$ = M_y/m = 3.04005773455, $k_y = (I_y/m)^{1/2}$ = 3.09307811219, and $k_x = (I_x/m)^{1/2}$ = 0.985351404481.

The volume and exterior area of the solid of revolution are calculated using the following

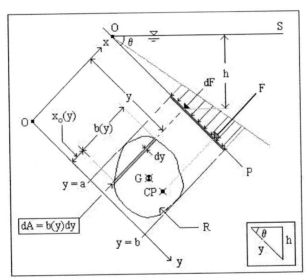

integrals:

The results are V = 12.0257015609, and A_s = 17.2872588354.

Hydrostatics: force over a flat surface submerged in a liquid

Consider the flat surface R located along the plane OP inclined by an angle θ with respect to the horizontal free surface OS of a liquid at rest.

The pressure in a liquid at rest is given by

$$p = p_0 + \gamma \cdot h,$$

where p_0 is the pressure at the free surface γ is the specific weight of the liquid (weight/volume), and h is the depth measured from the free surface. If the free surface OS is open to the atmosphere, and we use gage pressures, p_0 = 0, and

$$p = \gamma \cdot h.$$

Since pressure depends on depth only, a differential of force dF acting on the differential of area

67

of the surface R will be given by

$$dA = b(y)dy$$

where the relationship

$$dF = pdA = \gamma \cdot h \cdot dA = \gamma \cdot h \cdot b(y) \cdot dy = \gamma \cdot y \cdot \sin \theta \cdot b(y) \cdot dy,$$

$$h = y \cdot \sin \theta$$

has been used.   The force on the surface will be calculated through the integral

$$F = \int_R dF = \int_R p \cdot dA = \int_R \gamma \cdot h \cdot dA = \gamma \cdot \sin \theta \cdot \int_a^b y \cdot dA = \gamma \cdot \sin \theta \cdot \int_a^b y \cdot b(y) \cdot dy.$$

To find the point of application of the force we can take the moment of the differential of force dF with respect to the x and y axes as

$$dM_x = y \cdot dF = y \cdot p \cdot dA = \gamma \cdot h \cdot y \cdot dA = \gamma \cdot h \cdot y \cdot b(y) \cdot dy = \gamma \cdot y^2 \cdot \sin \theta \cdot b(y) \cdot dy,$$

and

$$dM_y = [x_o(y) + b(y)/2] \cdot dF = [x_o(y) + b(y)/2] \cdot p \cdot dA = [x_o(y) + b(y)/2] \cdot \gamma \cdot h \cdot dA = [x_o(y) + b(y)/2] \cdot \gamma \cdot y \cdot \sin \theta \cdot dA$$

$$dM_y = [x_o(y) + b(y)/2] \cdot \gamma \cdot y \cdot \sin \theta \cdot b(y) \cdot dy$$

where $x_o(y)$ is the distance from the y-axis to the left edge of the differential of area, and $b(y)$ is the width of the differential of area. The moments with respect to the x- and y-axes are given, respectively, by the following integrals

$$M_x = \int_R y \cdot dF = \int_R y \cdot p \cdot dA = \int_R \gamma \cdot y \cdot h \cdot dA = \gamma \cdot \sin \theta \cdot \int_a^b y^2 \cdot dA = \gamma \cdot \sin \theta \cdot \int_a^b y^2 \cdot b(y) \cdot dy.$$

and

$$M_y = \gamma \cdot \sin \theta \cdot \int_a^b [x_o(y) + \frac{1}{2} \cdot b(y)] \cdot y \cdot dA = \gamma \cdot \sin \theta \cdot \int_a^b [x_o(y) + \frac{1}{2} \cdot b(y)] \cdot y \cdot b(y) \cdot dy.$$

The point of application of the total force F is known as the center of pressure of the surface (point CP in figure above). Its coordinates are given as the arm of the force with respect to each axes that produce the same moments Mx and My. So, if the coordinates of CP are (x_{CP}, y_{CP}) we can write:

$$x_{CP} = M_y/F, \text{ and } y_{CP} = M_x/F.$$

Example 1 - Hydrostatic force on a triangular shape

Consider the triangular-shaped region located along the plane OP inclined by an angle θ from the free surface OS of a liquid at rest.   The dimensions of the triangular surface and its location with respect to the x- and y-axes are indicated in the sketch.   Find expressions for the force F, and the moments M_y and M_x produced by the hydrostatic pressure distribution on the triangular surface. Also find the coordinates of the center of pressure x_{CP} and y_{CP}.

68

To find an expression for $x_o(y)$ we use the coordinates of points A and B. The slope of the line AB can be found from

$$m_{AB} = (y_B - y_A)/(x_B - x_A) = (a + H - a)/(d - d - b_1) = -H/b_1.$$

The equation of a straight line going through point A with slope m_{AB} is $y - y_A = m_{AB}(x - x_A)$, or

$$y = y_A + m_{AB}(x - x_A) = a - (H/b_1)(x - d - b_1).$$

Using the calculator you can isolate x as follows:

'y=a-(H/b1)*(x-d-b1)' [ENTER] 'x' [ENTER] [↵][S.SLV][ISOL]

The result is: 'x = ((d+b1)*H+(b1*a-y*b1))/H'

To define this result as the function 'xo(y) = ((d+b1)*H+(b1*a-y*b1))/H', use the equation writer as follows:

[▼][▼][⇦][ALPHA][↵][O] [↵][( )] [ALPHA][↵][Y] [ENTER] [↵][DEF]

This operation creates the variable [xo   ].

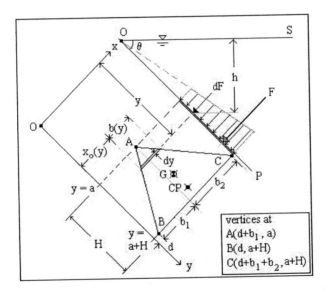

Similarly, the slope of line AC can be found from

$$m_{AC} = (y_C - y_A)/(x_C - x_A) = (a + H - a)/(d + b_1 + b_2 - d - b_1) = H/b_2,$$

and the equation of the line AC is

$$y = y_A + m_{AC}(x - x_A) = a + (H/b_2)(x - d - b_1).$$

Let's isolate x = x(y) by using the HP 49 G calculator:

'y=a+(H/b2)*(x-d-b1)'[ENTER] 'x' [ENTER] [↰][S.SLV][ISOL]

The result is: `x = -(((a-y)*b2-(d+b1)*H)/H'.

This result represents an outer value of x that we can define as xf(y). To define this function use:

[▼][▼][⇦][ALPHA][↰][F] [↰][( )] [ALPHA][↰][Y] [ENTER] [↰][DEF]

This operation creates the variable [xf].

⚓ The width of the element of area b(y) is by definition b(y) = xf(y) - xo(y), thus, we can define b(y) with the HP 49 G calculator by using:

'xf(y) - xo(y)' [ENTER][EVAL] [↦]['] [ALPHA][↰][B] [↰][( )] [ALPHA][↰][Y] [ENTER] [▶][↦][=]

This results in   `b(y) = -(((a-y)*b1+(a-y)*b2)/H)'.

Use [↰][DEF] to define the function b(y).

Having defined xo(y) and b(y) we can proceed to calculate the force F, moments M_y and M_x, and coordinates of the center of pressure x_{CP}, y_{CP}, as follows:

Note: The Greek letter γ is available in the HP 49 G calculator's character set by using [↦][CHAR], selecting γ, and pressing [ECHO1].

⚓ Force:

$$\gamma \cdot \text{SIN}(\theta) \cdot \int_{a}^{a+H} y \cdot b(y)\,dy$$

| EDIT | CURS | BIG■ | EVAL | FACTO | TEXPR |

Press [ENTER] [↦][EVAL].   After about 20 seconds you get the following result:

`((2*γ*H^2+3*γ*a*H)*b1+(2*γ*H^2+3*γ*a*H)*b2)*SIN(θ)/6'

Use [↦][ALG][FACTO] to get
`SIN(θ)*H*γ*((2*H+3*a)*b1+(2*H+3*a)*b2)/(3*2)'.

In the latter expression you can recognize another common factor (2*H+3*a) that has not yet been factored out.   You can factor it out by using the equation writer as follows:

[▼][▼][▼][▼][▼] [▶][▶][▶] [▲][▲][▲][▲][▲] [FACTO] [ENTER]

The result is now   `SIN(θ)*H*γ*((b1+b2)*(2*H+3*a))/(3*2)', i.e..

$$F = \frac{1}{6} \cdot \gamma \cdot H \cdot \sin \theta \cdot (b_1 + b_2) \cdot (2 \cdot H + 3 \cdot a).$$

Save this result into variable F by using [↦]['][ALPHA][F][STO▶]

🔸 Moment about the x axis:

Press [ENTER] [↦][EVAL].   After about 40 seconds you get the following result:

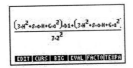

To factorize this expression use [↦][ALG][FACTO] .   Press [▼] to activate the equation writer.   If the option [BIG■] is selected, press the corresponding button to de-select it. This will let you see the current expression in a smaller font.   There is a common factor that has not been factored out.   To move about the equation writer screen, use the following: [▼][▼][▼][▼].   This will change the cursor to a rectangular shape that you can move from term to term.   Press [▶] twelve times to place the rectangular cursor over the term b1.   The screen should look like this:

$$\frac{\left(3 \cdot H^2 + 8 \cdot a \cdot H + 6 \cdot a^2\right) \cdot b1 + \left(3 \cdot H^2 + 8 \cdot a \cdot H + 6 \cdot a^2\right)}{3 \cdot 2^2}$$

EDIT CURS BIG EVAL FACTO TEXPR

This screen lets you see the common factor that is still distributed in the expression. This common factor is $(3 \cdot H^2 + 8 \cdot a \cdot H + 6 \cdot a^2)$.   To factor it out, use: [▲][▲][▲][FACTO].   Press [ENTER]. The resulting expression can be translated in paper as

$$M_x = \frac{1}{12} \cdot \gamma \cdot H \cdot \sin \theta \cdot (b_1 + b_2) \cdot (3 \cdot H^2 + 8 \cdot a \cdot H + 6 \cdot a^2).$$

Save this result in variable Mx using: [↦]['][ALPHA][M] [ALPHA][↤][X] [STO▶].

71

⬇ Moment about the y axis:

$$M(\phi) \cdot \int_{a}^{a+H} \left(x_0(y) + \tfrac{1}{2} \cdot b(y)\right) \cdot y \cdot b(y) \, dy$$

Press [ENTER] [↦][EVAL]. This calculation will take more than a minute since it involves multiplying out and integrating a more complicated expression. The beginning of the resulting expression is presented in the following screen:

```
RAD XYZ HEX R= 'X'
<HOME>
1: '((5*γ*H^2+8*γ*a*H)
   *b1^2+((8*γ*H^2+12*
   γ*a*H)*b2+(8*γ*d*H^
   2+12*γ*d*a*H))*b1+(
   (3*γ*H^2+4*γ*a*H)*
EXPAN FACTO LNCOL LIN SOLVE SUBST
```

To factorize this expression use [↦][ALG][FACTO]. The result is now:

```
RAD XYZ HEX R= 'X'
<HOME>
1: 'SIN(θ)*H*γ*((5*H+8
   *a)*b1^2+((8*H+12*a
   )*b2+8*d*H+12*d*a)*
   b1+(3*H+4*a)*b2^2+(
   8*d*H+12*d*a)*b2)/(
EXPAN FACTO LNCOL LIN SOLVE SUBST
```

In this last result we can see some common factors still not factored out, e.g., *(8*H+12*a)* and *(8*d*H+12*d*a)*. Press [▼] to activate the equation writer. (If the option [BIG■] is selected, press the corresponding button to de-select it. This will let you see the current expression in a smaller font. To move about the equation writer screen, use the following: [▼][▼][▼][▼]. This will change the cursor to a rectangular shape that you can move from term to term. Press [▶] fourteen times to place the rectangular cursor over the term 8. The

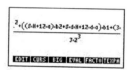

screen should look like this:

Now, press [▲][▲][▲] to select the expression (8·H+12·a)·b2+8·d·H+12·d·a. Press [FACTO] to factor this expression to (b2+d)· (8·H+12·a). Now, press [▼][▶] to highlight the term (8·H+12·a). Press [FACTO] to convert this expression to (2·H+3·a)·4. Next, press [▶][▶] to highlight the last term in the numerator: (8·d·H+12·d·a)·b2. Press [FACTO] to obtain for this last term b2·d· (8·H+12·a). We can factor this term even further by using [▼][▶][▶][FACTO] to highlight the term (8·H+12·a) and factor it out to (2·H+3·a)·4. Press [▼] until you obtain the rectangular cursor. Then, use the left- and right-arrow keys to move about the expression. The expression can be translated into paper as follows:

72

$$\frac{SIN(\theta) \cdot H \cdot \gamma \cdot ((5 \cdot H + 8 \cdot a) \cdot b1^2 + (b2 + d) \cdot (2 \cdot H + 3 \cdot a) \cdot b2^2 + b2 \cdot d \cdot (2 \cdot H + 3 \cdot a) \cdot 4)}{3 \cdot 2^2}$$

There is still the factor (2H+3a) that can be factored out of the last two terms in the numerator. Press [▼] until the rectangular cursor is available. Then move the cursor on top of the term b2 contained in (b2+d). Next, press [▲][▲][▲][▲][FACTO]. This result in the expression:

$$\frac{SIN(\theta) \cdot H \cdot \gamma \cdot (b1 + b2) \cdot ((5 \cdot H + 8 \cdot a) \cdot b1 + (3 \cdot H + 4 \cdot a) \cdot b2 + 8 \cdot d \cdot H + 12 \cdot d \cdot a)}{3 \cdot 2^2}$$

This is an improvement as we were able to identify the factor (b1+b2), however, within the second set of parentheses in the numerator we still have some factoring to do, particularly, in the last two terms. Press [▼] until the rectangular cursor is available. Then move the cursor on top of the term 8 contained in 8d·H Press [▲][▲][▲] until the term 8d·H is highlighted. Next, press [↦][▶] to highlight the last two terms, and press [FACTO]. The highlighted term is converted to d· (2···H+3a)4. The entire expression now looks like this:

$$\frac{SIN(\theta) \cdot H \cdot \gamma \cdot (b1 + b2) \cdot ((5 \cdot H + 8 \cdot a) \cdot b1 + (3 \cdot H + 4 \cdot a) \cdot b2 + d \cdot (2 \cdot H + 3 \cdot a) \cdot 4)}{3 \cdot 2^2}$$

Press [ENTER] and save the result into variable M_y, by using:

[↦]['][ALPHA][M] [ALPHA][↩][Y] [STO▶].

Press [VAR]. You should have in your soft-menu key labels the following keys:

[My][Mx][F].

♣ Coordinates of the center of pressure:

To calculate the coordinate $x_{CP} = M_y/F$ use:

[My][F] [÷] [↦][ALG][FACTO]

After about 30 seconds the calculator returns the result:

'((5*H+8*a)*b1+((3*H+4*a)*b2+(8*d*H+12*d*a)))/(8*H+12*a)'.

This result can be factored even more using the equation writer to make it look like this:

$$\frac{(5 \cdot H + 8 \cdot a) \cdot b1 + (3 \cdot H + 4 \cdot a) \cdot b2 + d \cdot (2 \cdot H + 3 \cdot a) \cdot 4}{(2 \cdot H + 3 \cdot a) \cdot 4}$$

73

This latter result suggest that we can write:

$$x_{CP} = d + \frac{(5 \cdot H + 8 \cdot a) \cdot b1 + (3 \cdot H + 4 \cdot a) \cdot b2}{4 \cdot (2 \cdot H + 3 \cdot a)}.$$

To calculate the coordinate $y_{CP} = M_x / F$ use:

[Mx][F] [÷] [↵][ALG][FACTO]

After about 20 seconds the calculator returns the result:

` (3*H^2+8*a*H+6*a^2)/(4*H+6*a) '.

The denominator has a common factor of 2, but no other simplification is possible, so the result is:

$$y_{CP} = \frac{3 \cdot H^2 + 8 \cdot a \cdot H + 6 \cdot a^2}{2 \cdot (2 \cdot H + 3 \cdot a)}.$$

Now, check these results by hand.

Note: Just kidding!

74

The figure below illustrates a region R described by { $0 < r < f(\theta)$, $a < \theta < b$ }. The quasi-triangular infinitesimal element of area limited by the angle $d\theta$ and the curve has an area

$$dA = \tfrac{1}{2} \text{ (base)} \cdot \text{(height)} = \tfrac{1}{2} \cdot (r \cdot d\theta) \cdot (r) = \tfrac{1}{2} \cdot r^2 \cdot d\theta = \tfrac{1}{2} \cdot [f(\theta)]^2 \cdot d\theta.$$

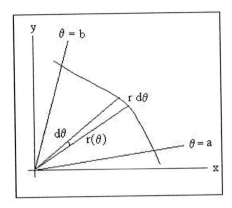

Therefore, the area of the region is given by

$$A = \int_R dA = \frac{1}{2} \cdot \int_{\theta=a}^{\theta=b} [f(\theta)]^2 \cdot d\theta.$$

Example 1 - Calculate the area of the region R = { $0 < r < a$, $0 < \theta < 2\pi$ }, i.e., the area of the circle of radius r = a centered at the origin. Type in the integral:

$$\frac{1}{2} \cdot \int_0^{2 \cdot \pi} a^2 \, d\theta$$

EDIT CURS BIG ◼ EVAL FACTO TEXPA

Press [▲][▲][▲][EVAL] to get the result $a^2 \cdot \pi.$

Fluid dynamics: calculating discharge in pipe for laminar flow

The figure below shows the profile of laminar flow velocity as a function of the radial distance r in a pipe.

The velocity distribution is given by the expression,

$$v(r) = v_c[1-(r/r_0)^2],$$

where v_c is the centerline velocity and r_0 is the radius of the pipe.

We can use this expression to obtain the discharge (volumetric flow) in the pipe by using the definition

75

$$Q = \int_R v \cdot dA.$$

Because the velocity distribution in a pipe depends on the radial distance only, we can use an element of area consisting of a ring of thickness dr and length $2\pi r$, thus, the area is

$$dA = 2\pi r dr.$$

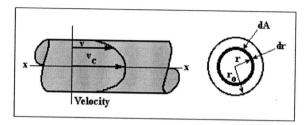

With this element of area, the discharge is calculated, in general, as

$$Q = \int_0^{r_o} v(r) \cdot 2 \cdot \pi \cdot r \cdot dr.$$

For the specific case of a laminar flow velocity distribution, you will need to set up the integral:

$$\int_0^{r0} vc \cdot \left[1 - \left(\frac{r}{r0} \right)^2 \right] \cdot 2 \cdot \pi \cdot r \, dr$$

| EDIT | CURS | BIG ◼ | EVAL | FACTO | TEXPA |

Then, press [ENTER][↦][EVAL]. The result is 'vc*r0^2*π/2'.

The mean velocity is defined as $V = Q/A$, with $A = \pi r_o^2$, then $V = v_c/2$ for laminar flow.

76

14 Multivariate and vector calculus

Multivariate calculus involve differentiation and integration using functions with more than one independent variables. The following definitions will be provided for functions of two variables. However, generalizing them to functions of more than two variables should be a straightforward. Set Exact mode before attempting any symbolic calculation.

Partial derivatives

Consider the function z = f(x,y), we define the partial derivative of z with respect to x as

$$\frac{\partial z}{\partial x} = z_x = \lim_{\Delta x \to 0} \frac{f(x + \Delta x, y) - f(x, y)}{\Delta x}.$$

Similarly, the partial derivative of z with respect to y is defined as

$$\frac{\partial z}{\partial y} = z_y = \lim_{\Delta y \to 0} \frac{f(x, y + \Delta y) - f(x, y)}{\Delta y}.$$

For practical purposes, a partial derivative with respect to any given independent variable is calculated the same way that you would calculate a total derivative with respect to that variable while treating all other variables in the function as you would constant values. Thus,

$$\frac{\partial}{\partial x}(2xy^2 - \exp(x) + \ln(y)) = \frac{\partial}{\partial x}(2xy^2) - \frac{\partial}{\partial x}(\exp(x)) + \frac{\partial}{\partial x}(\ln(y)) =$$

$$2y^2 - \exp(x) + 0 = 2y^2 - \exp(x)$$

The HP 49 G calculator uses the same functions DERIV and [→][∂] to calculate partial derivatives, as we did with total derivatives. Examples:

'2*X*Y^2-SIN(Y)' [ENTER] 'Y' [ENTER] [↰][CALC][DERIV][DERIV],

result = '2*X*(2*Y)-COS(Y)', i.e.,

$$\frac{\partial}{\partial x}(2xy^2 - \sin y) = 4xy - \cos y.$$

77

'2*EXP(-x*y*z)' [ENTER] 'z' [ENTER] [↦][∂] Result: '2*(EXP(-x*y*x)*(-x*y))', i.e.,

$$\frac{\partial}{\partial z}(2e^{-xyz}) = -2xye^{-xyz}.$$

Second order partial derivatives

Second order partial derivatives are defined by:

$$\frac{\partial^2 f}{\partial x^2} = \frac{\partial}{\partial x}\left(\frac{\partial f}{\partial x}\right) = f_{xx}, \quad \frac{\partial^2 f}{\partial x^2} = \frac{\partial}{\partial x}\left(\frac{\partial f}{\partial x}\right) = f_{xx},$$

$$\frac{\partial^2 f}{\partial x \partial y} = \frac{\partial}{\partial x}\left(\frac{\partial f}{\partial y}\right) = f_{yx} = \frac{\partial}{\partial y}\left(\frac{\partial f}{\partial x}\right) = \frac{\partial^2 f}{\partial y \partial x} = f_{xy}.$$

Notice the order of the variables in the two notations (using the partial derivative symbol or sub-indices) in the cross-derivative with respect ɓ x and y. Using the partial derivative symbol, the first derivative taken is the one located more to the right in the denominator, thus, $\partial^2 f/\partial x \partial y$ means $\partial f/\partial y$ is taken before $\partial/\partial x$. Using the sub-index notation, the first derivative taken is indicated by the sub-index closest to the function name f, thus, f_{xy} means the first derivative taken is the with respect to x and then with respect to y.

Here are some examples of second-order partial derivatives:

'SIN(X*Y)' [ENTER] 'X' [ENTER] [↦][∂] 'X' [ENTER] [↦][∂] Result: 'Y*-(Y*SIN(X*Y))', i.e.,

$$\frac{\partial^2}{\partial x^2}(\sin xy) = -y^2 \sin xy.$$

'X^2*LN(Y)' [ENTER] 'X' [ENTER] [↦][∂] 'Y' [ENTER] [↦][∂] Result: '2*X*(1/Y)'

$$\frac{\partial^2}{\partial y \partial x}(x^2 \ln y) = \frac{2x}{y}.$$

'X^2*LN(Y)' [ENTER] 'Y' [ENTER] [↦][∂] 'X' [ENTER] [↦][∂] Result: '2*X*(1/Y)'

$$\frac{\partial^2}{\partial x \partial y}(x^2 \ln y) = \frac{2x}{y}.$$

'Y+X*EXP(Y)' [ENTER] 'Y' [ENTER] [↦][∂] 'Y' [ENTER] [↦][∂] Result: 'X*EXP(Y)'

78

$$\frac{\partial^2}{\partial y \partial x}(y + xe^y) = xe^y.$$

Generalization of the definitions given above for third- or higher-order partial derivatives is straightforward.

The chain rule for partial derivatives

Consider the function z = f(x,y), such that x = x(t), y = y(t). The function z actually represents a composite function of *t* if we write it as z = f[x(t),y(t)]. The chain rule for the derivative dz/dt for this case is written as

$$\frac{dz}{dt} = \frac{\partial z}{\partial x} \cdot \frac{dx}{dt} + \frac{\partial z}{\partial y} \cdot \frac{dy}{dt}.$$

To see the expression that the HP 49 G calculator produces for this version of the chain rule use:

[EQW] [⊢][∂] [ALPHA][⬅][T] [▶] [ALPHA][⬅][Z] [⬅][( )] [ALPHA][⬅][X] [⬅][( )] [ALPHA][⬅][T]
[▶] [SPC] [ALPHA][⬅][Y] [⬅][( )] [ALPHA][⬅][T]

The derivative to be evaluated is

To expand this derivative use: [▲][▲][▲][▲] [EVAL]. The result provided by the calculator is

d1y(t)·d2z(x(t),y(t))+d1x(t)·d1z(x(y),y(t))

The term d1y(t) is to be interpreted as "the derivative of y(t) with respect to the 1st independent variable, i.e., t", or d1y(t) = dy/dt. Similarly, d1x(t) = dx/dt. On the other hand, d1z(x(t),y(t)) means "the first derivative of z(x,y) with respect to the first independent variable, i.e, x", or d1z(x(t),y(t)) = ∂z/∂x. Similarly, d2z(x(t),y(t)) = ∂z/∂y. Thus, the expression above is to be interpreted as:

dz/dt = (dy/dt)·(∂z/∂y) + (dx/dt)·(∂z/∂x).

Total differential of a function z = z(x,y)

From the last equation, if we multiply by dt, we get the total differential of the function z = z(x,y), i.e.,

dz = (∂z/∂x)·dx + (∂z/∂y)·dy.

79

Example: let's use $z = sin(xy)$, $x = t^2$, and $y = \sqrt{t}$ to verify the chain rule for the case z =f[x(t),y(t)] in the calculator.

♣ First, define the functions:

[EQW] [ALPHA][↤][Z] [↤][( )] [ALPHA][↤][X] [SPC] [ALPHA][↤][Y] [▶][↦][=] [SIN] [ALPHA][↤][X] [×] [ALPHA][↤][Y][ENTER] [↤][DEF]

[EQW] [ALPHA][↤][X] [↤][( )] [ALPHA][↤][T] [▶][↦][=] [ALPHA][↤][T] [y^x] [2] [ENTER] [↤][DEF]

[EQW] [ALPHA][↤][Y] [↤][( )] [ALPHA][↤][T] [▶][↦][=][√x] [ALPHA][↤][T] [ENTER] [↤][DEF]

You should have in your soft-menu key labels the functions [y   ],[x   ] and [z   ].

♣ Now, let's calculate the derivatives separately:

[EQW] [↦][∂][ALPHA][↤][T] [▶][ALPHA][↤][X] [↤][( )] [ALPHA][↤][T] [▲][▲][▲] [EVAL] [ENTER] [↦]['][ALPHA][↤][X][ALPHA][↤][T][STO▶]

[EQW] [↦][∂][ALPHA][↤][T] [▶][ALPHA][↤][Y] [↤][( )] [ALPHA][↤][T] [▲][▲][▲] [EVAL] [ENTER] [↦]['][ALPHA][↤][Y][ALPHA][↤][T][STO▶]

[EQW] [↦][∂][ALPHA][↤][X] [▶][ALPHA][↤][Z] [↤][( )] [ALPHA][↤][X] [SPC] [ALPHA][↤][Y] [▲][▲][▲] [EVAL]
[ENTER] [↦]['][ALPHA][↤][Z][ALPHA][↤][X][STO▶]

[EQW] [↦][∂][ALPHA][↤][Y] [▶][ALPHA][↤][Z] [↤][( )] [ALPHA][↤][X] [SPC] [ALPHA][↤][Y] [▲][▲][▲] [EVAL]
[ENTER] [↦]['][ALPHA][↤][Z][ALPHA][↤][Y][STO▶]

You should now have the soft-menu keys [zy   ][zx   ][xt   ][yt   ] corresponding to the derivatives $\partial z/\partial y$, $\partial z/\partial x$, dx/dt, and dy/dt, respectively.

♣ Using the notation of the variables we just stored, the chain rule for the derivative dz/dt will be written as dz/dt = zx*xt + zy*yt. Therefore, in the calculator we will use:

[zx   ][xt   ] [×] [zy   ][yt   ] [×] [+]. The result is:
'y*COS(x*y)*(2*t)+x*COS(x*y)*(1/2*√t)'

♣ Use [↦][ALG][FACTO] to simplify the expression to 'COS(x*y)*(4*y*t^2+x*√t)/(2*t)'

♣ To calculate the derivative directly, use:

[EQW] [↦][∂][ALPHA][↤][T] [▶] [ALPHA][↤][Z] [↤][( )] [ALPHA][↤][X] [↤][( )]
[ALPHA][↤][T] [▶] [SPC])] [ALPHA][↤][Y] [↤][( )] [ALPHA][↤][T] [▲][▲][▲][▲] [EVAL]
[ENTER]

The result in this case is 'COS(x(t)*y(t))*(2*t*y(t))+x(t)*(1/2*√t)))'.

♣ Use [↦][ALG][FACTO] to simplify the expression to 'COS(x(t)*y(t))*(√t*x(t)+ 4*t^2*y(t))/(2*t)'

80

The two results in your stack are basically the same except that the latest uses x(t) and y(t) instead of simply x and y.

A different version of the chain rule applies to the case in which $z = f(x,y)$, $x = x(u,v)$, $y = y(u,v)$, so that

$$z = f[x(u,v), y(u,v)].$$

The following formulas represent the chain rule for this situation:

$$\frac{\partial z}{\partial u} = \frac{\partial z}{\partial x} \cdot \frac{\partial x}{\partial u} + \frac{\partial z}{\partial y} \cdot \frac{\partial y}{\partial u}, \qquad \frac{\partial z}{\partial v} = \frac{\partial z}{\partial x} \cdot \frac{\partial x}{\partial v} + \frac{\partial z}{\partial y} \cdot \frac{\partial y}{\partial v}.$$

Determining extrema in functions of two variables

In order for the function $z = f(x,y)$ to have an extreme point (extrema) at (x_o,y_o), its derivatives $\partial f/\partial x$ and $\partial f/\partial y$ must vanish at that point. These are *necessary* conditions. The *sufficient conditions* for the function to have an extreme at point (x_o,y_o) are

$$\partial f/\partial x = 0, \; \partial f/\partial y = 0, \text{ and } \Delta = (\partial^2 f/\partial x^2) \cdot (\partial^2 f/\partial y^2) - [\partial^2 f/\partial x^2]^2 > 0.$$

The point (x_o,y_o) is a *maximum* if $\partial^2 f/\partial x^2 < 0$, or a *minimum* if $\partial^2 f/\partial x^2 > 0$. The value D is referred to as the *discriminant*.

If

$$\Delta = (\partial^2 f/\partial x^2) \cdot (\partial^2 f/\partial y^2) - [\partial^2 f/\partial x^2]^2 < 0,$$

we have a condition known as a *saddle point*, where the function would attain a maximum in x if we were to hold y constant, while, at the same time, attaining a minimum if we were to hold x constant, or vice versa.

Example 1 - Determine the extreme points (if any) of the function $f(x,y) = x^3 - 3x - y^2 + 5$.

⬇ First, define the function into the calculator: ʻF(X,Y) = X^3-3*X-Y^2+5ʼ [ENTER][↵][DEF]. This operation will create the variable [F].

⬇ Determine the first and second derivatives:

To evaluate and store $\partial f/\partial x$ use: ʻFX(X,Y)=∂X(F(X,Y))ʼ [ENTER][↦][EVAL][↵][DEF]

To evaluate and store $\partial f/\partial y$ use: ʻFX(X,Y)=∂Y(F(X,Y))ʼ [ENTER][↦][EVAL][↵][DEF]

To evaluate and store $\partial^2 f/\partial x^2$ use: ʻFXX(X,Y)=∂X(FX(X,Y))ʼ [ENTER][↦][EVAL][↵][DEF]

To evaluate and store $\partial^2 f/\partial y^2$ use: ʻFYY(X,Y)=∂Y(FY(X,Y))ʼ [ENTER][↦][EVAL][↵][DEF]

To evaluate and store $\partial^2 f/\partial y \partial x$ use: ʻFXY(X,Y)=∂Y(FX(X,Y))ʼ [ENTER] [↦][EVAL][↵][DEF]

⬇ To find the possible extrema, use [↦][FX] [▼], and edit it out so that only the expression, ʻ3*X^2-3ʼ remains. Then, enter [0][↦][=]. Next, do the same with [FY], namely, [→][FX] [▼], and edit out the program until only the expression '-(2*Y)' remains. Then, use [0][→][=]. You now have the two equations $\partial f/\partial x = 0$, $\partial f/\partial y = 0$.

⬇ To solve the equations use: [2] [⊣][PRG][TYPE][→ARRY]. Then, type the array ['X' 'Y'], and press [ENTER], and, finally, use [⊣][S.SLV][SOLVE] (second SOLVE key), to obtain the solution set:

$$\{[\ \ 'X=1'\ \ 'Y=0'\ \ ]\ \ [\ \ 'X=-1'\ \ 'Y=0'\ ]\}.$$

⬇ Let's define the discriminant function:

$$'D(X,Y) = FXX(X,Y)*FYY(X,Y)-FXY(X,Y)^2'\ \ [ENTER]\ \ [→][EVAL]\ \ [⊣][DEF]$$

⬇ Check the value of D(X,Y) at point (X,Y) = (1,0), by using: [1][SPC][0][VAR][D], it turns out that D(1,0) = -12 < 0, therefore, this point is a saddle point. No maximum or minimum occurs at this point.

⬇ Check the value of D(X,Y) at point (X,Y) = (-1,0), by using: [1][+/-][SPC][0][VAR][D], it turns out that D(-1,0) = 12 > 0, thus a maximum or minimum may exist at this point.

⬇ Check the value of FXX(X,Y) at point (X,Y) = (-1,0), by using: [1][+/-][SPC][0][VAR][FXX], it turns out that FXX(-1,0) = -6 < 0, thus the point (-1,0) corresponds to a maximum of the function.

⬇ To determine the value of the function at point (-1,0), use [1][+/-][SPC][0][VAR][F]. The result is F(-1,0) = 7.

⬇ To visualize the function use the option FAST3D in the plot types with view limits of X in (-2, 2), Y in (-2, 2), and Z in (-2,8). The figure below interprets the two points found earlier.

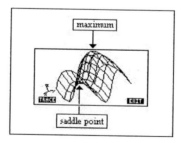

Derivative of a complex function

An interesting application of multi-variate calculus is to determine the derivative of a complex function. Complex variables were introduced in Chapter 5. Recall that a complex variable z = x +iy can be *mapped* into another complex variable w = Φ(x,y)+iΨ(x,y), through the complex function w = f(z). The derivative of the complex variable f(z), to be referred to as f'(z) = df/dz, is, by definition,

$$f'(z) = \frac{df}{dz} = \lim_{\Delta z \to 0} \frac{f(z + \Delta z) - f(z)}{\Delta z}.$$

The definition of a complex derivative requires us to evaluate the function f(z) at a point P(x,y) corresponding to z = x + iy, and at point Q(x+Δx, y+Δy), as illustrated in the figure below.

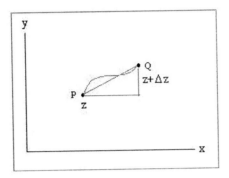

The figure also illustrates the fact that to get from point z to point z+Δz in the complex x-y plane you can follow a multitude of paths. In general, the value of the derivative will depend on the path we follow to define Δz. Because we want the derivative df/dz to be uniquely defined, we need to find some criteria such that, regardless of the path selected to define z, the value of df/dz remains the same. In general, we will write Δz = Δx+iΔy. Let's calculate the derivative df/dz utilizing paths for Δz along the x-axis alone, i.e, Δz = Δx, and along the y-axis alone, i.e., Δz = iΔy. Thus, for Δz = Δx, we can write

$$\frac{df}{dz} = \lim_{\Delta x \to 0} \frac{[\Phi(x + \Delta x, y) + i\Psi(x + \Delta x, y)] - [\Phi(x, y) + i\Psi(x, y)]}{\Delta x}$$

$$\frac{df}{dz} = \lim_{\Delta x \to 0} \left(\frac{[\Phi(x + \Delta x, y) - \Phi(x, y)]}{\Delta x} + i\frac{[\Psi(x + \Delta x, y) - \Psi(x, y)]}{\Delta x} \right)$$

i.e.,

$$\frac{df}{dz} = \frac{\partial \Phi}{\partial x} + i\frac{\partial \Psi}{\partial x}.$$

83

You can prove, by expressing the derivative in terms of $\Delta z = i\Delta y$, that

$$\frac{df}{dz} = \frac{\partial \Psi}{\partial y} - i\frac{\partial \Phi}{\partial y}.$$

In order for the last two expressions for df/dz to be the same, then we require that

$$\frac{\partial \Phi}{\partial x} = \frac{\partial \Psi}{\partial y}, \qquad \frac{\partial \Phi}{\partial y} = -\frac{\partial \Psi}{\partial x}.$$

These two equations are known as the Cauchy-Riemann differentiability conditions for complex functions (or, simply, the Cauchy-Riemann conditions). Thus, if the functions $\Phi(x,y) = Re[f(z)]$ and $\Psi(x,y) = Re[f(z)]$, satisfy the Cauchy-Riemann conditions, the derivative $f'(z)=df/dz$ is uniquely defined. In such case, the function f(z) is said to be an *analytical complex function*, and the functions $\Phi(x,y)$ and $\Psi(x,y)$ are said to be *harmonic functions*.

More importantly, if a complex function f(z) is analytical, the rules used for univariate derivatives can be applied to f(z). For example, in Chapter 5 we indicated that the function

$$w = f(z) = \ln(z) = \ln(r \cdot e^{i\theta}) = \ln(r) + i\theta.$$

can be written in terms of (x,y) as

$$\Phi = \Phi(x,y) = \ln[(x^2+y^2)^{1/2}] = (1/2)\ln(x^2+y^2), \text{ and } \Psi = \Psi(x,y) = \tan^{-1}(y/x).$$

Using the HP 49 G calculator, let's check if the functions $\Phi(x,y)$ and $\Psi(x,y)$ satisfy the Cauchy-Riemann conditions:

⬥ First, define the functions:

[EQW][ALPHA][ALPHA][P][H][I] [↩][( )][↩][X][SPC][↩][Y][▲][▲][ALPHA][→][=] [→][LN]
[ALPHA][↩][X][yˣ][2][▶] [+] [ALPHA][↩][Y][yˣ][2] [▲][▲][▲][▲] [÷][2] [ENTER]
[↩][DEF]

[EQW] [ALPHA][ALPHA][T][S][I][↩][( )][↩][X][SPC][↩][Y][▲][▲][ALPHA]
[→][=] [↩][ATAN] [ALPHA][↩][Y][▶] [÷] [ALPHA][↩][X] [ENTER]
[↩][DEF]

Soft-menu key labels [TSI] and [PHI] will now be available in your screen.

⬥ Next, calculate and store the four derivatives involved in the Cauchy-Riemann conditions:

[EQW] [→][∂] [ALPHA][↩][X] [▶] [VAR][PHI] [⇦] [↩][( )][ALPHA][↩][X]
[SPC][↩][ALPHA][Y][▲][▲][▲] [→][EVAL] [→][ALG][EXPAN][ENTER]
[VAR][→]['][PHI][ALPHA][↩][X][STO▶]

84

[EQW] [↱][∂] [ALPHA][↢][Y] [▶] [VAR][PHI] [⇦] [↢][( )][ALPHA][↢][X]
[SPC][↢][ALPHA][Y][▲][▲][▲] [↱][EVAL] [↱][ALG][EXPAN][ENTER]
[VAR][↱]['][PHI][ALPHA][↢][Y][STO▶]

[EQW] [↱][∂] [ALPHA][↢][X] [▶] [VAR][TSI] [⇦] [↢][( )][ALPHA][↢][X]
[SPC][↢][ALPHA][Y][▲][▲][▲] [↱][EVAL] [↱][ALG][EXPAN][ENTER]
[VAR][↱]['][TSI][ALPHA][↢][X][STO▶]

[EQW] [↱][∂] [ALPHA][↢][Y] [▶] [VAR][PHI] [⇦] [↢][( )][ALPHA][↢][X]
[SPC][↢][ALPHA][Y][▲][▲][▲] [↱][EVAL] [↱][ALG][EXPAN][ENTER]
[VAR][↱]['][TSI][ALPHA][↢][Y][STO▶]

At this point you will also have variables [TSIy], [TSIy], [PHIy], and [PHIx], representing Ψ_y, Ψ_x, Φ_y, and Φ_x, respectively.

⬥ Let's now check the Cauchy-Riemann conditions:

[VAR][PHIx][TSIy],   i.e., $\partial\Phi/\partial x = \partial\Psi/\partial y$, checks out ok.
[PHIy][TSIx],   also, $\partial\Phi/\partial y = -\partial\Psi/\partial x$, checks out ok.

The function f(z) = ln(z) is, therefore, analytical, and its derivative can be calculated by using:

$$\frac{df}{dz} = \frac{d}{dz}(\ln z) = \frac{1}{z}.$$

⬥ Use the calculator to obtain this derivative and express it in terms of (x,y) as follows:

[EQW] [↱][∂] [ALPHA][↢][Z] [▶] [↱][LN][ALPHA][↢][Z] [▲][▲][▲] [EVAL] [ENTER]
[↱]['] [ALPHA][↢][Z] [↱][=][ALPHA][↢][X] [+] [↢][i] [×] [ALPHA][↢][Y][ENTER]
[↱][ALG][SUBST]

The result is '1/(x+i*y)'.

⬥ To find the real and imaginary parts of this function use:

⬥ Real part: [ENTER][↢][MTH][NXT][CMPLX][RE], Result: 'x/(x^2+y^2)'
⬥ Imaginary part: [▶][IM][↱][ALG][EXPAN]   Result:
'y/(x^2+y^2)'.

⬥ Finally, check that Re[f'(z)] = $\partial\Phi/\partial x = \partial\Psi/\partial y$, and Im[f'(z)] = $\partial\Phi/\partial y = -\partial\Psi/\partial x$, by recalling the contents of variables [PHIx], [TSIy], [PHIy], and [TSIy][+/-]. This last check verifies the equations obtained earlier for f'(z) using $\Delta z = \Delta x$ and $\Delta z = i\Delta y$.

Note: Most of the functions that we commonly use with real variables, e.g., exp, ln, sin, cos, tan, asin, acos, atan, hyperbolic functions, polynomials, inverse, square root, etc., are analytical functions when used with the complex variable z = x +iy. Thus, the rules of derivatives for these functions are the same as in real variables, e.g., d(sin(z))/dz = cos(z), d(z^2+z)/dz = 2z+1, etc.

Multivariate calculus applications in potential flow

The concepts of partial derivatives and derivative of a complex variable have practical applications in the analysis of potential or ideal flow in two-dimensions. Ideal flow refers to the flow of a fluid that has no viscosity (inviscid fluid), while potential flow stands for a flow whose velocity components are obtained as partial derivatives of a function $\phi(x,y)$, called the flow potential function. Ideal flow and potential flow are synonyms.

Continuity equation

The equation of continuity is the mathematical expression of the law of conservation of mass for fluid flow. Considering an inviscid, incompressible (constant density) fluid flow in two dimensions. The equation of continuity for these flows is given by

$$\partial u/\partial x + \partial v/\partial y = 0,$$

Where $u = u(x,y)$, $v = v(x,y)$ are the x- and y-components of flow velocity in the plane.

Stream function

Let us define a function $\psi(x,y)$ such that the velocity components u and v are

$$u = \partial \psi/\partial y \text{ and } v = -\partial \psi/\partial x.$$

If we replace this function into the continuity equation we have

$$\partial(\partial \psi/\partial y)/\partial x + \partial(-\partial \psi/\partial x)/\partial y = 0,$$

or

$$\partial^2 \psi/\partial y \partial x - \partial^2 \psi/\partial x \partial y = 0,$$

which is satisfied by any continuous function $\psi(x,y)$. The function $\psi(x,y)$ is known as the *stream function* of the flow.

Curves defined by $\psi(x,y)$ = constant are known as the *streamlines* of the flow. The velocity vector

$$q(x,y) = u(x,y) \cdot i + v(x,y) \cdot j$$

at any point (x,y) on a streamline is tangent to the streamline.
The total differential for the stream function along a streamline $\psi(x,y)$ = constant is

$$d\psi = (\partial\psi/\partial x)\cdot dx + (\partial\psi/\partial y)\cdot dy = 0.$$

Therefore, the slope of the streamline at a point (x,y) is given by

$$m_\psi = dy/dx = -(\partial\psi/\partial x)/(\partial\psi/\partial y) = -(-v)/u = v/u.$$

Potential flow

A flow whose velocity components are obtained from

$$u = \partial\phi/\partial x, \text{ and } v = \partial\phi/\partial y,$$

where $\phi(x,y)$ is a scalar (i.e., non-vector) function, is referred to as a *potential flow*, and the function $\phi(x,y)$ is known as the *velocity potential*.

If we replace the definitions of u and v into the continuity equation, what results is the following partial differential equation known as Laplace's equation:

$$\partial^2\phi/\partial x^2 + \partial^2\phi/\partial y^2 = 0.$$

Curves defined by $\phi(x,y)$ = constant are known as the *iso-potential or equipotential lines* of the flow. The total differential for the velocity potential along a equipotential line $\phi(x,y)$ = constant is

$$d\phi = (\partial\phi/\partial x)\cdot dx + (\partial\phi/\partial y)\cdot dy = 0.$$

Therefore, the slope of the equipotential line at a point (x,y) is given by

$$m_\phi = dy/dx = -(\partial\phi/\partial x)/(\partial\phi/\partial y) = -u/v.$$

The flow net

The fact that the slope of a streamline is given by $m_\psi = v/u$, and that of an equipotential line is given by $m_\phi = -u/v$, indicates that at the point of intersection of any two of these lines the lines are normal to each other. This follows from the fact that

$$m_\psi \cdot m_\phi = (v/u)\cdot(-u/v) = -1,$$

which is the condition for two straight lines to be perpendicular to each other. In this case the straight lines of interest are the tangential lines to the streamline and to the equipotential line at the point of intersection.

A picture of a collection of equipotential lines and streamlines is known as a *flow net*.

Irrotational flow

87

When a fluid particle is subjected to motion it undergoes not only translation, but also suffers elongation (normal strains), shear strains, and rotation. In two dimensions, you can prove that the magnitude of the angular velocity of a fluid particle in a flow is given by

$$\omega = (\partial v/\partial x - \partial u/\partial y).$$

A fluid flow where the fluid particles undergo no rotation is called an *irrotational flow*. For such a flow we have $\omega = 0$, or

$$\partial v/\partial x - \partial u/\partial y = 0.$$

Replacing the velocity components in terms of the stream function ($u = \partial\psi/\partial y$, $v = -\partial\psi/\partial x$) reveals the fact that ψ (x,y) also satisfies Laplace's equation, i.e.,

$$\partial^2\psi/\partial x^2 + \partial^2\psi/\partial y^2 = 0.$$

Example 1 – Verify that a fluid flow whose velocity components are given by $u = x/(x^2+y^2)$, $v = -y/(x^2+y^2)$, satisfies the continuity equation and the condition of irrotationality. Also, determine expressions for the potential function $\phi(x,y)$ and the stream function $\psi(x,y)$.

Define the functions:

$$`u(x,y)=x/(x^2+y^2)` \qquad [ENTER][\leftharpoondown][DEF]$$
$$`v(x,y)=-y/(x^2+y^2)` \qquad [ENTER][\leftharpoondown][DEF]$$

These two operations create the variables [u] and [v].

Next, type in the continuity equation using the equation writer:

[EQW]
[→][∂] [ALPHA][↰][X] [▶] [ALPHA][↰][U] [↰][( )] [ALPHA][↰][X] [SPC] [ALPHA][↰][Y] [▶][▶]
[+][→][∂] [ALPHA][↰][Y] [▶] [ALPHA][↰][V] [↰][( )] [ALPHA][↰][X] [SPC] [ALPHA][↰][Y]

To evaluate the expression

$$\partial u/\partial x + \partial v/\partial y = 0,$$

enter [▲][▲][▲][▲][EVAL]. The result is indeed zero, thus proving that u(x,y) and v(x,y) satisfy the continuity equation.

The condition of irrotationality is given by the expression,

$$\partial v/\partial x - \partial u/\partial y = 0.$$

which, in the equation writer can be set up as

To find the <u>velocity potential</u> we start from $u(x,y) = \partial\phi/\partial x = x/(x^2+y^2)$, which we can integrate with respect to x to obtain

$$\phi(x,y) = \int u(x,y) \cdot dx + F(y) = \int \frac{x}{x^2 + y^2} \cdot dx + F(y)$$

By using

88

'u(x,y)' [ENTER]   Type in 'u(x,y)'
[→][EVAL]   Obtain the expression defining u(x,y), i.e.,
x/(x^2+y^2)
'x' [ENTER]   Type in 'x'
[↰][CALC][DERIV][NXT][RISCH] Integrate with respect to x (indefinite integral)

The result is '1/2*LN(x^2+y^2)'. In paper, this will be interpreted as $\phi(x,y) = \frac{1}{2} \cdot \ln(x^2+y^2) + F(y)$, although we do not include F(y) in the expression in the stack.

Next, we use the fact that $v(x,y) = \partial\phi/\partial y$. Therefore, let's take the derivative of the expression in stack level 1 with respect to y by using:

'y' [ENTER] [→][∂]   Derivative of '1/2*LN(x^2+y^2)' with respect to y
[→][EVAL]   To simplify the expression

In paper this means $\partial\phi/\partial y = y/(x^2+y^2) + F'(y)$. We can now modify this expression in the calculator as follows:

[▼] [+] [ALPHA][↰][D] [ALPHA][F] [▶][▶] [→][=] [ALPHA][↰][V] [↰][( )]
[ALPHA][↰][X] [SPC] [ALPHA][↰][Y] [ENTER]
[→]['] [ALPHA][↰][D] [ALPHA][F] [ENTER]
[↰][S.SLV][ISOL]

Here, dF represents F'(y). Press [→][EVAL] to simplify the expression in the stack, which results in 'dF=0', or, in paper, F'(y) = 0. This implies F(y) = K, where K is a constant. Thus, we can write

$$\phi(x,y) = \frac{1}{2} \cdot \ln(x^2+y^2) + K.$$

To find the <u>stream function</u> we start from $u(x,y) = \partial\psi/\partial y = x/(x^2+y^2)$, which we can integrate with respect to x to obtain

$$\psi(x,y) = \int u(x,y) \cdot dy + G(x) = \int \frac{x}{x^2+y^2} \cdot dy + G(x).$$

By using

'u(x,y)' [ENTER]   Type in 'v(x,y)'
[→][EVAL]   Obtain the expression defining v(x,y), i.e.,
x/(x^2+y^2)
'y' [ENTER]   Type in 'y'
[↰][CALC][DERIV][NXT][RISCH] Integrate with respect to x (indefinite integral)

The result is 'ATAN(y/x)'. In paper, this will be interpreted as $\psi(x,y) = \tan^{-1}(y/x) + G(x)$, although we do not include G(x) in the expression in the stack.

Next, we use the fact that $v(x,y) = -\partial\psi/\partial x$. Therefore, let's take the derivative of the expression in stack level 1 with respect to y by using:

'x' [ENTER] [→][∂]   Derivative of 'ATAN(y/x)' with respect to y
[→][EVAL]   To simplify the expression

In paper this means $\partial\psi/\partial x = -y/(x^2+y^2) + G'(x)$. We can now modify this expression in the calculator as follows (we need to change the sign of the expression first):

[▼] [+/-] [+] [ALPHA][↰][D] [ALPHA][G] [▶][▶] [↱][=] [ALPHA][↰][V] [↰][( )]
[ALPHA][↰][X] [SPC] [ALPHA][↰][Y] [ENTER]
[↱]['] [ALPHA][↰][D] [ALPHA][G] [ENTER]
[↰][S.SLV][ISOL]

Here, dG represents G'(x).   Press [↱][EVAL] to simplify the expression in the stack, which results in 'dG=0', or, in paper, G'(y) = 0. This implies G(y) = C, where C is a constant. Thus, we can write

$$\psi(x,y) = \tan^{-1}(y/x) + C.$$

To visualize the flow net for this case, first we need to select values of the constants K and C. We can stipulate that the point (x,y) = (0,0) belongs to the streamline ψ = 0, to make C = 0. Similarly, we can force point (0,0) into the equipotential line ϕ = 0, to make K = 0.   The result for the velocity potential and stream function for these conditions are

$$\phi(x,y) = \tfrac{1}{2}\cdot\ln(x^2+y^2) \text{ , and } \psi(x,y) = \tan^{-1}(y/x).$$

The flow net can be drawn by using a Ps-Contour plot as follows:

⚓ Press [↰][2D/3D], simultaneously to access to the PLOT SETUP window.

⚓ Change TYPE to Ps-Contour.

⚓ Press [▼] and type '(1/2)*LN(X^2+Y^2)' [OK]. This will plot $\phi(x,y)$.

⚓ Make sure that 'X' is selected as the Indep: and 'Y' as the Depnd: variables.

⚓ Press [NXT][OK] to return to normal calculator display.

⚓ Press [↰][WIN], simultaneously, to access the PLOT WINDOW screen.

⚓ Keep the default plot window ranges to read:

```
X-Left:-1  X-Right:1
Y-Near:-1  Y-Far: 1
Step Indep: 10  Depnd: 8
```

⚓ Press [ERASE][DRAW] to draw the contour plot. It is going to be slow and take some time, so be really patient here.

⚓ When the graph is finished, press [CANCL][ON], and then, press [↰][2D/3D], simultaneously, to access to the PLOT SETUP window.

⚓ Press [▼] and type 'ATAN(Y/X)' [OK]. This will plot $\phi(x,y)$.

⚓ Press [DRAW] (no ERASE here) to complete the flow net picture. Again, this is going to take some time.

⚓ Press [EDIT][NXT][LABEL][MENU] to see the graph with labels and ranges:

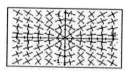

⬇ Press [NXT][NXT][PICT][CANCL] to return to the PLOT WINDOW environment.

⬇ Press [ON], or [NXT][OK], to return to normal calculator display.

Complex potential and complex velocity

The complex function

$$F(z) = \phi(x,y) + i \cdot \psi(x,y)$$

is referred to as the *complex potential* of the flow.

Recalling that the derivative of this complex function can be written as

$$dF/dz = \partial\phi/\partial x + i\cdot\partial\psi/\partial x = \partial\psi/\partial y - i\cdot\partial\phi/\partial y,$$

and from the definition of the velocity components u and v, it follows that dF/dz, referred to as the *complex velocity*, w(z), contains the velocity components in its real and imaginary parts. The complex velocity is written as

$$w(z) = dF/dz = u - i\cdot v.$$

Thus, $u = Re(w),$ and $v = -Im(w).$

Elementary two-dimensional potential flows

Because the equations governing the potential flow phenomena are linear equations (Laplace's equation), you can obtain the complex potential of a flow by adding the complex potentials of elementary flows. In this section we present the complex potentials of some elementary flows such as uniform flow, source and sink, vortex, and doublet. The last three are known as singularity flows since the velocities go to infinity at the location of the singularity generating the flow. A doublet is simply the combination of a source and a sink of the same strength that are infinitesimally close to each other. The strength of a singularity is a measure related to the flow discharge into a source or out of a sink, or to the angular velocity of a vortex.

The following are the complex potentials for these elementary flows:

Uniform flow with streamlines parallel to the x-axis: $F(z) = U \cdot z$

Source (m>0) or sink (m<0) of strength m located at (0,0): $F(z) = m \cdot \ln z$

Vortex of strength G (G>0, counterclockwise) at (0,0): $F(z) = i \cdot G \cdot \ln z$

Doublet of strength μ (μ >0, if sink is located to the left of source in the doublet): $F(z) = \mu/z$

We can obtain the velocity potential and stream function of any of these flows by using

$$\phi = Re[F(z)] \text{ and } \psi = Re[F(z)].$$

91

Example 1 -- To find the real and imaginary part of F(z) = ln z, a source flow with strength m = 1, you could try entering the expression 'LN(x+i*y)', however, the RE and IM functions will not produce any meaningful result. Using the polar representation of the complex variable $z = r \cdot e^{i\theta}$ proves more successful. Thus, enter:

'LN(r*EXP(i*θ))' [ENTER]   Enter the expression to be decomposed
[↦][TRIG][NXT][TEXPA]   Expand the expression to 'LN(r)+LN(EXP(i*θ))'
[↤][MTH][NXT][CMPLX][RE]   Find real part of expression

The result produced is simply the expression `RE(LN(r))+RE(LN(EXP(i*θ)))`', and no further simplification is possible. You may wonder why that is so, particularly when it is known that the functions LN and EXP are inverse functions. The reason is the following:

⬇ In order to use the term i*θ in the expression, somewhere along the line, you had to select the complex mode for your calculator's CAS. (This is unavoidable, since you are using the unit imaginary number i in the expression.) Once you are in `Complex` mode, however, if you try to evaluate a symbolic expression, the calculator assumes that any variable involved (such as r or θ in this case) may be a complex variable. Since the functions LN or EXP when applied to a complex variable do not operate the same way as when applied to a real variable, the calculator simply refuses to simplify further any symbolic expression when the CAS is set to `Complex` mode.

How do we solve this problem? You trick the calculator by replacing the term i*θ with iθ while clearing the `Complex` mode as follows:

[1][0][3][+/-][SPC][ALPHA][ALPHA][C][F][ENTER]   Clear system flag 103 (`Complex`)
'LN(r*EXP(iθ))'[ENTER]   Enter the expression to be decomposed
[↦][TRIG][NXT][TEXPA]   Expand and simplify the expression

The result is, as expected, 'LN(r) + iθ'. To continue the calculation, we need to introduce a * sign between the i and the θ in the expression, by using:

[▼][EDIT][↦][▶][◀][◀][×][ENTER][ENTER]   Insert * sign
[ENTER]   Make an extra copy of the expression
[↤][MTH][NXT][CMPLX][RE]   Find real part of expression

Select `Complex` mode when asked. The result is 'RE(LN(r))'. Again, we have the same situation as above, the `Complex` mode is required because the original expression included the unit imaginary number i. However, once the `Complex` mode is selected, the calculator assumes that r could be a complex variable and cannot simplify the expression RE(LN(r)) any further. Clear up system flag 103 once more and evaluate the expression currently in stack level 1:

[1][0][3][+/-][SPC][ALPHA][ALPHA][C][F][ENTER]   Clear system flag 103 (`Complex`)
[↦][EVAL]   Evaluate 'RE(LN(r))' → 'LN(r)'

Now, let's find the imaginary component of 'LN(r)+i*θ' by using:

[⇦][↤][MTH][NXT][CMPLX][IM]   Drop level 1, find imaginary part

92

You are required again to change the mode to Complex, resulting in 'IM(LN(r))+θ'. We are faced again with the same conflict resulting from selecting Complex mode. To fix it, clear system flag 103 again and evaluate the expression:

[1][0][3][+/-][SPC][ALPHA][ALPHA][C][F][ENTER]   Clear system flag 103 (Complex)
[⟶][EVAL]   Evaluate 'RE(LN(r))' → 'LN(r)'

The result is 'θ'. Thus, we have $\phi = \text{Re}[F(z)] = \ln(r)$, and $\psi = \text{Im}[F(z)] = \theta$.

Note: This example is relatively simple, however, it served the purpose of illustrating a possible conflict when using Complex mode and symbolic expressions.

Example 2 - Find the velocity potential and stream function for the complex potential F(z) = U·z+m/z.

Use:
'U*LN(z)+m*z' [ENTER] 'z =r*EXP(iθ)' [ENTER]   Enter F(z) and z = r·e$^{i\theta}$
[⟶][ALG][SUBST] [NXT][TEXPA]   Substitute z and expand expression
'iθ = i*θ' [ENTER] [⟶][ALG][SUBST]   Replace i θ with i* θ
[EXPAN]   Expand products in expression
[NXT][TEXPA]   Try to expand term EXP(i*θ)

TEXPA fails to expand the term EXP(i*θ) as part of the overall expression. We will have to replace it on our own by using Euler's formula EXP(i*θ) = COS(θ) + i*SIN(θ) as follows:

[▼]   Trigger the equation writer
[▼][▼][▼][▶][▶][▲][▲][▲]   Select term EXP(i*θ)
[EDIT]   Trigger line editor

Edit the term 'EXP(i*θ)' by using the right- left-arrows [◀] [▶], as well as the backspace arrow [⇦], until it has been replaced by the expression 'COS(θ) + i*SIN(θ)'. When done press

[ENTER][ENTER]   Enter expression and return to stack
[ENTER]   Make extra copy of the expression

[1][0][3][+/-][SPC][ALPHA][ALPHA][C][F][ENTER]   Clear system flag 103 (Complex)
[⟵][MTH][NXT][CMPLX][RE]   Find real part of expression

The Complex mode is forced again upon us, so try the following:

[1][0][3][+/-][SPC][ALPHA][ALPHA][C][F][ENTER]   Clear system flag 103 (Complex)
[⟶][EVAL]   Evaluate expression

The result is 'r*m*COS(θ)+U*LN(r)', i.e., the velocity potential, $\phi = \text{Re}[F(z)]$, is

$$\phi(r, \theta) = m{\cdot}r{\cdot}\cos\theta + U{\cdot}\ln r, \quad \text{or,} \quad \phi(x,y) = m{\cdot}x + U{\cdot}\ln(x^2+y^2)^{1/2}.$$

To find the stream function, $\psi = \text{Im}[F(z)]$, use:

[⟵][MTH][NXT][CMPLX][IM]   Find imaginary part of expression

Complex mode warning again! Don't loose your temper, here is how to handle it:

93

[1][0][3][+/-][SPC][ALPHA][ALPHA][C][F][ENTER]   Clear system flag 103 (Complex)
[↱][EVAL]   Evaluate expression

The result is '$r*m*SIN(\theta)+\theta*U$', i.e, the velocity potential, ψ = Re[F(z)], is

$$\psi(r, \theta) = m \cdot r \cdot \sin \theta + U \cdot \theta, \quad or, \quad \psi(x,y) = m \cdot y + U \cdot \tan^{-1}(y/x).$$

Example 3 - For the complex potential used in Example 2 obtain expressions for the components of velocity u and v.

Enter:

'$U*LN(z)+m*z$' [ENTER] 'z ' [ENTER] [↱][∂]   Enter F(z) and z , obtain w = dF/dz =
$U/z+m$
'$z=x+i*y$' [ENTER][↱][ALG][SUBST][ENTER]   Substitute z = x + iy, make extra copy
[↰][MTH][NXT][CMPLX][RE]   Find real part of expression
[1][0][3][+/-][SPC][ALPHA][ALPHA][C][F][ENTER]   Clear system flag 103 (Complex)
[↱][EVAL]   Evaluate expression

The result is '$(x*U+(x^2+y^2)*m)/(x^2+y^2)$'. This expression can be simplified further by using the command PARTFRAC:

[CAT][ALPHA][P] (find PARTFRAC) [OK]   Expand into partial fractions

The final result is '$x/(x^2+y^2)*U+m$', i.e.,

$$u(x,y) = x \cdot U / (x^2+y^2) + m.$$

To obtain an expression for v(x,y) = - Im(w), use:

[⇦][↰][MTH][NXT][CMPLX][IM]   Drop level 1, find imaginary part

This requires us to select the Complex mode. To clear up the result use:

[1][0][3][+/-][SPC][ALPHA][ALPHA][C][F][ENTER]   Clear system flag 103 (Complex)
[↱][EVAL][+/-]   Evaluate expression, change sign

The result is '$y*U/(x^2+y^2)$', i.e.,

$$v(x,y) = y \cdot U / (x^2+y^2) + m.$$

Plotting the complex potential

To plot the real and imaginary parts of the complex potential you can use the Gridmap type of plots, which require as input a complex function.

For example, to produce a Gridmap plot for the function F(z) = 1/z, use the following:

⬇ Press [↰][2D/3D], simultaneously to access to the PLOT SETUP window.

⬇ Change TYPE to Gridmap.

⬇ Press [▼] and type '$1/(X+i*Y)$' [OK].

⬇ Make sure that 'X' is selected as the Indep: and 'Y' as the Depnd: variables.

94

⬇ Press [NXT][OK] to return to normal calculator display.

⬇ Press [↰][WIN], simultaneously, to access the PLOT WINDOW screen.

⬇ Change the plot window ranges to read:

```
X-Left:-2  X-Right:2
Y-Near:-1  Y-Far: 1
XXLeft:-2  XXRight:2
YYNear:-1  yyFar: 1
Step Indep: 10  Depnd: 8
```

⬇ Press [ERASE][DRAW] to draw the gridmap plot.   The result is a grid of functions corresponding to the real and imaginary parts of the complex function.

⬇ Press [EDIT][NXT][LABEL][MENU] to see the graph with labels and ranges:

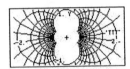

The graph shows the equipotential lines and streamlines of the doublet flow $F(z) = 1/z$. Because there is a singularity at $z = 0$ (i.e., $1/z$ is not defined at $z = 0$), the calculator avoids plotting lines near the origin.

⬇ Press [NXT][NXT][PICT][CANCL] to return to the PLOT WINDOW environment.

⬇ Press [ON], or [NXT][OK], to return to normal calculator display.

Complex potential for combinations of elementary flows

When we add complex potentials of elementary flows we can obtain the picture of more complicated flows. Some of those combined flows are presented here.

Example 1 - Find the velocity components for the combination of two sources both of strength $m = 1$, one located at $x = -1$ (source s_1), the other at $x = +1$ (source s_2). The complex potentials corresponding to the two sources are

$$F_1(z) = \ln (z +1), \; F_2(z) = \ln(z-1).$$

The combined complex potential is

$$F(z) = F_1(z) + F_2(z) = \ln (z +1) + \ln(z-1).$$

Use:

95

'LN(z+1)+LN(z-1)'[ENTER] 'z' [ENTER] [↰][∂]   Calculate w = dF/dz
'z = x+i*y' [ENTER] [↰][ALG][SUBST][ENTER]   Substitute z = x + iy, make extra copy
[↩][MTH][NXT][CMPLX][RE]   Find u = Re(w)
[▼] (using small font)   Show expression in equation writer

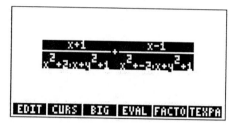

To obtain the component v(x,y), use:

[ENTER][⇦][IM]   Obtain imaginary part
[▼] (using small font)   Show expression in equation writer

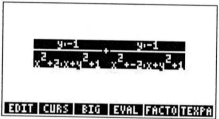

Press [ENTER] to return to normal calculator display.

Example 2 - Sketch the flow given by the combination of a uniform flow with U = 1, and a doublet with strength μ = 1, i.e, F(z) = z - 1/z .

➕ Press [↩][2D/3D], simultaneously to access to the PLOT SETUP window.

➕ Change TYPE to Gridmap.

➕ Press [▼] and type '(X+i*Y)+1/(X+i*Y)' [OK].

➕ Press [▲][NXT][CALC][↰][EVAL][OK]

➕ Make sure that 'X' is selected as the Indep: and 'Y' as the Depnd: variables.

➕ Press [NXT][OK] to return to normal calculator display.

➕ Press [↩][WIN], simultaneously, to access the PLOT WINDOW screen.

➕ Change the plot window ranges to read:

96

```
X-Left:-4  X-Right:4
Y-Near:-2  Y-Far: 2
XXLeft:-4  XXRight:4
YYNear:-2  yyFar: 2
```
Step Indep: 20 Depnd: 16

⬇ Press [ERASE][DRAW] to draw the gridmap plot.   The result is a grid of functions corresponding to the real and imaginary parts of the complex function.

⬇ Press [EDIT][NXT][LABEL][MENU] to see the graph with labels and ranges:

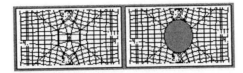

The graph shows the equipotential lines and streamlines of the combination of a uniform flow (U=1) and a negative doublet of strength μ = 1 (i.e., the source is located to the left of the sink in the doublet on the x-axis).   The graph on the right-hand side has been modified by shadowing the region within a circle of radius 1, which happens to constitute a closed streamline. (**Note:** this was not done in the calculator).   For all practical purposes you can replace the flow within the closed streamline with a solid body, in this case a cylinder.   Thus, the combination of this uniform flow and negative doublet produces the flow net corresponding to a uniform flow U = 1past a cylinder of radius 1.

⬇ Press [NXT][NXT][PICT][CANCL] to return to the PLOT WINDOW environment.

Press [ON], or [NXT][OK], to return to normal calculator display.

A word of warning on plotting combined flows in the calculator

While the calculator can be used to produce flow net graphics, the user should be warned that the more complicated the complex potential, the longer it will take for the calculator to produce a graph.   Also, functions such as 'LN(X+i*Y)' seem to behave strangely when producing graphs.   My advice is to use these graphs as guidelines only, and only for simple flows.   A different approach will be to obtain the velocity potential and stream functions separately, and to plot them, separately, as contour plots.   Such approach is left as an exercise to the reader.

97

Multiple integrals

Integrals of one variable were interpreted earlier as representing the area under the curve y = f(x), $a<x<b$. A double integral can be interpreted as representing the volume under the surface z = f(x,y) over a region R in the x-y plane. The figure below shows an element of that volume in the shape of a parallelepiped of base, dA = dx·dy, and height, f(x,y). The differential of volume is dV = f(x,y)·dA = f(x,y)·dy·dx.

The total volume is given by the double integral,

$$\iint_R dV = \iint_R f(x,y)dA = \iint_R f(x,y)dydx,$$

The region *R* over which a double integral is calculated can be described, in general, by the following inequalities: *R* = {a<x<b, g(x)<y<h(x)}, or *R* = {c<y<d, p(y)<x<q(y)}, as illustrated in the figures shown two pages ahead.

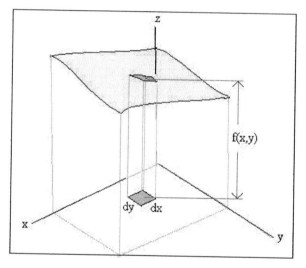

Having identified the limits for x and y that describe the region, the double integral

$$\iint_R f(x,y)dydx,$$

can be calculated using an iterated integral of the form

$$\int_a^b \int_{g(x)}^{h(x)} f(x,y)\,dy\,dx$$

or of the form

98

$$\int_c^d \int_{p(y)}^{q(y)} f(x, y) \, dx \, dy.$$

The last two integrals are known as iterated integrals because you integrate one level at a time. For example, the iterated integral

$$\int_a^b \int_{g(x)}^{h(x)} f(x, y) \, dy \, dx$$

Is typically calculated by integrating f(x,y) with respect to y, first. Which results in a function of x, only, i.e.,

$$\int_{g(x)}^{h(x)} f(x, y) dy = F(x).$$

Then, this function of x is integrated with respect to x within the limits a and b:

$$\int_a^b F(x) dx = \int_a^b \int_{g(x)}^{h(x)} f(x, y) dy dx.$$

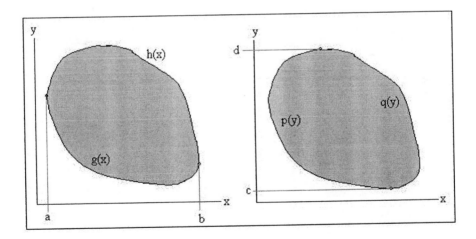

Calculating a double integral in the HP 49 G calculator

To calculate a double integral in the HP 49 G calculator, we can proceed by integrating one level at a time, as in the following example:
Let's calculate

$$\int_0^1 \int_x^{x^2} xy\,dy\,dx$$

Use the following:

[EQW] [→][∫] [ALPHA][↰][X] [►][ALPHA][↰][X][y^x][2] [►]
[ALPHA][↰][X][×][ALPHA][↰][Y] [►] [ALPHA][↰][Y]
[►][EVAL]

The result is

$$\frac{x^5 - x^3}{2}.$$

To proceed to the next level of integration try this:

[→][∫] [0][►] [1] [►][►][►][►][►][►] [ALPHA][↰][X]
[▲][▲][EVAL]

The result is -1/24.

You could also type the double integral directly in the equation writer as:

[EQW] [→][∫] [0][►] [1] [►] [→][∫] [ALPHA][↰][X] [►][ALPHA][↰][X][y^x][2] [►]
[ALPHA][↰][X][×][ALPHA][↰][Y] [►] [ALPHA][↰][Y] [►] [ALPHA][↰][X]

The equation writer will now look like this:

To evaluate the double integral use: [▲][▲][EVAL]

The result is -1/24.

Note: If the region of integration is a rectangle in the x-y plane defined by $a<x<b$, $c<y<d$, and if the function to be integrated is such that $f(x,y) = g(x)h(y)$, then

$$\int_a^b \int_c^d f(x,y)dydx = \int_a^b \int_c^d g(x)h(y)dydx = \left(\int_a^b g(x)dx\right)\cdot\left(\int_c^d h(y)dy\right)$$

Check the result shown in the note above by calculating:

$$\int_1^2 \int_{-1}^1 \exp(x)\ln(y)dxdy = \left(\int_1^2 \ln(y)dy\right)\cdot\left(\int_{-1}^1 \exp(x)dx\right)$$

The left-hand side of this equation is calculated by using:

[EQW] [↦][∫] [1][▶] [2] [▶] [↦][∫] [1][+/-][▶] [1][▶]
[↤][eˣ][ALPHA][↤][X] [▲][▲] [×][↦][LN][ALPHA][↤][Y]
[▶] [ALPHA][↤][Y] [▶] [ALPHA][↤][X]

The double integral to be calculated looks like this in the equation writer screen:

$$\int_1^2 \int_{-1}^1 EXP(x)\cdot LN(y)dx\ dy$$

To evaluate this double integral use: [▲][▲][EVAL]. The result is

$$\frac{(2\ln 2 - 1)\exp(1)^2 - (2\ln 2 - 1)}{\exp(1)}.$$

To simplify the result use [↦][→NUM]. The final result is 0.907947188573.

The right-hand side of the equation above can be calculated as follows:

[EQW] [↦][∫] [1][▶] [2] [▶] [↦][LN][ALPHA][↤][Y] [▶] [ALPHA][↤][Y] [▲][▲][×]
[↦][∫] [1][+/-][▶] [1][▶][↤][eˣ][ALPHA][↤][X] [▶] [ALPHA][↤][X]

The product of the two integrals will look as follows in the equation writer screen:

$$\int_1^2 LN(y)dy \cdot \int_{-1}^1 EXP(x)dx$$

To evaluate this product of integrals: [▲][▲][▲][EVAL].   The result is now

$$\frac{(2\ln 2 - 1)\exp(1)\exp(1) - (2\ln 2 - 1)}{\exp(1)}.$$

To simplify the result use [↦][→NUM]. The final result is, again, 0.907947188573.

Area properties in Cartesian coordinates using double integration

Double integration somewhat simplifies the calculation of area properties in two dimensions by identifying a generic element of area corresponding to a particular coordinate system.   For example, the figure below identifies the typical element of area in Cartesian coordinates that is used for calculating double integrals. The area of this infinitesimal area is dA = dx·dy.

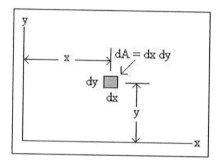

Having identified this differential of area we can re-write any generic double integral over a region R as an iterated integral once the limits of integration are determined.   Typically, in Cartesian coordinates, the region of integration R will be described as

R = { a < x < b, g₁(x) < y < g₂(x) },

or as

R = { c < y < d, h₁(y) < x < 2(x)}.

Thus, the double integral ∬_R f(x,y) dA can be written in any of these two forms:

$$\int_a^b \int_{g_1(x)}^{g_2(x)} f(x,y)\,dy\,dx\,, \qquad or\,, \qquad \int_c^d \int_{h_1(x)}^{h_2(x)} f(x,y)\,dx\,dy\,.$$

Area properties can be calculated by replacing the function f(x,y) with different expressions as indicated below:

⬥ Area   A = ∬_R dA,   i.e., f(x,y) = 1.0.

⬥ First moment with respect to the y-axis M_y = ∬_R x·dA,   i.e., f(x,y) = x.

⬥ First moment with respect to the x-axis M_x = ∬_R y·dA,   i.e., f(x,y) = y.

- Coordinates of the centroid $\qquad$ $\bar{x} = M_y/A, \quad \bar{y} = M_x/A$

- Moment of inertia with respect to the y-axis $\quad I_y = \iint_R x^2 \cdot dA \qquad$ i.e., $f(x,y) = x^2$.

- Moment of inertia with respect to the x-axis $\quad I_x = \iint_R y^2 \cdot dA, \qquad$ i.e., $f(x,y) = y^2$.

- Moment of inertia with respect to the origin $\quad I_o = \iint_R (x^2 + y^2) \cdot dA \qquad$ i.e., $f(x,y) = x^2 + y^2$

- Radii of gyration of the area with respect to the x-axis, y-axis, and origin:

$$k_y = (I_y/A)^{1/2}, \; k_x = (I_x/A)^{1/2}, \text{ and } k_o = (I_o/A)^{1/2}.$$

Example 1 -- Consider the area defined by the semi-circle R = { -R < x < R, 0 < y < $(R^2-x^2)^{1/2}$ }. Determine the area, first moments, and moments of inertia of the area by using integration. Also, determine the coordinates of the centroid and the radii of gyration.

The way that the region R is described is such that in the generic formulas developed above we can identify a = 0, b = R, g1(x) = 0, and g2(x) = $(R^2-x^2)^{1/2}$. To simplify typing the formulas in the calculator define the following variables:

[↱]['] [ALPHA][R][+/-] [↱]['] [ALPHA][↰][A] [STO▶]
[↱]['] [ALPHA][R] [ENTER]] [↱]['] [ALPHA][↰][B] [STO▶]
[0] [↱]['] [ALPHA][↰][G][1]
[EQW] [√x] [ALPHA][R] [yˣ][2] [▶][−] [ALPHA][↰][X][yˣ][2] [ENTER] [↱]['][ALPHA][↰][G][2]
[STO▶]

Next, we will show you how to evaluate, step-by-step, the generic equations that you will be entering in your calculator using as example the evaluation of the area. Type the following double integral:

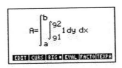

The screen above shows the way the double integral looks after you typed the x in dx. First, let's replace the generic integration limits a, b, g1, and g2, with their current definitions, using the following:

[▶][▼][EVAL] $\qquad$ Replaces a with -R
[▶][EVAL] $\qquad$ Replaces b with R
[▶][▼][EVAL] $\qquad$ Replaces g1 with 0
[▶][EVAL] $\qquad$ Replaces g2 with $\sqrt{(R^2-x^2)}$

Next, we will evaluate the innermost integral by using:

[▶][▲][EVAL] $\qquad$ Select innermost integral and evaluate it, resulting in $\sqrt{(R^2-x^2)}$
[▲][EVAL] $\qquad$ Select innermost integral and evaluate it, resulting in the
expression:

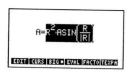

Because this is a symbolic expression, the calculator returns a generic result including the term ASIN(R/|R|), which allows for R to be a positive or negative real number, or even a complex number. We are interested, however, in the specific case in which R is real and R >0, which makes |R| = R. Thus, we will replace |R| by R, in the current expression, and re-evaluate it as follows:

[▼][►][▼][▼][►]   Move cursor about expression to select term
|R|
[EDIT]   Trigger the line editor
[↵][►][◄][⇦][◄][⇦][⇦][⇦]   Edit 'ABS(R)' to read 'R'
[ENTER]   Return to equation writer screen
[▲][▲][EVAL]   Select the term ASIN(R/R) and evaluate it

The final result is A = $R^2 \cdot (\pi/2)$, as expected for a semicircle.   Press [ENTER] and keep this result in the stack for future use.

The next integral to be calculated is

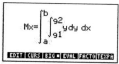

You can proceed step-by-step as in the previous integral, or simply select and evaluate the entire double integral, by using [▲][▲][EVAL]. While the calculator is evaluating the expression selected you will see the small hourglass icon active at the top of the screen. It takes the calculator about 20 seconds to produce the result: My = 0. Press [ENTER] and keep this result in the stack for future use.

$$Mx = \int_a^b \int_{g1}^{g2} y\, dy\, dx$$

Let's evaluate the next integral, i.e.,

Press [▲][▲][EVAL] to evaluate the double-integral at once. The result is Mx = $2 \cdot R^3/3$. Press [ENTER] and keep this result in the stack for future use.
The next integral to be calculated is the moment of inertia with respect to the y axis:

$$Iy = \int_a^b \int_{g1}^{g2} x^2\, dy\, dx ◄$$

104

Let's evaluate this integral step-by-step by using:

[►][▼][EVAL]   Replaces a with –R
[►][EVAL]   Replaces b with R
[►][▼][EVAL]   Replaces g1 with 0
[►][EVAL]   Replaces g2 with $\sqrt{(R^2-x^2)}$
[►][▲][EVAL]   Select innermost integral and evaluate it, resulting in $x^2 \cdot \sqrt{(R^2-x^2)}$

[▲][EVAL]   Select innermost integral and evaluate it, resulting in the
expression:

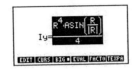

which includes the term ASIN(R/|R|). Here is another way to replace this term with $\pi/2$, by using a substitution:

[▼][▼][►]   Select the term ASIN(R/|R|).
[↵][|][ALPHA][R][►][1]   Insert evaluation at R = 1 in the term ASIN(R/|R|).
[▲][▲][EVAL][EVAL]   Replaces ASIN(R/|R|)|$_{R=1}$ with $\pi/2$.
[▲][▲][EVAL]   Re-arrange result to Iy = $R^4 \cdot \pi/8$.
[ENTER]   Keep this result in the stack for future use.

The last integral to evaluate is

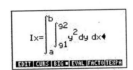

Evaluate the double integral at once by using [▲][▲][EVAL]. The result is

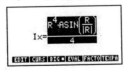

Use any of the methods shown above to replace ASIN(R/|R|) with $\pi/2$, and simplify the result to Iy = $R^4 \cdot \pi/8$. Press [ENTER] to keep this result in the stack.

Your stack should now look like this:

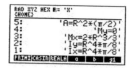

```
RAD XYZ HEX R= 'X'
{HOME}
5:                    'A=R^2*(π/2)'
4:                           'My=0'
3:                    'Mx=2*R^3/3'
2:                    'Iy=R^4*π/8'
1:                    'Ix=R^4*π/8'
PRTMI CASIN REALN   a    b    #1
```

To calculate centroidal coordinates and radii of gyration you can use the following:

[5][↤][PRG][LIST][→LIST][ENTER]	Place all results in a list, making extra copy
[ELEM][NXT][TAIL]	Reduce list to My, Mx, Iy, Ix only
[▶][HEAD]	Swap lists, and isolate value of A from list in stack level
1	
[÷]	Divide list in stack level 2 by value of A in stack level 1
[↦][EVAL]	Separate elements of list

The result in stack level 1 is Ix/A, press [↦][EVAL] to simplify the right-hand side of the current equation, resulting in 'Ix/A = R^2/4'. Press [√x] to obtain the radius of gyration, k_x, in the right-hand side of the equation, and press [↦][EVAL] to simplify the expression further. Because we are working with a symbolic result, you will see a couple of ABS functions inserted in the result. Since we restrict ourselves to real positive values of A and R, the actual result should be $k_x = R/2$. Press [⇐] to drop this result from the stack.

To obtain the radius of gyration k_y, use [↦][EVAL] [√x] [↦][EVAL]. The result, after ignoring the absolute values, is $k_y = R/2$. Press [⇐] to drop this result from the stack.

The result currently in stack level 1 is the y-coordinate of the centroid, $\bar{y}$. To evaluate it, simply use [↦][EVAL]. The result is $\bar{y}$ = '4*R/(3*π)'. Press [⇐] to drop this result from the stack.

The final result left in the stack is 'My/A=0', which produces $\bar{x}$ = '0'.

Mass properties of thin plates using double integration

If we think of a region R in the x-y plane as representing a plate of uniform thickness Δh, we can take f(x,y) = ρ(x,y)·Δh, where r(x,y) is the density (mass/volume) of the material in the plate. The function f(x,y) represents an areal density of the plate's material (mass/area). Thus, the mass of the plate can be calculated as

$$m = \iint_R f(x,y) \, dA = \iint_R \rho(x,y) \cdot \Delta h \, dA.$$

To simplify the notation we can take Δh =1.0, and simple replace f(x,y) = ρ(x,y), specifying an areal rather than volume density for ρ(x,y). Using such notation, we can work in terms of mass, rather than area, properties of a plate. A differential of mass will be defined as

$$dm = \rho(x,y) \cdot dA,$$

Thus, we can define the following quantities:

- 🔸 Mass $\qquad m = \iint_R dm = \iint_R \rho(x,y) \cdot dA,$

- 🔸 First moment with respect to the y-axis $M_y = \iint_R x \cdot dm = \iint_R x \cdot \rho(x,y) \cdot dA,$

- 🔸 First moment with respect to the x-axis $M_x = \iint_R y \cdot dm = \iint_R y \cdot \rho(x,y) \cdot dA,$

106

⚓ Coordinates of the center of mass $\qquad \bar{x} = M_y/m, \quad \bar{y} = M_x/m$

⚓ Moment of inertia with respect to the y-axis $\qquad I_y = \iint_R x^2 \cdot dm = \iint_R x^2 \cdot \rho(x,y) \cdot dA$

⚓ Moment of inertia with respect to the x-axis $\qquad I_x = \iint_R y^2 \cdot dm = \iint_R y^2 \cdot \rho(x,y) \cdot dA$,

⚓ Moment of inertia with respect to the origin $\qquad I_o = \iint_R (x^2 + y^2) \cdot dm = \iint_R (x^2 + y^2) \cdot \rho(x,y) \cdot dA$

⚓ Radii of gyration of the plate with respect to the x-axis, y-axis, and origin:

$$k_y = (I_y/m)^{1/2}, \; k_x = (I_x/m)^{1/2}, \; \text{and} \; k_o = (I_o/m)^{1/2}.$$

Example 2 -- Consider the triangle defined by R = { 0 < x < B, 0 < y < (H/B)x }. Assume that the triangle represents the face of a plate of constant thickness so that the areal density (mass/area) of the material is given by $\rho(x,y) = x + y$. Determine the mass of the plate, the first moments, and moments of inertia with respect to the two axes. Also, determine the coordinates of the plate's center of mass and the radii of gyration of the plate with respect to the x- and y-axes.

Following the generic definition of the region R, given earlier, we identify a = 0, b = B, g_1 = 0, g_2 = H*x/B, and are given the value $\rho(x,y) = x + y$ for the material's areal density. We can store all these values and functions in memory as follows:

[0] [→]['] [ALPHA][←][A] [STO▶]
[→]['] [ALPHA][B] [ENTER]] [→]['] [ALPHA][←][B] [STO▶]
[0] [→]['] [ALPHA][←][G][1] [STO▶]

[EQW] [ALPHA][H] [×] [ALPHA][←][X] [▶] [÷][ALPHA][B] [ENTER] [→]['][ALPHA][←][G][2] [STO▶]
[EQW] [→][CHARS] (select ρ) [ECHO1] [←][( )] [ALPHA][←][X] [SPC] [ALPHA][←][Y] [▶][→][=][ALPHA][←][X] [+][ALPHA][←][Y] [ENTER] [←][DEF]

Then, enter each of the following integrals in your calculator, and evaluate and simplify them using techniques similar to those presented in the previous exercise:

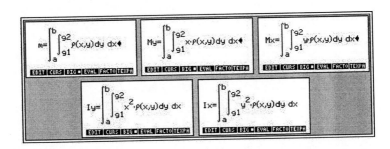

After evaluating each of the integrals, press [ENTER]. When finished, you should have the following (factorized) expressions in your stack, shown here in small font:

```
RAD XYZ HEX R= 'X'
{HOME}
7:
6:
5:          'M=B×H×(2×B+H)/(3×2)'
4:         'My=B^2×H×(2×B+H)/2^3'
3:      'Mx=B×H^2×(3×B+2×H)/(3×2^3)'
2:        'Iy=B^3×H×(2×B+H)/(5×2)'
1:    'Ix=B×H^3×(4×B+3×H)/(5×3×2^2)'
 P   PRINI CASIN REALA  q    b
```

To calculate center-of-mass coordinates and radii of gyration you can use the following:

[5][↰][PRG][LIST][→LIST][ENTER]	Place all results in a list, making extra copy
[ELEM][NXT][TAIL]	Reduce list to My, Mx, Iy, Ix only
[▶][HEAD]	Swap lists, and isolate value of A from list in stack level
1	
[÷]	Divide list in stack level 2 by value of A in stack level 1
[↱][EVAL]	Separate elements of list
[↱][EVAL]	Right-hand side = k_x^2 = '(4*H^2+3*H^3)/(20*B+10*H)'
[↰][↱][EVAL]	Right-hand side = k_y^2 = '3*B^2/5'
[↰][↱][EVAL]	Right-hand side = $\bar{x}$ = '(3*H*B+H^2)/(8*B+4*H)'
[↰][↱][EVAL]	Right-hand side = $\bar{x}$ = '3*B/4'

Double integrals in polar coordinates

In general, the double integral $\iint_R f(x,y) \, dA$ can be visualized as the volume of the solid contained between the x-y axis and the curve $z = f(x,y)$ and whose base is the region R in the x-y plane. To emphasize that we are dealing with the Cartesian coordinates system (x,y,z), we replace R with R(x,y) in the double integral, and write it as $\iint_{R(x,y)} f(x,y) \, dA$. Since any region R(x,y) in the xy plane in Cartesian coordinates can be transformed into a region R*(r,θ) in polar coordinates through the transformations

$$x = r \cos \theta, \quad y = r \sin \theta,$$

we should be able to write the double integral in polar (cylindrical) coordinates as

$$\iint_{R^*(r,\theta)} f^*(r,\theta) \, dA .$$

In this expression, the function $f^*(r,\theta)$ is the function that results from replacing the proper coordinate transformations in f(x,y), and dA is a differential of area in polar coordinates as shown below.

The polar differential of area incorporates an increment in the radial direction, dr, as well as the corresponding increment, rdθ, in the transversal direction. This element being nearly rectangular, its area is approximated by

$$dA = (r \cdot d\theta) \cdot (dr) = r \cdot dr \cdot d\theta.$$

108

Thus, the double integral can be written as

$$\iint_{R^*(r,\theta)} f^*(r,\theta)\, dA = \iint_{R^*(r,\theta)} f^*(r,\theta)\cdot r \cdot dr \cdot d\theta.$$

If the region of integration in the r- θ plane is described as $R^*(r, \theta)$ = { a < θ < b, $r_1(\theta)$ < r < $r_2(\theta)$ } , then the double integral in polar coordinates can be written as the following iterated integral

$$\iint_{R^*(r,\theta)} f^*(r,\theta)\,dA = \int_a^b \int_{r_1(\theta)}^{r_2(\theta)} f^*(r,\theta)\cdot r \cdot dr \cdot d\theta.$$

Thus, double integrals in polar coordinates need to include the term r in their integrand in addition to the function f*(r,θ) that is being integrated.

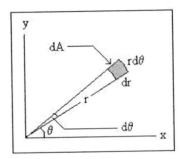

Example 1 - Calculate the integral of $f(r,\theta) = r\cdot e^\theta$ on the region $R^*(r,\theta)$ = {0< θ < π /4, 0< r < 1- sin θ } .

Start by typing in the integral shown below in the equation writer (small font):

$$\int_0^{\frac{\pi}{4}} \int_0^{1-\sin(\theta)} (r\cdot EXP(\theta))\cdot r\, dr\, d\theta$$

| EDIT | CURS | BIG | EVAL | FACTO | TEXPA |

As you can see, the function to integrate r EXP(θ) is multiplied by r, as required by the definition of $dA_{r\theta}$. To see the integration step-by-step, use:

[▲][▲][▶][▶][EVAL]   Highlight and evaluate innermost integral
[FACTO]   Factorize the resulting expression
[▲][EVAL]   Highlight and evaluate the remaining integral

Give the calculator some time to obtain the following result:

109

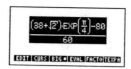

The Jacobian of a coordinate transformation

When expressing a double integral in Cartesian coordinates we used dA = dx·dy. Notice that in this case the area of the infinitesimal element is the product of the increments in the independent variables, dx and dy. Suppose that we want to emphasize the use of the x-y coordinates by writing dA_{xy} = dx·dy. Similarly, in polar coordinates we may want to write a polar differential of area consisting of the product of the increments of the independent variables as $dA_{r\theta}$ = dr·dθ. If we use this notation, then the double integrals in Cartesian and polar coordinates are related by

$$\iint_{R(x,y)} f(x,y) \cdot dx \cdot dy = \iint_{R(x,y)} f(x,y) \cdot dA_{xy} = \iint_{R^*(r,\theta)} f^*(r,\theta) \cdot r \cdot dr \cdot d\theta = \iint_{R^*(r,\theta)} f^*(r,\theta) \cdot r \cdot dA_{r\theta}.$$

Thus, the relationship between the differentials of area in x-y and r-θ is

$$dA_{xy} = r \cdot dA_{r\theta}.$$

This latter relationship is used to convert the differential of area in Cartesian coordinates to an equivalent expression in polar coordinates.

Suppose that you use other system of coordinates, say φ–ψ, where φ = φ (x,y) and ψ = ψ (x,y), whose differential of area is defined as $dA_{\phi\psi}$ = dφ·dψ. The relationship between the differential of area in Cartesian coordinates, dA_{xy}, and $dA_{\phi\psi}$ will be given by

$$dA_{xy} = \left| J\left(\frac{x,y}{\phi,\psi} \right) \right| \cdot dA_{\phi\psi}.$$

where the quantity between the absolute value sign is referred to as *the Jacobian of the coordinate transformation (x,y)* → *(φ,ψ)*. The Jacobian is defined by the following determinant:

$$J = J\left(\frac{x,y}{\phi,\psi} \right) = \begin{vmatrix} \dfrac{\partial x}{\partial \phi} & \dfrac{\partial x}{\partial \psi} \\ \dfrac{\partial y}{\partial \phi} & \dfrac{\partial y}{\partial \psi} \end{vmatrix} = \left(\frac{\partial x}{\partial \phi} \right)\left(\frac{\partial y}{\partial \psi} \right) - \left(\frac{\partial x}{\partial \psi} \right)\left(\frac{\partial y}{\partial \phi} \right)$$

Using the Jacobian, the following relationship exists between the double integral in Cartesian x-y coordinates and in the transformed coordinate system φ–ψ:

110

$$\iint\limits_{R(x,y)} f(x,y) \cdot dA_{xy} = \iint\limits_{R^*(\phi,\psi)} f^*(\phi,\psi) \cdot |J| \cdot dA_{\phi\psi}$$

In this equation, $f^*(\phi,\psi)$ represents the function $f(x,y)$ with the transformation $x = x(\phi,\psi)$, $y = y(\phi,\psi)$ incorporated. Also, $R^*(\phi,\psi)$ is the region in the ϕ–ψ plane corresponding to region $R(x,y)$ in the x-y plane.

To illustrate the use of the Jacobian, let's select $\phi = r$ and $\psi = \theta$, i.e., we want to calculate the Jacobian corresponding to the transformation of coordinates from Cartesian to polar. We know that the two systems of coordinates are related by $x(r, \theta) = r \cdot \cos\theta$, $y(r, \theta) = r \cdot \sin\theta$.

$$J = J\left(\frac{x,y}{r,\theta}\right) = \begin{vmatrix} \dfrac{\partial x}{\partial r} & \dfrac{\partial x}{\partial \theta} \\ \dfrac{\partial y}{\partial r} & \dfrac{\partial y}{\partial \theta} \end{vmatrix} = \begin{vmatrix} \cos\theta & -r \cdot \sin\theta \\ \sin\theta & r \cdot \cos\theta \end{vmatrix} = r \cdot \cos^2\theta + r \cdot \sin^2\theta = r \cdot (\cos^2\theta + \sin^2\theta) = r.$$

Therefore, the Jacobian is calculated as

Thus, $|J| = r$, and

$$\iint\limits_{R(x,y)} f(x,y) \cdot dA_{xy} = \iint\limits_{R^*(r,\theta)} f^*(r,\theta) \cdot r \cdot dA_{r\theta}.$$

Jacobian functions can be obtained for any coordinate transformations in systems of three or more coordinates. Thus, a generalized definition of the Jacobian corresponding to the transformation
$(x_1, x_2, ..., x_n) \rightarrow (\phi_1, \phi_2, ..., \phi_n)$, is

$$J = J\left(\frac{x_1,x_2,...,x_n}{\phi_1,\phi_2,...,\phi_{n\ 1}}\right) = \begin{vmatrix} \dfrac{\partial x_1}{\partial \phi_1} & \dfrac{\partial x_1}{\partial \phi_2} & \cdots & \dfrac{\partial x_1}{\partial \phi_n} \\ \dfrac{\partial x_2}{\partial \phi_1} & \dfrac{\partial x_2}{\partial \phi_2} & \cdots & \dfrac{\partial x_2}{\partial \phi_n} \\ \vdots & \vdots & \ddots & \vdots \\ \dfrac{\partial x_n}{\partial \phi_1} & \dfrac{\partial x_2}{\partial \phi_n} & \cdots & \dfrac{\partial x_n}{\partial \phi_n} \end{vmatrix}.$$

The n-multiple integral of a function $f(x_1, x_2, ..., x_n)$ over a "region" $R(x_1, x_2, ..., x_n)$ that gets transformed into a function $f^*(\phi_1, \phi_2, ..., \phi_n)$ over the transformed "region" $R^*(\phi_1, \phi_2, ..., \phi_n)$ will be written as

$$\iint\limits_{R(x_1,x_2,...,x_n)}\!\!\!...\int f(x_1,x_2,...,x_n)dx_1 \cdot dx_2 \cdots dx_n = \iint\limits_{R^*(\phi_1,\phi_2,...,\phi_n)}\!\!\!...\int f^*(\phi_1,\phi_2,...,\phi_n) \cdot |J| \cdot d\phi_1 \cdot d\phi_2 \cdots d\phi_n.$$

111

A program for calculating the Jacobian of a transformation

The following program can be used to calculate the Jacobian of the transformation

$(x_1, x_2, ..., x_n) \rightarrow (\phi_1, \phi_2, ..., \phi_n),$

given the vectors f and x

$['x_1(\phi_1, \phi_2, ..., \phi_n)'$ $'x_2(\phi_1, \phi_2, ..., \phi_n)'$ ... $'x_n(\phi_1, \phi_2, ..., \phi_n)']$
$['x_1', 'x_2', ..., 'x_n']$

The listing of the program is the following:

<u>Program JACOBIAN:</u>

<<	Start main program JACOBIAN
DUP SIZE EVAL	Obtain value of n (size of vector $['x_1' 'x_2' ...'x_n']$)
→ f x n	Pass vectors f and x, and value n
<<	Start first sub-program within JACOBIAN
n n 2 →LIST 0 CON → J	Create n×n matrix filled with zeroes, pass it on
as J	
<<	Start second sub-program within JACOBIAN
1 n FOR i	Start first FOR loop with i = 1,2, ..., n
1 n FOR j	Start second (interior) FOR loop with j = 1,2, ...,
n	
i j 2 →LIST	Create list { i j } for future use
F i GET x j ∂ GET EVAL EVAL	Calculate $\partial f_i / \partial x_j$
2 →LIST J SWAP EVAL PUT 'J' STO	Place $\partial f_i / \partial x_j$ in element (I,j) of J, store new J
NEXT	End inner FOR loop (j)
NEXT	End outer FOR loop (I)
J DET EVAL EVAL	Evaluate determinant of matrix J
>>	End second sub-program within JACOBIAN
>>	End first sub-program within JACOBIAN
>>	End program JACOBIAN

> **Notes**: (1) J and j are not the same within the program.   The HP 49 G is case sensitive.
> (2) i is used here as an index and not as the unit imaginary number.

Save the program in a variable called JACOBIAN.   Press [VAR] to check that a soft-menu key labeled [JACOB] is present.

Example 1 - Recalculate the Jacobian for the (x,y) → (r,q) using the calculator:

Enter the vectors:

    ['r*COS(θ) ''r*SIN(θ)']   [ENTER]
    ['r' 'θ']   [ENTER]

Then, press [JACOB]. The result is 'r*SIN(θ)^2+r*COS(θ)^2'. To simplify this result use:

    [↱][TRIG][NXT][NXT][TRIG].

The final result is 'r'.

Example 2 - Calculate the Jacobian of the transformation $(x,y,z) \rightarrow (\rho,\phi,\theta)$, i.e., the transformation between Cartesian to spherical coordinates in three-dimensions, if it is known that

$$x = \rho \sin \phi \cos \theta, \qquad\qquad y = \rho \sin \phi \sin \theta, \qquad\qquad z = \rho \cos \phi.$$

Enter the vectors:

['ρ*SIN(φ)*COS(θ)''ρ*SIN(φ)*SIN(θ)''ρ*COS(φ)']   [ENTER]
['ρ''φ''θ']   [ENTER]

Then, press [JACOB]. Finally, to simplify this result, use: [→][TRIG][NXT][NXT][TRIG]. The final result is 'ρ^2*SIN(φ)'.

Area properties in polar coordinates

Area properties in polar coordinates can be calculated by using the following integrals:

⬧ Area

$$A = \iint_R dA_{xy} = \iint_{R^*} r \cdot dA_{r\theta} = \iint_{R^*} r \cdot dr \cdot d\theta,$$

⬧ First moment with respect to the y-axis

$$M_y = \iint_R x \cdot r \cdot dA = \iint_{R^*} (r \cos \theta) \cdot (r \cdot dA_{r\theta}) = \iint_{R^*} r^2 \cdot \cos \theta \cdot dr \cdot d\theta,$$

⬧ First moment with respect to the x-axis

$$M_x = \iint_R y \cdot r \cdot dA = \iint_{R^*} (r \sin \theta) \cdot (r \cdot dA_{r\theta}) = \iint_{R^*} r^2 \cdot \sin \theta \cdot dr \cdot d\theta,$$

⬧ Coordinates of the centroid $\bar{x} = M_y/A, \quad \bar{y} = M_x/A$

⬧ Moment of inertia with respect to the y-axis

$$I_y = \iint_R x^2 \cdot dA = \iint_{R^*} (r \cos \theta)^2 \cdot r \cdot dA_{r\theta} = \iint_{R^*} r^3 \cdot \cos^2 \theta \cdot dr \cdot d\theta,$$

⬧ Moment of inertia with respect to the x-axis

$$I_x = \iint_R y^2 \cdot dA = \iint_{R^*} (r \sin \theta)^2 \cdot r \cdot dA_{r\theta} = \iint_{R^*} r^3 \cdot \sin^2 \theta \cdot dr \cdot d\theta,$$

⬧ Moment of inertia with respect to the origin

$$I_o = \iint_R (x^2 + y^2) \, dA = \iint_{R^*} (r^2) \cdot (r dA_{r\theta}) = \iint_{R^*} r^3 \cdot dr \cdot d\theta.$$

⬧ Radii of gyration of the area with respect to the x-axis, y-axis, and origin:

$$k_y = (I_y/A)^{1/2}, \, k_x = (I_x/A)^{1/2}, \text{ and } k_o = (I_o/A)^{1/2}.$$

Example 1 -- Calculate the area, first moments, and moments of inertia of the region in polar coordinates described by R* = {0<θ<2π, 0<r<1-cos θ}.

First, let's plot the region by using the following settings for the plot setup and plot window:

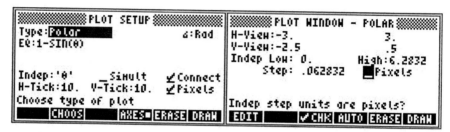

When ready, press [ERASE][DRAW].

The result is the following cardiod:

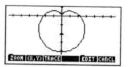

The area properties are calculated with the following integrals:

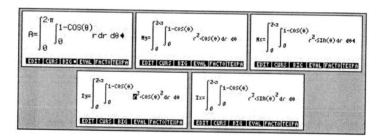

Evaluate them in the order shown above to get the following results:

To obtain centroidal coordinates and radii of gyration use the following:

114

[5][↰][PRG][LIST][→LIST][ENTER]	Place all results in a list, making extra copy
[ELEM][NXT][TAIL]	Reduce list to My, Mx, Iy, Ix only
[▶][HEAD]	Swap lists, and isolate value of A from list in stack level
1	
[÷]	Divide list in stack level 2 by value of A in stack level 1
[↱][EVAL]	Separate elements of list
[↱][EVAL]	Right-hand side = k_x^2 = '7/16'
[↰][↱][EVAL]	Right-hand side = k_y^2 = '49/48'
[↰][↱][EVAL]	Right-hand side = $\bar{x}$ = 0 (symmetry about y-axis)
[↰][↱][EVAL]	Right-hand side = $\bar{x}$ = '-5/6'

115

Vector differentiation and integration

In this section we present differentiation and integration using functions that can be expressed as vectors. Functions, in general, are also referred to as *fields*. A function, or field, that evaluates to a number is referred to as a *scalar field*. Examples of scalar fields are the temperature of a point in the plane or in space, the density or pressure in a fluid flow at a given point, etc. Some physical quantities, such as velocity, acceleration, and forces require for their description not only their magnitude, but also a direction. These quantities, when they depend on the coordinates of a point in space or on time, or both, would be referred to as *vector fields*. There are some quantities, such as the stresses at a particle presented in Chapter 9, that require for their full description their magnitude and two directions. Quantities such as this are referred to as second order tensors or *second-order tensor fields*. In general, if *n* directions are associated with a magnitude, the magnitude can be thought of as a *n*-th order tensor. In that sense a vector is a first-order tensor, and a scalar a zeroth-order tensor.

Derivatives of vector fields

Some of the simplest vector fields to differentiate or integrate are those representing position, velocity, and acceleration of a particle in three-dimensional space. In general, the position vector of a particle **r** is a function of time t, and can be written as

$$\mathbf{r}(t) = x(t)\mathbf{i}+y(t)\mathbf{j}+z(t)\mathbf{k}.$$

The velocity of the particle is defined as

$$\mathbf{v}(t) = v_x\mathbf{i}+v_y\mathbf{j}+v_z\mathbf{k}$$

and

$$\mathbf{v}(t) = d\mathbf{r}/dt = dx/dt\cdot\mathbf{i}+dy/dt\cdot\mathbf{j}+dz/dt\cdot\mathbf{k}.$$

The acceleration of the particle is given by

$$\mathbf{a}(t) = d\mathbf{v}/dt = a_x\mathbf{i}+a_y\mathbf{j}+a_z\mathbf{k},$$

$$\mathbf{a}(t) = d\mathbf{v}/dt = dv_x/dt\cdot\mathbf{i}+dv_y/dt\cdot\mathbf{j}+dv_z/dt\cdot\mathbf{k},$$

and

$$\mathbf{a}(t) = d^2\mathbf{r}/dt^2 = d^2x/dt^2\cdot\mathbf{i}+d^2y/dt^2\cdot\mathbf{j}+d^2z/dt^2\cdot\mathbf{k}.$$

From these definitions it follows that you can deal separately with the x-, y-, and z-components of the motion by writing:

$$v_x= dx/dt, \; v_y = dy/dt, \; v_z = dz/dt,$$

and

$$a_x = dv_x/dt = d^2x/dt^2, \; a_y = dv_y/dt = d^2y/dt^2.$$

116

In the HP 49 G calculator you can write a vector field by simply writing its components as components of an array. For example, if the position vector of a particle is given by

$$r(t) = (\sin t)\cdot i + (\ln t)\cdot j + (e^t)\cdot k,$$

you can write this vector in the calculator as

['SIN(t)' 'LN(t)' 'EXP(t)'] [ENTER]

However, you cannot simply take the derivative with respect to t. Try it: 't' [ENTER] [→][∂]

You will get an error labeled: |<!> ∂ Error: Bad Argument Type|

You will need to convert the vector into a list. Try:

[←][MATRICES][OPER][AXL] 't' [ENTER] [→][∂][AXL]

The result is   ['COS(t)' '1/t''EXP(t)'], i.e.,

$v(t) = (\cos t)\cdot i + (1/t)\cdot j + (e^t)\cdot k.$

To get the acceleration use: [AXL] 't' [ENTER] [→][∂][AXL] to get

['COS(t)' '1/t''EXP(t)'], i.e.,

$$a(t) = (-\sin t)\cdot i + (-1/t^2)\cdot j + (e^t)\cdot k.$$

Next, we develop a program for vector function derivatives. Create a sub-directory to be called VCALC (Vector CALCulus), and, within that sub-directory, enter the following program:

Program _VDeriv_:

<< INDER DCALC >>

The program consists of the two sub-programs listed below:

Sub-program _INDER_:

<<	Start sub-prog. INDER (INput data for
DERivative)	
"Enter deriv. info.:"	Prompt title for inputting data
{ "↵ : func: ↵ : var: ↵" {2 0 } V }	Input string
INPUT	INPUT function using two previous lines
OBJ→	Decomposes input string into three tagged
values	
1 2 FOR j	Start FOR loop to de-tag values, j = 1,2,3,4
DTAG	De-tag last value in stack
2 ROLLD	Roll-down two elements in stack
NEXT	End of FOR loop
2 →LIST	Create list with the two de-tagged values
>>	End of sub-program INDAT

Sub-program *DCALC*:

```
<<
EVAL SWAP AXL SWAP ∂ AXL
VSIMP
>>
```

Start program DCALC (Derivative CALCulation)
Swap, convert to list, take derivative, convert back
Call sub-program VSIMP
End program DCALC

Sub-program *VSIMP*

```
<<
DUP SIZE EVAL → L n
  <<
  L
  1 n FOR j
    L j GET EVAL FACTOR
    j SWAP  PUT
  NEXT
  >>
>>
```

Start program VSIMP(Vector SIMPlification)
Duplicate vector, find size, pass vector and size
Start first sub-program within VSIMP
Place array in stack
Start FOR loop with j = 1,2, ..., n
Get element j, evaluate and simplify
Place evaluated value back in array at pos. j
End FOR loop (j)
End first sub-program within IINTCALC
End program IINTCALC

Sub-program VSIMP simplifies each element of the vector and puts the simplified vector together.

Test the program on the vector $\qquad$ **r**(t) = (at^2)·**i**+ (√t)·**j**+ (sin^{-1}t)·**k**,

['a*t^2' '√t' 'ASIN(t)'][ENTER] 't' [ENTER][VDeri].

The result is $\qquad$ ['2*t*a' '√t /(2*t)' '(-√-(t^2-1)/(t^2-1))'], i.e.,

v(t) = (2at)·**i**+ (√t /(2t))·**j**+ (-√-(t^2-1)/(t^2-1))·**k**.

To get the acceleration you would use: 't' [VDeri]. The result is

['2*a' '-√t/(4*t^2)' '√-(t^2-1)*t/((t+1)^2*(t-1)^2)'], i.e.,

a(t) = (2a)·**i**+ (√t /(4t^2))·**j**+ (-√-(t^2-1)t/((t+1)^2(t+1)^2)·**k**.

Integrals of vector functions

Integration of the acceleration or velocity functions is straightforward, e.g., from

d**v** = **a**(t) dt ,

you can write

$$\int_{\mathbf{v_o}}^{\mathbf{v}} d\mathbf{v} = \int_{t_o}^{t} \mathbf{a}(t)dt = \int_{t_o}^{t} [a_x(t)\cdot\mathbf{i} + a_y(t)\cdot\mathbf{j} + a_z(t)\cdot\mathbf{k}]dt$$

$$= \left(\int_{t_o}^{t} a_x(t)dt\right)\cdot\mathbf{i} + \left(\int_{t_o}^{t} a_y(t)dt\right)\cdot\mathbf{j} + \left(\int_{t_o}^{t} a_z(t)dt\right)\cdot\mathbf{k}$$

118

Or, you can integrate the three components separately, i.e.,

$$\int_{v_{ox}}^{v_x} dv_x = \int_{t_o}^{t} a_x(t)dt, \quad \int_{v_{oy}}^{v_y} dv_y = \int_{t_o}^{t} a_y(t)dt, \quad \int_{v_{oz}}^{v_z} dv_z = \int_{t_o}^{t} a_z(t)dt,$$

where

$$v_o = v_{xo} \cdot i + v_{yo} \cdot j + v_{zo} \cdot k = v(t_o),$$

is the initial velocity of the particle.

To integrate, you need to convert the vector into a list before performing the integration.

Example 1 - Indefinite integral

Given $v(t) = (e^t)i + (-t^3)j + (1/t)k$, obtain a general expression for the position vector r(t).   No initial conditions are given.

Try this:

['EXP(t)' '-t^3' '1/t'][ENTER]	Enter vector to be integrated
[↰][MATRICES][OPER][AXL]	Convert vector to list
't' [ENTER] [↰][CALC][DERIV][NXT][RISCH]	Enter integration variable, integrate
[↰][MATRICES][OPER][AXL]	Convert vector to list

The result is   ['EXP(t)' '-(1/4*t^4)' 'LN(t)'], i.e.,

$$r(t) = (e^t)i + (-t^4/4)j + (\ln t)k + C,$$

where **C** is a constant vector.

The following program will take care of calculating an indefinite integral:

Program *VIntI* (*V*ector calculus *I*ntegration *I*ndefinite - wow! That was a mouthful):

<< IINDAT IINTCALC >>

The two sub-programs involved are listed below:

Sub-program *IINDAT* (Indefinite integral INput DATa):

<<	Start sub-prog. IINDAT
"Enter integr. info.:"	Prompt title for inputting data
{ "↵ : func: ↵ : var: ↵" { 2 0 } V }	Input string
INPUT	INPUT function using two previous lines
OBJ→	Decomposes input string into 3 tagged values
1 2 FOR j	Start FOR loop to de-tag values, j = 1,2,3,4
DTAG	De-tag last value in stack
2 ROLLD	Roll-down two elements in stack
NEXT	End of FOR loop
2 →LIST	Create list with the two de-tagged values
>>	End of sub-program IINDAT

Sub-program *IINTCALC* (Indefinite INTegral CALCulation):

```
<<                                          Start program IINTCALC
EVAL SWAP AXL SWAP RISCH AXL                Swap, convert to list, integrate, convert back
VSIMP                                       Call sub-program VSIMP (defined earlier)
>>                                          End program IINTCALC
```

Try the following exercise using the indefinite integral program: integrate $v(s) = s \cdot i + s^2 \cdot j + s^3 \cdot k$ as an indefinite integral. In the calculator, use the following:

[VIntl] [←][[ ]] [→]['] [ALPHA][←][S] [▶] [→]['] [ALPHA][←][S] [y^x][2] [▶]
[→]['] [ALPHA][←][S] [y^x][3] [▼] [→]['] [ALPHA][←][S] [ENTER]

The result is   ['s^2/2' 's^3/3' 's^4/2^2'], i.e.,

$$\int v(s)ds = (s^2/2)\cdot i + (s^3/3)\cdot j + (s^4/4)\cdot k + C,$$

where **C** (a constant vector) is a constant of integration.

Example 2 - Definite integral

Given $a(t) = (e^{1/t})i + (\tan^{-1} t)j + (t^2)k$, and the initial velocity $v_o = 2i - 5j + 3k$ at $t = 0$, determine the velocity $v(t)$.

We are to evaluate the integral:

$$\int_{v_o}^{v} dv = \int_0^t a(t)dt.$$

In this case, it is better to work only with lists. To integrate the right-hand side of the equation use:

```
{'EXP(1/t)' 'ATAN(t)' 't^2'}[ENTER]     Enter list to be integrated
{ 0 0 0 } [ENTER][▶]                    Enter list of initial values (*), swap order
{ t t t } [ENTER] [▶]                   Enter list of upper limit of integration(*)
{ t t t } [ENTER]                       Enter list of variables of integration (*)
[→][ ∫ ]                                Calculate the integrals
```

The result is the list: { '∫ (0,t,EXP(1/tt),tt)' '-((LN(t^2+1)-2*t*ATAN(t))/2''t^3/3' }. The first element in the list has no closed-form expression.

The left-hand side of the equation is obviously $v - v_o$, thus, the value of $v(t)$ is

$$v(t) = v_O + \int_0^t a(t)dt,$$

With the right-hand side given by the list we found earlier. To obtain a list representing $v(t)$, therefore, type in the list of the constant value and added to the existing list as follows:

{ 2 -5 3} [ENTER] [←][MTH][LIST][ADD]

120

the result is   {'∫(0,t,EXP(1/tt),tt)+2' '-((LN(t^2+1)-2*t*ATAN(t))/2+-5''t^3/3+3' },

Which can be interpreted as:

$$\mathbf{v}(t) = \left(\int_0^t \exp(1/\tau)d\tau + 2\right)\mathbf{i} + \left(-\frac{\ln(t^2+1)-2t\cdot\tan^{-1}t}{2}-5\right)\mathbf{j} + \left(\frac{t^3}{3}+3\right)\mathbf{k}.$$

We can let the calculator take care of the details of the integration by putting together the following program:

Program *VIntD* (*V*ector calculus *Int*egration *D*efinite – Another mouthful):

<< DINDAT DINTCALC >>

Sub-program *DINDAT* (Definite integral INput DATa):

<<	Start sub-prog. DINDAT
"Enter integr. info.:"	Prompt title for inputting data
{ "↵ : low: ↵ : high: ↵ : func: ↵ : var: ↵" {2 0 } V }	Input string
INPUT	INPUT function using two previous lines
OBJ→	Decomposes input string
1 4 FOR j	Start FOR loop to detag values, j=1..4
DTAG	De-tag last value in stack
4 ROLLD	Roll-down four elements in stack
NEXT	End of FOR loop
4 →LIST	Create list with the 4 detagged values
>>	End of sub-program DINDAT

Sub-program *DINTCALC* (*Ind*efinite *INT*egral *CALC*ulation):

<<	Start program DINTCALC
EVAL SWAP DUP SIZE EVAL → a b v f n	Determine vector size, pass values
<<	Start first sub-program within DINTCALC
n 1 →LIST a CON AXL	Create list with lower limit repeated
n 1 →LIST b CON AXL	Create list with upper limit repeated
F AXL	Convert vector function to a list
n 1 →LIST v CON AXL	Create list with integration variable repeated
∫ AXL	Integrate list, convert to vector
VSIMP	Call sub-program VSIMP
>>	End first sub-program within DINTCALC
>>	End program DINTCALC

Try the following exercise using the definite integral program: integrate the right-hand side of

$$\mathbf{a}(\theta) = \sin\theta\cdot\mathbf{i} + \theta^2\cdot\mathbf{j} + (1/\theta)\cdot\mathbf{k}$$

between the limits θ = π/4 and θ = π/2. In the calculator, use the following:

[VIntD] [→]['][→][π] [÷] [4] [▼] [→]['][→][π] [÷] [2] [▼]
[→][[]] [→]['] [SIN][ALPHA][→][T] [▶][▶] [→]['] [ALPHA][→][T] [yˣ][2] [▶]
[→]['] [1][÷][ALPHA][→][T] [▼]
[→]['] [ALPHA][→][T] [ENTER]

121

The result is $['\sqrt{2}/2'$ $'7*\pi^3/192'$ $'LN(\pi/2)-LN(\pi/4))']$, i.e.,

$$\int_{\pi/4}^{\pi/2} \mathbf{a}(\theta)d\,\theta = (\sqrt{2}/2)\cdot\mathbf{i}+(7\pi^3/192)\cdot\mathbf{j}+\ln(2)\cdot\mathbf{k} \ .$$

Curves

A curve in the Cartesian space can be represented by a vector function in its parametric representation, for example, x = 5 sin t, y = 3 cos t, z = 2t.   Alternatively, you can have a curve in space by specifying y = f(x) and z = g(x), for example, $y = 0.02x^2$, z = exp(0.05x). Another way to represent a curve is as the intersection of the three-dimensional surfaces, F(x,y,z) = 0, G(x,y,z) = 0. For example, F(x,y,z) $=x^2+y^2+z^2$-25, G(x,y,z) = x-5*y+3*z-1=0.

Arc Length

Let $\mathbf{r}$ = r(t) = x(t)$\mathbf{i}$+y(t)$\mathbf{j}$+z(t)$\mathbf{k}$ be a vector in parametric representation describing a curve C in space, the length of the curve corresponding to values of a<t<b is given by:

$$l = \int_a^b \sqrt{\dot{\mathbf{r}} \bullet \dot{\mathbf{r}}}\, dt, \quad where \ \dot{\mathbf{r}} = \frac{d\mathbf{r}}{dt}, \ \dot{\mathbf{r}} \bullet \dot{\mathbf{r}} = \left|\frac{d\mathbf{r}}{dt}\right|.$$

We can define an arc length function s(t) by replacing the upper limit of the integration with t:

$$s(t) = \int_a^t \sqrt{\dot{\mathbf{r}} \bullet \dot{\mathbf{r}}}\, dt = \int_a^t \sqrt{\left(\frac{dx}{dt}\right)^2 + \left(\frac{dy}{dt}\right)^2 + \left(\frac{dz}{dt}\right)^2}\, dt$$

From the definition of the arc length function it follows that

$$\frac{ds}{dt} = \sqrt{\dot{\mathbf{r}} \bullet \dot{\mathbf{r}}}, \quad \left(\frac{ds}{dt}\right)^2 = \left(\frac{dx}{dt}\right)^2 + \left(\frac{dy}{dt}\right)^2 + \left(\frac{dz}{dt}\right)^2.$$

We can also write,

$$dr = dx\cdot\mathbf{i}+dy\cdot\mathbf{j}+dz\cdot\mathbf{k},$$

and

$$ds^2 = dx^2 + dy^2 + dz^2,$$

where ds is called the linear element of the curve C.

122

For a plane curve represented by y = f(x), the arc length function can be written as

$$s(x) = \int_a^x \sqrt{1 + \left(\frac{dy}{dx}\right)^2}\,.$$

Example1 - Circular helix in space. This curve can be represented in parametric form as x(t) = a·cos(t), y(t) = a·sin(t), and z(t)= c·t. The plot of the curve for values a = 2, c = 1, is shown below. This graph was produced in Maple V because the calculator does not provide for three-dimensional curve plots.

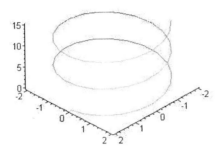

To obtain an expression of the arc length of this curve using the calculator, we use:

‘x(t) = a*COS(t)’ [↵][DEF]
‘y(t) = a*SIN(t)’ [↵][DEF]
‘z(t) = c*t’ [↵][DEF]

Then, using the equation writer put together the following function:

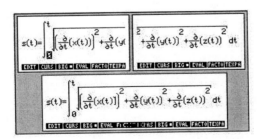

(The top two figures show the expression split in two parts, as you would see it in your calculator. The bottom figure results from combining the top two figures.)

123

Using the cursor you can select and evaluate the derivatives step-by-step. For example, you could select the derivative $\partial x(t)/\partial t$ as shown in the left-hand side figure below, and press [EVAL] to get the result shown in the right-hand figure below.

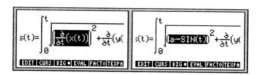

The evaluation of the other two derivatives contained under the square-root sign, is shown in the figures shown below.

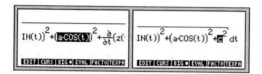

The next step is to select the expression under the square-root sign and press [EVAL]. The result is shown below:

$$s(t)=\int_{0}^{t} \sqrt{a^2 \cdot \sin(t)^2 + a^2 \cdot \cos(t)^2 + c^2}\, dt$$

Now, the first two terms can be simplified to a^2 by selecting the quantity under the square-root and using [→][TRIG][NXT][NXT][TRIG]. The next step is to select and evaluate the integral by using [→][EVAL]. The figure below shows the results of the two steps just described.

Therefore, if we take $K = t \cdot (a^2+c^2)^{1/2}$, $s(t) = K \cdot t$, the new parametric representation of the curve, in terms of the arc length, s, is

$$x(s) = a \cdot \cos(s/K),\ y(s) = a \cdot \sin(s/K),\ \text{and}\ z(s) = c \cdot s/K.$$

The following program can be used to automatically calculate the arc length of a curve described by x = x(t), y = y(t), z = z(t).

Program *ArcLength*: << INDARC INICCALC >>

Sub-program *INDARC* (INput DAta for ARC length calculation):

<<	Start sub-prog. INDARC
"Enter x(t)y(t)z(t):"	Prompt title for inputting data
{ " ↵ :x(t): ↵ :y(t): ↵ :z(t): " { 2 0 } V }	Input string
INPUT	INPUT function using two previous lines
OBJ→	Decomposes input string
1 3 FOR j	Start FOR loop to detag values, j = 1..4
DTAG	De-tag last value in stack
3 ROLLD	Roll-down four elements in stack
NEXT	End of FOR loop
3 →LIST	Create list with the 4 detagged values
{ 'x(t)' 'y(t)' 'z(t)' } SWAP = DEFINE	Define functions x(t), y(t), z(t) [*]
>>	End of sub-program INDARC

[*] This operation creates variables [x][y][z] in your sub-directory

Sub-program *INICCALC* (INItial Conditions and CALCulation of arc length):

<<	Start sub-program INICCALC
"Enter init. cond.:"	Prompt title for inputting data
{ " ↵ : s: ↵ :at t: " { 2 0 } V }	Input string
INPUT	INPUT function using two previous lines
OBJ→ DTAG SWAP DTAG SWAP	Decomposes input, de-tags elements
't'	Place 't' in stack
' (∂t(x(t))^2+∂t(y(t))^2+∂t(z(t))^2)' EVAL TRIG	Calculate integrand for s(t)
't' ∫ EVAL TRIG +	Place 't' in stack, integrate, init. cond.
's(t)' SWAP =	Place 's(t) =' in front of integral result
>>	End sub-program INICCALC

Example 1 -- Test the program with the parametric equations of the circular helix:

[ArcLe]	Start program *ArcLength*
[→]['] [ALPHA][↵][A] [×] [COS] [ALPHA][↵][T] [▼]	Enter 'a*COS(t)' for x(t)
[→]['] [ALPHA][↵][A] [×] [SIN] [ALPHA][↵][T] [▼]	Enter 'a*SIN(t)' for y(t)
[→]['] [ALPHA][↵][C] [×] [ALPHA][↵][T]	Enter 'c*t' for z(t)
[ENTER]	Enter input string
[0] [▼] [0] [ENTER]	Enter s = 0 at t = 0, enter input string

After what seems an eternity (about 20 seconds) the calculator returns the value:

$$'s(t) = t*\sqrt{(a^2+c^2)}'$$

Example 2 - Run program *ArcLength* with x(t) = t, y(t) = t^2, z(t) = z_0 (a plane parallel to the x-y axis), using the initial conditions s = s_0 at t = t_0. Use:

125

[ArcLe]	Start program *ArcLength*
[→]['] [ALPHA][←][T] [▼]	Enter 't' for x(t)
[→]['] [ALPHA][←][T] [yˣ][2] [▼]	Enter 't^2' for y(t)
[→]['] [√x] [ALPHA][←][Z][0]	Enter 'z0' for z(t)
[ENTER]	Enter input string
[→]['] [ALPHA][←][S][0]	Enter s = s0
[→]['] [ALPHA][←][T][▼] [0] [ENTER]	at t = t0, enter input string

This time the calculator will take some time to produce the following result:

Press [▼] to activate the equation writer and use the cursor to see the resulting equation in its entirety.

Tangent, normal, and bi-normal vectors, curvature and torsion

Let **r** = **r**(t) = x(t)**i**+y(t)**j**+z(t)**k** be a vector in parametric representation describing a curve C in space. The vector **v** = d**r**/dt at a point P on the curve C is a vector tangent to the curve (or trajectory) C at P. A *unit tangent vector* at P is given by

$$\mathbf{T} = \mathbf{v}/|\mathbf{v}| .$$

If **r** = **r**(s), then

$$\mathbf{T} = d\mathbf{r}/ds.$$

The *curvature* of C is given by

$$\kappa(s) = | \, d\mathbf{T}/ds \, | = | \, d^2\mathbf{r}/ds^2 \, |,$$

where s is the arc length.

The *unit normal vector* is defined as

$$\mathbf{N} = d\mathbf{T}/dt/|d\mathbf{T}/dt|,$$

or, in terms of s, as

$$\mathbf{N} = (1/\kappa)(d\mathbf{T}/ds).$$

The radius of curvature,

$$\rho(s) = 1/\kappa(s),$$

at any point of the curve, is the radius of a circle tangent to the curve at that point. The center of the curvature circle is located along the normal direction **N**.

The *unit binormal vector* is defined as the cross-product of **T** and **N**,

$$\mathbf{B} = \mathbf{T} \times \mathbf{N}.$$

126

The triad of vectors **N**, **T**, and **B** are orthogonal to each other and they form what is called the *trihedron* of C at point P. Each pair of vectors define a plane. The three planes defined by the **N**, **T**, and **B** are called: *normal plane* (defined by N and B), *rectifying plane* (defined by T and B), and *osculating plane* (defined by T and N). The vector triad and the corresponding planes are illustrated in the figure below.

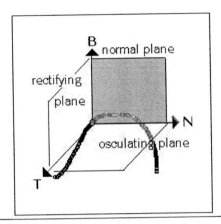

The *torsion* of the curve is defined as

$$\tau(s) = -\mathbf{N}(s) \bullet \frac{d\mathbf{B}(s)}{ds}.$$

For a curve in the plane given by y = f(x), the curvature is given by

$$\kappa(x) = \left| \frac{f''(x)}{\sqrt{1 + [f'(x)]^{3/2}}} \right|.$$

Example 1 -- Earlier we found that a circular helix in space can be described in terms of the arc-length s as x(s) = a·cos(Ks), y(s) = a·sin(Ks), z(s) = c·s/K, where K = $(a^2+c^2)^{1/2}$. Using such representation determine the tangent, normal, and bi-normal vectors, the curvature and torsion of the curve.

Start by defining the functions:

'x(s) = a*COS(s/K)' [↵][DEF]   'y(s) = a*SIN(s/K)' [↵][DEF]   'z(s) = c*s/K' [↵][DEF]

To determine the unit tangent vector, **T** = dr/ds, we can use the program [VDeriv] defined earlier, as follows:

[VDeri] [↵][[ ]] [→]['] [ALPHA][↵][X] [↵][( )] [ALPHA][↵][S] [▶][▶]
[→]['] [ALPHA][↵][Y] [↵][( )] [ALPHA][↵][S] [▶][▶]
[→]['] [ALPHA][↵][Z] [↵][( )] [ALPHA][↵][S] [▼]
[→]['] [↵][( )] [ALPHA][↵][S] [ENTER]

The result is $\qquad$ $\mathbf{T} = -(a/K)\cdot\sin(s/K)\cdot\mathbf{i} + (a/K)\cdot\cos(s/K)\cdot\mathbf{j} + (c/K)\cdot\mathbf{k}$.

Store this result in a variable T: $\qquad$ [↱]['][ALPHA][T][STO▶].

The curvature, $\kappa(s) = |\ dT/ds\ |$, can be calculated using the following:

[VAR][VDeri] [↱]['][T] [▼][↱]['] [↰][( )] [ALPHA][↰][S] [ENTER]   Calculate dT/ds
[ENTER]   Keep extra copy
[↰][ABS]   Calculate $\kappa = |\ dT/ds\ |$

The resulting expression is '√ (SIN(s/K)^2+COS(s/K)^2)*ABS(a)*K^2)/K^4'. To simplify it, use

[↱][TRIG][NXT][NXT][TRIG]

resulting in 'ABS(a)/K^2', i.e., $\qquad$ $\kappa(s) = |a|/K$.

This result indicates that the circular helix has constant curvature.

Since we already have dT/ds in stack level 2, simply press [÷] to obtain the normal unit vector $\mathbf{N} = dT/ds/|dT/ds|$. The result of this division does not simplify each component. Therefore, to produce the simplification we use the following:

[↰][MATRICES][CREAT][NEXT]   Get this menu ready for use

[ENTER]   Make extra copy of the vector
[1][GET]   Get first element of vector
[↱][EVAL]   Simplify element, result = '-
(a*COS(s/K)/ABS(a))'
[1] [ENTER][▶]   Place a 1 in stack, swap levels 1 and 2
[PUT]   Replace first element of vector

[ENTER]   Make extra copy of the vector
[2][GET]   Get second element of vector
[↱][EVAL]   Simplify element, result = '-
(a*SIN(s/K)/ABS(a))'
[2] [ENTER][▶]   Place a 2 in stack, swap levels 1 and 2
[PUT]   Replace second element of vector

[ENTER]   Make extra copy of the vector
[3][GET]   Get third element of vector

The last term is equal to zero, thus, it needs not be modified. The next step is to store the result in variable N:
[⇦][↱]['][ALPHA][N] [STO▶][VAR]

To calculate $\mathbf{B} = \mathbf{T} \times \mathbf{N}$, use:
$\qquad\qquad\qquad\qquad$ [T][N] [↰][MTH][VECT][CROSS]

The result, as in the case of N, needs to be simplified. This time, however, we will use the program VSIMP, that was defined earlier as a sub-program of [VDeriv].

Using [VAR][VSIMP] with the result from the calculation of B produces (after about 30 seconds):

['c*a*SIN(s/K)/(K*ABS(a))' '-(c*a*COS(s/K)/(K*ABS(a)))' 'a^2/(K*ABS(a))'], i.e.,

128

$$B = a \cdot c \cdot \sin(s/K)/(K \cdot |a|) \cdot \mathbf{i} - a \cdot c \cdot \cos(s/K)/(K \cdot |a|) \cdot \mathbf{j} + a^2/(K \cdot |a|) \cdot \mathbf{k}.$$

Store this result in variable B, by using:

[↵]['][ALPHA][B] [STO▶][VAR]

Note: For a>0, the vector B, in this case, will simplify to $\mathbf{B} = c \cdot \sin(s/K)/K \cdot \mathbf{i} - c \cdot \cos(s/K)/K \cdot \mathbf{j} + a/K \cdot \mathbf{k}$.

A program to calculate unit vector triad, curvature, radius of curvature, and torsion

I suggest you create a sub-directory called TRIAD (TRIAD of vectors **T,N,B**) to develop the program and sub-programs presented in this section. The program *GetTNB* can be used to automatically calculate the unit vectors: tangential, normal, and bi-normal, as well as curvature, radius of curvature, and torsion of a curve described by x = x(s), y = y(s), z=z(s), where s is the arc length. The program basically repeats the steps used in the example shown above.

Program GetTNB: << INCURVE GETT GETNk GETBτ SHOWALL >>

Sub-program INCURVE:

<<	Start sub-prog. INDARC
"Enter x(s)y(s)z(s):"	Prompt title for inputting data
{ "↵ :x(s): ↵ :y(s): ↵ :z(s): " { 2 0 } V }	Input string
INPUT	INPUT function using two previous lines
OBJ→	Decomposes input string
1 3 FOR j	Start FOR loop to detag values, j = 1..4
DTAG	De-tag last value in stack
3 ROLLD	Roll-down four elements in stack
NEXT	End of FOR loop
3 →LIST	Create list with the 4 de-tagged values
{ 'x(s)' 'y(s)' 'z(s)' } SWAP = DEFINE	Define functions x(s), y(s), z(s) [*]
>>	End of sub-program INDARC

[*] This operation creates or replaces variables [x][y][z]

Sub-program *GETT*:

<<	Start SUB-program GETT
{ 'x(s)' 'y(s)' 'z(s)' } 's' ∂ AXL VSIMP 'T' STO	Calculate dr/dt, store in variable T
"T done" MSGBOX	Calculation of **T** is complete
>>	End of program GETT

Sub-program *GETNk*:

<<	Start sub-program GETNk
T AXL 's' ∂ AXL VSIMP	Calculate dT/dt
DUP ABS EVAL FACTOR TRIG DUP 'kappa' STO	Calculate curvature, store in *kappa*
/ VSIMP 'N' STO "N done" MSGBOX	Calculate N, indicate ending of process
>>	End sub-program GETNk

Sub-program GETBτ:

129

```
<<
T  N CROSS VSIMP DUP
AXL 's' ∂  AXL VSIMP
N  SWAP DOT NEG EVAL FACTOR TRIG 'τ' STO
'B' STO  "B done" MSGBOX
>>
```

Start sub-program GETBτ
Calculate **B** = **T** × **N**, duplicate result
Calculate dB/dt
Calculate torsion, τ
Indicate calculation of B is done
End sub-program GETBτ

Sub-program *SHOWALL*:

```
<<
T  "T"  →TAG  N  "N"  →TAG
kappa "k"  →TAG  kappa INV "r"  →TAG
B  "B"  →TAG  τ  "τ"  →TAG
>>
```

Start sub-program SHOWALL
Tag T and N
Tag k, calculate r = 1/k, tag r
Tag B and t
End sub-program SHOWALL

Sub-program VSIMP is exactly the same as that defined in sub-directory VCALC, therefore, you can simply copy it from that sub-directory to sub-directory TRIAD.

Example 1 - repeat the calculation of the vector triad and related measures (curvature, torsion) for the case of the circular helix, $x(s) = a \cdot \cos(K \cdot s)$, $y(s) = a \cdot \sin(K \cdot s)$, $z(s) = c \cdot s/K$, where $K = (a^2 + c^2)^{1/2}$.

[GetTN]
[↱]['] [ALPHA][↰][A] [×] [COS] [ALPHA][K] [×] [ALPHA][↰][S] [▼]
[↱]['] [ALPHA][↰][A] [×] [SIN] [ALPHA][K] [×] [ALPHA][↰][S] [▼]
[↱]['] [ALPHA][↰][C] [×] [ALPHA][↰][S] [÷] [ALPHA][K]
[ENTER]

Press [OK] after every message. These were included for the user's sake, to keep him or her informed of the program's progress. When the last message B done shows up, the next step is to present the results in the stack. The result for this case, in small case, shows up like this:

After dropping the first 4 levels of the stack in the screen above, we get:

Velocity and acceleration as a function of arc length

In terms of the arc length s, we can write for the velocity:

$$v = dr/dt = (dr/ds) \cdot (ds/dt) = |v| \cdot (dr/ds) = v \cdot (dr/ds),$$

where $v = |v|$ is the magnitude of the velocity (the speed).

130

For the acceleration we can write:

$$a = dv/dt = d/dt[(dr/ds)\cdot(ds/dt)] = d/ds[(dr/ds)\cdot(ds/dt)]\cdot(ds/dt) =$$
$$= (d^2r/ds^2)\cdot(ds/dt)^2 + (dr/ds)\cdot(d^2s/dt^2) = v^2\cdot(d^2r/ds^2) + a\cdot(dr/ds),$$

If we replace the definitions of the unit tangent and normal vectors, T=dr/ds, and

$$N=(1/\kappa)\cdot(dT/ds) = \rho\cdot(d^2r/ds^2),$$

into the expression for the acceleration we find

$$a = (v^2/\rho)\cdot N + (d^2s/dt^2)\cdot T = a_N\cdot N + a_T\cdot T,$$

where

$$a_N = v^2/\rho$$

is the normal component of the acceleration, and

$$a_T = d^2s/dt^2 = dv/dt$$

is the tangential component.

Line integrals

A line integral is an integral calculated along a curve C, in space or in the plane, with the integrand defined at each point of C. Suppose that the curve C has the vector representation

$$r(s) = x(s)\ i + y(s)\ j + z(s)\ k,$$

in the interval $a \le s \le b$, so that r(s) is continuous and has a non-zero, continuous first derivative dr/ds in the interval. Then C is said to be a *smooth curve*, i.e., C has a unique tangent at each point of C, whose direction varies continuously as we travel along the curve. Let f(x,y,z) be a function defined (at least) at each point of C, and let f be a continuous function of s, i.e.,

$$f[x(s),y(s),z(s)] = f^*(s).$$

Then, the line integral of f along C from A to B (where s = a, and s = b, respectively) is calculated as

$$\int_C f(x, y, z)\cdot ds = \int_a^b f(x(s), y(s), z(s))\cdot ds = \int_a^b f^*(s)\cdot ds.$$

The variable s represents the distance along the curve from an arbitrary point (where s = 0). The curve C is called the path of integration. In the exercises presented in next sub-section is it assumed that all the integration paths are piecewise smooth, i.e., it consists of finitely many smooth curves.

131

For a line integral over a closed path C, the symbol

$$\oint_C f(x, y, z) \cdot ds$$

is sometimes used in the literature.

If the curve is given in terms of a parameter t, which is not the distance along the curve (t could be time, for example), then the line integral over the curve C will be calculated as

$$\int_C f(x, y, z) \cdot ds = \int_a^b f(x(t), y(t), z(t)) \cdot \left(\frac{ds}{dt}\right) \cdot dt.$$

If t represents time, then ds/dt = v_s is the speed (magnitude of the velocity) of a particle whose motion describes the curve C.

Example 1 - Determine the line integral of the function f(x,y,z) = xyz, along the curve described by x = sin(s), y = cos(s), z = s, between s = 0, and s = π.

Type:

'x*y*z' [ENTER] { 'x' 'SIN(s)' 'y' 'COS(s)' 'z' 's' } [ENTER] [→][|][ENTER]
0 [ENTER] [▶] 'π' [ENTER] [▶] 's' [ENTER] [→][∫]

The result is   '-(π/4)'.

Example 2 - Determine the line integral of the function f(x,y,z) = x+y+z, along the curve described by the motion of a particle: x = 2t², y = t, z = ln(t), between t = 1 and t = 10, where t is time. The particle moves along the curve as a constant speed ds/dt = 2.5.

Type: 'x+y+z' [ENTER] { 'x' '2*t^2' 'y' 't' 'z' 'LN(t)' } [ENTER] [→][|] [ENTER] 2.5 [×]
1 [ENTER] [▶] 10 [ENTER] [▶] 't' [ENTER] [→][∫]

Accept the change to Approx mode, if asked. The result is 1823.81462732.

In many applications, the integrands of the line integrals are of the form g(x,y,z)·(dx/ds), g(x,y,z)·(dy/ds), or g(x,y,z)· (dz/ds), where s is a variable representing a length on the integration path, and x=x(s), y=y(s), z=z(s). Then, the line integrals are written as

$$\int_C g(x, y, z) \cdot \frac{dx}{ds} \cdot ds = \int_C g(x, y, z) \cdot ds,$$

with similar expression for the other two integrals.

For sums of these types of integrals along the same path C we use the following notation:

$$\int_C f \cdot dx + \int_C g \cdot dy + \int_C h \cdot dz = \int_C (f \cdot dx + g \cdot dy + h \cdot dz).$$

132

Example 3 -- Evaluate the line integral whose integrand is $[x^2ydx +(x-z)dy+xyzdz]$ where C is the arc of the parabola $y = x^2$ in the plane $z = 2$ from A[0,0,2] to B[1,1,2]. Here is a picture of the path of integration:

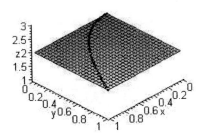

The solution to this problem consists in turning the differentials dy and dz into functions of x. First of all, since the curve is located in the plane $z = 2$, then dz = 0, throughout the integration path. Also, since the curve is described by $y = x^2$, then dy = 2xdx, thus the integrand is now:

$$x^2ydx +(x-z)dy+xyzdz = x^2(x^2)dx +(x-2)(2xdx)+xy(0)dz = (x^4+2x^2-2x)dx,$$

which is to be integrated from $x = 0$ to $x = 1$. In the calculator this is entered as:

$$\int_0^1 \left(x^4+2\cdot x^2-2\cdot x\right)dx$$

| EDIT | CURS | BIG ■ | EVAL | FACTO | TEXPR |

The integral evaluates to -2/15.

Vector notation

If the functions f(x,y,z), g(x,y,z), and h(x,y,z), are the components of a vector function F(x,y,z), i.e.,

$$\mathbf{F}(x,y,z) = f(x,y,z) \mathbf{i} +g (x,y,z) \mathbf{j} + h(x,y,z) \mathbf{k},$$

you can prove that if a differential position vector is defined as

$$d\mathbf{r} = dx\, \mathbf{i} + dy\, \mathbf{j} + dz\, \mathbf{k},$$

then

$$\int_C (f \cdot dx + g \cdot dy +h \cdot dz) = \int_C \mathbf{F} \bullet d\mathbf{r} = \int_C (\mathbf{F} \bullet \frac{d\mathbf{r}}{ds})\, ds.$$

133

Example 4 -- Work performed by a force. Determine the work performed by the force given by

$$F = a \cdot s^2 \cdot i + a \cdot \exp(-s/K) \cdot j - K \cdot s \cdot k,$$

while moving a particle on the circular helix path

$$x(s) = a \cdot \cos(K \cdot s), \ y(s) = a \cdot \sin(K \cdot s), \ z(s) = c \cdot s/K,$$

from point A, where s = 0, to point B, where s = s_o,

To begin with, define the functions

'x(s) = a*COS(s/K)' [↤][DEF]   'y(s) = a*SIN(s/K)' [↤][DEF]   'z(s) = c*s/K' [↤][DEF]

Next, put together the vector **r** as:

[↤][[ ]] [↦]['] [ALPHA][↤][X] [↤][( )] [ALPHA][↤][S] [▶][▶]
[↦]['] [ALPHA][↤][Y] [↤][( )] [ALPHA][↤][S] [▶][▶]
[↦]['] [ALPHA][↤][Z] [↤][( )] [ALPHA][↤][S]
[ENTER]

Evaluate the vector using the program VSIMP within sub-directory VCALC, to obtain:

['a*COS(s/K)' 'a*SIN(s/K)' 'c*s/K'].

Now, type the force vector:

['a*s^2' 'a*EXP(-s/K)' 'K*s'] [ENTER].

Next, take the dot product of these two vectors by using [↤][MTH][VECTR][DOT]. Also, use [↦][EVAL] to simplify the expression, if possible.

To proceed with the integral use:

[0][ENTER][▶]   [↦]['][ALPHA][↤][S][0][ENTER][▶] [↦]['][ALPHA][↤][S][ENTER] [↦][∫]

Being patient with the calculator, after about 40 seconds it produces a result that occupies the entire screen. In small font, such result is shown as:

```
RAD XYZ HEX R= 't'
{HOME VCALC}

3:
2:
1: '(((6×a^2×K×s0^2-12×a^2×K^3)×
    EXP(s0/K)-3×a^2×K)×SIN(s0/K)+(
    (12×a^2×K^2×s0×EXP(s0/K)-3×a^2
    ×K)×COS(s0/K)+(2×c×s0^3+3×a^2×
    K)×EXP(s0/K)))/(6×EXP(s0/K))'
EXPAN FACTO LNCOL  LIN  SOLVE SUBST
```

Attempts to use EVAL or FACTOR on this expression did not help in simplifying the expression. You can see the expression in the equation writer by using [▼]. This is what you will see (after moving left and right on the screen):

134

$$\frac{\left[\left(6 \cdot a^2 \cdot K \cdot s\theta^2 - 12 \cdot a^2 \cdot K^3\right) \cdot EXP\left(\frac{s\theta}{K}\right) - 3 \cdot a^2 \cdot K\right] \cdot SIN\left(\frac{s\theta}{K}\right) + \left(12 \cdot a^2 \cdot K^2 \cdot s\theta \cdot EXP\left(\frac{s\theta}{K}\right) - 3 \cdot a^2 \cdot K\right) \cdot COS\left(\frac{s\theta}{K}\right) + \left(2 \cdot c \cdot s\theta^3 + 3 \cdot a^2 \cdot K\right) \cdot EXP\left(\frac{s\theta}{K}\right)}{6 \cdot EXP\left(\frac{s\theta}{K}\right)}$$

Exact differentials

An expression of the form

$$f(x,y,z) \cdot dx + g(x,y,z) \cdot dy + h(x,y,z) \cdot dz$$

is known as a *first-order differential form*. If

$$f = \partial u/\partial x, \ g = \partial u/\partial y, \text{ and, } h = \partial u/\partial z,$$

then the differential form shown above is said to be an *exact differential* of a function $u(x,y,z)$, i.e.,

$$du = f(x,y,z) \cdot dx + g(x,y,z) \cdot dy + h(x,y,z) \cdot dz = (\partial u/\partial x) \cdot dx + (\partial u/\partial y) \cdot dy + (\partial u/\partial z) \cdot dz.$$

To check that the expression is an exact differential, check that

$$\partial f/\partial y = \partial g/\partial x, \ \partial f/\partial z = \partial h/\partial x, \text{ and } \partial g/\partial z = \partial h/\partial y.$$

The following example shows how to obtain the function $u(x,y,z)$ given an exact differential form.

Example 5 -- Check whether the following first-order differential form is an exact differential.

$$(y+z+2x)dx+(x+z)dy+(x+y)dz.$$

We identify

$$f(x,y,z) = y+z+2x, \ g(x,y,z) = x+z, \ h(x,y,z) = x+y.$$

Define them in the calculator as:

'f(x,y,z) = y+z+2*x'[↰][DEF] 'g(x,y,z) = x+z' [↰][DEF] 'h(x,y,z) =x+y' [↰][DEF]

Now, check the conditions for an exact differential as follows:

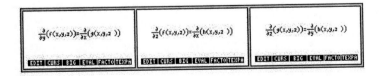

The results obtained were '1=1', '1=1', and '1=1', checking that the conditions $\partial f/\partial y = \partial g/\partial x$, $\partial f/\partial z = \partial h/\partial x$, and $\partial g/\partial z = \partial h/\partial y$, are indeed satisfied.

Example 6 – Obtain the function u(x,y,z) whose differential du = (y+z+2x)dx+(x+z)dy+(x+y)dz was verified to be an exact differential in Example 6, above.

Since the differential is exact, then we have

$$\partial u/\partial x = f(x,y,z) = y+z+2x,$$

$$\partial u/\partial y = g(x,y,z) = x+z,$$

and

$$\partial u/\partial z = h(x,y,z) = x+y.$$

First, let's integrate, $\partial u/\partial x = f(x,y,z) = y+z+2x$, with respect to x. In the calculator we will proceed as follows:

'g(x,y,z)' [→][EVAL] 'x' [ENTER] [↰][CALC][DERIV][NXT][RISCH]

This suggest that

$$u(x,y,z) = yx+zx+x^2+K(y,z).$$

The function K(y,z) acts like an integration "constant" that accounts for the dependency of u on y and z. The result in the calculator, of course, does not contain K(y,z).

The next step is to take the derivative of this expression with respect to y, using the calculator, i.e.,
'y' [→][∂], which results in 'x'. This is interpreted in paper as,

$$\partial u/\partial y = x + \partial K(y,z)/\partial y.$$

This result is now made equal to g(x,y,z), i.e.,

$$\partial u/\partial y = x + \partial K(y,z)/\partial y = x+z = g(x,y,z),$$

from which

$$\partial K(y,z)/\partial y = z.$$

Now, integrating this later result with respect to y, by using:

'z'[ENTER] 'y' [ENTER] [↰][CALC][DERIV][NXT][RISCH]

which results in 'z*y'. Or, in paper,

$$K(y,z) = zy + C(z).$$

Here, again, we need to add C(z) because we integrated only with respect to y. Now, replacing K(y,z) into u(x,y,z) results in

$$u(x,y,z) = xy+zx+zy+x^2+C(z).$$

Next, take the derivative of this expression with respect z in the calculator

'x*y+z*x+z*y+x^2' [ENTER] 'z' [ENTER] [→][∂],

136

this results in 'x+y', which is interpreted, in paper, as

$$\partial u/\partial z = x+y+C'(z).$$

This result should be equal to h(x,y,z), i.e.,

$$\partial u/\partial z = x+y+C'(z) = x+y = h(x,y,z),$$

from which,

$$C'(z) = 0, \text{ and } C(z) = D$$

where D is a constant of integration.

With C(z) into the expression for u(x,y,z) , we get

$$u(x,y,z) = xy+zx+zy+x^2+C(z).$$

Line integrals independent of path

In general, a line integral of a differential form, i.e., $\int_C(fdx+gdy;+hdz)$, over a path C will depend not only on the endpoints of the integration (say from point P to point Q), but also on the path followed to perform that integration, i.e., on the curve C. However, if the integrand is an exact differential, then the line integral is independent of the path and we can write:

$$\int_C (f \cdot dx + g \cdot dy + h \cdot dz) = \int_P^Q du = u(Q) - u(P).$$

Example 6 – Check that the integral $\int_C(fdx+gdy;+hdz)$, using the differential from Examples 4 and 5, above, is independent of the path by calculating the integral on the path x(s) = s, y(s) = s^2, z(s) = $\sqrt{s}$, from s = 0 to s = 4, and then evaluate u(Q)-u(P), where Q(x(0),y(0),z(0)) = Q(0,0,0), and P(x(4),y(4),z(4)) = P(4,16,2).

Define the functions

'x(s) = s' [ENTER][↰][DEF] 'y(s) = s^2' [ENTER][↰][DEF] 'z(s) = √s' [ENTER][↰][DEF]

Then, we calculate dx, dy, dz, and put together the differential as follows:

'x(s)' [ENTER] 's' [ENTER] [↱][∂] 'f(x(s),y(s),z(s))' [↱][EVAL] [×]
'y(s)' [ENTER] 's' [ENTER] [↱][∂] 'g(x(s),y(s),z(s))' [↱][EVAL] [×] [+]
'z(s)' [ENTER] 's' [ENTER] [↱][∂] 'h(x(s),y(s),z(s))' [↱][EVAL] [×] [+]

Then, use [↱][EVAL] to simplify the differential.

The integral then is calculated as:

0 [ENTER][▶] 4 [ENTER][▶] [↱]['][ALPHA][↰][S] [↱][∫].

The result is 120.

137

On the other hand, we have $u(x,y,z) = yz+zx+x^2$. Let's define,

'u(x,y,z) = x*y+y*z+z*x+x^2' [ENTER][↩][DEF]

Then evaluate $u(Q)-u(P)$ by using:

4 [SPC] 16 [SPC] 2 [ENTER] [u] 0 [SPC] 0 [SPC] 0 [ENTER] [u] [-]

The result is $u(Q)-u(P) = 120$, as expected.

A program to check and integrate an exact differential

We use the vector notation for the first-order differential

$$f \cdot dx + g \cdot dy + h \cdot dz = \mathbf{F} \bullet d\mathbf{r},$$

with

$$\mathbf{F}(x,y,z) = f(x,y,z) \, \mathbf{i} + g \, (x,y,z) \, \mathbf{j} + h(x,y,z) \, \mathbf{k},$$

and

$$d\mathbf{r} = dx \, \mathbf{i} + dy \, \mathbf{j} + dz \, \mathbf{k}.$$

To put together a program for automatic check and integration of exact differentials, firs create a sub-directory to be called *ExDiff* (*Ex*act *Diff*erentials).   Within that sub-directory create a program called *Chk&Int* (*Chk*eck & *Int*egrate) that takes as input a vector corresponding to $\mathbf{F}(x,y,z)$, i.e,

$$[\text{ 'f(x,y,z)' 'g(x,y,z)' 'h(x,y,z)'}],$$

and a vector with the variables corresponding to

$$\mathbf{r} = x \, \mathbf{i} + y \, \mathbf{j} + z \, \mathbf{k},$$

i.e.,   ['x' 'y' 'z'].

The output of the program consists of two items:

⬇ A message indicating whether the resulting first-order differential, $\mathbf{F} \bullet d\mathbf{r}$, is exact or not.

⬇ The integrated function $u(x,y,z)$, so that $du = \mathbf{F} \bullet d\mathbf{r}$, if the differential is exact.

The value of $\mathbf{F}$ is also displayed at program conclusion.

Here is the listing of the program and sub-programs

Program *Chk&Int* (*Check & Int*egrate):

`<<`	Start program *Chk&Int*
`→ f x`	Take values of **F** (as f) and **r** (as x)
`  <<`	Start first sub-program within *Chk&Int*
`  f x XCTDIFF`	Call XCTDIFF - check exact differential
`  3 == IF  THEN`	IF result of XCTDIFF = 3 THEN
`     "Exact" MSGBOX`	Message indicating Exact differential
`     f f x INTXD`	Place f, call INTXD – integrate diff.
`  ELSE`	ELSE
`     "Not Exact" MSGBOX`	Message: Not Exact differential
`     f`	Place f
`  END`	END IF
`  f`	Place value of **F** in stack
`  >>`	End first sub-program within *Chk&Int*
`>>`	End program within *Chk&Int*

Sub-program XCTDIFF (e**X**a**CT** **DIFF**erential):

`<<`	Start sub-program XCTDIFF
`→ f x`	Take values of **F** (as f) and **r** (as x)
`  <<`	Start first sub-program within XCTDIFF
`  0`	Place a zero in stack
`  1 2 f x CHKDER`	Check $\partial f/\partial y = \partial g/\partial x$, if true 1, if false 0
`  +`	Add result from check to value in lev. 1
`  1 3 f x CHKDER`	Check $\partial f/\partial z = \partial h/\partial x$, if true 1, if false 0
`  +`	Add result from check to value in lev. 1
`  2 3 f x CHKDER`	Check $\partial g/\partial z = \partial h/\partial y$, if true 1, false 0
`  +`	Add result from check to value in lev. 1
`  >>`	End first sub-program within XCTDIFF
`>>`	End program XCTDIFF

Note: If the first order differential **F•dr** is exact, the result of XCTDIFF must be 3. Any other result (0,1, or 2) means **F•dr** is not an exact differential.

Sub-program CHKDER (Chec**K** **DER**ivatives)

`<<`	Start sub-program CHKDER
`→ i j f x`	Take values of i, j, **F** (as f) and
`r (as x)`	**r** (as x)
`  <<`	Start first sub-program within CHKDER
`  f i GET x j GET ∂`	Calculate $\partial f_i/\partial x_j$.
`  f j GET x i GET ∂`	Calculate $\partial f_j/\partial x_i$.
`  − ABS`	Calculate $\|\partial f_i/\partial x_j - \partial f_j/\partial x_i\|$
`  0 == IF  THEN`	IF $\|\partial f_i/\partial x_j - \partial f_j/\partial x_i\| = 0$ THEN
`     1`	place a 1 in stack
`  ELSE`	ELSE
`     0`	place a 0 in stack
`  END`	END IF
`  >>`	End first sub-program within CHKDER
`>>`	End sub-program CHKDER

139

Sub-program INTXD (INTegrate eXact Differential):

```
<<                                            Start sub-program INTXD
→ f x                                         Take values of F (as f) and r (as x)
  <<                                           Start first sub-program within INTXD
  f 1 GET x 1 GET RISCH SIMP DUP              Calculate integral of f(x,y,z)dx
  x 2 GET ∂ SIMP NEG f 2 GET + SIMP          Use ∂u/∂y with previous result
  x 2 GET RISHC + SIMP DUP                    Calculate integral with respect to y
  x 3 GET ∂ SIMP NEG f 3 GET + SIMP          Use ∂u/∂z with previous result
  x 3 GET RISHC + SIMP                        Calculate integral with respect to z
  >>                                           End first sub-program within INTXD
>>                                            End sub-program INTXD
```

Sub-program SIMP (SIMPlify expression)

```
<< EVAL FACTOR TRIG >>
```
To simplify expression as much as possible.

Now, to test the program we developed the following program that lets you produce the vector F out of the function u(x,y,z). The input to the program is the function u(x,y,z) and the vector r = ['x' 'y' 'z']:

Program GETDiff (GET exact *Diff*erential):

```
<<                                            Start program GETDiff
DUP  SIZE  EVAL → f x n                       Duplicate r, get its size, pass values
  <<                                           Start first sub-program within GETDiff
  1 n FOR j                                    Start FOR loop with j = 1, 2, ..., n
      f  x  j GET ∂ SIMP                      Get f/xj, and simplify it
  NEXT                                         End FOR loop
  3 →ARRY                                      Create array F
  f  SWAP                                      Place f back in stack, swap levels 1 and
2                                              
  >>                                           End first sub-program within GETDiff
>>                                            End program GETDiff
```

Example 1 -- As an exercise, try the following:

                    'LN(z)*SIN(x)/EXP(y)' [ENTER] ['x' 'y' 'z'] [ENTER] [GETDi]
The result is:
            ['LN(z)*COS(x)/EXP(y)' '-(LN(z)*SIN(x)/EXP(y))' 'SIN(x)/(z*EXP(y))'].

This is an exact differential. To check that and integrate it use:

                            ['x' 'y' 'z'] [ENTER] [Chk&I]

The result, after some time (be patient, there are lots of operations involved), and after reporting "Exact", is:
                            'LN(z)*SIN(x)/EXP(y)',
as expected.

Example 2 - Repeat the exercise worked previously by hand, i.e.,

$$(y+z+2x)dx+(x+z)dy+(x+y)dz.$$

Use: ['y+z+2*z' 'x+z' 'x+y'][ENTER]['x' 'y' 'z'][ENTER][Chk&I].

The result is: 'x^2+(y+z)*x+z*y'.

Example 3 - This is a non-exact differential: ydx + ydy + ydz. Check it out:

['y' 'y' 'y'][ENTER]['x' 'y' 'z'][ENTER][Chk&I].

The result is the message "Not exact."

Transformation of double integrals into line integrals

Let R be a close region in the x-y plane bounded by the curve C. Then,

$$\iint_R \left(\frac{\partial g}{\partial x} - \frac{\partial f}{\partial y} \right) dxdy = \int_C (fdx + gdy).$$

This result is known as Green's theorem in the plane. One consequence of this theorem is that you can calculate the area of a region by calculating a line integral around its boundary, as

$$A = \frac{1}{2} \int_C (xdy - ydx).$$

The latter result is obtained by taking f(x,y) = x, and g(x,y) = -y.

Thus, to determine the area enclosed by the curve x(t) = R cos t, y(t) = R sin t, 0 < t < 2π, using Green's theorem, take dx = - R sin t dt, dy = R cos t dt. The integrand, xdy - ydx, now becomes =(R cos t)·(-R cos t dt) - (R sin t) · (-R sin t dt) = R^2 dt, and,

$$A = \frac{1}{2} \int_C (xdy - ydx) = \frac{1}{2} \int_0^{2\pi} R^2 dt = \pi R^2.$$

Vector Analysis

Vector analysis refers to the analysis of multi-variate vector fields. In this section we study the use of the operation "del" or "nabla", ∇, in defining the operations of gradient of a scalar function, divergence and curl of a vector function, and the laplacian operator ∇^2.

The del *operator*

The differential operator *del* (or *nabla*) is defined as

$$\nabla[] = \frac{\partial[]}{\partial x} \cdot \mathbf{i} + \frac{\partial[]}{\partial y} \cdot \mathbf{j} + \frac{\partial[]}{\partial z} \cdot \mathbf{k}.$$

Thus, the operator is similar to a vector, where the x-, y-, and z-components of the vector are the derivatives with respect to x, y, and z, respectively, of the function enclosed between the square brackets [ ] as shown above.

Directional derivative and gradient

The first partial derivatives of a scalar field, f(x,y,z), in space provide the rate of change of the function f with respect to each of the coordinate directions. We can think of $\partial f(x,y,z)/\partial x$ as the rate of change of f(x,y,z) along the x direction. We can define the rate of change of the function f with respect to an arc length, s, measured along an arbitrary straight line in the plane as

$$\partial f(x(s),y(s),z(s))/\partial s = [\partial f(x,y,z)/\partial x] \cdot [dx(s)/dt] + [\partial f(x,y,z)/\partial x] \cdot [dy(s)/dt] + [\partial f(x,y,z)/\partial x] \cdot [dy(s)/dt].$$

This derivative is referred to as the _directional derivative_ of f along a given trajectory. You can prove that a straight line in space can be represented as a vector by

$$\mathbf{r}(s) = x(s)\mathbf{i} + y(s)\mathbf{j} + z(s)\mathbf{k} = \mathbf{a} + s \cdot \mathbf{b},$$

where a and b are constant vectors, say,

$$\mathbf{a} = x_a \mathbf{i} + y_a \mathbf{j} + z_a \mathbf{k},$$

and

$$\mathbf{b} = x_b \mathbf{i} + y_b \mathbf{j} + z_b \mathbf{k}.$$

Therefore,

$$x(s) = x_a + x_b \cdot s, \ y(s) = y_a + y_b \cdot s, \text{ and } z(s) = z_a + z_b \cdot s,$$

and

$$d\mathbf{r}/ds = x_b \mathbf{i} + y_b \mathbf{j} + z_b \mathbf{k} = \mathbf{b} = \text{constant}.$$

We can think of the derivative $\partial f(x,y,z)/\partial s$, defined above, as the dot product of $d\mathbf{r}/ds$ and a vector that we will define as the _gradient_ of the function f(x,y,z) with respect to the coordinates (x,y,z), i.e.,

$$\partial f/\partial s = (\mathbf{grad}\ f) \bullet (d\mathbf{r}/ds),$$

where

$$\mathbf{grad}\ f = \partial f(x,y,z)/\partial x \cdot \mathbf{i} + \partial f(x,y,z)/\partial y \cdot \mathbf{j} + \partial f(x,y,z)/\partial z \cdot \mathbf{k}.$$

142

Notice that **b** = d**r**/ds is the unit tangent vector, **T**, defined earlier. Since our curve is a straight line, **b** here represents a unit vector along the line. Therefore, the directional derivative,

$$\partial f / \partial s = (\mathbf{grad}\ f) \bullet \mathbf{b},$$

is the projection of the vector grad f over the unit vector **b**.

Using the *del* operator, ∇, we can define the gradient as:

$$\mathbf{grad}\ f = \nabla f = \frac{\partial f}{\partial x} \cdot \mathbf{i} + \frac{\partial f}{\partial y} \cdot \mathbf{j} + \frac{\partial f}{\partial z} \cdot \mathbf{k}.$$

Determining the gradient in the HP 49 G calculator – the function HESS

The function HESS can be used to obtain the gradient of a function.. The function takes as input a function of *n* independent variables $f(x_1, x_2, ..., x_n)$, and a vector of the functions [$'x_1'$ $'x_2'...'x_n'$]. The function returns the *Hessian matrix* of the function, defined as the matrix

$$H = [h_{ij}] = [\partial f / \partial x_i \partial x_j],$$

the gradient of the function with respect to the n-variables,

$$\mathbf{grad}\ f = [\ \partial f / \partial x_1\ \ \partial f / \partial x_2\ ...\ \partial f / \partial x_n],$$

and the list of variables [$'x_1'$ $'x_2'...'x_n'$].

The function Hess is available through the keystroke sequence: [↰][CALC][DERIV][HESS].

Example 1 -- An example of a function of four variables is

'x^2*t^3*y*z^4' [ENTER] ['x' 'y' 'z' 't'] [ENTER] [↰][CALC][DERIV][HESS].

The result is

To obtain the gradient of a function of three variables, you could create a program GRADIENT by using:

<< HESS DROP SWAP DROP >>

You can add this variable to your sub-directory VCALC, since it is related to vector calculus. The program basically eliminates the first and third output lines from the function HESS, leaving only the gradient in the screen. The program GRADIENT uses the same input as HESS, i.e., the function f and the vector of variables.

Example 2 – Use the program GRADIENT ([GRADI]) to calculate the gradient of the function $f(x,y,z) = x*\sin y + y*\cos z + x*y$.

143

Use: 'x*SIN(y)+y*COS(z)+x*y' [ENTER] ['x''y''z'][ENTER][GRADI].

The result is: ['SIN(y)+y' 'x*COS(y)+COS(z)+x' 'y*-SIN(z)'], i.e.,

$$\textbf{grad } f = (\sin y + y)\ \textbf{i} + (x \cos y + \cos z + x)\ \textbf{j} - y \sin z\ \textbf{k}.$$

Direction of maximum increase of a function at a given point

Because the directional derivative represents the projection of the gradient vector over a unit vector, **b**, in a pre-selected direction, the magnitude of the directional derivative can be written as:

$$\partial f/\partial s = |\textbf{b}| \cdot |\textbf{grad } f| \cdot \cos \gamma,$$

where γ is the angle between the vectors **grad** f and **b**. Since **b** is a unit vector, $|\textbf{b}| = 1$, regardless of the direction selected. Therefore, the maximum value of $\partial f/\partial s$ is reached when $\gamma = \pi/2$, for which $\cos \gamma = 1$, and

$$(\partial f/\partial s)_{max} = |\textbf{grad } f| = |\nabla f|$$

In conclusion, we can state that if at a point P the gradient of a function f is not a zero vector, it has the direction of maximum increase of f at P. That direction can be defined by the unit vector,

$$\textbf{e}_g = \textbf{grad } f / |\textbf{grad } f|.$$

Example 3 - Determine the direction of maximum increase of f(x,y,z) from Example 2 at point (-1,0,1).

We have the result for grad f in the stack. Use:
[ENTER]   Get an additional copy.
[↰][ABS]   Get magnitude of the gradient.
[÷]   Calculate **grad** f/|**grad** f|.

To evaluate this unit vector at point (-1,0,1), enter the list

{ 'x' -1 'y' 0 'z' 1}[ENTER],
then, use:

'x=-1'[ENTER][↱][ALG][SUBST]   'y=0' [SUBST]   'z=1' [SUBST].

Finally, use the program [VSIMP], defined within the sub-directory VCALC to simplify vectors. The result is [0 -1 0].

Consider a function f(x,y,z) in three-dimensional space. An equation of the form

$$f(x,y,z) = c = \text{constant}$$

represents a surface S in space known as a level surface of the function f. Let the curve C represented by the parametric equations x = x(t), y = y(t), and z = z(t), i.e.,

$$r(t) = x(t)\ \mathbf{i} + y(t)\ \mathbf{j} + z(t)\ \mathbf{k}.$$

If the curve C is to be contained in the level surface S, then x(t), y(t), z(t), must satisfy the equation of the curve, namely, f[x(t),y(t),z(t)] = c. Taking the derivative df/dt and using the chain rule we have:

$$df/dt = (\partial f/\partial x)\cdot(dx/dt) + (\partial f/\partial x)\cdot(dy/dt) + (\partial f/\partial x)\cdot(dz/dt) = (\mathbf{grad}\ f)\bullet(dr/dt) = 0.$$

where the vector

$$\mathbf{v} = dr/dt$$

is tangent to the curve C. The vector **v** is contained in a plane that is tangent to the level surface of the function at a given point of interest. Also, the result

$$\mathbf{grad}\ f\ .\ \mathbf{v} = 0$$

indicates that the vectors **grad** f and **v** are perpendicular. Therefore, the vector **grad** f(x,y,z) is normal to the tangent plane at the point P(x,y,z), and therefore, normal to the curve at that point. This is illustrated in the figure below.

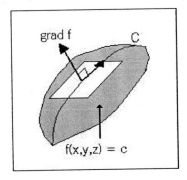

In 2D space, the function f will be defined as f(x,y). The object defined by f(x,y) = c is a curve in the plane. The grad f now represents a vector normal to the tangent line to the curve f(x,y) = c at a given point that belongs in the curve.

Example 4 -- Determine the equation of a plane tangent to the surface f(x,y,z) = $x^2+y^2+z^2$-50 = 0, at the point A(0,-5,5).

The gradient of the function f(x,y,z) produces a vector normal to the surface f(x,y,z) = 0, i.e.,

'x^2+y^2+z^2-50 ' [ENTER]   ['x' 'y' 'z'] [ENTER] [GRADI]

145

The result is   ['2*x' '2*y' '2*z']

To evaluate at point (0,-5,5), use:

'x=0'[ENTER][→][ALG][SUBST] 'y=-5' [SUBST] 'z=5' [SUBST] [VAR][VSIMP]

The result is [0 -10 0], i.e.,   **n = -10j +10k**

To obtain the equation of the tangential plane, we follow the approach presented in Chapter 9:

['x' 'y' 'z'] [ENTER]   Enter generic point P(x,y,z) as a vector
[0 -5 5] [ENTER]   Enter point P(5, 0, -1) as a vector
[-]   Calculate r$_{P/A}$
[←][MTH][VECTR][DOT]   Calculate n•r$_{P/A}$

which results in '10*(z-5)+-10*(y--5)'. Use [→][ALG][EXPA] to obtain '-(10-*y-(10*z-100))'.

The equation of the plane, of course, can be expanded, by hand, to read: -y+z - 10 = 0.

To verify that the point A(0,-5,5) satisfies the equation, first, press [ENTER] to keep a second copy of the expression available for future use. Then, enter the list

{'x' 0 'y' -5 'z' 5}[ENTER],

and use

[→][|][ENTER]

to replace the values in the expression. The result is ' 3*5+(2*0-(-1+16))'. Press [→][EVAL] to get 0.

Gradient of a potential

In many physical problems it is possible to define a function, $\phi(x,y,z)$, known as the *potential function* or, simply, the potential, such that the gradient of ϕ represents a vector field. As an example, take the case of a two-dimensional frictionless flow presented earlier. The potential of the flow is a function, $\phi(x,y)$, such that the velocity field, **q** = u(x,y)**i** + v(x,y)**j**, is obtained from, **q** = **grad** ϕ.

Example 5 -- Determine the velocity vector corresponding to the velocity potential f(x,y,z) = $x^2y^2z^2$.

Use: '(x*y*z)^2' [ENTER] ['x' 'y' 'z'][ENTER] [VAR][GRADI][VSIMP].

The result is: ['2*z^2*y^2*x' '2*z^2*y*x^2' '2*z*y^2*x^2'], i.e.,

q = $(2xy^2z^2)$**i**+$(2x^2yz^2)$**j**+$(2x^2y^2z)$**k**.

146

The following formulas apply to the calculation of gradients:

(a) $\mathbf{grad}(c \cdot f) = c \cdot \mathbf{grad}(f)$, c = constant
(b) $\mathbf{grad}(f \cdot g) = f \cdot \mathbf{grad}(g) + g \cdot \mathbf{grad}(f)$.
(c) $\mathbf{grad}(f/g) = (1/g^2)[g \cdot \mathbf{grad}(f) + f \cdot \mathbf{grad}(g)]$
(d) $\mathbf{grad}(f^n) = n \cdot f^{(n-1)} \cdot \mathbf{grad}(f)$

Example 6 -- Check the formula for the gradient of the product of two functions:

'f(x,y,z)*g(x,y,z)' [ENTER] ['x' 'y' 'z'] [ENTER] [VAR][GRADI].

The result is:

['d1f(x,y,z)*g(x,y,z)+f(x,y,z)*d1g(x,y,z)"d2f(x,y,z)*g(x,y,z)+f(x,y,z)*d2g(x,yz)'
'd3f(x,y,z)*g(x,y,z)+f(x,y,z)*d3g(x,yz)']

Compare with:

'f(x,y,z)' [ENTER] 'g(x,y,z)' ['x' 'y' 'z'] [ENTER] [GRADI] [×]
'g(x,y,z)' [ENTER] 'f(x,y,z)' ['x' 'y' 'z'] [ENTER] [GRADI] [×] [+]

The result is the same as above.

Divergence of a vector field

Consider the vector function $\mathbf{v}(x,y,z;) = v_1(x,y,z) \cdot \mathbf{i} + v_2(x,y,z) \cdot \mathbf{j} + v_3(x,y,z) \cdot \mathbf{k}$. The function

is called the divergence of the vector field v or, simply, the divergence of **v**.

$$div\,\mathbf{v} = \nabla \bullet \mathbf{v} = \frac{\partial v_1}{\partial x} + \frac{\partial v_2}{\partial y} + \frac{\partial v_3}{\partial z}$$

The HP 49 G provides the function DIV to calculate the divergence of a vector function. The function DIV takes as input a vector function ['v_1(x,y,z)' 'v_3(x,y,z)' 'v_3(x,y,z)'] and a vector of independent variables ['x' 'y' 'z'], and returns the divergence of the vector function, i.e., $\partial v_1/\partial x + \partial v_2/\partial y + \partial v_3/\partial z$.

Example 1 - Determine the divergence of the vector function $\mathbf{v} = e^x \sin x\, \mathbf{i} + y^2 \sin y\, \mathbf{j} + z\, e^z\, \mathbf{k}$. Use:

['EXP(x)*SIN(x)' 'y^2*SIN(y)' 'z*EXP(z)'] [ENTER] ['x' 'y' 'z'][ENTER][←][CALC][DERIV][DIV]

The result is: 'EXP(x)*SIN(x)+EXP(x)*COS(x)+(2*y*SIN(y)+y^2*COS(y)+(EXP(z)+z*EXP(z)))'

147

To simplify this result use: [→][EVAL]. The final result is:

'EXP(x)*SIN(x)+(2*y*SIN(y)+(EXP(x)*COS(x)+(y^2*COS(y)+(z+1)*EXP(z))))', i.e.,

$$\text{div } v = e^x \sin x + (2 y \sin y + (e^x \cos x + (y^2 \cos y + (z + 1) e^z))).$$

Formulas for the divergence

The following formulas apply to the calculation of divergence of vector fields:

(a) div($c\mathbf{v}$) = c div($\mathbf{v}$)
(b) div($f\mathbf{v}$) = f div($\mathbf{v}$) + $\mathbf{v}$•grad(f)
(c) div(f grad(g)) = f div(grad(g)) + grad(f) • grad(g)
(d) div(f grad g - g grad f) = f ∇^2g - g ∇^2f

A physical interpretation of the divergence: mass flux of fluids

Consider the flow of a fluid through the differential volume shown in the figure below. In the analysis of fluid flow, such volume is referred to as a differential control volume, and its outer surface is known as the control surface.

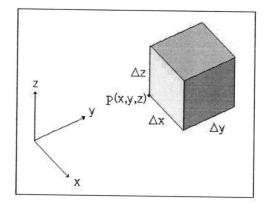

Let the velocity field of the fluid flow be given by the function

$$q(x,y,z,t;) = u(x,y,z,t) \mathbf{i} + v(x, y, z, t) \mathbf{j} + w(x, y, z, t) \mathbf{k}.$$

This expression will be used to represent the function at point P(x,y,z) corresponding to the corner of the differential element that is closest to the origin, as shown in the figure below.

148

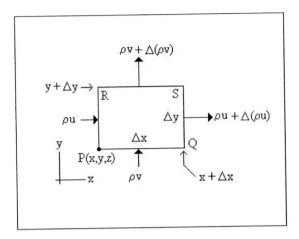

The mass flux of the fluid through the face of the control volume parallel to the xz plane, for example, is given by $\rho v\, \Delta x\, \Delta$, where $\rho(x,y,z,t)$ is the fluid density, defined as mass per unit volume. (The mass flux has units of mass per unit volume). The function $\rho v = f(x,y,z,t)$ represents the product of density, $\rho(x,y,z,t)$, and the y-component of the velocity, $v(x,y,z,t)$, on the face of interest. We can use a Taylor series expansion along each coordinate direction to write out an expression for the products ρu and ρv at the different faces of the differential volume. The figure above shows how the product ρu changes by an amount $\Delta(\rho u)$ as we move from face PR, located at x, to face SQ, located at x + Δx. The figure also shows how the product ρv changes by an amount $\Delta(\rho v)$ as we move from face PQ, located at y, to face RS, located at y+Δy. From the Taylor series expansions of the corresponding functions along each of the coordinate axes, we can show that the increases in the functions ρu and ρv are approximated by

$$\Delta\,(\rho u) = (\partial(\rho u)/\,\partial x)\cdot\Delta x, \quad \text{and} \quad \Delta(\rho v) = (\partial\,(\rho v)/\partial y)\cdot\Delta y,$$

respectively.

The net mass flux out of the control volume along the x direction is given by

$$F_x= [\rho u+(\partial(\rho u)/\,\partial x)\cdot\Delta x)\Delta y\cdot\Delta z]-(\rho u)\,\Delta y\cdot\Delta x \;=\; (\partial(\rho u)/\,\partial x)\cdot\Delta x\cdot\Delta y\cdot\Delta z \;=\; (\partial(\rho u)/\,\partial x)\cdot\Delta V,$$

where, $\Delta V= \Delta x\cdot\Delta y\cdot\Delta z$, is the (constant) volume of the differential element. We can prove that the net mass fluxes out of the control volume in the y- and z-directions are given by

$$F_y = (\partial(\rho v)/\partial y)\cdot\Delta V, \quad \text{and} \quad F_z = (\partial(\rho w)/\,\partial z)\cdot\Delta V,$$

respectively. The net mass flux out of the control volume is then given by:

$$F_{\text{total}} = F_x+F_y+F_z = [\partial(\rho u)/\,\partial x + \partial(\rho v)/\partial y + \partial(\rho w)/\partial z]\cdot\Delta V = \text{div}(\rho\cdot\mathbf{q})\cdot\Delta V.$$

Therefore, the divergence of the vector function, $\rho\cdot\mathbf{q} = f(x,y,z)$, is interpreted for fluid flow as the total mass flux per unit volume out of a differential control volume, i.e.,

$$\text{div}(\rho\mathbf{q}) = F_{\text{total}}\,/\,\Delta V.$$

149

Assuming that there are not sources or sinks of fluid mass within the differential control volume, the net mass flux out of the control volume must be equal to the rate of decrease with respect to time of the mass within the control volume. This is a statement of the _law of conservation of mass_ for the elementary control volume, and it is written as:

$$F_{total} = -(\partial\rho/\partial t)\cdot\Delta V, \quad \text{or} \quad div(\rho\mathbf{q})\cdot\Delta V = -(\partial\rho/\partial t)\cdot\Delta V.$$

Simplifying this equation, by dividing by ΔV, and rearranging terms results in the differential form of the continuity equation for a compressible fluid flow, namely,

$$\partial\rho/\partial t + div(\rho\mathbf{q}) = 0.$$

Most liquids at normal pressures are incompressible, meaning that their density, $\rho(x,y,z,t)$; is constant. For a constant value of ρ, the continuity equation reduces to

$$div(\mathbf{q}) = \nabla\bullet\mathbf{q} = \partial u/\partial x + \partial v/\partial y + \partial w/\partial z = 0.$$

The Laplacian operator

The gradient of a scalar function, $f(x,y,z)$, is a vector function,

$$\mathbf{grad}\ f = (\partial f/\partial x)\mathbf{i} + (\partial f/\partial x)\ \mathbf{j} + (\partial f/\partial x)\ \mathbf{k}.$$

The divergence of this vector function produces a differential operator known as the _Laplacian_ of the function f, namely:

$$\nabla^2 f = div(\mathbf{grad}\,f) = \nabla\bullet(\nabla f) = \frac{\partial^2 f}{\partial x^2} + \frac{\partial^2 f}{\partial y^2} + \frac{\partial^2 f}{\partial z^2}.$$

The function LAPL

The function LAPL takes as input a scalar function '$f(x,y,z)$' and a vector of independent variables ['x' 'y' 'z'], and calculates the Laplacian of the function.

Example 1 - Determine the Laplacian of the function $f(x,y,z) = x\ e^y \sin z$.

Use:

'x*exp(y)*sin(z)' [ENTER] ['x' 'y' 'z'][ENTER] [↤][CALC][DERIV][LAPL]

The result is 'x*EXP(y)*SIN(z)+x*EXP(y)*-SIN(z)'. Press [↦][EVAL] to simplify the expression to 0, i.e., $\nabla^2 f=0$.

150

Curl (rotational) of a vector function

Consider the vector function $v(x,y,z;) = v_1(x,y,z) \cdot i + v_2(x,y,z) \cdot j + v_3(x,y,z) \cdot k$. The function

$$curl \; \mathbf{v} = \nabla \times \mathbf{v} = \begin{vmatrix} \mathbf{i} & \mathbf{j} & \mathbf{k} \\ \dfrac{\partial}{\partial x} & \dfrac{\partial}{\partial y} & \dfrac{\partial}{\partial z} \\ v_1(x,y,z) & v_2(x,y,z) & v_3(x,y,z) \end{vmatrix} = $$

$$= \left(\frac{\partial v_3}{\partial y} - \frac{\partial v_2}{\partial z} \right) \cdot \mathbf{i} + \left(\frac{\partial v_1}{\partial z} - \frac{\partial v_3}{\partial x} \right) \cdot \mathbf{j} + \left(\frac{\partial v_2}{\partial x} - \frac{\partial v_1}{\partial y} \right) \cdot \mathbf{k}.$$

is called the _curl_ of the vector field $\mathbf{v}$ or, simply, the curl of $\mathbf{v}$.

The function CURL

The function CURL takes as input a vector function ['v1(x,y,z)' 'v2(x,y,z)' 'v3(x,y,z)'] and a vector of independent variables ['x' 'y' 'z'], and returns the curl of the vector function. This function is available through [←][CALC][DERIV][CURL].

Example 1 - Determine the curl of the vector function $\mathbf{v} = (x^2 y)\mathbf{i} + (y^2 z)\mathbf{j} + (z^2 x)\mathbf{k}$.

Use: ['x^2*y' 'y^2*z' 'z^2*x'][ENTER] ['x' 'y' 'z'][ENTER] [←][CALC][DERIV][CURL].

The result is ['-y^2' '-z^2' '-x^2'], i.e., $\nabla \times v = - (y^2 \mathbf{i} + z^2 \mathbf{j} + x^2 \mathbf{k})$.

Physical interpretation of the curl: rotation of a rigid body

Consider a body rotating with constant angular velocity, $\mathbf{\Omega} = \omega_1 \mathbf{i} + \omega_2 \mathbf{j} + \omega_3 \mathbf{k}$. Let $\mathbf{r} = x\mathbf{i} + y\mathbf{j} + z\mathbf{k}$ represent the position of a point $P(x,y,z)$ in the solid body measured with respect to the origin $(0,0,0)$. The velocity of that point can be determined by the cross product, $\mathbf{v} = \mathbf{\Omega} \times \mathbf{r}$. Using the HP 49 G calculator to enter this operation we write:

['ω1' 'ω 2' 'ω3']   [ENTER] ['x' 'y' 'z'] [ENTER] [←][MTH][VECTR][CROSS].

151

The result is

$$['x^*\omega2 - y^*\omega3' \ '\omega3^*x - z^*\omega1' \ 'y^*\omega1 - \omega2^*x'].$$

Let's now calculate the curl of the velocity field v(x,y,z) calculated above. In the calculator use:

$$['x' \ 'y' \ 'z'][ENTER] \ [\neg][CALC][DERIV][CURL].$$

The result is $\quad [\ '\omega1 + \omega1' \ '\omega2 + \omega2' \ '\omega3 + \omega3'] = ['2^*\omega1' \ '2^*\omega2' \ '2^*\omega3'],$ i.e.,

$$\nabla\times\mathbf{r} = 2\mathbf{\Omega}.$$

This result indicates that curl $\mathbf{v} = 2\mathbf{\Omega}$, i.e., the curl of the velocity field v(x,y,z) representing the velocity of point (x,y,z) for a rigid body subject to pure rotation with an angular $\mathbf{\Omega} = \omega_1\mathbf{i} + \omega_2\mathbf{j} + \omega_3\mathbf{k}$., is equal to twice the angular velocity. This is a physical interpretation of the curl for a particular type of motion.

Vorticity and circulation in fluid motion

Given a fluid motion characterized by the velocity vector $\mathbf{q} = u\mathbf{i} + v\cdot\mathbf{j} + w\cdot\mathbf{k}$, we define the _vorticity vector_ as

$$\mathbf{\zeta} = \nabla\times\mathbf{q}.$$

A flow for which $\mathbf{\zeta} = 0$ is said to be _irrotational_.

Associated with the vorticity of a flow is the concept of _circulation_ of the flow, G, defined as

$$\Gamma = \oint_C \mathbf{q} \bullet d\mathbf{r}$$

Example 1 - Given the three-dimensional velocity vector $\mathbf{q} = (x^2\mathbf{i} + x\cdot y\cdot\mathbf{j} + z\cdot\mathbf{k})$, determine the vorticity vector for the flow.

Use:

$$['x^2' \ 'x^*y' \ 'z'][ENTER]['x' \ 'y' \ 'z'][ENTER] \ [\neg][CALC][DERIV][CURL].$$

The result is $[\ 0 \ 0 \ 'y']$, i.e., $\mathbf{\zeta} = y\mathbf{k}$. Since, $\mathbf{\zeta} \neq 0$ the flow is not irrotational.

Vector differential operations in generalized orthogonal coordinates

So far, we have defined and used the operations of gradient, divergence, and curl in Cartesian coordinates. In this section we present a general approach to define these operations in other systems of orthogonal coordinates.

152

Cartesian, cylindrical, and spherical coordinate systems are called _orthogonal coordinates_ because it is possible to define a triad of unit orthogonal vectors associated with each of the three coordinates (q_1, q_2, q_3) that form a vector basis. A _vector basis_ in three dimensions is a set of three (unit) vectors e_1, e_2, e_3, so that any vector A in space can be written as a linear combination of the basis vectors, i.e.,

$$A = A_1 \cdot e_1 + A_2 \cdot e_2 + A_3 \cdot e_3,$$

where A_1, A_2, A_3, are the components of the vector A in the coordinate system under consideration.

The following table shows the coordinates, unit vectors, and vector components for the Cartesian, cylindrical, and spherical coordinates:

Coordinate system	Variables	Unit vectors	Components
	$[q_1, q_2, q_3]$	$[e_1, e_2, e_3]$	$[A_1, A_2, A_3]$
Cartesian	$[x, y, z]$	$[i, j, k]$	$[A_x, A_y, A_z]$
Cylindrical	$[r, \theta, z]$	$[e_r, e_\theta, e_z]$	$[A_r, A_\theta, A_3]$
Spherical	$[\rho, \phi, \theta]$	$[e_\rho, e_\phi, e_\theta]$	$[A_\rho, A_\phi, A_\theta]$

The figure below shows the unit vectors for cylindrical and spherical coordinates at a generic point P. While the unit vectors in Cartesian coordinates, $[i, j, k]$, are constant, the unit vectors in cylindrical coordinates (except for $e_z = k$) and spherical coordinates change from point to point. Because of the fact that its unit vector basis is constant, the Cartesian coordinate system is the easiest to use. Most other orthogonal coordinate systems are eventually referred to the Cartesian system.

Given a system of orthogonal coordinates (q_1, q_2, q_3) with unit vectors (e_1, e_2, e_3), the absolute value of the partial derivative of a position vector,

$$r = q_1 \cdot e_1 + q_2 \cdot e_2 + q_3 \cdot e_3,$$

with respect to the coordinate q, is know as the _i-th scale factor of the coordinate system_, i.e.,

$$h_i = |\partial r / \partial q_i|$$

The derivative of the position vector with respect to the coordinate q_i can be written as,

$$\partial r / \partial q_i = h_i \cdot e_i.$$

Therefore, the unit vector e_i is defined in terms of its Cartesian components as

$$e_i = \partial r / \partial q_i \, / \, |\partial r / \partial q_i| = (e_i)_x \cdot i + (e_i)_x \cdot j + (e_i)_x \cdot k.$$

153

The differential of length in generalized orthogonal coordinates is written, in terms of the scale factors, as

$$ds^2 = h_1{}^2 \cdot dq_1{}^2 + h_2{}^2 \cdot dq_2{}^2 + h_3{}^2 \cdot dq_4{}^2.$$

Also, the differential of volume is

$$dV = (h_1 \cdot dq_1) \cdot (h_2 \cdot dq_2) \cdot (h_3 \cdot dq_3) = h_1 \cdot h_2 \cdot h_3 \cdot dq_1 \cdot dq_2 \cdot dq_3.$$

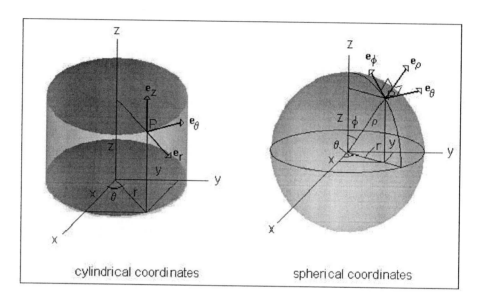

cylindrical coordinates   spherical coordinates

The scale factors for cylindrical and spherical coordinates are:

- Cylindrical (r, θ, z): $h_1 = 1,$ $h_2 = r,$ $h_3 = 1$

- Spherical (ρ, θ, ϕ): $h_1 = 1,$ $h_2 = \rho,$ $h_3 = \rho \sin \phi$

We can check that the differentials of volumes for these two coordinate systems are

$$(dV)_{cyl} = r \cdot dr \cdot d\theta \cdot dz, \quad \text{and} \quad (dV)_{sph} = \rho^2 \cdot \sin \phi \cdot d\rho \cdot d\theta \cdot d\phi$$

154

Using the scale factors (h_1, h_2, h_3) and unit vector basis (e_1, e_2, e_3), the following vector differential operations are defined:

➤ Gradient

$$\mathbf{grad}\, f = \nabla f = \sum_{i=1}^{3} \frac{1}{h_i} \cdot \frac{\partial f}{\partial q_i} \cdot \mathbf{e}_i.$$

➤ Divergence

$$div\, \mathbf{A} = \nabla \bullet \mathbf{A} = \frac{1}{h_1 \cdot h_2 \cdot h_3} \cdot \sum_{i=1}^{3} \frac{\partial}{\partial q_i} \left(\frac{h_1 \cdot h_2 \cdot h_3 \cdot A_i}{h_i} \right)$$

➤ Curl

$$curl\, \mathbf{A} = \nabla \times \mathbf{A} = \frac{1}{h_1 \cdot h_2 \cdot h_3} \cdot \begin{vmatrix} h_1 \cdot \mathbf{e}_1 & h_2 \cdot \mathbf{e}_2 & h_3 \cdot \mathbf{e}_3 \\ \dfrac{\partial}{\partial q_1} & \dfrac{\partial}{\partial q_2} & \dfrac{\partial}{\partial q_3} \\ h_1 \cdot A_1 & h_2 \cdot A_2 & h_2 \cdot A_2 \end{vmatrix}.$$

➤ Laplacian

$$\nabla^2 f = \frac{1}{h_1 \cdot h_2 \cdot h_3} \cdot \sum_{i=1}^{3} \frac{\partial}{\partial q_i} \left(\frac{h_1 \cdot h_2 \cdot h_3}{h_i^2} \cdot \frac{\partial f}{\partial q_i} \right)$$

Create a sub-directory to be called *OrtCoord* (*Ort*hogonal *Coord*inates). Within that sub-directory enter the following programs:

Program INFO (INFOrmation):

<<	Start program INFO
"Enter f,[h],[q] for GRADC & LAPLC" MSGBOX	Show info on gradient and Laplacian
"Enter [A],[h],[q] for DIVC & CURLC" MSGBOX	Show info on divergence and curl
>>	End program INFO

155

Program GRADC (GRADient for generalized orthogonal Coordinates):

`<<`	Start program GRADC
`→ f h q`	Enter $f(q_1,q_2,q_3)$, $[h_1, h_2, h_3]$, $[q_1, q_2,$
`q_3]`	
`<<`	Start first sub-program within GRADC
`h AXL INV AXL`	Calculate a vector containing $[1/h_i]$
`f q HESS DROP SWAP DROP`	Calculate gradient of f with variables q
`HADAMARD`	Multiply vectors $[1/h_i][\text{grad } f]$
`VSIMP`	Simplify vector
`>>`	End first sub-program within GRADC
`>>`	End program GRADC

Program DIVC (DIVergence for generalized orthogonal Coordinates):

`<<`	Start program DIVC
`→ A h q`	Enter $A(q_1,q_2,q_3)$, $[h_1, h_2, h_3]$, $[q_1, q_2,$
`q_3]`	
`<<`	Start first sub-program within DIVC
`h AXL ΠLIST → K`	Calculate $K = h_1 \cdot h_2 \cdot h_3$
`<<`	Start second sub-program within DIVC
`0`	Place a zero in stack
`1 3 FOR j`	Start FOR loop with j = 1,2,3
`A j GET h j GET / K *`	Calculate $K \cdot A_j / h_j$
`q j GET ∂`	Calculate $\partial(K \cdot A_j / h_j) / \partial q_j$
`+`	Add term to the divergence
`NEXT`	End FOR loop (j)
`K / EVAL  FACTOR  TRIG`	Simplify expression
`>>`	End second sub-program within DIVC
`>>`	End first sub-program within DIVC
`>>`	End program DIVC

Program CURLC (CURL for generalized orthogonal Coordinates):

`<<`	Start program CURLC
`→ A h q`	Enter $A(q_1,q_2,q_3)$, $[h_1, h_2, h_3]$, $[q_1, q_2, q_3]$
`<<`	Start first sub-program within CURLC
`h  A HADAMARD  CURL h q HADAMARD`	Calculate determinant in eq. for curl A
`h AXL ΠLIST / VSIMP`	Find $K=h_1 \cdot h_2 \cdot h_3$, divide by K, simplify
`>>`	Ender first sub-program within CURLC
`>>`	End program CURLC

Program LAPLC (LAPLacian for generalized orthogonal Coordinates):

`<<`	Start program LAPLC
`→ f h q`	Enter $f(q_1,q_2,q_3)$, $[h_1, h_2, h_3]$, $[q_1, q_2, q_3]$
`<<`	Start first sub-program within DIVC
`h AXL ΠLIST → K`	Calculate $K = h_1 \cdot h_2 \cdot h_3$
`<<`	Start second sub-program within LAPLC
`0`	Place a zero in stack
`1 3 FOR j`	Start FOR loop with j = 1,2,3
`f g  j GET ∂ K * h j GET 2 ^ / q  j GET ∂ +`	Calculate Laplacian
`NEXT`	End FOR loop (j)
`K / EVAL FACTOR TRIG`	Divide by $K = h_1 \cdot h_2 \cdot h_3$, simplify expression
`>>`	End second sub-program within LAPLC
`>>`	End first sub-program within LAPLC
`>>`	End program LAPLC

156

Also, copy the program VSIMP from sub-directory VCALC into this sub-directory.

Before operating the programs, order the variables by using:

{ INFO GRADC DIVC CURLC LAPLC VSIMP } [ENTER] [↩][PRG][MEM][DIR][NXT][ORDER],

so that the soft-menu key labels in your sub-directory now look like this:

[INFO][GRADC][DIVC][CURLC][LAPLC][VSIMP].

The programs GRADC (gradient) and LAPLC (Laplacian) use as input a function 'f(q1,q2,q3)', a vector of scale factors ['h1' 'h2' 'h3'], and a vector of independent variables ['q1' 'q2' 'q3']. For example, using cylindrical coordinates, try the following exercise:

Example 1 -- Find expressions for the gradient, divergence, curl, and Laplacian in cylindrical coordinates.

Since we are going to be using the vectors h = [1 'r' 1], and q = ['r' 'θ' 'z'], several times, create the following list in the stack:

{'f(r,θ,z)' [1 'r' 1] ['r' 'θ' 'z'] }

and press [ENTER] three times to make three copies of this list.

Next, press [↩][EVAL] to separate the terms of the last copy of the list, followed by:

2 [ENTER] [↩][PRG][TYPE][→LIST] [▶] [⇦]

Also, put together a vector **A** as follows:

'A1(r,θ,z)' [ENTER] 'A2(r,θ,z)' [ENTER] 'A3(r,θ,z)' [ENTER] 3 [ENTER] [↩][PRG][TYPE][→ARRY]

Next, swap this vector with the list in stack level 2, add the vector to the list, and make extra copy of the new list, by using:

[▶][+][ENTER].

First, we calculate the <u>divergence</u> of **A** by using:

[↩][EVAL][VAR][DIVC]

The result is:

'(r*d1A1(r,θ,z)+(d2A2(r,θ,z)+(r*d3A3(r,θ,z)+A1(r,θ,z))))/r', i.e.,

$$\nabla \bullet \mathbf{A} = \frac{r \cdot \dfrac{\partial A_r}{\partial r} + (\dfrac{\partial A_\theta}{\partial \theta} + (r \cdot \dfrac{\partial A_z}{\partial z} + A_r))}{r} = \frac{1}{r}\frac{\partial}{\partial r}(r \cdot A_r) + \frac{1}{r}\frac{\partial A_\theta}{\partial \theta} + \frac{\partial A_z}{\partial z}.$$

♣ Next, we calculate the <u>curl</u> of **A** by using:

[⇦][↦][EVAL][VAR][CURLC]

The result is:

```
['-((r*d3A2(r,θ,z)-d2A3(r,θ,z))/r'     'd3A1(r, θ,z)-d1A3(r, θ,z)'
                          '-((d2A1(r, θ,z)-(r*d1A2(r,q,z)+A2(r, θ,z)))/r'],
```
i.e.,

$$\nabla \times \mathbf{A} = (\frac{1}{r}\frac{\partial A_z}{\partial \theta} - \frac{\partial A_\theta}{\partial z})\mathbf{e}_r + (\frac{\partial A_z}{\partial r} - \frac{\partial A_r}{\partial z})\mathbf{e}_\theta + [\frac{\partial}{\partial r}(r \cdot A_\theta) - \frac{\partial A_r}{\partial \theta}]\mathbf{e}_z$$

♣ Next, we calculate the <u>gradient</u> of f by using:

[⇦][↦][EVAL][VAR][GRADC]

There will be an error message reported. This is because of a conflict in using EVAL with symbolic derivatives. Press [ON] [⇦][⇦][⇦][⇦][⇦][⇦]. The remaining vector is the result we want:

```
['d1f(r,θ,z)'  'd2f(r,θ,z)/r'  'd3f(r,θ,z)'], i.e.,
```

$$\nabla f = \frac{\partial f}{\partial r} \cdot \mathbf{e}_r + \frac{1}{r} \cdot \frac{\partial f}{\partial \theta} \cdot \mathbf{e}_\theta + \frac{\partial f}{\partial z} \cdot \mathbf{e}_z .$$

♣ Finally, the Laplacian is calculated by using:

[⇦][↦][EVAL][VAR][GRADC]

The result is:

```
'(r^2*d1d1'f'(r,q,z)+d2d2'f'(r,q,z)+r^2*d3d3'f'(r,q,z)+r*d1'f'(r,q,z))/r^2',
```

i.e.,

$$\nabla^2 f = \frac{r^2\frac{\partial^2 f}{\partial r^2}+\frac{\partial^2 f}{\partial \theta^2}+r^2\frac{\partial^2 f}{\partial z^2}+r\frac{\partial f}{\partial r}}{r^2} = \frac{1}{r}\frac{\partial}{\partial r}\left(\frac{\partial f}{\partial r}\right)+\frac{1}{r^2}\frac{\partial^2 f}{\partial \theta^2}+\frac{\partial^2 f}{\partial z^2} .$$

158

Example 2 – Determine the gradient and the Laplacian of the function $f(\rho,\theta,\phi) = \rho \sin \theta \cos \phi$ in spherical coordinates.

Use:

'ρ*SIN(θ)*COS(φ)' [ENTER] [1 'ρ' 'ρ*SIN(φ)'][ENTER]   ['ρ' 'θ' 'φ'][ENTER]

To keep an additional copy of the input lines, let's create a list, by using: 3 [↰][PRG][TYPE][→LIST]. Then, press [ENTER][ENTER] (Keep two copies of the list in the stack, just in case you loose one accidentally).

⬇ To calculate the gradient, use: [↱][EVAL] [VAR][GRADC]. The result is:

['COS(φ)*SIN(θ)' 'COS(φ)*SIN(θ)' '-SIN(θ)']

i.e., $\nabla f = \cos \phi \sin \theta\, \mathbf{e}_\rho + \cos \phi \sin \theta\, \mathbf{e}_\theta - \sin \theta\, \mathbf{e}_\phi = \sin \theta\, [\cos \phi\, (\mathbf{e}_\rho + \mathbf{e}_\theta) - \mathbf{e}_\phi]$.

⬇ To calculate the Laplacian, use: [↰][↱][EVAL] [VAR][GRADC]. The result is:

'COS(φ)*SIN(θ)/ρ'

i.e., $\nabla^2 f = \cos \phi \sin \theta / \rho$.

159

Surfaces

Surfaces in space can be represented implicitly as

$$f(x,y,z) = 0,$$

or explicitly as

$$z = g(x,y).$$

The latter can be converted into an implicit representation by writing,

$$f(x,y,z) = z - g(x,y) = 0.$$

Surfaces described by $z = g(x,y)$ can be plotted in the HP 49 G calculator by using *Fast3D* or *Wireframe* graphs. Examples of these type of graphics are presented also in Chapter 11.

A parametric representation of a surface in terms of the two parameters u and v is,

$$r(u,v) = x(u,v) \, \mathbf{i} + y(u,v) \, \mathbf{j} + z(u,v) \, \mathbf{k}.$$

Parametric representations of surfaces can be plotted in the HP 49 G calculator by using *Pr-Surface* graphs. This type of graphs was also introduced in Chapter 11.

Example 1 – Plot the surface $z = \sin(x)\cos(y)$ using a *Fast3D* graph.

* Press [←][2D/3D], simultaneously to access to the PLOT SETUP window.

➤ Change TYPE to Fast3D.

➤ Press [▼] and type 'SIN(X)*COS(Y)' [OK].

➤ Make sure that 'X' is selected as the Indep: and 'Y' as the Depnd: variables.

➤ Press [NXT][OK] to return to normal calculator display.

* Press [←][WIN], simultaneously, to access the PLOT WINDOW screen.

➤ Change the plot window ranges to read:

```
X-Left:-3.15      X-Right:3.15
Y-Near:-3.15      Y-Far: 3.15
Z-Low: -1         Z-High: 1

Step Indep: 15  Depnd: 12
```

➤ Press [ERASE][DRAW] to draw the three-dimensional surface. The following figure shows one view of the FAST3D plot for this example:

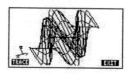

➤ Press [EXIT] to return to the PLOT WINDOW environment.

➤ Press [CANCL] to return to PLOT WINDOW.

➤ Press [ON], or [NXT][OK], to return to normal calculator display.

Example 2 - Plot the surface represented parametrically by x = x(X,Y) = X sin Y, y = y(X,Y) = x cos Y,

Pr-Surface (parametric surface) plots are used to plot a three-dimensional surface whose coordinates (x,y,z) are described by x = x(X,Y), y = y(X,Y), z=z(X,Y), where X and Y are independent parameters.

> **Note:** The equations x = x(X,Y), y = y(X,Y), z=z(X,Y) represent a parametric description of a surface. X and Y are the independent parameters. Most textbooks will use (u,v) as the parameters, rather than (X,Y). Thus, the parametric description of a surface is given as x = x(u,v), y = y(u,v), z=z(u,v).

For example, to produce a Pr-Surface plot for the surface x = x(X,Y) = X sin Y, y = y(X,Y) = X cos Y, z=z(X,Y)=X^2, use the following:

• Press [↰][2D/3D], simultaneously to access to the PLOT SETUP window.

➤ Change TYPE to Pr-Surface.

➤ Press [▼] and type '{X*SIN(Y) X*COS(Y) X^2}' [OK].

➤ Make sure that 'X' is selected as the Indep: and 'Y' as the Depnd: variables.

➤ Press [NXT][OK] to return to normal calculator display.

• Press [↰][WIN], simultaneously, to access the PLOT WINDOW screen.

➤ Change the plot window ranges to read:

```
X-Left:-1  X-Right:1
Y-Near:-1  Y-Far: 1
Z-Low: -1  Z-High:1
XE:  -8    YE:-8    zE:-8
Step Indep: 15 Depnd: 15
```

➤ Press [ERASE][DRAW] to draw the three-dimensional surface.   The result is a tree-dimensional surface that looks like a symmetric watermelon.   Ideally, this should be the plot of a sphere. The distortion occurs because of the rectangular shape of the calculator's screen. By the way, it is going to take the calculator a couple of minutes to finish the plot. So, be patient. Here is what the surface looks like:

> Press [EDIT][NXT][LABEL][MENU] to see the graph with labels and ranges.

> Press [NXT][NXT][PICT][CANCL] to return to the PLOT WINDOW environment.

> Press [ON], or [NXT][OK], to return to normal calculator display.

Area of a parametric surface

The areas A of a surface S: r(u,v) is defined by the double integral

$$A = \iint_R dA = \iint_R | \mathbf{r}_u \times \mathbf{r}_v | \, du \cdot dv,$$

where

$$\mathbf{r}_u = \partial r / \partial u, \qquad \mathbf{r}_v = \partial r / \partial v,$$

and R is the region of the u-v plane corresponding to the surface.

The expression

$$dA = | r_u \times r_v | \, du \cdot dv,$$

is called the element or differential of area of the surface.

Example 1 -- Consider the surface S: $r = r(u,v) = [R \cdot \sin u \cdot \cos v, R \cdot \sin u \cdot \sin v, R \cdot \cos u;], 0<u<\pi/2, 0<v<\pi$. To obtain the integrand $|r_u \times r_v|$ we use the program _VDeriv_ within sub-directory VCALC, as well as the HP 49 G function CROSS, as follows:

['R*SIN(u)*COS(v)' 'R*SIN(u)*SIN(v)' 'R*COS(u)'] [ENTER] 'r' [STO►]	Store r
[VDeri] 'r' [▼] 'u' [ENTER]	Calculate r_u
[VDeri] 'r' [▼] 'u' [ENTER]	Calculate r_v
[↩][MTH][VECTR][CROSS] [↩][ABS]	Calculate $|r_u \times r_v|$
[↪][EVAL][↪][ALG][FACTO][↪][TRIG][NXT][NXT][TRIG]	Simplify last result

The result is   'R^2*SIN(u)'.

To create the double integral required for calculating the area, we will use the equation writer as follows:

[▼]	Enter eq. writer, expression is highlighted.
[↪][∫][0] [►] [↩][π]	Place expression in integral, enter limits
[►][►] [ALPHA][↩][V]	Enter variable of integration for inner integral
[▲][▲][↪][∫][0] [►] [↩][π][÷][2]	Select/place expression in integral, enter limits
[►][►] [ALPHA][↩][U]	Enter variable of integration for outer integral

162

The integral should look like this:

$$\int_0^\pi \int_0^\pi R^2 \cdot SIN(u) \, dv \, du$$

The integral is calculated by using [▲][▲][EVAL]. The result is '2*R^2*π', which is the area of the hemisphere defined by the surface S.

Area of a surface z = g(x,y)

A surface S represented by z = g(x,y) can also be written as

$$r(u,v) = u\, \mathbf{i} + v\, \mathbf{j} + g(u,v)\, \mathbf{k},$$

with

$$r_u = \mathbf{i} + g_u\mathbf{k}, \quad r_v = \mathbf{i} + g_v\mathbf{k},$$

and

$$|\, r_u \times r_v \,|^2 = 1 + g_u{}^2 + g_v{}^2 = 1 + (\partial g/\partial u)^2 + (\partial g/\partial v)^2.$$

Replacing u = x and v = y in this result we have:

$$A = \iint_{S^*} dA = \iint_{S^*} \sqrt{1 + \left(\frac{\partial g}{\partial x}\right)^2 + \left(\frac{\partial g}{\partial y}\right)^2}\, dx \cdot dy,$$

where S* is the projection of S on the x-y plane.

Example 1 - Determine the side area of the cone described by S: { z = $(x^2+y^2)^{1/2}$, 0<z<1 }.

The surface can be plotted in the HP 49 G calculator using a Fast3D graph to look as follows:

TRACE   EXIT

The projection of the surface on the x-y plane is obtained by replacing z = 1 in the expression z = $(x^2+y^2)^{1/2}$, resulting in x^2+y^2 =1, or S* = { $-(1-x^2)^{1/2}$ < y < $(1-x^2)^{1/2}$, -1 < x < 1}. To put together the integral use the following:

'√ (x^2+y^2)'[ENTER][ENTER]	Enter g(x,y), make extra copy
'x' [ENTER][↱][∂] [2] [y^x][ENTER] [↱][EVAL]	Calculate $(\partial g/\partial x)^2$
[►]	Swap levels 1 and 2, g(x,y) is now in level 1
'y' [↱][∂][↰][x^2][↱][EVAL]	Calculate $(\partial g/\partial y)^2$
[+]	Calculate $(\partial g/\partial x)^2 + (\partial g/\partial y)^2$
[1] [+][√x]	Calculate $[1+ (\partial g/\partial x)^2 + (\partial g/\partial y)^2]^{1/2}$

163

The result is '√2'.

Now, put together the following integral:

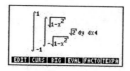

Finally, press [▲][▲][EVAL], within the equation writer, to obtain the result '√2*π'.

Surface integrals

As a line integral is a generalization of the univariate integral, the surface integral is a generalization of the double integral.   Let S be a surface represented by r(u,v), with dA = | r_u × r_v | du·dv, then the surface integral of f(x,y,z) over S is calculated as

$$\iint_S f(x,y,z)dA = \iint_S f[x(u,v),y(u,v),z(u,v)] \cdot |\, \mathbf{r}_u \times \mathbf{r}_v \,| \, du \cdot dv.$$

If S is represented in the form z = g(x,y), then

$$\iint_{S^*} f(x,y,z) \cdot dA = \iint_{S^*} f[x,y,g(x,y)] \cdot \sqrt{1 + \left(\frac{\partial g}{\partial x}\right)^2 + \left(\frac{\partial g}{\partial y}\right)^2} \, dx \cdot dy,$$

Orientation of a surface

Let S be a smooth surface. At any point P on S we can select a unit normal vector n. The direction of n is called the positive normal direction of S at P. There are, obviously, two possibilities in choosing n for any given surface in space. The two expressions for the normal vector can be obtained from

$$\mathbf{n} = \pm \frac{\mathbf{r}_u \times \mathbf{r}_v}{|\, \mathbf{r}_u \times \mathbf{r}_v \,|}.$$

A smooth surface is said to be *orientable* if the positive normal direction, when given at an arbitrary point P of S, can be continued in a unique and continuous way over the entire surface.   The external surface of a sphere, for example, will be an orientable surface. Classical examples of no-orientable surfaces are the Moebius strip, and Klein's bottle.

If a smooth surface is orientable, then we may orient the S by choosing one of the two possible directions of the normal vector.

164

Evaluating surface integrals over a parametric surface

Depending on the sign selected for the normal vector **n**, the integral of a function f(x,y,z) over a surface r(u,v) can be calculated as

$$\iint_S f(x,y,z)dxdy = \pm\iint_R f[x(u,v),y(u,v),z(u,v)] \cdot J(\frac{x,y}{u,v}) \cdot dudv,$$

Where R is the region corresponding to S in the u-v plane.

Example 1 -- Determine the value of the integral, $\iint_R [x^2+y^2+(z-a)^2]^{-1/2}dA$, on the hemisphere $S:x^2+y^2+z^2= a^2$, z>0. [Hint: represent S by **r**(u,v) = a sin u cos v **i** + a sin u sin v **j** + a cos u **k**.]

Start by putting together the Jacobian, using the program JACOBIAN developed earlier:

['a*SIN(u)*COS(v)' 'a*SIN(u)*SIN(v)' 'a*COS(u)'] [ENTER]Enter vector ['x(u,v)' 'y(u,v)']
['u' 'v'][ENTER] [JACOB]   Enter vector ['u' 'v']
[↵][EVAL][↵][ALG][FACTO][↵][TRIG][NXT][NXT][TRIG] Simplify the expression

The result is 'a^2*COS(u)*SIN(u)'. Next, evaluate the function in terms of u,v, as follows:

'1/√ (x^2+y^2+(z-a)^2)'   [ENTER]   Enter   expression   for
function
'x = a*SIN(u)*COS(v)'   [ENTER][↵][ALG][SUBST]   Substitute x = x(u,v)
'y = a*SIN(u)*SIN(v)'   [ENTER][↵][ALG][SUBST]   Substitute y = y(u,v)
'z = a*COS(v)'   [ENTER][↵][ALG][SUBST]   Substitute z = z(u,v)
[↵][EVAL][↵][ALG][FACTO][↵][TRIG][NXT][NXT][TRIG] Simplify the expression

The result is '1/(√ -(2*(COS(u)-1)*ABS(a))'. Multiply the two terms and simplify the result, by using:

[×][↵][EVAL].

Next, put together the following double integral using the equation writer:

[▼]   Enter   equation   writer,   expression   is
highlighted.
[↵][∫][0] [▶] [←][π]   Place expression in integral, enter limits
[▶][▶] [ALPHA][←][V]   Enter the variable of integration for inner
integral
[▲][▲][↵][∫][0] [▶] [←][π][÷][2]   Select and place expression in integral,
enter limits
[▶](12 times) [ALPHA][←][U]   Enter the variable of integration for outer
integral

To evaluate the integral, step-by-step, use:

[▲][▲]   Select entire double integral
[▼][▼]   Select lower limit of outer integral, change
cursor
[▶][▶][▶][▶][▶]   Move cursor to integrand expression
[▲][▲][▲][▲][▲]   Select inner integral

165

The screen should look like this:

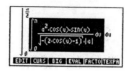

Then, press [EVAL]. Highlight the remaining integral, and press [EVAL] again. Because the calculator does not know that a is a real number, it will request to change settings to Complex, accept the change as requested. The result is:

Considering the complicated expression that we are integrating, you should allow the calculator a few minutes to achieve the result.

166

15 Differential equations

Differential equations are equations involving derivatives of a function. Because many physical quantities are given in terms of rates of change of a certain quantity with respect to one or more independent quantities, derivatives appear frequently in the statement of physical laws. For example, the flux of heat, q $[J/m^2]$, in a one-dimensional direction is given by

$$q = -k \cdot (dT/dx),$$

where T[K or $^\circ$C] is the temperature, x [m] is positions, and k $[J/(m\ K)$ or $J/(m\ oC)]$. This equation can be considered as a differential equation if q and k are known, and we are trying to solve for the temperature as a function of x, i.e., T = T(x). The equation of conservation of energy for heat transfer in one-dimension, where there are no sources or sink of heat, requires that the rate of change of the heat flux across an area perpendicular to the x-axis be zero, i.e., dq/dx = 0,or,

$$\frac{d}{dx}\left[-k \cdot \frac{dT}{dx}\right] = 0.$$

If k is a constant, i.e., not a function of x, then, the equation of conservation of energy reduces to

$$d^2T/dx^2 = 0.$$

The last two expressions are also differential equations. The solution for these equations will be the temperature T = T(x).

Entering differential equations in the HP 49 G calculator

The key to using differential equations in the HP 49 G calculator is typing in the derivatives in the equation. The easiest way to enter a differential equation is to type it in the equation writer. For example, to type the following ODE :

$$(x-1) \cdot (dy/dx)^2 + 2 \cdot x \cdot y = e^{-x} \sin x.$$

use:

[EQW] [↰][( )] [ALPHA][↰][X] [-] [1] [▶][▶][▶] [×] [↱][∂] [ALPHA][↰][X] [▶][ALPHA]
[↰][Y]
[↰][( )] [ALPHA][↰][X] [▶][▶] [y^x][2] [▶][▶] [+] [2] [×] [ALPHA][↰][X] [×] [ALPHA][↰][Y]
[▶][▶][▶] [↱][=] [↰][e^x] [ALPHA][↰][X] [▶] [×] [SIN] [ALPHA][↰][X] [ENTER]

The result is

'(x-1)*∂x(y(x))^2+2*x*y-EXP(x)*SIN(x)'.

167

The derivative dy/dx is represented by $\partial x(y(x))$. For solution or calculation purposes, you need to specify y(x) in the derivative, i.e., the dependent variable must include its independent variable(s) in any derivative in the equation.

You can type an equation directly into the stack by using the symbol ∂ in the derivatives. For example, to type the following ODE involving second-order derivatives:

$$d^2u/dx^2 + 3 \cdot u \cdot (du/dx) + u^2 = 1/x,$$

directly into the stack, use:

[→]['] [→][∂] [ALPHA][↰][X] [↰][( )] [→][∂] [ALPHA][↰][X] [↰][( )] [ALPHA] [↰][U] [↰][( )] [ALPHA][↰][X] [▶][▶][▶] [+] [3] [×] [ALPHA][↰][U] [×][→][∂][ALPHA][↰][X] [↰][( )] [ALPHA][↰][U] [↰][( )] [ALPHA][↰][X] [▶][▶] [+][ALPHA][↰][U] [yˣ][2] [→][=] [1] [÷] [ALPHA][↰][X][ENTER]

The result is

'$\partial x(\partial x(u(x))) + 3*u*\partial x(u(x)) + u^2 = 1/x$ '.

Press [▼] to see the equation in the equation writer:

Partial differential equations can also be entered in the calculator by using the equation writer or by typing directly into the stack. The only difference is that the dependent variable will have more than one independent variable. For example, using the equation writer you could write the equation

$$\partial^2 C/\partial t^2 - u(x,t) \cdot (\partial C/\partial x) = 0,$$

as follows:

[EQW] [→][∂] [ALPHA][↰][T] [▶] [→][∂] [ALPHA][↰][T] [▶] [ALPHA][C] [↰][( )] [ALPHA] [↰][X] [SPC] [ALPHA] [↰][T] [▶][▶][▶] [-][ALPHA][↰][U] [↰][( )] [ALPHA] [↰][X] [SPC] [ALPHA] [↰][T] [▶] [→] [×] [∂] [ALPHA][↰][X] [▶] [ALPHA][C] [↰][( )] [ALPHA] [↰][X] [SPC] [ALPHA] [↰][T] [▶][▶][▶][▶][▶][→][=] [0] [ENTER]

In the stack, the result is:

'$\partial t(\partial t(C(x,y,t))) - u(x,t) * \partial t(C(x,t)) = 0$'.

An alternative notation for derivatives typed directly in the stack is to use 'd1' for the derivative with respect to the first independent variable, 'd2' for the derivative with respect to the second independent variable, etc. A second-order derivative, e.g., d^2x/dt^2, where x = x(t), would be written as 'd1d1x(t)', while $(dx/dt)^2$ would be written 'd1x(t)^2'. Thus, the PDE

$$\partial^2 y/\partial t^2 - g(x,y) \cdot (\partial^2 y/\partial x^2)^2 = r(x,y),$$

would be written, using this notation, as

'd2d2y(x,t)-g(x,y)*d1d1y(x,t)^2=r(x,y)'.

168

The notation using 'd' and the order of the independent variable, as demonstrated in this example, is the notation preferred by the calculator when taking derivatives. For example, write the following equation and make an extra copy:

$$\text{'x*f(x,t)+g(t,y) = h(x,y,t)' [ENTER][ENTER],}$$

then, use 't' [ENTER] [◄][CALC][DERIV][DERIV] to obtain the implicit derivatives with respect to t. The result is:

$$\text{'x*d2f(x,t)+d1g(t,y)=d3h(x,y,t)',}$$

i.e.,

$$x \cdot (\partial f / \partial t) + \partial g / \partial t = \partial h / \partial t.$$

Because the order of the variable t is different in f(x,t), g(t,y), and h(x,y,t), derivatives with respect to t have different indices, i.e., d2f(x,t), d1g(t,y), and d3h(x,y,t). All of them, however, represent derivatives with respect to the same variable.

Expressions for derivatives using the order-of-variable index notation do not translate into derivative notation in the equation writer, as you can check by pressing [▼] while the last result is in stack level 1. However, the calculator understands both notations and operates accordingly regarding of the notation used.

Definitions

The following definitions allow us to classify equations, thus providing general guidelines for obtaining solutions.

Ordinary and partial differential equations

When the dependent variable is a function of a single independent variable, as in the cases presented above, the differential equation is said to be an _ordinary differential equation (ODE)._ If the dependent variable is a function of more than one variable, a differential equation involving derivatives of this dependent variable is said to be a _partial differential equation (PDE)._ An example of a partial differential equation would be the time-dependent would be the Laplace's equation for the stream function, $\psi(x,y,z)$, of a three-dimensional, inviscid flow:

$$\partial^2 \psi / \partial x^2 + \partial^2 \psi / \partial y^2 + \partial^2 \psi / \partial x^2 = 0.$$

Order and degree of an equation

The _order_ of a differential equation is the order of the highest-order derivative involved in the equation. Thus, the ODE

$$dy/dx + 3xy = 0$$

is a first-order equation, while Laplace's equation (shown above) is a second-order equation.

The _degree_ of a differential equation is the highest power to which the highest-order derivative is raised. Therefore, the equation

$$(d^3y/dt^3)^2+(d^2y/dx^2)^5\text{-}xy = e^x,$$

is a third-order, second-degree ODE, while the equation

$$\partial y/\partial t = c\cdot(\partial y/\partial x),$$

is a first-order, first-degree PDE.

Linear and non-linear equations

An equation in which the dependent variable and all its pertinent derivatives are of the first degree is referred to as a _linear differential equation_. Otherwise, the equation is said to be _non-linear_. Examples of linear differential equations are:

$$d^2x/dt^2 + \beta\cdot(dx/dt) + \omega_o\cdot x = A \sin \omega_f\, t,$$

and

$$\partial C/\partial t + u\cdot(\partial C/\partial x) = D\cdot(\partial^2 C/\partial x^2).$$

Constant or variable coefficients

The following equation:

$$d^3y/dt^3+\pi\cdot(d^2y/dx^2)^2\text{-}5\cdot y = e^x,$$

where all the coefficients accompanying the dependent variable and its derivative are constant, would be classified as a third-order, linear ODE _with constant coefficients_. Instead, the equation

$$\partial^2 C/\partial t^2 - u(x,t)\cdot(\partial C/\partial x) = 0,$$

would be classified as a second-order, linear PDE _with variable coefficients_.

Homogeneous and non-homogeneous equations

Typically, differential equations are arranged so that all the terms involving the dependent variable are placed on the left-hand side of the equation leaving only constant terms or terms involving the independent variable(s) only in the right-hand side. When arranged in this fashion, a differential equation that has a zero right-hand side is referred to as a _homogeneous equation_. Examples of homogeneous equations are:

$$d^2x/dt^2 + \beta\cdot(dx/dt) + \omega_o\cdot x = 0,$$

and

$$(x\text{-}1)\cdot(dy/dx) + 2\cdot x\cdot y = 0.$$

On the other hand, if the right-hand side of the equation, after placing the terms involving the dependent variable and its derivatives on the left-hand side, is non-zero, the equation is said to be _non-homogeneous_. Non-homogeneous versions of the last two equations are:

$$d^2x/dt^2 + \beta\cdot(dx/dt) + \omega_o\cdot x = A_o\cdot e^{-t/\tau},$$

and

$$(x\text{-}1)\cdot(dy/dx) + 2\cdot x\cdot y = x^2\text{-}2x.$$

170

Solutions

A _solution_ to a differential equation is a function of the independent variable(s) that, when replaced in the equation, produces an expression that can be reduced, through algebraic manipulation, to the form 0 = 0.   For example, the function

$$y = \sin x,$$

is a solution to the equation

$$d^2y/dx^2 + y = 0,$$

because when we replace y into the equation we have

$$-\sin x + \sin x = 0,$$

or, 0 = 0, for all values of x. This follows from the fact that $dy/dx = \cos x$, and $d^2y/dx^2 = -\sin x$.

General and particular solutions

A _general solution_ is one involving integration constants so that any choice of those constants represents a solution to the differential equation.   For example, the function

$$x = C \cdot e^{-t},$$

is a general solution to the equation

$$dx/dt + x = 0,$$

because, substituting $C \cdot e^{-t}$ for x in the equation produces

$$-C \cdot e^{-t} + C \cdot e^{-t} = 0.$$

A _particular solution_ is a solution corresponding to a specific value of the integration constants. For example, the function

$$y = x^2/2$$

is a particular solution to the equation,

$$dy/dx - x = 0.$$

A general solution for this equation would be

$$y = x^2/2 + C,$$

where C is an arbitrary integration constant.

171

Initial conditions and boundary conditions

To determine the specific value of the constant(s) of integration, we need to provide values of the solution, or of one or more of its derivatives, at specific points. These values are referred to as the _conditions_ of the solution. For example, we could specify that the solution to the equation

$$d^2y/dt^2 + y = 0,$$

must satisfy the conditions

$$y(0) = -5,$$

and

$$dy/dt = -1 \text{ at } t = 5.$$

Initial conditions are provided at a single value of the independent variable so that after evaluating those conditions at that point all the integration constants are uniquely specified. In general, first order differential equations include only one integration constant, requiring only one condition to be evaluated to uniquely determine the solution. Thus, these type of equations needs only one initial condition. The term "initial condition" is used because many first order equations involve a derivative with respect to time, and the condition given to specify the solution is typically the value of the function at time equal to zero, i.e., an initial value of the function. _Boundary conditions_, on the other hand, are provided at more then one value of the independent variable(s). The term "boundary conditions" is used because the function is evaluated at the "boundaries" of the solution domain in order to specify the solution.

An example of _initial conditions_ used in a solution will be to solve the equation

$$d^2u/dt^2 + 2 \cdot (du/dt) = 0,$$
given
$$u(0) = 1, \ du/dt|_{t=0} = -1.$$

An example of boundary conditions used in a solution will be to solve the equation

$$d^2y/dx^2 + y = A \sin x,$$

using

$$y(0) = A/2, \text{ and } y(1) = -A/2.$$

Checking solutions in the HP 49 G calculator

To check if a function satisfy a certain equation using the HP 49 G calculator, first enter the differential equation, then enter the function in the form 'y = f(x)' or 'y = f(x,t)', etc., and use [↦][ALG][SUBST]. You may need to simplify the result by using [↦][EVAL]. For example, to check that

$$u = A \sin \omega_0 t$$

is a solution of the equation

$$d^2u/dt^2 + \omega_0^2 \cdot u = 0,$$

use:

'd1d1u(t)+ ω0^2*u(t) = 0' [ENTER] 'u=A*SIN (ω0*t)'[ENTER] [↦][ALG][SUBST] [↦][EVAL].

172

The result is   '0=0'.

For this example, you could also use:

'∂t(∂t(u(t)))+)+ ω0^2*u(t) = 0' [ENTER] 'u=A*SIN (ω0*t)'[ENTER] [⇨][ALG][SUBST] [⇨][EVAL].

Slope field plots for visualization of solutions

Slope field plots, introduced in Chapter 11, are used to visualize the solutions to a differential equation of the form dy/dx = f(x,y). A slope field plot shows a number of segments tangential to the solution curves, y = f(x). The slope of the segments at any point (x,y) is given by dy/dx = f(x,y), evaluated at any point (x,y), represents the slope of the tangent line at point (x,y).

Example 1 -- Trace the solution to the differential equation y' = f(x,y) = sin x cos y, using a slope field plot. Proceed as follows:

- Press [⇦][2D/3D], simultaneously to access to the PLOT SETUP window.

➢ Change TYPE to Slopefield.

➢ Press [▼] and type 'SIN(X)*COS(Y)' [OK].

➢ Make sure that 'X' is selected as the Indep: and 'Y' as the Depnd: variables.

➢ Press [NXT][OK] to return to normal calculator display.

- Press [⇦][WIN], simultaneously, to access the PLOT WINDOW screen.

➢ Change the plot window ranges to read:

```
X-Left:-5 X-Right:5
Y-Near:-5 Y-Far: 5
```

➢ Press [ERASE][DRAW] to draw the slope field plot. Press [EDIT][NXT][LABEL][MENU] to see the plot unencumbered by the menu and with identifying labels. The graph should look like this:

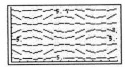

➢ Press [NXT][NXT][PICT] to leave the EDIT environment.

➢ Press [NXT][CANCL] to return to the PLOT WINDOW environment. Then, press [ON], or [NXT][OK], to return to normal calculator display.

If you could reproduce the slope field plot in paper, you can trace by hand lines that are tangent to the line segments shown in the plot. This lines constitute lines of y(x,y) = constant, for the solution of y' = f(x,y). Thus, slope fields are useful tools for visualizing particularly difficult equations to solve.

Try also a slope field plot for the function y' = f(x,y) = tan^{-1}(y/x), by using:

- Press [←][2D/3D], simultaneously to access to the PLOT SETUP window.

➢ Change TYPE to Slopefield.

➢ Press [▼] and type 'ATAN (Y/X)' [OK].

➢ Press [ERASE][DRAW] to draw the slope field plot.   Press [EDIT][NXT][LABEL][MENU] to see the plot unencumbered by the menu and with identifying labels.   Here is the graph:

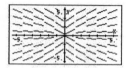

➢ Press [NXT][NXT][PICT] to leave the EDIT environment.

➢ Press [NXT][CANCL] to return to the PLOT WINDOW environment.   Then, press [ON], or [NXT][OK], to return to normal calculator display.

In summary, slope fields are graphical aids to sketch the curves y = g(x) that correspond to solutions of the differential equation dy/dx = f(x,y).

Symbolic solutions to ordinary differential equations

By symbolic solutions we understand those solutions that can be expressed as a closed-form function of the independent variable. Because solution of first-order differential equations imply integrating the derivative involved in the equation, many of the techniques used for solving first-order ODEs follow from integration techniques. Details of some techniques used for solving ordinary differential equations follow.

Solution techniques for first-order, linear ODEs with constant coefficients

A first order equation is an equation of the form

$$a \cdot (dy/dx)^n + b \cdot y^m = f(x),$$

where a, b, n and m are, in general, real numbers. Some specific techniques for <u>linear equations</u>, i.e., when n = m = 1, follow:

Equations of the form: dy/dx = f(x) -- Direct integration

An equation of the form dy/dx = f(x) can be re-written as

$$dy = f(x)dx,$$

and a general solution found by direct integration,

$$\int dy = \int f(x)dx,$$

or

$$y = \int f(x)dx + C.$$

If an initial condition $y(x_o) = y_o$, is given, then the integration can be calculated as

$$\int_{y_o}^{y} dy = \int_{x_o}^{x} f(x)dx,$$

or,

$$y - y_0 = \int_{x_o}^{x} f(x)dx.$$

Example 1 - Determine a general solution for the equation, $dy/dx = e^{-x} \sin x$. Since the integration is indefinite, we want to use the RISCH function as follows:

‘EXP(-x)*SIN(x)’ [ENTER] ‘x’ [ENTER] [⌐][CALC][DERIV][NXT][RISCH].

The result is:

‘(-1/2*SIN(x)+-1/2*COS(x))*EXP(-x)’,

i.e.,

$$y(x) = (-e^{-x}/2)(\sin x + \cos x) + C.$$

175

Example 2 – Determine the solution of the equation, dy/dx = tan^{-1} x, if at x = 0, y = 1. The integration is now definite, thus we can set up the integrals in the equation writer to read:

$$\int_{1}^{y} 1\,dy = \int_{0}^{x} \text{ATAN}(x)\,dx \blacklozenge$$

EDIT CURS BIG ▪ EVAL FACTO TEXPR

Next, press [ENTER][→][EVAL]. The result is: `'y-1=-(LN(x^2+1)-2*x*ATAN(x))/2)'`. To solve for y, we can use: `'y'[ENTER][↰][S.SLV][ISOL]`. The final result is:

`'y=-(2*x*ATAN(x)-(LN(x^2+1)-2))/2'`.

Equations of the form: dy/dx = g(y) -- Inversion and direct integration

Equations of the form dy/dx = g(y), can be re-written as

dy/g(y) = dx.

Thus, an indefinite integral will be given by

$$\int dy/g(y) = \int dx,$$

or

$$\int dy/g(y) = x + C.$$

From the latter expression, the dependent variable y may be solved for.   A similar approach is followed when using a definite integral, i.e., one with initial condition y(x$_o$) = y$_o$. The integration in this case reads:

$$\int_{y_o}^{y} \frac{dy}{g(y)} = \int_{x_o}^{x} dx = x - x_o.$$

Example 3 – Determine a general solution for the equation dy/dx = y ln y. To solve it, we re-write the equation as

dy/(y ln y) = dx,

and integrate

$$\int dy/(y \ln y) = x + C.$$

The left-hand side integral can be calculated using the RISCH function:

`'1/(y*LN(y))'[ENTER] 'y' [ENTER] [↰][CALC][DERIV][NXT][RISCH]`.

The result is

`'LN(ABS(LN(y)))'`,

i.e.,

ln|ln y| = x + C.

To isolate y, edit the result to read:

`'LN(ABS(LN(y)))=x+C'`.

176

Then, use [⤺][e^x]. This result in
$$\text{'ABS(LN(y))=EXP(x+C)'.}$$

Since the absolute value implies two possible solutions for the left-hand side of the equation, namely, ± ln(y), we select one of the two signs, the positive one, for the absolute value to continue with the solution. Selecting ln(y)>0 means that we set y > 1. We need to edit the latter result to read simply:
$$\text{'LN(y)=EXP(x+C)'.}$$

Use [⤺][e^x] once more to get:
$$\text{'y = EXP(EXP(x+C))'.}$$

Example 4 - Determine the solution to the equation $dy/dx = 1+y^2$, if for $x = 0$, $y = 1$. The equation can be re-written as $dy/(1+y^2) = dx$, and integrated by writing:

$$\int_1^y \frac{1}{1+y^2} dy = \int_0^x 1\, dx$$

EDIT CURS BIG ∎ EVAL FACTO TEXPR

Press [ENTER][→][EVAL] to get the result:
$$\text{'(4*ATAN(y)−π)/4=x'.}$$

To solve for y use: 'y' [ENTER][⤺][S.SLV][ISOL].

The solution is: 'y=TAN((π+4*x)/4)'.

Equations of the form: dy/dx = f(x)g(y) -- Separation of variables

Equations of the form $dy/dx = f(x)g(y)$, can be separated into
$$dy/g(y) = dx/g(x),$$

and then integrated using indefinite integrals for general solutions, or definite integrals with initial conditions for particular solutions.

Example 5 -- Find a general solution for the equation $dy/dx = y^2/x$. Separating variables, we have
$$dy/y^2 = dx/x,$$

which can be integrated as follows:

Left-hand side: '1/y^2'[ENTER]'y'[⤺][CALC][DERIV][RISCH].   Result: '-(1/y)'

Right-hand side: '1/x'[ENTER] 'x' [⤺][CALC][DERIV][RISCH].   Result: 'LN(ABS(x))'

Combining the two results by using: 'C' [+] [→][=], we get:

$$'-(1/y) = \text{LN(ABS}(x))+C'.$$

To solve for y use: 'y' [ENTER][←][S.SLV][ISOL].

The final result is:

$$'y=-1/(C+\text{LN(ABS}(x)))'.$$

Example 6 - Find the solution to the equation dy/dx = sin x·cos y, subject to the condition y = 0 when x = 0. Separating variables we have, dy/cos y = sin x dx. Using the initial condition as lower limit of integration we can write:

$$\int_0^y \frac{1}{\cos(y)}dy = \int_0^x \text{SIN}(x)dx$$

Press [ENTER][→][EVAL] to get the result:

$$'(\text{LN(ABS(SIN}(y)+1))-\text{LN(ABS(SIN}(y)-1)))/2=-(\text{COS}(X)-1)'.$$

To solve for y, first combine the two log functions by using: [←][EXP&LN][LNCOL].

Next, enter [2][×][→][EVAL], to move the 2 in the denominator in the left-hand side to the right-hand side.

Next, use [←][e^x] to eliminate the LN function from the expression.

Next, edit the expression so as to eliminate the ABS functions out (i.e., selecting the positive sign of ABS only).

The result now reads:

$$'(\text{SIN}(y)+1)/(\text{SIN}(y)-1))=1/\text{EXP}(2*\text{COS}(X)-2)'.$$

At this point, we can try to isolate y by using: 'y' [ENTER][←][S.SLV][ISOL]. The result is the following list:

$$'\{ \ 'y=-((2*n1-1)*\pi-\text{ASIN}((\text{EXP}(2*\text{COS}(x)-2)+1)/(\text{EXP}(2*\text{COS}(x)-2)-1)))'$$
$$'y = 2*n1*\pi -\text{ASIN}((\text{EXP}(2*\text{COS}(x)-2)+1)/(\text{EXP}(2*\text{COS}(x)-2)-1)))' \ \}'.$$

The term n1 introduced in these expressions accounts for the periodicity of the function sine.

Equations of the form: dy/dx = g(y/x)

Using the change of variable

$$u = y/x,$$

we have

$$y = u·x,$$

$$dy = u·dx + x·du,$$

then

178

$$(u \cdot dx + x \cdot du)/dx = g(u),$$

$$u \cdot dx + x \cdot du = g(u) \cdot dx,$$

$$[g(u)-u] \cdot dx = x \cdot du,$$

from which the variables x and u can be separated as

$$du/[g(u)-u] = dx/x.$$

After integration, we replace
$$u = y/x$$

back in the result, and isolate, if possible, y(x).

Example 7 - Determine the solution of the equation

$$dy/dx = y/x + x/y.$$

With
$$u = y/x,$$

we have
$$y = u \cdot x,$$

$$dy/dx = u + x \cdot (du/dx),$$

$$u + x \cdot (du/dx) = u + 1/u,$$

$$x \cdot (du/dx) = 1/u ,$$

and
$$udu = dx/x,$$

integration results in
$$u^2/2 = \ln x + C/2,$$

or
$$(y/x)^2 = 2 \cdot \ln x + C,$$

$$y/x = (2 \cdot \ln x + C)^{1/2},$$

Finally,
$$y = x \cdot (2 \cdot \ln x + C)^{1/2}.$$

To verify the result, use:

‘d1y(x) - y(x)/x-x/y(x)’ [ENTER] ‘y(x) = x*√ 2*(LN(x)+C)’[ENTER] [↵][ALG][SUBST][↵][EVAL]

The result is ‘0’.

Equations of the form: a·(dy/dx)+ b·y = f(x) -- Integrating factors

The expression
$$a \cdot (dy/dx) + b \cdot y = f(x)$$

constitutes the most general form of a first-order, linear, ordinary differential equation. The equation can be re-written as
$$dy/dx + (b/a) \cdot y = (1/a) \cdot f(x),$$

You can prove that, by multiplying both sides of this form of the equation by a function,

179

$$IF(x) = \exp(b \cdot x/a),$$

known as an *integrating factor*, the equation becomes:

$$\frac{d}{dx}\left(a \cdot \exp\left(\frac{b \cdot x}{a}\right) \cdot y(x)\right) = \frac{1}{a} \cdot \exp\left(\frac{b \cdot x}{a}\right) \cdot f(x).$$

This equation can be easily integrated to read:

$$y(x) = \exp\left(-\frac{b \cdot x}{a}\right)\left(\frac{1}{a} \cdot \int \exp\left(-\frac{b \cdot x}{a}\right) \cdot f(x) + C\right)$$

In terms of the integrating factor, this solution will be:

$$y(x) = (1/FI(x)) \cdot [(1/a) \cdot \int FI(x) \cdot f(x) \cdot dx + C].$$

Example 8 - Find a general solution to the equation $dy/dx - 3 \cdot y = x^2$, by using an integrating factor. The integrating factor to use, with $a = 1$, and $b = -3$ is,

$$FI(x) = \exp(b \cdot x/a) = \exp(-3x).$$

The solution can be obtained by first finding the integral of the function

$$FI(x) \cdot f(x) = x^2 \cdot \exp(-3x),$$

as follows:

'x^2*EXP(-3*x)' [ENTER] 'x' [ENTER] [↰][CALC][DERIV][NXT][RISCH].

To verify that this result satisfies the equation use:

'y(x)' [ENTER] [▶][↦][=] 'd1y(x)-3*y(x)=x^2' [ENTER][▶] 'y(x)' [↦][ALG][SUBST][↦][EVAL].

The result is

'x^2=x^2'.

Example 9 – Determine the solution to the equation: $2 \cdot (dy/dx) + 5 \cdot y = \sin(x)$, subject to the conditions $y = 0$, when $x = 0$. This equation can be integrated in a similar manner as that in example 8, by selecting the integrating factor $FI = \exp(5x/2)$, and then integrating the function $(1/a)FI(x)f(x) = (1/2) \exp(5x/2) \sin(x)$, as follows:

'(1/2)*EXP(5*x/2)*SIN(x)' [ENTER] 'x' [ENTER] [↰][CALC][DERIV][NXT][RISCH].

Next, we add an integration constant, by using:

'C' [ENTER] [+]

Then, we divide by FI(x), by using:

'EXP(5*x/2)' [ENTER] [÷].

180

The result is: '((5/29*SIN(x)+-2/29*COS(x))*EXP(5*x/2)+C)/ EXP(5*x/2)', i.e.,

$$y(x) = (5 \sin x - 2 \cos x)/29 + Ce^{-5x/2}.$$

To verify that this result satisfies the equation use:

'y(x)' [ENTER] [▶][↱][=] '2*d1y(x)+5*y(x)=SIN(x)' [ENTER][▶] 'y(x)'
[↱][ALG][SUBST][↱][EVAL].

Note: the simplification takes about one minute. The result is   'SIN(x)=SIN(x)'.

Solution techniques for first-order, linear ODEs with variable coefficients

An equation with variable coefficients such as

$$K_1(x)(dy/dx) + K_2(x)y(x) = K_3(x),$$

can be reduced to the form,

$$dy/dx + g(x)y(x) = f(x),$$

by dividing the entire equation by $K_1(x)$. This latter equation can be solved by multiplying both sides of the equation by the integrating factor

$$IF(x) = \exp(\int g(x)dx).$$

After identifying the integrating factor, IF(x), the solution procedure is very similar to the case of a first-order, constant-coefficient ODEs, i.e.,

$$y(x) = (1/FI(x)) \cdot [\int FI(x) \cdot f(x) \cdot dx + C].$$

Example 10 -- Solve the equation dy/dx + (1/x)y = x, using an integrating factor. The integrating factor to use is

$$IF(x) = \exp(\int (1/x)dx) = \exp(\ln x) = x.$$

Thus, multiplying both sides of the equation by x produces,

$$x(dy/dx) + y = x^2,$$

or

$$\frac{d}{dx}(xy) = x^2.$$

Integrating with respect to x, produces

$$xy = x^3/3 + C, \text{ and } y = x^2/3 + C/x.$$

To verify that the solution satisfies the equation, try:

'd1y(x)+y(x)/x=x'[ENTER] 'y(x)=x^2/3+C/x'[ENTER] [↱][ALG][SUBST][↱][EVAL].

The result is   'x^2 = x^2'.

181

Exact differential equations

In Chapter 14 we introduced the concepts of a first-order differential in three-dimensions, i.e., an expression of the form:

$$f(x,y,z)dx+g(x,y,z)dy+h(x,y,z)dz,$$

and the conditions under which this first-order differential was an exact differential, i.e., the differential of a function $u(x,y,z)$, so that

$$f(x,y,z) = \partial u/\partial x, \; g(x,y,z) = \partial u/\partial y, \; h(x,y,z) = \partial u/\partial z.$$

We also developed a procedure, and an User RPL program, to integrate the exact differential to obtain the solution $u(x,y,z)$.

An expression of the form,

$$F(x,y) \cdot dx + G(x,y) \cdot dy = 0,$$

will be considered an exact differential equation in two dimensions, if the components $F(x,y)$ and $G(x,y)$ satisfy the conditions

$$\partial F/\partial y = \partial G/\partial x.$$

In such case, it is possible to find a function $u(x,y)$, such that

$$F(x,y) = \partial u/\partial x, \; G(x,y) = \partial u/\partial y.$$

The equation, $u(x,y) = C$, where C is a constant, will represent a solution to the exact differential equation:

$$F(x,y) \cdot dx + G(x,y) \cdot dy = 0.$$

You can use the program *Chk&Int* within sub-directory *ExDiff*, as developed in Chapter 14, to obtain the function $u(x,y)$, as shown in the following example.

Example 1 – Determine a solution, if possible, to the equation
$$dy/dx = -(\sin y - y \cos x)/(x \cos y - \sin x).$$

This expression can be written as

$$(\sin y - y \cos x)dx + (x \cos y - \sin x)dy = 0,$$

with

$$F(x,y) = x \cos y - \cos x,$$

and

$$G(x,y) = \sin y + y \sin x.$$

The program Chk&Int was developed to check and integrate a three-dimensional first-order differential, therefore, to solve this two-dimensional problem, use:

['SIN(Y)-Y*COS(X)' 'X*COS(Y)−SIN(X)' 0][ENTER] ['X' 'Y' 'Z'][ENTER][Chk&In]

The result, provided after receiving the message that the first-order differential is exact, is given by:

182

'X*SIN(Y)-Y*SIN(X)'.

The solution to the differential equation is now,

$$x \sin y - y \sin x = C.$$

Because y cannot be isolated from the expression, the solution is said to be an *implicit* expression.

Solutions of homogeneous linear equations of any order with constant coefficients

Consider the linear, constant-coefficient, homogeneous ODE of order n:

$$d^{(n)}y/dx^{(n)} + b_{n-1} \cdot (dy^{(n-1)}/dx^{(n-1)}) + \ldots + b_2 \cdot (d^2y/dx^2) + b_1 \cdot (dy/dx) + b_0 \cdot y = 0.$$

where the coefficients b_0, b_1, ..., b_{n-1}, are constant. We can use the operator $D^{(k)} = d^{(k)}/dx^{(k)}$, to re-write the equation as

$$D^{(n)}y + b_{n-1} \cdot D^{(n-1)}y + \ldots + b_2 \cdot D^2 y + b_1 \cdot Dy + b0 \cdot y = f(x).$$

Treating the operators $D^{(k)}$, (k = n, n-1, ..., 1), as algebraic terms, the equation is re-written as

$$[D^{(n)} + b_{n-1} \cdot D^{(n-1)} + \ldots + b_2 \cdot D^2 + b_1 \cdot D + b_0] \cdot y = 0.$$

The idea is that the linear combination of the operators, shown above in square brackets, is applied to the function y(x), in a similar manner as algebraic terms would be multiplied to it.

Associated with the latter expression is a polynomial known as the *characteristic equation* of the ODE, and written as

$$\lambda^n + b_{n-1} \cdot \lambda^{n-1} + \ldots + b_2 \cdot \lambda^2 + b_1 \cdot \lambda + b_0 = 0.$$

Suppose that the characteristic equation has n independent roots, then the general solution of the linear, constant-coefficient, homogeneous ODE of order n given earlier is

$$y = C_1 \cdot e^{\lambda_1 x} + C_2 \cdot e^{\lambda_2 x} + \ldots + C_{n-1} \cdot e^{\lambda_{n-1} x} + C_n \cdot e^{\lambda_n x}.$$

If out of the n roots there is one that has multiplicity m, then the m terms corresponding to this root λ in the solution, will be

$$C_{(1)} \cdot e^{\lambda x} + C_{(2)} \cdot x \cdot e^{\lambda x} + C_{(1)} \cdot x^2 \cdot e^{\lambda x} + \ldots + C_{(1)} \cdot x^{m-1} \cdot e^{\lambda x}.$$

Example 1 - Determine the general solution to the homogeneous equation

$$d^3y/dx^3 - 4 \cdot (d^2y/dx^2) - 11 \cdot (dy/dx) + 30 \cdot y = 0.$$

In terms of the D operator, this ODE can be written as

$$[D^3 - 4 \cdot D^2 - 11 \cdot D + 30]y = 0.$$

The characteristic equation corresponding to this ODE is

$$\lambda^3 - 4 \cdot \lambda^2 - 11 \cdot \lambda + 30 = 0.$$

183

To obtain solutions to this equation in the HP 49 G calculator, we can enter the equivalent equation in terms of X (assuming that VX = 'X', where VX is the default independent variable for the calculator's CAS):

'X^3-4*X^2-11*X+30 = 0' [ENTER] [↵][S.SLV][SOLVE] (first [SOLVE] key). The result is the list:

$$\{ \text{'X=-3' 'X=5' 'X=2'} \}.$$

Thus, a general solution to the ODE under consideration is

$$y = C_1 \cdot e^{-3x} + C_2 \cdot e^{5x} + C_3 \cdot e^{2x}.$$

To verify that this general solution satisfies the equation use:

'd1d1d1Y(X)-4*d1d1Y(X)-11*d1Y(X)+30*Y(X) = 0'[ENTER]
'Y(X)=C1*EXP(-3*X)+C2*EXP(5*X)+C3*EXP(2*X)' [ENTER]
[↵][ALG][SUBST] [↵][EVAL]

Allow the calculator about twenty seconds to produce the result: '0=0'.

Example 2 - Determine the general solution to the homogeneous ODE:

$$d^4y/dx^4 - 7 \cdot (d^3y/dx^3) + 18 \cdot (d^2y/dx^2) - 20 \cdot (dy/dx) + 8 \cdot y = 0.$$

In terms of the D operator, this ODE can be written as:

$$[D^4 - 7 \cdot D^3 + 18 \cdot D^2 - 20 \cdot D + 8]y = 0.$$

Thus, the characteristic equation is

$$\lambda^4 - 7 \cdot \lambda^3 + 18 \cdot \lambda^2 - 20 \cdot \lambda + 8 = 0.$$

To obtain the solution of this equation using the HP 49 G calculator, use:

'X^4-7*X^3+18*X^2-20*X+8 = 0' [ENTER] [↵][S.SLV][SOLVE] (first [SOLVE] key).

The result is the list: { 'X=1' 'X=2' }. However, because the characteristic equation is of order 4, the product '(X-1)*(X-2)' cannot generate the characteristic equation just solved. Obviously, one or both of the roots have multiplicity larger than one. To figure out the multiplicity we will use the function FACTOR to see the actual expansion of the characteristic equation. To recover the equation use:

[↵][UNDO]

Then,

[↵][ALG][FACTO].

The result is: '(X-1)*(X-2)^3'.

Thus, the root $\lambda = 2$ has multiplicity 3, and will produce the terms $C_1 \cdot e^{2x} + C_2 \cdot x \cdot e^{2x} + C_3 \cdot x^2 \cdot e^{2x}$, in the solution. The other term corresponds to the root $\lambda = 1$, which produces the term $C_4 \cdot e^x$. Thus, the general solution to the ODE under consideration is:

$$y = (C_1 + C_2 \cdot x + C_3 \cdot x^2) \cdot e^{2x} + C_4 \cdot e^x.$$

184

To verify that this is a solution of the original ODE, use:

'd1d1d1d1Y(X)-7*d1d1d1Y(X)+18*d1d1Y(X)-20*d1Y(X)+8*Y(X) = 0' [ENTER]
'Y(X) = (C1+C2*X+C3*X^3)*EXP(2*X)+C4*EXP(X)'[ENTER]
[↬][ALG][SUBST] [↬][EVAL]

Allow the calculator about twenty seconds to produce the result: '0=0'.

The function LDEC: HP 49 G's solution of linear equations of any order with constant coefficients

The method presented in the previous section dealt only with homogeneous linear ODEs with constant coefficients. The HP 49 G calculator provides the function LDEC (Linear Differential Equation Command) that lets you find the general solution to a linear ODE of any order with constant coefficients, whether it is homogeneous or not. This function requires you to provide two piece of input:

the right-hand side of the ODE
the characteristic equation of the ODE

Both of these inputs must be given in terms of the default independent variable for the calculator's CAS (typically X). The output from the function is the general solution of the ODE. The function LDEC is available through the keystroke sequence: [↤][CALC][DIFF][LDEC].

Example 1 – To solve the homogeneous ODE

$$d^3y/dx^3 - 4 \cdot (d^2y/dx^2) - 11 \cdot (dy/dx) + 30 \cdot y = 0.$$

Enter:

0 [ENTER] 'X^3-4*X^2-11*X+30' [ENTER] [↤][CALC][DIFF][LDEC].

The solution is:

'-(6*C0-(C1+C2))/24*EXP(5*X)+(10*C0-(7+C1-C2))/40*EXP(-(3*X))+(15*C0+(2*C1-C2))/15*EXP(2*X)'

Now, this latter result looks way more complicated than the result obtained earlier, i.e.,

$$y = C_1 \cdot e^{-3x} + C_2 \cdot e^{5x} + C_3 \cdot e^{2x}.$$

However, the two results are equivalent if you realize that the terms accompanying the exponential terms in the result provided by LDEC are combinations of constants. Thus, if we take

K1 = (10*C0-(7+C1-C2))/40, K2 = -(6*C0-(C1+C2))/24, and K3 = (15*C0+(2*C1-C2))/15,

we can write the result provided by LDEC as

$$y = K_1 \cdot e^{-3x} + K_2 \cdot e^{5x} + K_3 \cdot e^{2x}.$$

The reason why the result provided by LDEC shows such complicated combination of constants is because, internally, to produce the solution, LDEC utilizes Laplace transforms (to be presented later in this chapter), which transform the solution of an ODE into an algebraic

185

solution. The combination of constants result from factoring out the exponential terms after the Laplace transform solution is obtained.

Example 2 -- To solve the homogeneous ODE:

$$d^4y/dx^4 - 7\cdot(d^3y/dx^3) + 18\cdot(d^2y/dx^2) - 20\cdot(dy/dx) + 8\cdot y = 0.$$

Enter:

0 [ENTER] 'X^4-7*X^3+18*X^2-20*X+8' [ENTER] [↰][CALC][DIFF][LDEC].

The solution is:

'(8*C0-(12*C1-(6*C2-C3)))*EXP(X)+(-((4*C0-(8*C1-(5*C2-C3)))/2*X^2)+(6*C0-(11*C1-(6*C2-C3)))*X-(7*C0-(12*C1-(6*C2-C3))))*EXP(2*X)'

Again, if we replace the combination of constants as follows:

K_1= -(7*C0-(12*C1-(6*C2-C3))) , K_2 =(6*C0-(11*C1-(6*C2-C3))), K_3 = -(4*C0-(8*C1-(5*C2-C3)))/2,

and

K_4 = (8*C0-(12*C1-(6*C2-C3))),

we get a simpler result:

$$y = (K_1 + K_2\cdot x + K_3\cdot x^2)\cdot e^{2x} + K_4\cdot e^x.$$

Example 3 - Using the function LDEC, solve the non-homogeneous ODE:

$$d^3y/dx^3 - 4\cdot(d^2y/dx^2) - 11\cdot(dy/dx) + 30\cdot y = x^2.$$

Enter:

'X^2' [ENTER] 'X^3-4*X^2-11*X+30' [ENTER] [↰][CALC][DIFF][LDEC].

The solution is:

'-(750*C0-(125*C1+125*C2+2))/3000*EXP(5*X)+(270*C0-(189*C1-(27*C2-2)))/1080*EXP(-(3*X))+(450*X^2+330*X+241)/13500+(60*C0+3*C1-(4*C2+1))/60*EXP(2*X)'

Replacing the combination of constants accompanying the exponential terms with simpler values, such as K_3 = -(750*C0-(125*C1+125*C2+2))/3000, results in the expression

$$y = K_1\cdot e^{-3x} + K_2\cdot e^{5x} + K_3\cdot e^{2x} + (450\cdot x^2 + 330\cdot x + 241)/13500.$$

We recognize the first three terms as the general solution of the homogeneous equation (see Example 1, above). If y_h represents the solution to the homogeneous equation, i.e.,

$$y_h = K_1\cdot e^{-3x} + K_2\cdot e^{5x} + K_3\cdot e^{2x},$$

you can prove that the remaining terms in the solution shown above, i.e.,

$$y_p = (450\cdot x^2 + 330\cdot x + 241)/13500,$$

constitute a particular solution of the ODE.

Note: This result is general for all non-homogeneous linear ODEs, i.e., given the solution of the homogeneous equation, $y_h(x)$, the solution of the corresponding non-homogeneous equation, $y(x)$, can be written as

186

$$y(x) = y_h(x) + y_p(x),$$

where $y_p(x)$ is a particular solution to the ODE.

To verify that $y_p = (450 \cdot x^2 + 330 \cdot x + 241)/13500$, is indeed a particular solution of the ODE, use the following:

'd1d1d1Y(X)-4*d1d1Y(X)-11*d1Y(X)+30*Y(X) = X^2'[ENTER]
'Y(X)=(450*X^2+330*X+241)/13500' [ENTER]
[↱][ALG][SUBST] [↱][EVAL]

Allow the calculator about ten seconds to produce the result: 'X^2 = X^2'.

Obtaining the particular solution for a second-order, linear ODE with constant coefficients

Thus, how do we come up with a particular solution, y_p, to complete the solution to a non-homogeneous equation, $y = y_h + y_p$, given the solution to the homogeneous equation, y_h? In this section we present a general method to obtain y_p for second-order, linear ODEs with constant coefficients. The reason why we choose second-order equations is not only because they are the simpler equations to solve (not including first-order equations, which were discussed in great detail in an earlier section), but also because they are useful to model a number of real-life situations. Typical systems modeled by second-order ODEs are the damped and undamped oscillatory behavior in spring-mass and electric circuit systems.

The general expression for a second-order, linear, non-homogeneous ODE with constant coefficients is

$$d^2y/dx^2 + b_1 \cdot (dy/dx) + b_0 \cdot y = h(x).$$

The first step is to obtain the solution to the homogeneous equation

$$d^2y/dx^2 + b_1 \cdot (dy/dx) + b_0 \cdot y = 0,$$

by using the solutions to the characteristic equation

$$\lambda^2 + b_1 \cdot \lambda + b_0 = 0.$$

Consider the case in which the solutions to the characteristic equation are real numbers. The solutions to this quadratic equation can be two different values of λ, say λ_1 and λ_2, in which case the homogeneous solution is written as

$$y_h(x) = C_1 \cdot \exp(\lambda_1 \cdot x) + C_2 \cdot \exp(\lambda_2 \cdot x),$$

or a single solution of multiplicity 2, say λ_0, in which case we write

$$y_h(x) = (C_1 + C_2 \cdot x) \exp(\lambda_0 \cdot x).$$

If the two solutions to the quadratic (characteristic) equation are complex numbers, they must be complex conjugates of each other as required by the fundamental theorem of algebra. In this case we can write

$$\lambda_1 = \alpha + \beta i, \text{ and } \lambda_2 = \alpha - \beta i,$$

187

where α and β are real numbers. Thus, the solution $C_1 \cdot \exp(\lambda_1 \cdot x) + C_2 \cdot \exp(\lambda_2 \cdot x)$, becomes

$$C_1 \cdot e^{(\alpha+\beta i)x} + C_2 \cdot e^{(\alpha-\beta i)x} = C_1 \cdot e^{\alpha x} \cdot e^{i\beta x} + C_2 \cdot e^{\alpha x} \cdot e^{-i\beta x} = e^{\alpha x} \cdot (C_1 \cdot \cos \beta x + i \cdot C_1 \cdot \sin \beta x + C_2 \cdot \cos \beta x - i \cdot C_2 \cdot \sin \beta x)$$
$$= e^{\alpha x} \cdot [(C_1+C_2) \cdot \cos \beta x + i \cdot (C_1-C_2) \cdot \sin \beta x] = e^{\alpha x} \cdot (K_1 \cdot \cos \beta x + K_2 \cdot \sin \beta x),$$

where

$$K_1 = (C_1+C_2), \text{ and } K_2 = i \cdot (C_1-C_2).$$

Thus, for the case of two complex solutions to the characteristic equation, the homogeneous solution is a sinusoidal function whose amplitude grows ($\alpha > 0$) or decreases ($\alpha < 0$) with x:

$$y_h(x) = e^{\alpha x} \cdot (K_1 \cdot \cos \beta x + K_2 \cdot \sin \beta x).$$

If the solutions are imaginary numbers, i.e., if $\alpha = 0$ in the previous result, the homogeneous solution is a pure sinusoidal function:

$$y_h(x) = K_1 \cdot \cos \beta x + K_2 \cdot \sin \beta x.$$

To obtain the particular solution, $y_p(x)$, that will produce the overall solution of the non-homogeneous ODE, $y(x) = y_h(x) + y_p(x)$, follow this rule that refers to the sub-sequent table of functions:

If $h(x)$, in the general non-homogeneous ODE, is given by one of the functions in the first column of the table shown below, choose for $y_p(x)$ a linear combination of $h(x)$ and its linearly independent derivatives, as shown in the second column of the table.

If $h(x)$ is the sum of some of the functions shown in column 1 of the table below, choose for $y_p(x)$ the sum of the functions in the corresponding lines.

If a term in $h(x)$ is a solution of the homogeneous equation corresponding to the ODE under consideration, modify your choice of $y_p(x)$ by multiplying the appropriate line of column 2 by x or x^2, depending on whether the root of the characteristic equation (column 3) is simple or double.

Term in h(x)	Choice for $y_p(x)$	Root of char. eqn.
$c \cdot e^{\alpha x}$	$C_0 \cdot e^{\alpha x}$	α, real
$c \cdot x^n$ (n = 0, 1, ...)	$C_n \cdot x^n + C_{n-1} \cdot x^{n-1} + ... + C_1 \cdot x + C_0$	0
$c \cdot \sin \beta x$	$C_1 \cdot \sin \beta x + C_2 \cdot \sin \beta x$	$i\beta$, imaginary
$c \cdot \cos \beta x$	$C_1 \cdot \sin \beta x + C_2 \cdot \sin \beta x$	$i\beta$, imaginary

Once the particular solution is set up by following the rule above, the undetermined coefficients in $y_p(x)$ can be determined by substituting yp(x) into the ODE.

Example 1 - Obtain the general solution to the non-homogeneous, second-order, linear ODE:

$$d^2y/dx^2 - 5 \cdot (dy/dx) + 6 \cdot y = x^2.$$

The characteristic equation of the homogeneous equation is

$$\lambda^2 - 5 \cdot \lambda + 6 = 0,$$

or

188

$$(\lambda-3)\cdot(\lambda-2) = 0,$$

with solutions

$$\lambda = 2, \text{ and } \lambda = 3.$$

Thus, the homogeneous solution is

$$y_h(x) = K_1 \cdot e^{2x} + K_2 \cdot e^{3x}.$$

Since the right-hand side of the non-homogeneous equation is

$$h(x) = x^2,$$

from the table above we select

$$y_p(x) = C_2 x^2 + C_1 x + C_0.$$

To obtain the values of C_0, C_1, and C_2, replace the solution $y_p(x)$ into the ODE. In the HP 49 G calculator this is accomplished by using:

'd1d1Y(X)-5*d1Y(X)+6*Y(X) - X^2' [ENTER]
'Y(X) = C0+C1*X+C2*X^2'[ENTER]
[↱][ALG][SUBST]

This produces the result:

'2*C2-5*(C1+C2*(2*X))+6*(C0+C1*X+C2*X^2)-X^2'.

To solve for C0, C1, and C2, using the calculator we will have to use the equation editor as follows:

[▼]	Launch equation editor
[▼][▼][▼]	Select first term (2) in equation, cursor -> rectangle
[▶][▶][▶][▲][▲][▲][▲][EVAL]	Expand term $5\cdot(C1+C2\cdot(2\cdot X))$
[▶][EVAL]	Expand term $6\cdot(C0+C1\cdot X+C2\cdot X^2)$
[▲][EVAL]	Expand entire left-hand side of equation

Now, we need to put together terms in X^0, X, and X^2, by using selecting the proper terms to move, and then using [↱][CUT], and [↱][PASTE]. Press [ENTER] when done. The expression, after these changes, should look like this:

'2*C2-5*C1+6*C0+6*X*C1-10*X*C2+6*X^2*C2-X^2'.

Going back to the equation editor you can factor out the terms X, and X^2, by using:

[▼]	Launch equation editor
[▼][▼][▼]	Select first term (2) in equation, changing cursor to rectangle
[▶][▶][▶][▶][▶][▶]	Moves cursor to the 6 in the first term with X
[↱] (hold this key) [▶][▶][▶]	Select the two terms with X
[FACTO]	Factor out X from these two terms
[▶][↱] [▶]	Select the two terms with X^2
[FACTO]	Factor out X^2 from these two terms
[ENTER]	Return to main calculator display

The result now looks like this:

'2*C2-5*C1+6*C0+X*(6*C1-10*C2) +X^2*(6*C2-1)'.

This is equivalent to

$$2\cdot C_2-5\cdot C_1+6\cdot C_0+(6\cdot C_1-10\cdot C_2)\cdot X+(6\cdot C_2-1)\cdot X_2 = 0,$$

or,

189

$$6 \cdot C_0 - 5 \cdot C_1 + 2 \cdot C_2 = 0,$$
$$6 \cdot C_1 - 10 \cdot C_2 = 0,$$
$$6 \cdot C_2 = 1.$$

The solution of this system can be calculated by using:

$$[0\ 0\ 1][ENTER]\ [[6\ \text{-}5\ 2][0\ 6\ \text{-}10][0\ 0\ 6]][ENTER]\ [\div].$$

The result is
$$C_0 = 19/108,\ C_1 = 5/18,\ \text{and}\ C_2 = 1/6.$$

Thus,
$$y_p(x) = x^2/6 + (5/18)x + 19/108,$$

and the general equation to the non-homogeneous equation becomes:

$$y(x) = y_h(x) + y_p(x) = K_1 \cdot e^{2x} + K_2 \cdot e^{3x} + x^2/6 + (5/18)x + 19/108.$$

Of course, we don't need to go through all these details in the calculation if we use the function LDEC as follows:
'X^2'[ENTER] 'X^2-5*X+6'[ENTER][↰][CALC][DIFF][LDEC].

The result is: '-(54*C0-(27*C1+2))/27*EXP(3*X)+(18*X^2+30*X+19)/108+(12*C0-(4*C1+1))/4*EXP(2*X)'.

With
$$K_1 = (12 \cdot C0 - (4 \cdot C1 + 1))/4,\ K_2 = -(54 \cdot C0 - (27 \cdot C1 + 2))/27,$$

the result is
$$y(x) = K_1 \cdot e^{2x} + K_2 \cdot e^{3x} + (18x^2 + 30x + 19)/108,$$

which, you can check, is the same result as obtained earlier using the step-by-step approach.

Applications of ODEs I : analysis of damped and undamped free oscillations

Consider the mass-spring system shown in the figure below.   The mass is removed from its equilibrium position (x = 0) and released at a position $x = x_0$ at t=0.   At the moment of its release the body was moving with a speed $v = v_0$.

The diagram shows the body of mass m being acted upon by the restoring force of the spring,

$$Fs = -k \cdot x,$$

and by a viscous damping force,

$$Fv = -\beta \cdot v = -\beta \cdot (dx/dt).$$

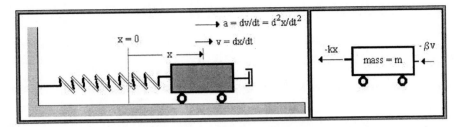

Newton's second law, when applied in the x-direction to the mass m is written as:

$$-kx - \beta\,(dx/dt) = m\,(d^2x/dt^2),$$

which results in the second-order, linear, ordinary differential equation:

$$d^2x/dt^2 + (\beta/m)\cdot(dx/dt) + (k/m)\cdot x = 0.$$

Let us first consider the case in which the motion is undamped, i.e., b = 0. The equation in this case reduces to

$$d^2x/dt^2 + (k/m)\cdot x = 0.$$

The corresponding characteristic equation is

$$\lambda^2 + (k/m) = 0,$$

with solutions,

$$\lambda = \pm\,i\cdot\sqrt{(k/m)} = \pm i\cdot\omega_0.$$

This result suggest a solution of the form

$$x(t) = C_1\cos\omega_0 t + C_2\sin\,\omega_0 t.$$

Alternatively, by taking

$$C_1 = A\cos\phi,\ \text{and}\ C_2 = -A\sin\phi,$$

the solution can be written as

$$x(t) = A\cdot\cos(\omega_0 t + \phi).$$

The quantity

$$\omega_0 = \sqrt{(k/m)}$$

is known as the *natural angular frequency* of the harmonic motion that results when no viscous damping is present. The frequency of the oscillation can be calculated from

$$f = 2\pi/\omega_0 = 1/T,$$

where T is the period of the oscillation (i.e., the time that the mass takes to return to a pre-defined position in the motion). The quantity ϕ is known as the angular phase of the oscillation, and A is known as the amplitude.

The velocity of the motion is given by

$$v = dx/dt = -\omega_0\cdot A\sin(\omega_0 t + \phi),$$

and its acceleration, is

$$a = dv/dt = -\omega_0^2\cdot A\cos(\omega_0 t + \phi),$$

191

The initial conditions, $x(0) = x_o$, $v(0) = v_o$, can be used to evaluate the constants A and f, as follows:

$$x_o = x(0) = A \cos \phi,$$

and

$$v_o = v(0) = -\omega_b \cdot A \sin \phi.$$

Thus,

$$\tan \phi = - v_o/(\omega_b \, x_o), \text{ or } \phi = \tan^{-1}(-v_o/(\omega_b \, x_o)),$$

and

$$A = [x_o^2 + (v_o/\omega_b)^2]^{1/2}.$$

If damping occurs ($\beta \neq 0$), the characteristic equation becomes

$$\lambda^2 + (\beta/m) \cdot \lambda + \omega_b^2 = 0,$$

whose solutions are

$$\lambda = -(\beta/(2 \cdot m)) \pm \sqrt{([\beta/(2 \cdot m)]^2 - \omega_b^2)} = - \alpha \pm \sqrt{(\alpha^2 - \omega_b^2)},$$

where

$$\alpha = \beta/(2 \cdot m).$$

The nature of the solution will depend on the relative size of the coefficients α and ω_b, as follows:

- If $\alpha < \omega_b$, then $\sqrt{(\alpha^2 - \omega_b^2)} = i \cdot \omega_1$, where

$$\omega_1 = \sqrt{(\omega_b^2 - \alpha^2)}$$

  is real, and the solutions of the characteristic equation are

$$\lambda_1 = -\alpha + i \cdot \omega_1, \text{ and } \lambda_2 = -\alpha - i \cdot \omega_1.$$

The solution to the ODE, therefore, is written as

$$x(t) = e^{-\alpha t} (C_1 \cos \omega_1 t + C_2 \cdot \sin \omega_1 t) = A_o \cdot e^{-\alpha t} \cdot \cos(\omega_1 t + \phi_1).$$

The parameter

$$\omega_1 = \sqrt{(\omega_b^2 - \alpha^2)} = \sqrt{[(k/m)^2 - (\beta/(2m))^2]} = \sqrt{(4k^2 - \beta^2)}/(2m),$$

represents the damped angular frequency of the oscillation, and ϕ_1 represents the corresponding angular phase. A_o is the amplitude of the oscillation at $t = 0$. If we define a variable amplitude,

$$A(t) = A_o \cdot e^{-\alpha t},$$

then the solution to the ODE, also known as the signal, can be written as

$$x(t) = A(t) \cdot \cos(\omega_1 t + \phi_1).$$

Please notice that this solution is very similar to the case of an undamped oscillation, except for the fact that in a damped oscillation the amplitude decreases with time. The amplitude decreases, or decays, with time because the parameter $\alpha = \beta/(2m)$ is positive. Therefore, the function $\exp(-\alpha t)$ decreases with time.

- If $\alpha = \omega_b$, then the characteristic equation produces the solution $\lambda = -\alpha$, with multiplicity 2, in which case the solution becomes

$$x(t) = e^{-\alpha t} (C_1 + C_2 \cdot t).$$

192

This solution represents a linear function of t subjected to a decay factor, $\exp(-\alpha t)$.

- If $\alpha > \omega_b$, then $\sqrt{(\alpha^2-\omega_b^2)} = K$ is real, and $K < \alpha$, the solutions of the characteristic equation become

$$\lambda_1 = -\alpha + K = -c_1, \text{ and } \lambda_2 = -\alpha - K = -c_2,$$

both negative. Therefore, the resulting signal can be written as:

$$x(t) = C_1 \cdot \exp(-c_1 t) + C_2 \cdot \exp(-c_2 t).$$

Notice that the last two cases, namely, $\alpha = \omega_b$ and $\alpha > \omega_b$, produce signals that decay with time. These cases correspond to harmonic motions that are said to be *over-damped*, i.e., the viscous damping is large enough to quickly damp out any oscillation after the body of mass m is released.

To illustrate an example of a damped oscillatory motion, we will plot the signals that result from a motion having the following parameters:

Example 1 - Damped oscillatory motion: Plot position, velocity, and acceleration corresponding to the following parameters: m = 1 kg, β = 0.1 N·s/m, k = 0.5 N/m. With these values,

$$\omega_b = (k/m)^{1/2} = (0.5N/1kg\cdot m)^{1/2} = (0.5 \ s^{-2})^{1/2} = 0.7071 \ s^{-1} = 0.7071 \ rad/s,$$

and

$$\alpha = \beta/(2m) = 0.1 \ N\cdot s/ \ (2\times 1 \ kg\cdot m) = 0.05 \ s^{-1} = 0.05 \ rad/s.$$

Since, $\alpha < \omega_b$, the resulting signal is that of a damped oscillation with

$$\omega_1 = \sqrt{(\omega_b^2-\alpha^2)} = \sqrt{(0.7071^2-0.05^2)} = 0.7053 \ rad \ /s.$$

The resulting equation is

$$x(t) = A_o \exp(-0.05t) \cos(0.7053t - \phi_1).$$

The position x(t) for this motion can be entered into the HP 49 G calculator by using:

'A0*EXP(-0.05*t)*COS(0.7053*t-φ1)' [ENTER]

The velocity, v = dx/dt, is obtained by

[ENTER]'t'[ENTER][→][∂]

To determine the constants A_o and ϕ_1, we use initial conditions, x(0) = 1.5 m, and v(0) = -5.0 m/s. Using the calculator, we will enter:

't=0'[ENTER][→][ALG][SUBST][→][EVAL],

which produces an expression for v(0). Make this expression equal to -5.0, by entering:

-5 [ENTER][→][=].

Next, swap contents of levels 1 and two, replace the value 't=0' in the expression for x(t), and make it equal to 1.5, by using:

[▶] 't = 0' [ENTER][→][ALG][SUBST][→][EVAL] '1.5' [ENTER][→][=].

I suggest that you keep a copy of these two equations by using the following:

193

2 [ENTER][⇦][PRG][TYPE][→LIST].

This create the list

{ '.7053*A0*SIN(ϕ1)-.05*A0*COS(ϕ1)=-5.' 'A0*COS(ϕ1) = 1.5}.

Press [ENTER] to keep an extra copy of the list, then press [→][EVAL] to decompose the list back into the two original equations.   Next, press [÷] to divide the two expressions term by term, the result is:

'(.7053*A0*SIN(ϕ1)-.05*A0*COS(ϕ1))/(A0*COS((ϕ1))=-3.333333333333'

Now, press [▼] to activate the equation writer. Use small font (i.e., de-select the soft-menu key [BIG]), and press [▼] to select the left-hand side of the equation. Press [▼] once more to select the numerator of the left-hand side, then press [EDIT], and edit out the expression to read:

.7053*TAN(ϕ1)-.05 = -3.333333333.

Next, store this result in variable EQ:

'EQ'[STO▶].

Make sure your calculator's angle measurement is set to radians, and launch the numerical equation solver,

[→][NUM.SLV][OK].

Press [▼][SOLVE] to obtain the value,   ϕ1: -1.3592.

Press [ENTER]. The result will be shown in stack level 1 as a tagged object. Transform the tagged object into an equality by using:

[⇦][PRG][TYPE][OBJ→]	Decompose tagged object
[▼]	Trigger line editor to edit string "ϕ1"
[ALPHA][→]['] [▶][▶] [ALPHA][→]['] [ENTER] "	Edit line to read 'ϕ1', entered as " 'ϕ1'
[OBJ→]	Transform string into algebraic 'ϕ1'
[▶] [→][=]	Swap levels 1 and 2, form equality

The result is: 'ϕ1 = -1.3592'.

Now, in stack level 2 we should have the extra copy of the two equations we left in the stack. To access those equations, and solve for A0, try the following:

[▶]	Swap levels 1 and 2
[→][EVAL]	Decompose list
[▶][⇦]	Swap levels 1 and 2, drop second
equation	
[▶][→][ALG][SUBST]	Swap levels 1 and 2, substitute value of
ϕ1	
[→][EVAL]	Evaluate equation numerically
[→]['][ALPHA][A][0][ENTER][⇦][S.SLV][ISOL]	Isolate A0

The result is   'A0 = 7.142136'.

194

So, we have the results $A_o = 7.142136$, and $\phi 1 = -1.3592$, which allows us to write the oscillatory signal as:

$$x(t) = 7.142136 \exp(-0.05t) \cos(0.7053t + 1.3592).$$

Let's plot the signal, $x(t)$, and its first two derivatives, $v(t) = dx/dt$, and $a(t) = dv/dt$, by using the following:

'7.142136*EXP(-.05*t)*COS(.7053*t+1.3592)' [ENTER][ENTER]	Enter x(t), make copy
't' [ENTER][↱][∂][↱][EVAL][ENTER]	Calculate v(t), make
copy	
't' [ENTER] [↱][∂][↱][EVAL]	Calculate a(t)
3 [ENTER][↰][PRG][TYPE][→LIST]	Create list
{x(t),v(t),a(t)}	
'EQ' [STO▶]	Store list in EQ for plots

Next, prepare the plot by using:

[↰][2D/3D] (simultaneously)	To set up plot
[▼][▼] [ALPHA][↰][T] [OK]	Change independent variable to
't'	
[NXT][OK]	Accept changes
[↰][WIN] (simultaneously)	To set up plot window
[1][+/-][OK] [4][0][OK]	Change t-range to (-1,40)
[8][+/-][OK] [8][OK]	Change vertical range to (-8,8)
[ERASE][DRAW]	Erase plot window, plot x,v,a
[EDIT][NXT][LABEL][MENU]	Show the graphs w/o key labels

The graphics screen should look like this:

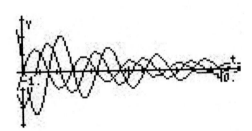

Notice the oscillatory nature of the three functions, as well as their amplitudes decay with time as expected.

To cancel the graphics screen and return to normal calculator display, use:

[NXT][NXT][PICT][CANCL][ON].

195

A program to create phase portraits of oscillatory motion

A phase portrait for oscillatory, or any kind of, motion is a plot involving the dependent variable and one of its derivatives, or two derivatives of the dependent variable. For example, a plot of velocity, v(t), versus position, x(t), represents a phase portrait. Other phase portraits would be a(t) vs. x(t), and a(t) vs. v(t). To produce a phase portrait we will make use of the ΣDAT matrix for statistical calculations. We will load this matrix with four columns corresponding to 100 values of time (column 1), position (column 2), velocity (column 3), and acceleration (column 4). Then, plots of x-vs-t, v-vs-t, and a-vs-t, as well as phase portraits can be generated as scatterplots of the proper combinations of columns in the ΣDAT matrix.

Create a sub-directory to be called PPORT (for Phase PORTraits), and, within that sub-directory create the following programs:

Program GETΣ (GET ΣDAT):

`<<`	Start program GETΣ
`INPHASE`	Call sub-program INPHASE
`→ x t0 tf`	Pass values as x (signal), t0, tf
`  <<`	Start first-subprogram within GETΣ
`  x DEFFCTS`	Place signal, define functions x, v, t
`  t0 tf  '(tf - t0)/100' EVAL GETtLIST`	Place t0, tf, Δt, call GETtLIST
`  CRΣDAT`	Call sub-program CRΣDAT to set up ΣDAT
`  "ΣDAT ready" MSGBOX`	Announce completion of program
`  >>`	End first sub-program within GETΣ
`>>`	End program GETΣ

Sub-program INPHASE (INput data for PHASE portraits, etc.):

`<<`	Start program INPHASE
`"Enter x(t),t0,tf:"`	
`{" ↵  :x(t):↵  : t0: ↵  : tf:" {2 0} V } INPUT`	Input string
`OBJ→`	Decompose input string
`1 3 FOR j`	Start FOR loop with j = 1, 2, 3
`  DTAG 3 ROLLD`	Detag, roll down three levels
`NEXT`	End FOR loop (j)
`>>`	End sub-program INPHASE

Sub-program DEFFCTS (DEFine FunCTionS):

`<<`	Start sub-program DEFFCTS
`→ x`	Get x(t) as input
`  <<`	Start first sub-program within DEFFCTS
`  x 's(t)' SWAP = DEFINE`	Define 's(t) = x', position
`  x 't' ∂ EVAL DUP 'v(t)' SWAP = DEFINE`	Define 'v(t) = ds/dt', velocity
`  't' ∂ EVAL 'a(t)' SWAP = DEFINE`	Define 'a(t) = dv/dt', acceleration
`  >>`	End first sub-program within DEFFCTS
`>>`	End sub-program DEFFCTS

196

Sub-program GETtLIST (*GET* the *time LIST*):

```
<<                              Start sub-program  GETtLIST
→ t0  tf  Δt                    Input data t0, tf, Δt
 <<                             Start first sub-program within GETtLIST
 t0  1  →LIST t0                Create a list { t0 }, place t0 after list
 1 100 FOR j                    Start FOR loop with j = 1, 2, …, 100
    Δt  +  DUP 3 ROLLD  + SWAP  Add Δt to level 1, add result to list
 NEXT                           End FOR loop (j)
 +                              Add last value of t to the list
 >>                             Close sub-program within GETtLIST
>>                              End sub-program GETtLIST
```

Sub-program CRΣDAT (Create ΣDAT):

```
<<                              Start sub-program CR ΣDAT
DUP AXL SWAP                    Creates a vector and a list with values of t
DUP 's' LSTEVAL AXL SWAP       Produce vector of values of x(t)
DUP 'v' LSTEVAL AXL SWAP       Produce vector of values of v(t)
'a' LSTEVAL AXL                Produce vector of values of a(t)
4  COL→ STOΣ                   Create 4-column matrix, store it in ΣDAT
>>                              End sub-program CR ΣDAT
```

Sub-program LSTEVAL (LiSt EVALuation):

```
<<                              Start sub-program LSTEVAL
→ L  f                          Input list L and function f
 <<                             Start first sub-program within LSTEVAL
 { } L SIZE                     Place empty list in stack, get size of L
 1 SWAP FOR j                   Start FOR loop with j = 1, 2, … SIZE(L)
    L j GET f EVAL +            Evaluate f(Lj), add it to list on stack
 NEXT                           End FOR loop (j)
 >>                             End first sub-program within LSTEVAL
>>                              End sub-program LSTEVAL
```

Program TPLOTS (Time PLOTS, i.e., x-vs-t, v-vs-t, a-vs-t):

```
<<                              Start program TPLOTS
"x vs. t" MSGBOX                Announce upcoming plot x-vs-t
1 2 "t" "s" SCTPnm             Place data to plot using SCTPnm
DRAX LABEL PICTURE              Draw axes, labels, recall picture
"v vs. t" MSGBOX                Announce upcoming plot v-vs-t
1 3 "t" "v" SCTPnm            Place data to plot using SCTPnm
DRAX LABEL PICTURE              Draw axes, labels, recall picture
"v vs. t" MSGBOX                Announce upcoming plot a-vs-t
1 4 "t" "a" SCTPnm            Place data to plot using SCTPnm
DRAX LABEL PICTURE              Draw axes, labels, recall picture
>>                              End program TPLOTS
```

Program PPLOTS (Phase portrait PLOTS, i.e., v-vs-x, a-vs-x, a-vs-v):

<<	Start program TPLOTS
"v vs. x" MSGBOX	Announce upcoming plot x-vs-t
2 3 "x" "v" SCTPnm	Place data to plot using SCTPnm
PICTURE	Recall picture (no axes or labels)
"a vs. x" MSGBOX	Announce upcoming plot v-vs-t
2 4 "x" "a" SCTPnm	Place data to plot using SCTPnm
PICTURE	Recall picture (no axes or labels)
"a vs. v" MSGBOX	Announce upcoming plot a-vs-t
3 4 "v" "a" SCTPnm	Place data to plot using SCTPnm
PICTURE	Recall picture (no axes or labels)
>>	End program TPLOTS

Sub-program SCTPnm (*SCaTterPlot* using columns *n* and *m* of ΣDAT)

<<	Start sub-program SCTPnm
→ n m sX sY	Get column numbers n,m, and labels
sX, sY	
<<	Start first sub-program within SCTPnm
(0, 0) # Ah sX sY 4 →LIST AXES	Load axes information for current plot
n XCOL m YCOL	Select n-th col. for x, m-th col. for y
MINΣ MAXΣ 2 →LIST	Min and max values in ΣDAT put in list
DUP EVAL n GET SWAP n GET SWAP XRNG	Set x-axis range from data in column n
EVAL m GET SWAP m GET SWAP YRNG	Set y-axis range from data in column m
SCATRPLOT	Select graph type as scatterplot
>>	End of first sub-program within SCTPnm

Example 1 – Plots time plots and phase portraits for the oscillatory motion: $x = 2e^{-t/10} \cdot \sin(t/20)$, for t = 0 to 30.

Use:

[GETΣ]	Start program to produce ΣDAT
'2*EXP(-t/10)*SIN(t/20)' [▼]	Enter expression for x(t)
0 [▼] 80 [▼] [ENTER]	Enter initial and final values of time

Wait about one minute to get the message box: | ΣDAT ready   . |

[OK]	Clears message box
[TPLOT]	Shows plots of functions
[OK]	To see the x-vs-t plot
[CANCL]	To move to next plot
[OK]	To see the v-vs-t plot
[CANCL]	To move to next plot
[OK]	To see the a-vs-t plot
[CANCL]	To end program TPLOT
[PPLOT]	Shows phase portraits
[OK]	To see the v-vs-x plot
[CANCL]	To move to next plot
[OK]	To see the a-vs-x plot
[CANCL]	To move to next plot
[OK]	To see the a-vs-v plot
[CANCL]	To end program TPLOT

The figures produced are shown below. The labels were added in the computer. In the calculator, the labels are shown before each plot.

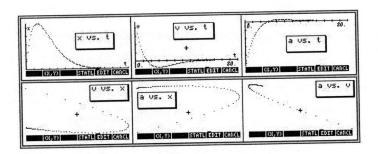

You can see from these plots that the x-vs-t plot shows one relatively large oscillation, and then x goes to zero. The v-vs-t and a-vs-t plots show the same trend. The phase portraits all show curve orbits that quickly go to a fixed point, reflecting the fact that x, v, and a go to zero after t > 70 or thereabouts.

Example 2 – Plot the time-dependent plots and phase portraits for the signal obtained in Example 1 in the previous section, i.e.,

$$x(t) = 7.142136 \exp(-0.05t) \cos(0.7053t +1.3592).$$

Use:

[GETΣ]	Start program to produce ΣDAT
'7.142136*EXP(-.05*t)*COS(.7053*t+1.3592)' [▼]	Enter expression for x(t)
0 [▼] 40 [▼] [ENTER]	Enter initial and final values of time

Wait about one minute to get the message box:

	ΣDAT ready .

[OK]	Clears message box
[TPLOT]	Shows plots of functions
[OK]	To see the x-vs-t plot
[CANCL]	To move to next plot
[OK]	To see the v-vs-t plot
[CANCL]	To move to next plot
[OK]	To see the a-vs-t plot
[CANCL]	To end program TPLOT
[PPLOT]	Shows phase portraits
[OK]	To see the v-vs-x plot
[CANCL]	To move to next plot
[OK]	To see the a-vs-x plot
[CANCL]	To move to next plot
[OK]	To see the a-vs-v plot
[CANCL]	To end program PPLOT

The plots generated in this exercise are shown in the figure below.

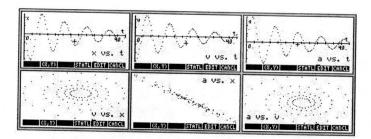

These figures depict a damped oscillation that produces a good number of oscillations before the amplitude becomes negligible. The figure for x-vs-t shows 4 complete oscillations for t < 40. The typical behavior of the damped oscillation is also shown in the v-vs-t and a-vs-t graphs. The phase portraits of v-vs-x and a-vs-v show orbits spiraling inwards towards the center of the picture, i.e., towards (0,0). This is because the amplitude of both variables included in the phase portrait decreases at about the same rate with time. The phase portrait a-vs-x shows data following a straight-line pattern, however, if you watch the plots being plotted, you will notice that the trend is also an inward spiral, although the extension of the spiral in space is quite narrow.

200

Applications of ODEs II : analysis of damped and undamped forced oscillations

Earlier we presented the analysis of damped and undamped free oscillations, meaning that, once the particle subjected to oscillatory motion is released, all forces acting on it are internal to the system, i.e., the restoring force of the spring, and the damping force from the dashpot. If the particle is continuously subjected to an external force (an excitation), then the type of oscillations thus generated are termed *forced oscillations*. Of interest are excitations that are themselves oscillatory. The simplest case will be an external force,

$$F_e(t) = F_o \cos \omega t.$$

The differential equation for the mass-spring-dashpot system, including the excitation, $F_e(t)$, is now written as:

$$d^2x/dt^2 + (\beta/m)\cdot(dx/dt)+(k/m)\cdot x = (F_o/m)\cdot\cos \omega t.$$

Let's assume that the values of the parameters m, b, and k are such that the solution of the homogeneous equation is

$$x_h(t) = A_o\cdot e^{-at}\cdot\cos(\omega_o\cdot t+\phi).$$

Also, because the term *cos ωt* shows up in the right-hand side term, the table for selecting the particular solution (shown earlier in this chapter), suggest that we try

$$x_p(t) = C_1 \cos \omega t + C_2 \sin \omega t.$$

Because this particular solution must satisfy the governing ODE, we can write

$$d^2x_p/dt^2 + (\beta/m)\cdot(dx_p/dt)+(k/m)\cdot x_p = (F_o/m)\cdot\cos \omega t.$$

Let's use the calculator to determine the values of C_1 and C_2 as follows (use $\omega0^2 = k/m$):

$$\text{'d1d1xp(t)+(b/m)*d1xp(t)+ }\omega0^2\text{*xp(t)' [ENTER]}$$
$$\text{'xp(t) = C1*COS(}\omega\text{*t)+C2*SIN(}\omega\text{*t)'[ENTER]}$$
$$[\rightarrow][\text{ALG}][\text{SUBST}].$$

The result is:

$$\text{'-(((}\beta\text{*}\omega\text{*C1-(m*}\omega0^2\text{- }\omega^2\text{*m)*C2)*SIN(}\omega\text{*t)-((m*}\omega0\text{-}\omega^2\text{*m)*C1+}\beta\text{*}\omega\text{*C2)*COS(}\omega\text{*t))/m)'}$$

This result must be equal to the right-hand side of the equation, which in the calculator would be written as:

$$\text{'F0/m*COS(}\omega\text{*t)'.}$$

Thus, the coefficients of SIN(ω*t) and COS(ω*t) in both sides of the equation should be the same, i.e.,

'-(β*ω*C1-(m*$\omega0^2$- ω^2*m)*C2)/m = 0'   [coefficients of SIN(ω*t)]
'((m*$\omega0$-ω^2*m)*C1+β*ω*C2)/m) = F0/m'   [coefficients of COS(ω*t)]

You can put together these two equations in the calculator by cutting and pasting terms from the result above, of just by typing the equations in the stack or using the equation writer. In any event, once you have the two equations in stack levels 1 and 2, as shown, enter:

2 [ENTER] [↰][PRG][TYPE][→ARRY].

This creates an array with the two equations for the coefficients of SIN and COS. Next, enter the array:

['C1' 'C2'][ENTER].

Finally, to solve the linear system of equations for C1 and C2, use:

[↰][S.SLV][LINSO]

The solution is:

{ ['C1= -((F0*m*ω^2-F0*ω0^2*m)/(ω^2*β^2+(m^2*ω^4-2*ω0*m^2*ω^2+ ω0^4*m^2)))'
'C2 = F0*ω*b/(ω^2*β^2+(m^2*ω^4-2*ω0*m^2*ω^2+ ω0^4*m^2))'] }

To decompose the list and the array from this result use:

[↱][EVAL][↰][PRG][TYPE][OBJ→][↰].

The expression for C2 should now be in stack level 1. To factor this expression, use the equation writer (press [▼]), highlight the last three terms in the denominator of the right hand-side of the equation, and press [FACTO]. Press [ENTER] when done. The equation has been simplified to:

'C2 = F0*ω*β/(ω^2*β^2+m^2*(ω0-ω)^2*(ω0+ ω)^2)', i.e.,

$$C_2 = \frac{F_0 \omega \beta}{\omega^2 \beta^2 + m^2 (\omega_0^2 - \omega^2)^2}.$$

Press [▶] to swap results, and [▼] to trigger the screen writer. Select first the numerator in the right-hand side of the equation, and press [FACTO]. Then, select the last three terms in the denominator, and press [FACTO]. The denominator is exactly the same as for C_1. Press [ENTER] when done. The expression gets simplified to:

'C1 = -(-(F0*m*(ω0^2-ω^2))/(ω^2*β^2+m^2*(ω0-ω)^2*(ω0+ ω)^2)', i.e.,

$$C_1 = \frac{F_0 m(\omega_0^2 - \omega^2)}{\omega^2 \beta^2 + m^2 (\omega_0^2 - \omega^2)^2}.$$

The particular solution can be written now as

$$x_p(t) = F_0 \cdot \frac{m(\omega_0^2 - \omega^2) \cdot \cos(\omega \cdot t) + \omega \beta \cdot \sin(\omega \cdot t)}{\omega^2 \beta^2 + m^2 (\omega_0^2 - \omega^2)^2}.$$

202

Suppose that we want to write this solution as

$$x_p(t) = A_p \cos (\omega t + \phi_p) = A_p \cos \omega t \cos \phi_p - A_p \sin \omega t \sin \phi_p,$$

by comparing the last two expressions we find that

$$A_p \cos \phi_p = F_0 m(\omega_0{}^2 - \omega^2)/[\ \omega^2\beta^2 + m^2\ (\omega_0{}^2 - \omega^2)\ ^2],$$

and

$$A_p \sin \phi_p = - F_0 \omega\beta/[\ \omega^2\beta^2 + m^2\ (\omega_0{}^2 - \omega^2)\ ^2],$$

from which,

$$A_p{}^2 = F_0{}^2/[\ \omega^2\beta^2 + m^2\ (\omega_0{}^2 - \omega^2)\ ^2],$$

and

$$\tan \phi_p = - \omega\beta/(m(\omega_0{}^2 - \omega^2)).$$

Thus, the particular solution can be written as:

$$x_p(t) = \frac{F_0}{\sqrt{\omega^2\beta^2 + m^2(\omega_0^2 - \omega^2)^2}} \cdot \cos(\omega \cdot t + \phi_p).$$

To analyze the behavior of this particular solution, first we study the case in which no damping is present, i.e., b = 0. In such case, ϕ_p = 0, and the particular solution becomes

$$x_p(t) = \frac{F_0}{m(\omega_0^2 - \omega^2)} \cdot \cos \omega \cdot t = \frac{F_0 /(m \cdot \omega_0)}{1 - (\omega / \omega_0)^2} \cdot \cos \omega \cdot t = A_p(\omega) \cdot \cos \omega \cdot t.$$

For this case, the amplitude of the oscillation, $A_p(\omega)$, becomes infinity as $\omega \to \omega_0$. This condition is known as _resonance_. Thus resonant conditions will occur if the exciting force has the same frequency as the natural frequency of the system. In practice, the amplitude of the undamped oscillations grows without bound until the system is severely damaged or destroyed. This is important for analyzing building response to earthquakes. Every building has a natural frequency of vibration. If a building is subjected for a long period of time to an earthquake with a frequency similar or equal to its natural frequency, the building may suffer severe damages as consequence of the earthquake.

If damping is present, then the amplitude of the oscillation is given by

$$A_p(\omega) = \frac{F_0}{\sqrt{\omega^2\beta^2 + m^2(\omega_0^2 - \omega^2)^2}},$$

which has a maximum

$$A_p(\omega) = \frac{2mF_0}{\beta\sqrt{4m^2\omega^2 - \beta^2}},$$

when

$$\beta^2 = 2m^2\ (\omega_0{}^2 - \omega^2).$$

203

Since the general solution of the damped equation,

$$x_h(t) = A_o \cdot e^{-at} \cdot \cos(\omega_b \cdot t + \phi),$$

decreases with time, it will eventually become negligible when compared to the particular solution. Thus, it is said that the general solution represents the _transient (temporary) response_ of the system to the exciting force, $F_e(t)$. The particular solution, which turns out to be a sinusoidal wave, represents _the steady-state response_ of the system.

The function DESOLVE

So far we have used the function LDEC to solve linear ordinary differential equations. The HP 49 G calculator provides the function DESOLVE (Differential Equation SOLVEr) to solve certain types of differential equations. The function requires as input the differential equation and the unknown function, and returns the solution to the equation if available. You can also provide a vector containing the differential equation and the initial conditions, instead of only a differential equation, as input to DESOLVE. The function DESOLVE is available in the menu [↰][CALC][DIFF]. Examples of DESOLVE applications are shown below.

Example 1 - Solve the first-order ODE:

$$dy/dx + x^2 \cdot y(x) = 5.$$

In the calculator use:

'd1y(x)+x^2*y(x)=5' [ENTER] 'y(x)' [ENTER] [↰][CALC][DIFF][DESOL].

The solution provided is {'y = (INT(5*EXP(xt^3/3),xt,x)+C0)*1/EXP(x^3/3))' }, i.e.,

$$y(x) = \exp(-x^3/3) \cdot \left(\int 5 \cdot \exp(x^3/3) \cdot dx + C_0 \right).$$

The variable ODETYPE

You will notice in the soft-menu key labels a new variable called [ODETY] (ODETYPE). This variable is produced with the call to the DESOL function and holds a string showing the type of ODE used as input for DESOLVE. Press [ODETY] to obtain the string "1st order linear".

Example 2 -- Solve the second-order ODE:

$$d^2y/dx^2 + x (dy/dx) = \exp(x).$$

In the calculator use:

'd1d1y(x)+x*d1y(x) = EXP(x)' [ENTER] 'y(x)' [ENTER] [↰][CALC][DIFF][DESOL].

The calculator responds with the message: <!> DESOLVE error: Unable to solve ODE.

This means that the calculator's CAS is not set to recognize this type of equations and provide a solution to them. For this particular equation, however, we realize that the left-hand side of the equation represents d/dx(x dy/dx), thus, the ODE is now written:

$$d/dx(x\, dy/dx) = \exp x,$$

and

$$x \, dy/dx = \exp x + C.$$

Next, we can write

$$dy/dx = (C + \exp x)/x = C/x + e^x/x.$$

In the calculator, you may try to integrate:

'd1y(x) = (C + EXP(x))/x' [ENTER] 'y(x)' [ENTER] [↰][CALC][DIFF][DESOL].

The result is   { 'y(x) = INT((EXP(xt)+C)/xt,xt,x)+C0' }, i.e.,

$$y(x) = \int \cdot \frac{e^x + C}{x} dx + C_0.$$

Performing the integration by hand, we can only get it as far as:

$$y(x) = \int \cdot \frac{e^x}{x} dx + C \cdot \ln x + C_0,$$

because the integral of exp(x)/x is not available in closed form.

Example 3 – Solving an equation with initial conditions.   Solve

$$d^2y/dt^2 + 5y = 2\cos(t/2),$$

with initial conditions

$$y(0) = 1.2, \ y'(0) = -0.5.$$

In the calculator, use:

['d1d1y(t)+5*y(t) = 2*COS(t/2)' 'y(0) = 6/5' 'd1y(0) = -1/2'][ENTER] 'y(t)'
[ENTER][↰][CALC][DIFF][DESOL].

Notice that the initial conditions were changed to their Exact expressions, 'y(0) = 6/5', rather than 'y(0)=1.2', and 'd1y(0) = -1/2', rather than, 'd1y(0) = -0.5'. If you don't make these changes, you will be asked to change to Approx mode, and then, the calculator will refuse to solve the differential equation under the argument that the result is not exact.   Just one of those quarks of the calculator.

The solution is:

{ 'y(t) = 8/19*COS(-1/2*t)+((19*(6/5)-8)/19*COS(√5*t)+ √5*(-1/2)/5*SIN(√5*t))' }.

Press [↱][EVAL][↱][EVAL] to simplify the result to

'y(t) = -((19*5*SIN(√5*t)-(148*COS(√5*t)+80*COS(t/2)))/190)'.

Press [VAR][ODETY] to get the string "Linear w/ cst coeff" for the ODE type in this case.

205

Laplace Transforms

The Laplace transform of a function f(t) produces a function F(s) in the image domain that can be utilized to find the solution of a linear differential equation involving f(t) through algebraic methods. The steps involved in this application are three:

1. Use of the Laplace transform converts the linear ODE involving f(t) into an algebraic equation.

2. The unknown F(s) is solved for in the image domain through algebraic manipulation.

3. An inverse Laplace transform is used to convert the image function found in step 2 into the solution to the differential equation f(t).

Definitions

The _Laplace transform_ for function f(t) is the function F(s) defined as

$$L\{f(t)\} = F(s) = \int_0^\infty f(t) \cdot e^{-st} dt.$$

The image variable s can be, and it generally is, a complex number.

Many practical applications of Laplace transforms involve an original function f(t) where t represents time, e.g., control systems in electric or hydraulic circuits. In most cases one is interested in the system response after time t>0, thus, the definition of the Laplace transform, given above, involves an integration for values of t larger than zero.

The _inverse Laplace transform_ maps the function F(s) onto the original function f(t) in the time domain, i.e.,

$$L^{-1}\{F(s)\} = f(t).$$

The _convolution integral_ or _convolution product_ of two functions f(t) and g(t), where g is shifted in time, is defined as

$$(f * g)(t) = \int_0^t f(u) \cdot g(t-u) \cdot du.$$

Laplace transform and inverses in the HP 49 G calculator

The HP 49 G calculator provides the functions LAP and ILAP to calculate the Laplace transform and the inverse Laplace transform, respectively, of a function f(VX), where VX is the CAS default independent variable (typically X). The calculator returns the transform or inverse transform as a function of X. The functions LAP and ILAP are available under the menu [↰][CALC][DIFF].

Example 1 - You can get the definition of the Laplace transform use the following:

'f(X)' [ENTER][←][CALC][DIFF][LAP]. The calculator returns the result:

'∫ (0, ∞,f($t)*EXP(-$t)*X,$t)'.

Press [▼] to activate the equation writer. The result is shown now as follows:

$$\int_0^\infty f(\$t)\text{EXP}(-(\$t\cdot X))d\$t$$

EDIT | CURS | BIG ■ | EVAL | FACTO | TEXPR

Compare this expression with the one given earlier in the definition of the Laplace transform,

$$L\{f(t)\} = F(s) = \int_0^\infty f(t)\cdot e^{-st}dt,$$

i.e.,

$$F(s) = L\{e^{2t}\cdot\sin t\} = \frac{1}{s^2 - 4\cdot s + 5}.$$

and you will notice that the CAS default variable X in the equation writer screen replaces the variable s in this definition. Therefore, when using the function LAP you get back a function of X, which is the Laplace transform of f(X).

Example 2 - Determine the Laplace transform of f(t) = e^{2t}·sin(t). Use:

'EXP(2*X)*SIN(X)' [ENTER] [←][CALC][DIFF][LAP]. The calculator returns the result:

'1/(X^2+(-4,0)*X+(5,0))'.

The terms (-4,0) and (5,0) are complex number representation of -4 and 5, respectively, therefore, you translate this result in paper as

Example 3 - Determine the inverse Laplace transform of F(s) = sin(s). Use:

'SIN(X)' [ENTER] [←][CALC][DIFF][ILAP].

The calculator returns the result: 'ILAP(SIN(X))', meaning that there is no closed-form expression f(t), such that f(t) = Λ⁻¹{sin(s)}.

Example 4 - Determine the inverse Laplace transform of F(s) = $1/s^3$. Use:

'1/X^3' [ENTER] [←][CALC][DIFF][ILAP]. The calculator returns the result: '.5*X^2', which is interpreted as

$$L^{-1}\{1/s^3\} = t^2/2.$$

Example 5 - Determine the Laplace transform of the function f(t) = cos (a·t+b). Use:

207

'COS(a*X+b)' [ENTER] [↰][CALC][DIFF][LAP]. The calculator returns the result:

$$\text{'-((a*SIN(b)-X*COS(b))/(X\^2+(1,0)*a\^2))'},$$

which is interpreted as:

$$\Lambda\{a\cdot t+b\} = (s\cdot \cos b - a\cdot \sin b)/(s^2+a^2).$$

Laplace transform theorems

To help you determine the Laplace transform of functions you can use a number of theorems, some of which are listed below. A few examples of the theorem applications are also included.

- _Differentiation theorem for the first derivative_. Let f_0 be the initial condition for $f(t)$, i.e., $f(0) = f_0$, then

$$L\{df/dt\} = s\cdot F(s) - f_0.$$

Example 1 - The velocity of a moving particle $v(t)$ is defined as $v(t) = dr/dt$, where $r = r(t)$ is the position of the particle. Let $r_0 = r(0)$, and $R(s) = L\{r(t)\}$, then, the transform of the velocity can be written as

$$V(s) = L\{v(t)\}=L\{dr/dt\}= s\cdot R(s)-r_0.$$

- _Differentiation theorem for the second derivative_. Let $f_0 = f(0)$, and $(df/dt)_0 = df/dt|_{t=0}$, then

$$L\{d^2f/dt^2\} = s^2\cdot F(s) - s\cdot f_0 - (df/dt)_0.$$

Example 2 - As a follow up to Example 1, the acceleration $a(t)$ is defined as $a(t) = d^2r/dt^2$. If the initial velocity is $v_0 = v(0) = dr/dt|_{t=0}$, then the Laplace transform of the acceleration can be written as:

$$A(s) = L\{a(t)\} = \Lambda\{d^2r/dt^2\}= s^2\cdot R(s) - s\cdot r_0 - v_0.$$

- _Differentiation theorem for the n-th derivative_. Let $f^{(k)}_0 = d^kf/dx^k|_{t=0}$, and $f_0 = f(0)$, then

$$L\{d^nf/dt^n\} = s^n\cdot F(s) - s^{n-1}\cdot f_0 -...- s\cdot f^{(n-2)}_0 - f^{(n-1)}_0.$$

- _Linearity theorem_. $\qquad\qquad L\{af(t)+bg(t)\} = a\cdot\Lambda\{f(t)\} + b\cdot\Lambda\{g(t)\}.$

- _Differentiation theorem for the image function_. Let $F(s) = L\{f(t)\}$, then $d^nF/ds^n = \Lambda\{(-t)^n\cdot f(t)\}$.

208

- *Integration theorem.* Let F(s) = Λ{f(t)}, then

$$L\left\{\int_0^t f(u)du\right\} = \frac{1}{s} \cdot F(s).$$

- *Convolution theorem.* Let F(s) = Λ{f(t)} and G(s) = Λ{g(t)}, then

$$L\left\{\int_0^t f(u)g(t-u)du\right\} = L\{(f * g)(t)\} = L\{f(t)\} \cdot L\{g(t)\} = F(s) \cdot G(s).$$

Example 4 - Using the convolution theorem, find the Laplace transform of (f*g)(t), if f(t) = sin(t), and g(t) = exp(t). To find F(s) = Λ{f(t)}, and G(s) = Λ{g(t)}, use:

'SIN(X)' [ENTER] [←][CALC][DIFF][LAP]. Result, '1/(X^2+1)', i.e., F(s) = 1/(s^2+1).

'EXP(X)' [ENTER] [←][CALC][DIFF][LAP]. Result, '1/(X-1)', i.e., G(s) = 1/(s-1).

Thus, Λ{(f*g)(t)} = F(s)·G(s) = 1/(s^2+1)·1/(s-1) = 1/((s-1)(s^2+1)) = 1/(s^3-s^2+s-1).

- *Shift theorem for a shift to the right.* Let F(s) = L{f(t)}, then L{f(t-a)}=e^{-as}·L{f(t)} = e^{-as}·F(s).

- *Shift theorem for a shift to the left.* Let F(s) = L{f(t)}, and a >0, then

$$L\{f(t+a)\} = e^{as} \cdot \left(F(s) - \int_0^a f(t) \cdot e^{-st} \cdot dt\right)$$

- *Similarity theorem.* Let F(s) = L{f(t)}, and a>0, then L{f(a·t)} = (1/a)·F(s/a).

- *Damping theorem.* Let F(s) = L{f(t)}, then L{e^{-bt}·f(t)} = F(s+b).

- _Division theorem_. Let F(s) = L{f(t)}, then

$$L\left\{\frac{f(t)}{t}\right\} = \int_s^\infty F(u)du.$$

- _Laplace transform of a periodic function of period T_:

$$L\{f(t)\} = \frac{1}{1-e^{-sT}} \cdot \int_0^T f(t) \cdot e^{-st} \cdot dt.$$

- _Limit theorem for the initial value_: Let F(s) = L{f(t)}, then

$$f_0 = \lim_{t\to 0} f(t) = \lim_{s\to\infty} [s \cdot F(s)].$$

- _Limit theorem for the final value_: Let F(s) = L{f(t)}, then

$$f_\infty = \lim_{t\to\infty} f(t) = \lim_{s\to 0} [s \cdot F(s)].$$

Dirac's delta function and Heaviside's step function

In the analysis of control systems it is customary to utilize a type of functions that represent certain physical occurrences such as the sudden activation of a switch (Heaviside's step function, H(t)) or a sudden, instantaneous, peak in an input to the system (Dirac's delta function, δ(t)). These belong to a class of functions known as _generalized or symbolic functions_ [e.g., see Friedman, B., 1956, _Principles and Techniques of Applied Mathematics_, Dover Publications Inc., New York (1990 reprint)].

The formal definition of **_Dirac's delta function_**, δ(x), is δ(x) = 0, for x ≠0, and

$$\int_{-\infty}^\infty \delta(x)dx = 1.0.$$

Also, if f(x) is a continuous function, then

$$\int_{-\infty}^\infty f(x)\delta(x-x_0)dx = f(x_0).$$

An interpretation for the integral above, paraphrased from Friedman (1990), is that the δ-function "picks out" the value of the function f(x) at x = x_0. Dirac's delta function is typically represented by an upward arrow at the point x = x0, indicating that the function has a non-zero value only at that particular value of x_0.

Heaviside's step function, H(x), is defined as

$$H(x) = \begin{cases} 1, & x > 0 \\ 0, & x < 0 \end{cases}$$

Also, for a continuous function f(x),

$$\int_{-\infty}^{\infty} f(x)H(x-x_0)dx = \int_{x_0}^{\infty} f(x)dx.$$

Dirac's delta function and Heaviside's step function are related by

$$dH/dx = \delta(x).$$

The two functions are illustrated in the figure below.

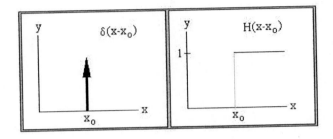

You can prove that

$$L\{H(t)\} = 1/s,$$

from which it follows that

$$L\{U_0 \cdot H(t)\} = U_0/s,$$

where U_0 is a constant. Also,

$$L^{-1}\{1/s\} = H(t),$$

and

$$L^{-1}\{U_0/s\} = U_0 \cdot H(t).$$

Also, using the shift theorem for a shift to the right, $\Lambda\{f(t-a)\} = e^{-as} \cdot \Lambda\{f(t)\} = e^{-as} \cdot F(s)$, we can write

$$L\{H(t-k)\} = e^{-ks} \cdot L\{H(t)\} = e^{-ks} \cdot (1/s) = (1/s) \cdot e^{-ks}.$$

Another important result, known as the _second shift theorem for a shift to the right_, is that

$$L^{-1}\{e^{-as} \cdot F(s)\} = f(t-a) \cdot H(t-a),$$

with $F(s) = L\{f(t)\}$.

In the HP 49 G calculator the Heaviside step function H(t) is simply referred to as '1'. To check the transform in the calculator use:

1 [ENTER] [↰][CALC][DIFF][LAP].

The result is '1/X', i.e.,

$$L\{1\} = 1/s.$$

Similarly,

'U0' [ENTER] [↰][CALC][DIFF][LAP],

produces the result 'U0/X', i.e.,

$$L\{U_0\} = U_0/s.$$

211

You can obtain Dirac's delta function in the HP 49 G calculator by using:

1 [ENTER] [↰][CALC][DIFF][ILAP].

The result is   'Delta(X)'.

This result is simply symbolic, i.e., you cannot find a numerical value for, say 'Delta(5)'.

This result can be defined the Laplace transform for Dirac's delta function, because from

$$L^{-1}\{1.0\} = \delta(t),$$

it follows that

$$L\{\delta(t)\} = 1.0$$

Also, using the shift theorem for a shift to the right, $L\{f(t-a)\} = e^{-as} \cdot L\{f(t)\} = e^{-as} \cdot F(s)$, we can write

$$L\{\delta(t-k)\} = e^{-ks} \cdot L\{\delta(t)\} = e^{-ks} \cdot 1.0 = e^{-ks}.$$

Applications of Laplace transform in the solution of linear ODEs

At the beginning of the section on Laplace transforms we indicated that you could use these transforms to convert a linear ODE in the time domain into an algebraic equation in the image domain. The resulting equation is then solved for a function F(s) through algebraic methods, and the solution to the ODE is found by using the inverse Laplace transform on F(s).

The theorems on derivatives of a function, i.e.,

$$L\{df/dt\} = s \cdot F(s) - f_o,$$

$$L\{d^2f/dt^2\} = s^2 \cdot F(s) - s \cdot f_o - (df/dt)_o,$$

and, in general,

$$L\{d^nf/dt^n\} = s^n \cdot F(s) - s^{n-1} \cdot f_o - \ldots - s \cdot f^{(n-2)}{}_o - f^{(n-1)}{}_o,$$

are particularly useful in transforming an ODE into an algebraic equation.

Example 1 - To solve the first order equation,

$$dh/dt + k \cdot h(t) = a \cdot e^{-t},$$

by using Laplace transforms, we can write:

$$L\{dh/dt + k \cdot h(t)\} = L\{a \cdot e^{-t}\},$$

$$L\{dh/dt\} + k \cdot \Lambda\{h(t)\} = a \cdot L\{e^{-t}\}.$$

> **Note:** 'EXP(-X)' [ENTER][↰][CALC][DIFF][LAP], produces '1/(X+1)', i.e., $L\{e^{-t}\} = 1/(s+1)$.

With $H(s) = L\{h(t)\}$, and $L\{dh/dt\} = s \cdot H(s) - h_o$, where $h_o = h(0)$, the transformed equation is

$$s \cdot H(s) - h_o + k \cdot H(s) = a/(s+1).$$

212

Use the calculator to solve for H(s), by writing:

'X*H-h0+k*H=a/(X+1)' [ENTER] 'H' [¬][S.SLV][ISOL].

The result is   'H=((X+1)*h0+a)/(X^2+(k+1)*X+k)'.

To find the solution to the ODE, h(t), we need to use the inverse Laplace transform, as follows:

[¬][PRG][TYPE][OBJ→][⇔][⇔]   Isolates right-hand side of last expression
[¬][CALC][DIFF][ILAP]   Obtains the inverse Laplace transform

The result is   'a/(k-1)*EXP(-X)+((k-1)*h0-a)/(k-1)*EXP(-(k*X))', i.e.,

$$h(t) = a/(k-1) \cdot e^{-t} + ((k-1) \cdot h_o - a)/(k-1) \cdot e^{-kt}.$$

Check what the solution to the ODE would be if you use the function LDEC:

'a*EXP(-X)' [ENTER] 'X+k' [ENTER] [¬][CALC][DIFF][LDEC]

The result is: 'a/(k-1)*EXP(-X)+((k-1)*C0-a)/(k-1)*EXP(-(k*X))', i.e.,

$$h(t) = a/(k-1) \cdot e^{-t} + ((k-1) \cdot C_o - a)/(k-1) \cdot e^{-kt}.$$

Thus, C0 in the results from LDEC represents the initial condition h(0).

Note: When using the function LDEC to solve a linear ODE of order n in f(X), the result will be given in terms of n constants C0, C1, C2, ..., C(n-1), representing the initial conditions f(0), f'(0), f''(0), ..., $f^{(n-1)}$ (0).

Example 2 - Use Laplace transforms to solve the second-order linear equation,

$$d^2y/dt^2 + 2y = \sin 3t.$$

Using Laplace transforms, we can write:

$$L\{d^2y/dt^2 + 2y\} = L\{\sin 3t\},$$

$$L\{d^2y/dt^2\} + 2 \cdot \Lambda\{y(t)\} = L\{\sin 3t\}.$$

Note: 'SIN(3*X)' [ENTER][¬][CALC][DIFF][LAP], produces '3/(X^2+9)', i.e., $L\{\sin 3t\}=3/(s^2+9)$.

With Y(s) = L{y(t)}, and $L\{d^2y/dt^2\} = s^2 \cdot Y(s) - s \cdot y_o - y_1$, where y_o = h(0) and y_1 = h'(0), the transformed equation is

$$s^2 \cdot Y(s) - s \cdot y_o - y_1 + 2 \cdot Y(s) = 3/(s^2+9).$$

Use the calculator to solve for Y(s), by writing:

'X^2*Y-X*y0-y1+2*Y=3/(X^2+9)' [ENTER] 'Y' [¬][S.SLV][ISOL].

The result is   'Y=((X^2+9)*y1+(y0*X^3+9*y0*X+3))/(X^4+11*X^2+18)'.

To find the solution to the ODE, y(t), we need to use the inverse Laplace transform, as follows:

213

[↰][PRG][TYPE][OBJ→][⇦][⇦]   Isolates right-hand side of last expression
[↰][CALC][DIFF][ILAP]   Obtains the inverse Laplace transform

The result is   '-1/7*SIN(3*X)+(y0*COS(√2*X)+(7*√2*y1+3*√2)/14*SIN(√2*X))', i.e.,

                       $y(t) = -(1/7) \sin 3x + y_o \cos \sqrt{2}x + (\sqrt{2}\,(7y_1+3)/14) \sin \sqrt{2}x.$

Check what the solution to the ODE would be if you use the function LDEC:

                'SIN(3*X)' [ENTER] 'X^2+2' [ENTER] [↰][CALC][DIFF][LDEC]

The result is: '-1/7*SIN(3*X)+(C0*COS(√2*X)+(7*√2*C1+3*√2)/14*SIN(√2*X))',

i.e., the same as before with C0 = y0 and C1 = y1.

Note: Using the two examples shown here, we can confirm what we indicated earlier, i.e., that the function ILAP uses Laplace transforms and inverse transforms to solve linear ODEs given the right-hand side of the equation and the characteristic equation of the corresponding homogeneous ODE.

Example 3 - Consider the equation

                                   $$d^2y/dt^2 + y = \delta(t-3),$$

where δ(t) is Dirac's delta function.

Using Laplace transforms, we can write:

                              $$L\{d^2y/dt^2 + y\} = L\{\delta(t-3)\},$$

                              $$L\{d^2y/dt^2\} + L\{y(t)\} = L\{\delta(t-3)\}.$$

Note: With 'Delta(t-3)' [ENTER][↰][CALC][DIFF][LAP], the calculator produces

                       '(0,∞,Delta($t-3)*EXP(-($t*X)),$t)', i.e.,

                       $$L\{\delta(t-3)\} = \int_0^\infty \delta(t-3) \cdot e^{-tX} \cdot dt.$$

The evaluation of the integral is not defined in the calculator. However, using the shift theorem for a shift to the right, can write

                                   $$L\{\delta(t-3)\} = e^{-3s}.$$

With Y(s) = L{y(t)}, and $\Lambda\{d^2y/dt^2\} = s^2 \cdot Y(s) - s \cdot y_o - y_1$, where $y_o = h(0)$ and $y_1 = h'(0)$, the transformed equation is

                              $$s^2 \cdot Y(s) - s \cdot y_o - y_1 + Y(s) = e^{-3s}.$$

Use the calculator to solve for Y(s), by writing:

                'X^2*Y-X*y0-y1+Y=EXP(-3*X)' [ENTER] 'Y' [↰][S.SLV][ISOL].

The result is   'Y=(X*y0+(y1+EXP(-(3*X))))/(X^2+1)'.

214

To find the solution to the ODE, y(t), we need to use the inverse Laplace transform, as follows:

[↰][PRG][TYPE][OBJ→][⇦][⇦]   Isolates right-hand side of last expression
[↰][CALC][DIFF][ILAP]   Obtains the inverse Laplace transform

The result is   'ILAP(X*y0+(y1+EXP(-(3*X))))/(X^2+1)'.

This means that the calculator threw its arms up and decided it can not find an inverse Laplace transform for the expression '(X*y0+(y1+EXP(-(3*X))))/(X^2+1)'. Let's see if we can help it by separating the expression into partial fractions, i.e.,

'y0*X/(X^2+1) + y1/(X^2+1) + EXP(-3*X)/(X^2+1)',

and use the linearity theorem of the inverse Laplace transform

$$L^{-1}\{a \cdot F(s)+b \cdot G(s)\} = a \cdot L^{-1}\{F(s)\} + b \cdot L^{-1}\{G(s)\},$$

to write,

$$L^{-1}\{y_0 \cdot s/(s^2+1)+y_1/(s^2+1)) + e^{-3s}/(s^2+1)) \} = y_0 \cdot L^{-1}\{s/(s^2+1)\}+ y_1 \cdot L^{-1}\{1/(s^2+1)\}+ L^{-1}\{e^{-3s}/(s^2+1))\},$$

Then, we use the calculator to obtain the following:

'X/(X^2+1)' [ENTER] [↰][CALC][DIFF][ILAP]. Result, 'COS(X)', i.e., $L^{-1}\{s/(s^2+1)\}$= cos t.
'1/(X^2+1)' [ENTER] [↰][CALC][DIFF][ILAP]. Result, 'SIN(X)', i.e., $L^{-1}\{1/(s^2+1)\}$= sin t.
'EXP(-3*X)/(X^2+1)' [ENTER] [↰][CALC][DIFF][ILAP].

The last result is 'ILAP(EXP(-3*X)/(X^2+1))', i.e., the calculator cannot find the inverse Laplace transform of this term.   In this case, however, we can use the symbolic result (second shifting theorem for a shift to the right)

$$L^{-1}\{e^{-as} \cdot F(s)\}=f(t-a) \cdot H(t-a),$$

if we can find an inverse Laplace transform for $1/(s^2+1)$. With the calculator, try

'1/(X^2+1)' [ENTER] [↰][CALC][DIFF][ILAP].

The result is '0.+1*SIN(X)', or, with [][EVAL], 'SIN(X)'.   Thus,

$$L^{-1}\{e^{-3s}/(s^2+1))\} = \sin(t-3) \cdot H(t-3),$$

Thus, the solution to the original ODE is to be written as:

$$y(t) = y_0 \cos t + y_1 \sin t + \sin(t-3) \cdot H(t-3).$$

Check what the solution to the ODE would be if you use the function LDEC:

'Delta(t-3)' [ENTER] 'X^2+1' [ENTER] [↰][CALC][DIFF][LDEC]

The result is: 'C0*COS(X)+(∫ (0,∞,Delta($t-3)*EXP(-($t*X)),$t)+C1)*SIN(X)'.

Please notice that the variable X in this expression actually represents the variable t in the original ODE, and that the variable $t in this expression is a dummy variable.

215

Thus, the translation of the solution in paper may be written as:

$$y(t) = Co \cdot \cos t + \left(\int_0^\infty \delta(u-3) \cdot e^{-ut} \cdot du + C_1 \right) \cdot \sin t.$$

When comparing this result with the previous result for y(t), we conclude that $C_o = y_o$, $C_1 = y_1$, and

$$L^{-1}\{ \frac{e^{-3s}}{s^2 + 1} \} = \int_0^\infty \delta(u-3) \cdot \sin t \cdot e^{-ut} \cdot du = \sin(t-3) \cdot H(t-3).$$

Defining and using Heaviside's step function in the HP 49 G calculator

The previous example provided some experience with the use of Dirac's delta function as input to a system (i.e., in the right-hand side of the ODE describing the system). In this example, we want to use Heaviside's step function, H(t). In the calculator we can define this function as:

'H(X) = IFTE(X>0, 1, 0)' [ENTER] [↰][DEF].

This definition will create the variable [H] in the calculator's soft menu key.

Example 1 -- To see a plot of H(t-2), for example, use the following:

- Press [↰][2D/3D], simultaneously to access to the PLOT SETUP window.

➢ Change TYPE to FUNCTION, if needed

➢ Change EQ to 'H(X-2)'.

➢ Make sure that Indep is set to 'X'.

➢ Press [NXT][OK] to return to normal calculator display.

- Press [↰][WIN], simultaneously, to access the PLOT window.

➢ Change the H-VIEW range to 0 to 20, and the V-VIEW range to -2 to 2.

➢ Press [ERASE][DRAW] to plot the function .

The resulting graph will look like this:

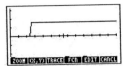

Unfortunately, use of the function H(X) with LDEC, LAP, or ILAP, is not allowed in the calculator. Thus, you have to use the main results provided earlier when dealing with the Heaviside step function, i.e.,

$$L\{H(t)\} = 1/s,$$

$$L^{-1}\{1/s\}=H(t),$$

$$L\{H(t-k)\}=e^{-ks}\cdot L\{H(t)\} = e^{-ks}\cdot(1/s) = \cdot(1/s)\cdot e^{-ks},$$

and

$$L^{-1}\{e^{-as}\cdot F(s)\}=f(t-a)\cdot H(t-a).$$

Example 2 -- The function $H(t-t_o)$ when multiplied to a function $f(t)$, i.e., $H(t-t_o)f(t)$, has the effect of switching on the function $f(t)$ at $t = t_o$. For example, the solution obtained in Example 3, above, was

$$y(t) = y_o \cos t + y_1 \sin t + \sin(t-3)\cdot H(t-3).$$

Suppose we use the initial conditions $y_o = 0.5$, and $y_1 = -0.25$. Let's plot this function to see what it looks like:

- Press [↩][2D/3D], simultaneously to access to the PLOT SETUP window.

➤ Change TYPE to FUNCTION, if needed

➤ Change EQ to '0.5*COS(X)-0.25*SIN(X)+SIN(X-3)*H(X-3)'.

➤ Make sure that Indep is set to 'X'.

➤ Press [ERASE][DRAW] to plot the function.

➤ Press [EDIT][NXT][LABEL] to see the plot.

217

The resulting graph will look like this:

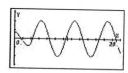

Notice that the signal starts with a relatively small amplitude, but suddenly, at t=3, it switches to an oscillatory signal with a larger amplitude. The difference between the behavior of the signal before and after t = 3 is the "switching on" of the particular solution $y_p(t)$ = sin(t-3)·H(t-3). The behavior of the signal before t = 3 represents the contribution of the homogeneous solution, $y_h(t)$ = y_o cos t + y_1 sin t.

The solution of an equation with a driving signal given by a Heaviside step function is shown below.

Example 3 - Determine the solution to the equation,

$$d^2y/dt^2 + y = H(t-3),$$

where H(t) is Heaviside's step function.

Using Laplace transforms, we can write:

$$L\{d^2y/dt^2 + y\} = L\{H(t-3)\},$$

$$L\{d^2y/dt^2\} + L\{y(t)\} = L\{H(t-3)\}.$$

The last term in this expression is:

$$L\{H(t-3)\} = (1/s)·e^{-3s}.$$

With Y(s) = L{y(t)}, and $L\{d^2y/dt^2\}$ = s^2·Y(s) - s·y_1 - y_1, where y_o = h(0) and y_1 = h'(0), the transformed equation is

$$s^2·Y(s) - s·y_o - y_1 + Y(s) = (1/s)·e^{-3s}.$$

Use the calculator to solve for Y(s), by writing:

'X^2*Y-X*y0-y1+Y=(1/X)*EXP(-3*X)' [ENTER] 'Y' [¬][S.SLV][ISOL].

The result is   'Y=(X^2*y0+(X*y1+EXP(-3*X)))/(X^3+X)'.

To find the solution to the ODE, y(t), we need to use the inverse Laplace transform, as follows:

[¬][PRG][TYPE][OBJ→][⇔][⇔]   Isolates right-hand side of last expression
[¬][CALC][DIFF][ILAP]   Obtains the inverse Laplace transform

The result is   'ILAP((X^2*y0+(X*y1+EXP(-3*X)))/(X^3+X))'.

This means that the calculator can not find an inverse Laplace transform for the expression separate the expression into partial fractions, i.e.,

'y0*X^2/(X^3+X) + y1*X/(X^3+X) + EXP(-3*X)/(X^3+X)',

and, use the calculator to obtain the following:

218

'X^2/(X^3+X)' [ENTER] [↵][CALC][DIFF][ILAP]. Result, 'COS(X)', i.e., $\Lambda^{-1}\{s^2/(s^3+s)\}=\cos t$.
'X/(X^3+X)' [ENTER] [↵][CALC][DIFF][ILAP]. Result, 'SIN(X)', i.e., $\Lambda^{-1}\{s/(s^3+s)\}=\sin t$.
          'EXP(-3*X)/(X^3+X)' [ENTER] [↵][CALC][DIFF][ILAP].

The last result is 'ILAP(EXP(-3*X)/(X^3+X))', i.e., the calculator cannot find the inverse Laplace transform of this term. Using the function PARTFRAC we can decompose the term X/(X^3+X) into '1/X-X/(X^2-1)', therefore, 'EXP(-3*X)/(X^3+X)' is decomposed into 'EXP(-3*X)/X - X*EXP(-3*X)/(X^2-1)'. However, use of ILAP on these terms will not produce a solution either. Thus, the solution to the original ODE is to be written as:

$$y(t) = y_0 \cos t + y_1 \sin t + \Lambda^{-1}\{ e^{-3s}/s \} + \Lambda^{-1}\{ e^{-3s}/(s^2+1)\}.$$

We recognize $\Lambda^{-1}\{ e^{-3s}/s \} = H(t-3)$, and $\Lambda^{-1}\{e^{-3s}/(s^2+1)\}= H(t-3)\cdot\sin(t-3)$. The remaining terms is similar to that found earlier in Example 4 in the previous section. Thus, we write as the solution:

$$y(t) = y_0 \cos t + y_1 \sin t + H(t-3)\cdot(1+\sin(t-3)).$$

Check what the solution to the ODE would be if you use the function LDEC:

          'H(t-3)' [ENTER] 'X^2+1' [ENTER] [↵][CALC][DIFF][LDEC]

The result is: 'C0*COS(X)+(∫ (0,∞,H($t-3)*EXP(-($t*X)),$t)+C1)*SIN(X)'.

Please notice that the variable X in this expression actually represents the variable t in the original ODE, and that the variable $t in this expression is a dummy variable. Thus, the translation of the solution in paper may be written as:

$$y(t) = Co \cdot \cos t + C_1 \cdot \sin t + \int_0^\infty H(u-3)\cdot \sin t \cdot e^{-ut} \cdot du.$$

Example 4 - Plot the solution to Example 3 using the same values of y_0 and y_1 used in the plot of Example 1, above. We now plot the function

$$y(t) = 0.5 \cos t - 0.25 \sin t + (1+\sin(t-3))\cdot H(t-3).$$

In the range 0 < t < 20, and changing the vertical range to (-1,3), the graph should look like this:

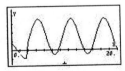

Again, there is a new component to the motion switched at t=3, namely, the particular solution

$$y_p(t) = [1+\sin(t-3)]\cdot H(t-3),$$

which changes the nature of the solution for t>3.

219

The Heaviside step function can be combined with a constant function and with linear functions to generate square, triangular, and sawtooth finite pulses, as follows:

- Square pulse of size U_o in the interval $a < t < b$:

$$f(t) = Uo[H(t-a)-H(t-b)].$$

- Triangular pulse with a maximum value Uo, increasing from $a < t < b$, decreasing from $b < t < c$:

$$f(t) = U_o \cdot ((t-a)/(b-a) \cdot [H(t-a)-H(t-b)]+(1-(t-b)/(b-c))[H(t-b)-H(t-c)]).$$

- Sawtooth pulse increasing to a maximum value Uo for $a < t < b$, dropping suddenly down to zero at $t = b$:

$$f(t) = U_o \cdot (t-a)/(b-a) \cdot [H(t-a)-H(t-b)].$$

- Sawtooth pulse increasing suddenly to a maximum of Uo at $t = a$, then decreasing linearly to zero for $a < t < b$:

$$f(t) = U_o \cdot [1-(t-a)/(b-1)] \cdot [H(t-a)-H(t-b)].$$

Examples of the plots generated by these functions, for Uo = 1, a = 2, b = 3, c = 4, x-range = (0,5), and y-range = (-1, 1.5), are shown in the figures below:

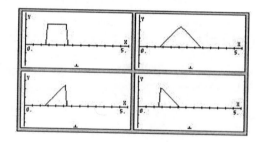

Fourier Series

Fourier series are series involving sine and cosine functions that are typically used to expand periodic functions. A function f(x) is said to be _periodic_, of period T, if f(x+T) = f(t). For example, because sin(x+2π) = sin x, and cos(x+2π) = cos x, the functions *sin* and *cos* are 2π-periodic functions. If two functions f(x) and g(x) are periodic of period T, then their linear combination h(x) = a·f(x) + b·g(x), is also periodic of period T.

A T-periodic function f(t) can be expanded into a series of sine and cosine functions known as a Fourier series given by

$$f(t) = a_0 + \sum_{n=1}^{\infty} \left(a_n \cdot \cos\frac{2n\pi}{T}t + b_n \cdot \sin\frac{2n\pi}{T}t \right)$$

where the coefficients a_n and b_n are given by

$$a_0 = \frac{1}{T}\int_{-T/2}^{T/2} f(t)\cdot dt, \quad a_n = \frac{2}{T}\int_{-T/2}^{T/2} f(t)\cdot\cos\frac{2n\pi}{T}t\cdot dt, \quad b_n = \frac{2}{T}\int_{-T/2}^{T/2} f(t)\cdot\sin\frac{2n\pi}{T}t\cdot dt.$$

Example 1 - Suppose that the function f(t) = t^2+t is periodic with period T = 2. Determine the coefficients a_0, a_1, and b_1 for the corresponding Fourier series.

Define f(t) as:

'f(t) = t^2+t' [ENTER] [↤][DEF]

Then, to calculate a_0, use: '(1/2)*∫(−1,1,f(t),t)' [ENTER] [→][EVAL]   Result: a_0 = 1/3.
To calculate a_1, use: '∫(−1,1,f(t)*COS(π*t),t)' [ENTER] [→][EVAL]   Result: a_1 = -4/π^2.
To calculate b_1, use: '∫(−1,1,f(t)*SIN(π*t),t)' [ENTER] [→][EVAL]   Result: b_1 = 2/π.

Thus, the first three terms of the function are:

$$f(t) \approx 1/3 - (4/\pi^2)\cdot\cos(\pi t) + (2/\pi)\cdot\sin(\pi t).$$

A graphical comparison of the original function with the Fourier expansion using these three terms shows that the fitting is acceptable for t < 1, or thereabouts. But, then, again, we stipulated that T/2 = 1. Therefore, the fitting is valid only between -1 < t < 1.

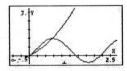

An alternative way to define a Fourier series is by using complex numbers as follows:

$$f(t) = \sum_{n=-\infty}^{+\infty} c_n \cdot \exp(\frac{2in\pi t}{T}),$$

where

$$c_n = \frac{1}{T} \int_0^T f(t) \cdot \exp(\frac{2 \cdot i \cdot n \cdot \pi}{T} \cdot t) \cdot dt, \quad n = -\infty, \dots, -2, -1, 0, 1, 2, \dots \infty.$$

The function FOURIER

The function FOURIER provides the coefficient c_n of the complex-form of the Fourier series given the function f(t) and the value of n. The function FOURIER requires you to store the value of the period (T) of a T-periodic function into the CAS variable PERIOD before calling the function. The function FOURIER is available in the menu [←][CALC][DERIV].

Example 1 -- Determine the coefficients c_0, c_1, and c_2 for the function f(t) = t^2+t, with period T = 2.

Note: Because the integral calculating the coefficients with the function FOURIER is calculated in the interval [0,T], while the one defined earlier was calculated in the interval [-T/2,T/2], we need to shift the function in the t-axis, by subtracting T/2 from t, i.e., we will use g(t) = f(t-1) = $(t-1)^2$+(t-1).

Using the calculator:

'g(t) = f(t-1)' [ENTER] [←][DEF]
2 [ENTER] [→]['] [ALPHA][ALPHA][P][E][R][I][O][D] [ENTER] [STO▶]
'g(X)' [ENTER] 0 [ENTER] [←][CALC][DERIV][FOURI]
[→][EVAL].

The result is $a_0 = 1/3$.

To calculate the coefficient c_1, we use:

'g(X)' [ENTER] 1 [ENTER] [←][CALC][DERIV][FOURI]
[→][EVAL].

The result is $a_1 = (\pi i + 2)/\pi^2$.

To calculate the coefficient c_2, use:

'g(X)' [ENTER] 2 [ENTER] [←][CALC][DERIV][FOURI]
[→][EVAL]..

The result is $a_2 = (\pi i + 1)/(2\pi^2)$.

The Fourier series with three elements will be written as

g(t) ≈ Re[(1/3) + $(\pi i + 2)/\pi^2 \cdot$exp(i·πt)+ $(\pi i + 1)/(2\pi^2) \cdot$exp(2·i·πt)].

222

A plot of the shifted function g(t) and the Fourier series fitting follows:

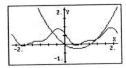

The fitting is somewhat acceptable for 0<t<2, although not as good as in the previous example.

A general expression for c_n

The function FOURIER can provide a general expression for the coefficient c_n of the complex Fourier series expansion. For example, using the same function g(t) as before, the general term c_n is given by

'g(X)' [ENTER]'n' [ENTER] [↰][CALC][DERIV][FOURI]
[↱][EVAL].

The general expression turns out to be:

$$c_n = \frac{(n\pi + 2i)\cdot e^{2in\pi} + 2i^2 n^2 \pi^2 + 3n\pi - 2i}{2n^3 \pi^3 \cdot e^{2in\pi}}.$$

We can simplify this expression even further by using Euler's formula for complex numbers, namely,

$$e^{2in\pi} = \cos(2n\pi) + i\cdot\sin(2n\pi) = 1 + i\cdot 0 = 1,$$

since $\cos(2n\pi) = 1$, and $\sin(2n\pi) = 0$, for n integer.
Using the calculator you can simplify the expression as follows:

[▼]	Trigger the equation writer
[▼][▼][▼][▼][▼][▼][►][►][►][►][▲][▲][▲]	Highlight the term EXP(2·i·n·π)
[1]	Replace EXP(2·i·n·π) with 1
[►][►][►] ... [►][►][►] (17 times)[▲][▲][▲]	Highlight the term EXP(2·i·n·π)
[1]	Replace EXP(2·i·n·π) with 1
[▲][▲][▲]	Highlight the entire expression
[EVAL]	Simplify the expression
[ENTER]	Return to normal calculator display

The result is now

$$c_n = (i\cdot n\cdot\pi + 2)/(n^2\cdot\pi^2).$$

223

Putting together the complex Fourier series

Having determined the general expression for c_n, we can put together a finite complex Fourier series by using the summation function (Σ) in the calculator as follows:

- First, define a function c(n) representing the general term c_n in the complex Fourier series.

[ALPHA] [↰][C] [↰] [( )] [ALPHA] [↰][N] [ENTER]	Type in 'c(n)'
[▶] [↦][=]	Swap levels, insert equal sign
[↰][DEF]	Define function c(n) = c_n

  This operation creates a variable [c] in the soft-menu key.

- Next, define the finite complex Fourier series, F(X, k), where X is the independent variable and k determines the number of terms to be used. Ideally we would like to write this finite complex Fourier series as

$$F(X,k) = \sum_{n=-k}^{k} c(n) \cdot \exp(\frac{2 \cdot i \cdot \pi \cdot n}{T} \cdot X),$$

However, because the function c(n) is not defined for n = 0, we will be better advised to re-write the expression as

$$F(X,k,c0) = c0 + \sum_{n=1}^{k} [c(n) \cdot \exp(\frac{2 \cdot i \cdot \pi \cdot n}{T} \cdot X) + c(-n) \cdot \exp(-\frac{2 \cdot i \cdot \pi \cdot n}{T} \cdot X)],$$

[EQW]	Start the equation writer
[ALPHA][F] [↰][( )] [X] [SPC] [ALPHA][↰][K]	Type in F(X,k....
[SPC][ALPHA][↰][C][0][▶] [↦][=]	Type in c0 =
[ALPHA][↰][C][0] [+]	Type in c0 +
[↦][Σ] [ALPHA][↰][N] [▶] [1]	Type in Σ, n = 1 (lower limit)
[▶] [ALPHA][↰][K]	Type in upper limit of sum
[▶] [↰][( )]	Open parentheses in summation
[ALPHA] [↰][C] [↰] [( )] [ALPHA] [↰][N] [▶] [×]	Type in c(n)*
[↰][e^x][2] [×] [↰][i] [×] [↰][π] [×][ALPHA] [↰][N] [×] [X]	Type in EXP(2·i·π·n·X...
[▲][▲] [÷] [ALPHA][ALPHA][P][E][R][I][O][D]	Type in /PERIOD
[▶][▶][▶] [+]	Type in +
[ALPHA] [↰][C] [↰] [( )] [+/-] [ALPHA][↰][N] [▶][▶] [×]	Enter c(n)*
[↰][e^x] [2] [×] [↰][i] [×] [↰][π] [×][ALPHA] [↰][N] [×] [X]	Enter EXP(2·i·π·n·X...
[▲][▲] [+/-] [÷] [ALPHA][ALPHA][P][E][R][I][O][D]	Enter /PERIOD
[ENTER]	

The stack now shows the function:

'F(X,k,c0) = c0+Σ(n=1,k,c(n)*EXP(2*i*π*n*X/PERIOD)+c(-n)*EXP(-(2*i*π*n*X/PERIOD)))'.

To define the function use: [↰][DEF].

This operation creates the variable [F].

The function [F] can be used to generate the expression for the complex Fourier series for a finite value of k. For example, for k = 2, c_0 = 1/3, and using t as the independent variable, use:

$$\text{'t' [ENTER] 2 [ENTER] '1/3' [VAR][F]}$$

Be warned that the calculator will take some time in returning a result due to the number of operations involved.

The result will look like this in the equation writer:

$$\frac{1}{3} + \frac{(0.2026, 0.3183) \cdot EXP\left(\frac{(0., 6.2832) \cdot t}{2}\right)^2 + (.2026, -0.3183)}{EXP\left(\frac{(0., 6.2832) \cdot t}{2}\right)}$$

$$+ \frac{(5.066E - 2, 0.1591) EXP\left(\frac{(0., 12.56) \cdot t}{2}\right)^2 + (5.066E - 2, -0.1591)}{EXP\left(\frac{(0., 12.56) \cdot t}{2}\right)}$$

This result can be written in paper as

$$\frac{1}{3} + (0.2026 + 0.3183 \cdot i) \cdot EXP(i \cdot \pi \cdot t) + (.2026 - 0.3183 \cdot i) \cdot EXP(-i \cdot \pi \cdot t)$$

$$+ (0.05066 + 0.1591 \cdot i) \cdot EXP(i \cdot 2 \cdot \pi \cdot t) + (0.05066 - 0.1591 \cdot i) \cdot EXP(-i \cdot 2 \cdot \pi \cdot t).$$

Since we are interested in the real function that results from the complex Fourier series, we want to modify the program [F] to produce only the real part of the function as follows:

[VAR][↱][F][▼]	Copy contents of F to stack, start editor
[↱][▼][◀] [↱][EVAL]	Evaluate F(X,k,c0), if possible
[↰][MTH][NXT][CMPLX][RE]	Get real part of result
[ENTER]	Enter modified expression in stack level 1
[↰][F]	Store new definition of F

The function F, thus defined, is fine for obtaining values of the finite Fourier series. For example, a single value of the series, e.g., F(0.5,2,1/3), can be obtained by using:

$$\text{0.5 [ENTER] 2 [ENTER] '1/3' [ENTER] [VAR][F]}$$

Accept change to Approx mode if requested. The result is the value -0.40467....

I should point out that the function generated with F(X,k,c0) evaluates too slowly for the purpose of generating tables or graphics. Therefore, I suggest creating the following programs to generate finite Fourier series.

A program to calculate a finite Fourier series

Instead of using the program F(X,k,c0) defined above, we will use the following program:

Program FReal (Fourier series *Real* component):

<<	Start program FReal
→ X k c0	Enter values X, k, c_0
<<	Start first sub-program within FReal
c0	Place value c0 in stack
1 k FOR n	Start FOR loop for n = 1,2, ..., k
'c(n)' EVAL 'EXP(i*2*π*n*X/PERIOD)' EVAL * RE	Get real part of $c_n \cdot \exp(i2\pi nX/T)$
'c(-n)' EVAL 'EXP(-i*2*π*n*X/PERIOD)' EVAL * RE	Get real part of $c_n \cdot \exp(-i2\pi nX/T)$
+ +	Add terms in series
NEXT	End FOR loop (n)
EVAL	Simplify result
>>	End first sub-program within FReal
>>	End program FReal

The program requires that you have previously determined the values of c0 and c(n), as shown earlier.

Example 1 -- Just to check the results produced by FReal(X,k,c0), use;

0.5 [ENTER] 2 [ENTER] '1/3' [ENTER] [VAR][FReal]

The result is the value -0.40467.

The actual value of the function g(0.5) is: 0.5 [ENTER] [g   ], i.e., g(0.5) = -0.25. The following calculations show how well the Fourier series approximates this value as the number of components in the series, given by k, increases:

k=0, the only component in the series is c_0 = 0.3333333333
k = 1, Use: 0.5 [ENTER] 1 [ENTER] '1/3' [ENTER] [FReal], FReal(0.5, 1, 1/3) = -0.303286439037
k = 2, Use: 0.5 [ENTER] 2 [ENTER] '1/3' [ENTER] [FReal], FReal(0.5, 2, 1/3) = -0.404607622677
k = 3, Use: 0.5 [ENTER] 3 [ENTER] '1/3' [ENTER] [FReal], FReal(0.5, 3, 1/3) = -0.192401031887
k = 4, Use: 0.5 [ENTER] 4 [ENTER] '1/3' [ENTER] [FReal], FReal(0.5, 4, 1/3) = -0.16707073598
k = 5, Use: 0.5 [ENTER] 5 [ENTER] '1/3' [ENTER] [FReal], FReal(0.5, 5, 1/3) = -0.294394690454
k = 6, Use: 0.5 [ENTER] 6 [ENTER] '1/3' [ENTER] [FReal], FReal(0.5, 6, 1/3) = -0.305652599744

Of course, as k increases so does the time that the calculator takes to produce a result.

226

A program to visualize Fourier series approximations for a fixed value of the independent variable

The following program will produce a table of values of the Fourier series for a fixed value of X as k increases. The table is placed in the statistical matrix ΣDAT, and can be plot using a scatterplot graph.

Program FAppx (Fourier series Approximation):

<<	Start program FAppx
→ X k c0	Enter values of X, k, c_0
<<	Start first sub-program within FAppx
0 c0 1 2 2 →LIST →ARRY DUP STOΣ →ROW	Set first row of ΣDAT
k FOR n	Start FOR loop with n = 1, 2, ..., k
1	Place a 1 in the stack
'c(n)' EVAL 'EXP(i*2*π*n*X/PERIOD)' EVAL * RE	Get real part of $c_n \cdot \exp(i2\pi nX/T)$
'c(-n)' EVAL 'EXP(-i*2*π*n*X/PERIOD)' EVAL * RE	Get real part of $c_n \cdot \exp(-i2\pi nX/T)$
+ EVAL	Calculate next term in series
2 →ARRY + DUP RCLΣ SWAP n 1 + ROW+	Set row (n+1) of ΣDAT
STOΣ	Store new ΣDAT
NEXT	End FOR loop (n)
DROP "ΣDAT Ready" MSGBOX	Announce end of program
>>	End first sub-program within FApprx
>>	End sub-program FApprx

To check your program enter the following:

0.5 [ENTER] 3 [ENTER] '1/3'[→][→NUM] [ENTER] [FAppx].

After about 30 seconds you will get a message indicating that SDAT is ready. Press [OK]. Press [ΣDAT] to see the contents of the statistics matrix:

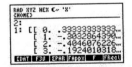

The following table shows the values of the Fourier series approximation F(0.5) corresponding to the function g(0.5). These values were obtained by using the program FAppx, with

0.5 [ENTER] 30 [ENTER] '1/3'[→][→NUM] [ENTER] [FAppx].

It took the calculator approximately 5 minutes to obtain these results:

n	F(0.5)	n	F(0.5)	n	F(0.5)
1	-0.3032	11	-0.2253	21	-0.2639
2	-0.4046	12	-0.2225	22	-0.2648
3	-0.1924	13	-0.2714	23	-0.2371
4	-0.1671	14	-0.2735	24	-0.2364
5	-0.2944	15	-0.2311	25	-0.2619
6	-0.3056	16	-0.2295	26	-0.2625
7	-0.2147	17	-0.2669	27	-0.2389
8	-0.2084	18	-0.2681	28	-0.2384
9	-0.2791	19	-0.2347	29	-0.2604
10	-0.2831	20	-0.2337	30	-0.2608

To see how the values of F(0.5) converges to the value g(0.5) = 0.25 using the data in SDAT for n = 30, select the command SCATTERPLOT from the catalog. To see the resulting graph, press [◄]. Here is a graph of the values of F(0.5) vs. n:

The graph shows the value of F(0.5) following a sort of damped oscillatory behavior while approaching the value of 0.25. From the table, you can see that the approximation, even after 30 terms in the series, is only -0.2608.

Plotting the Fourier series approximation

To plot the Fourier series approximation and the original function in the same graph we need to use a FUNCTION plot with EQ holding the list of functions { 'FReal(X,5,0.333333)' 'g(X)'}. In this case we are using n = 5. Remember that the higher the value of n you select the longer it will take to the graph to be generated. Also, when the calculator starts plotting the graphs you will see no output for about 40 seconds, while it calculates the series. Therefore, be patient while the calculator completes those steps The following graph shows the original function g(X) = (X-1)^2+(X-1), and its Fourier series approximation for n = 5. The plot ranges used were (-0.5,2.0) in x, and (-0.5,2.0) in y.

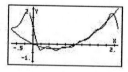

As you can see from this figure, there is good agreement between the two functions for 0<X<2, which is the period of the function under consideration.

228

Example: Fourier series approximation for a triangular periodic function

In this section we repeat the process used earlier to produce the Fourier series expansion for

$$g(x) = (x-1)^2+(x-1),$$

but this time applied to the 2-period function:

$$g(x) = \begin{cases} x, & \text{if } 0 < x < 1 \\ 2-x, & \text{if } 1 < x < 2 \end{cases}$$

First, we enter the period T = 2 into variable PERIOD, and define the function g(X) by using:

2 [ENTER] [ALPHA][ALPHA][P][E][R][I][O][D] [STO▶]
'g(X) = IFTE(X<1,X,2-X)' [ENTER] [↤][DEF]

Next, we generate c_0, by using:

'g(X)' [ENTER] 0 [ENTER] [↤][CALC][DERIV][FOURI] [↦][EVAL]

You will be asked to change mode to Approx. The result is $c_0 = 0.5$.

Change CAS mode back to Exact by using: -105 [ALPHA][ALPHA][C][F][ENTER]

The next step is to obtain a general expression for c_n as follows:

'g(X)' [ENTER] 'n' [ENTER] [↤][CALC][DERIV][FOURI]

You will be asked to change mode to Approx. Accept the change. The calculator produces the symbolic integral:

'0.5*∫ (0,2,IFTE(Xt<1,Xt,-(2-Xt))/EXP((0,1)*n*Xt*3.14159265359),Xt)'.

Change mode once more to exact by using:

-105 [ALPHA][ALPHA][C][F][ENTER],

and evaluate the integral with:[↦][EVAL].

The calculator simply repeats the symbolic integral replacing the dummy variable Xt with Xtt.

Basically, what the calculator is telling us is that it cannot produce a close-form expression for c_n for this function g(X). We will have to re-define the value of c_n by setting up the integral ourselves as follows:

$$\frac{1}{2} \cdot \left(\int_0^1 \frac{X}{EXP\left(\dfrac{i \cdot 2 \cdot n \cdot \pi \cdot X}{PERIOD}\right)} \cdot dX + \int_1^2 \frac{2-X}{EXP\left(\dfrac{i \cdot 2 \cdot n \cdot \pi \cdot X}{PERIOD}\right)} \cdot dX \right)$$

On the stack, this integral will look like this:

'1/2*(∫ (0,1,X/EXP(i*2*n*π*X/PERIOD),X)+ ∫ (0,1,X/EXP(i*2*n*π*X/PERIOD),X)))'.

Making sure that you set your CAS mode back to Exact, press [→][EVAL], and give the calculator about a minute, to produce the result:

'-(((EXP(i*n*π)-2)*EXP(2*i*n*π)+EXP(i*n*π))/(2*n^2*π^2*EXP(i*n*π)*EXP(2*i*n*π)))'.

This expression can be simplified further by using the fact that

EXP(2*i*n*π) = 1, and EXP(i*n*π) = (-1)^n.

These replacements can be performed within the equation writer by highlighting the corresponding term, e.g., EXP(i*n*π), and typing [←][( )] [1][+/-][▶][y^x][ALPHA][←][N]. The result, after simplification, is:

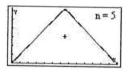

Use this expression to define c_n as the function:

'c(n) = -((-1)^n-1)/(n^2*π^2*(-1)^n)' [ENTER] [←][DEF].

To plot the Fourier series approximation, with n = 5 and c0 = 0.5, and the original function, store the list of functions

{ 'FReal(X,5,0.5)' 'g(X)'}

into variable EQ. Use the plot ranges (0,2) in x, and (0,1) in y. Remember that the calculator will produce no activity for the first 20 or 30 seconds. Here is the comparison of the two graphs with n = 5:

As you can see from the graph, the agreement between the two functions is excellent. The figure below shows the comparison between g(X) and its finite Fourier series approximation for

230

n = 2 and n = 3. You can see that even n = 2 produces an excellent fitting of the original function.

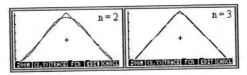

To verify that the Fourier series approximation indeed generates a periodic function, plot the function F(X,3,0.5) changing the x-range to (-2,4). The result is:

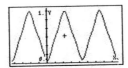

Example: Fourier series approximation for a square wave

This time we produce the Fourier series expansion for the square wave of period 4 defined by:

$$g(x) = \begin{cases} 0, & \text{if } 0 < x < 1 \\ 1, & \text{if } 1 < x < 3 \\ 0, & \text{if } 3 < x < 4 \end{cases}$$

First, we enter the period T = 3 into variable PERIOD, and define the function g(X) by using:

2 [ENTER] [ALPHA][ALPHA][P][E][R][I][O][D] [STO▶]
'g(X) = IFTE((X>1) AND (X<3),1,0)' [ENTER] [←][DEF]

Because g(X) is zero for X<1 and X>3, we can write our own expressions for c_0 and c_n as follows:

For c_0:

$$\frac{1}{T} \cdot \left(\int_1^3 1 \cdot dX \right)$$

In the calculator, this integral will be written as:

'1/PERIOD*(∫ (0,1,1,X))'.

Press [→][EVAL] to obtain c_0 = 1/2.

For c_n:

$$\frac{1}{T} \cdot \left(\int_1^3 EXP\left(-\frac{i \cdot 2 \cdot n \cdot \pi \cdot X}{T} \right) \cdot dX \right)$$

231

On the stack, this integral will look like this:

'1/PERIOD*($\int$ (0,1,EXP(-i*2*n*π*X/PERIOD),X))'.

Press [↵][EVAL][↵][↵] to obtain

c_n = '(-(i*EXP(3*i*n*π/2))+i*EXP(i*n*π/2))/(2*n*π*EXP(i*n*π/2)*EXP(3*i*n*π/2))'.

This expression could be simplified further if we can find a way to express

$$EXP(3 \cdot i \cdot n \cdot \pi/2) = \cos(3 \cdot n \cdot \pi/2) + i \cdot \sin(3 \cdot n \cdot \pi/2) = 0 + i \cdot \sin(3 \cdot n \cdot \pi/2) = i \cdot \sin(3 \cdot n \cdot \pi/2)$$

and

$$EXP(i \cdot n \cdot \pi/2) = = \cos(n \cdot \pi/2) + i \cdot \sin(n \cdot \pi/2) = 0 + i \cdot \sin(n \cdot \pi/2) = i \cdot \sin(n \cdot \pi/2).$$

One possibility is to use the fact that $3 \cdot n \cdot \pi/2 = n \cdot \pi + n \cdot \pi/2$, and write

$$\sin(3 \cdot n \cdot \pi/2) = \sin(n \cdot \pi + n \cdot \pi/2) = \sin(n \cdot \pi) \cdot \cos(n \cdot \pi/2) + \cos(n \cdot \pi) \cdot \sin(n \cdot \pi/2) = 0 \cdot \cos(n \cdot \pi/2) + (-1)^n \cdot \sin(n \cdot \pi/2),$$

i.e.,

$$\sin(3 \cdot n \cdot \pi/2) = (-1)^n \cdot \sin(n \cdot \pi/2),$$

and

$$EXP(3 \cdot i \cdot n \cdot \pi/2) = (-1)^n \cdot i \cdot \sin(n \cdot \pi/2).$$

Thus, the expression for c_n is (somewhat) simplified to

c_n = '(-(((-1)^n*i^2*SIN(n*π/2))+i^2*SIN(n*π/2))/(2*n*π*i*SIN(n*π/2)*(-1)^n*i*SIN(n*π/2))' =

'i^2*SIN(n*π/2)*(-(-1)^n+1)/((-1)^n*i^2*2*n*π*SIN(n*π/2)^2)' =

'-((-1)^n+1)/((-1)^n *2*n*π*SIN(n*π/2))',

i.e.,

$$c_n = \frac{1 - (-1)^n}{2 \cdot n \cdot \pi \cdot (-1)^n \cdot \sin(n \cdot \pi/2)}.$$

The simplified result, within the equation writer, is given by:

$$\frac{-\left((-1)^n - 1\right)}{2 \cdot n \cdot \pi \cdot (-1)^n \cdot \text{SIN}\left(\frac{n \cdot \pi}{2}\right)}$$

EDIT CURS BIG EVAL FACTO TEXPN

Notice that, when n is even, both the numerator and denominator of this expression become zero, i.e., we get an undetermined form. Also, we did not simplified the expression more by trying to evaluate $\sin(n \cdot \pi/2)$, since this expression takes the values 0, 1, 0, -1, 0, 1, 0, -1, etc., as n = 0, 1, 2, 3, 4, 5, 6, 7, etc.

232

Because the only values that are define correspond to odd numbers (besides, n = 0, of course), we can re-write the general expression for c_n by replacing n = 2m-1, with m = 1, 2, 3, 4, ..., etc. Because n or m are dummy variables in the Fourier series expansion, we can simply replace n with '2*n-1', so that the expression now reads:

$$\frac{-\left((-1)^{(2 \cdot n-1)}-1\right)}{2 \cdot (2 \cdot n-1) \cdot \pi \cdot (-1)^{(2 \cdot n-1)} \cdot \text{SIN}\left(\frac{(2 \cdot n-1) \cdot \pi}{2}\right)}$$

Use this expression to define c_n for positive values of n as the function:

'cp(n) = -((-1)^(2*n-1)-1)/(2*(2*n-1)^2*π*(-1)^(2*n-1)*SIN((2*n-1)*π/2)' [ENTER] [↵][DEF].

A similar expression needs to be defined for c_n corresponding to negative values of n, i.e.,

'cn(n) = -((-1)^(2*n+1)-1)/(2*(2*n+1)^2*π*(-1)^(2*n+1)*SIN((2*n+1)*π/2)' [ENTER] [↵][DEF].

We will have to modify the program that calculates the function *FReal*, by introducing cp(n) and cn(n), and by replacing n with (2*n-1) and (-2*+1) in the complex EXP functions within the program as shown below. Let's call the resulting program *FOdd*. The new program should read:

```
<< → X k c0 << c0 RE 1 k FOR n 'cp(n)' EVAL 'EXP(i*2*π*(2*n-1)*X/PERIOD)' EVAL * RE
   'cn(-n)' EVAL 'EXP(-i*2*π*(-2*n+1)*X/PERIOD)' EVAL * RE + + NEXT    EVAL    >> >>
```

To plot the Fourier series approximation, with n = 3 and c0 = 0.5, and the original function, store the list of functions
                    { 'FOdd(X,3,0.5)' 'g(X)'}

into variable EQ. Use the plot ranges (-0.5,4.5) in x, and (-0.5,1.5) in y. Remember that the calculator will produce no activity for the first 20 or 30 seconds. Here is the comparison of the two graphs with n = 3:

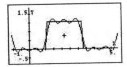

Notice that even for n = 3 the Fourier series approximation captures the general behavior of the square wave. There is no way to hide the oscillatory behavior of the Fourier series, in particular the small peaks near the sharp corners of the square wave. Such overshooting (or undershooting) near sharp corners is known as the *Gibss phenomenon*, and is a very well known feature of Fourier series approximations.

233

The following figure shows the approximation to the square wave using n = 10 in the Fourier series expansion. The fitting is much better than the previous example where only n = 3 was used. Still, the Gibbs phenomenon is observable near the sharp corners of the square wave.

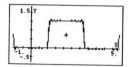

Fourier series applications in differential equations

Example 1 – Suppose we want to use the periodic square wave defined in the previous example as the excitation of an undamped spring-mass system whose homogeneous equation is:

$$d^2y/dX^2 + 0.25y = 0.$$

We can generate the excitation force by obtaining an approximation with n =3 out of the Fourier series, FOdd(X,n,0.5) by using:

'X' [ENTER] 3 [ENTER] 0.5 [ENTER] [FOdd]X

The result (using Approx and Complex modes) is a function of X. We can use this result as the first input to the function LDEC when used to obtain a solution to the system

$$d^2y/dX^2 + 0.25y = SquareWave(X)$$

Where *SquareWave*(X) is the function currently in the stack. The second input line will be the characteristic equation corresponding to the homogeneous ODE shown above, i.e.,

'X^2+0.25' [ENTER]

With these two lines of input available in the stack, obtain a solution to the non-homogeneous ODE by using:

[↰][CALC][DIFF][LDEC].

The result is a function of X involving integration constants C0 and C1. Assuming that C0 = 0.5 and C1 = -0.5, we can substitute these values in the expression in the stack by using:

'C0 = 0.5'[ENTER] [↱][ALG][SUBST]   'C1=-0.5' [ENTER] [SUBST] [↱][EVAL].

Next, to define this solution as a function h(X), use:

'h(X)' [ENTER][▶][↱][=] [↰][DEF].

This definition produces the variable [h] in the soft-menu keys. The definition needs to be modified by adding, at the very end of the program, the function RE, since we are interested only in the real part of the complex result. Once this modification has been made, you can proceed to produce a graph of the function.

Plot the function h(X) using a x-range of (0, 100) and a y-range of (-1,6). The result is the following graph:

234

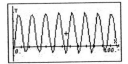

Example 2 - Suppose that we use the triangular periodic function defined earlier as the excitation to a damped spring-mass system whose homogeneous equation is given by:

$$d^2y/dX^2 + 0.1 \cdot (dy/dX) + 0.5 \cdot y = 0.$$

Recall that for the triangular periodic function, PERIOD = 2, $c0 = 1/3$, and

$$\text{'c(n)} = -((-1)^\wedge n-1)/(n^\wedge 2 \cdot \pi^\wedge 2 \cdot (-1)^\wedge n)\text{'}.$$

We can generate the excitation force by obtaining an approximation with n = 3 out of the Fourier series, FReal(X,n,0.333333333) by using:

'X' [ENTER] 3 [ENTER] 1[ENTER] [÷] [ENTER] [FReal]

The result (using `Approx` and `Complex` modes) is a complicated function of X We can use this result as the first input to the function LDEC when used to obtain a solution to the system

$$d^2y/dX^2 + 0.1 \cdot (dy/dX) + 0.5 \cdot y = TriangularWave(X)$$

where *TriangularWave*(X) is the function currently in the stack. The second input line will be the characteristic equation corresponding to the homogeneous ODE shown above, i.e.,

'X^2+0.1*X+0.5' [ENTER]

With these two lines of input available in the stack, obtain a solution to the non-homogeneous ODE by using:
[↰][CALC][DIFF][LDEC].

Given the complexity of the right-hand side of the ODE, it will take the calculator a couple of minutes to solve this equation. The result is a function of X involving integration constants C0 and C1. Assuming that the system is at rest and at its equilibrium position at t = 0, then C0 = 0 and C1 = 0, we can substitute these values in the expression in the stack by using:

'C0 = 0'[ENTER] [↦][ALG][SUBST]   'C1= 0' [ENTER] [SUBST] [↦][EVAL].

This solution involves complex numbers. Once more, due to the complexity of the function, it will take the

Next, to define this solution as a function h(X), use:

'h(X)' [ENTER][▶][↦][=] [↰][DEF].

235

This definition produces the variable [h] in the soft-menu keys, taking about another minute to finish. The definition needs to be modified by adding, at the very end of the program, the function RE, since we are interested only in the real part of the complex result.

Note: Solution of ODEs using Fourier series expansions as driving functions may result in too long a process for the HP 49 G, as illustrated below. Although the calculator has the ability to solve the equation and produce graphics of the solution, the time involved in producing the data for such plots may be more than you are willing to invest in plotting the solution. Cases like this may call for the use of a computer.

The graphs of the function presented below were produced using the programs GETΣ, TPLOT, and PPLOT in sub-directory PPORT (Phase PORTraits). It took about 30 minutes to generate the matrix ΣDAT with GETΣ. This is due to the fact that the function h(t) involves a large number of operations. Thus, if you have 20 minutes to check the results in your calculator, proceed (at your own risk) as follows:

- Copy function [f] into sub-directory PPORT

- Generate the matrix ΣDAT using: [GETΣ] 'h(t)' [▼] 0 [▼] 20 [ENTER]. Wait for about 30 minutes.

- Press [→][ΣDAT][▼] to see the contents of the matrix ΣDAT. Press [ENTER] when done.

- Press [TPLOT] to get the plots x-vs-t, v-vs-t, and a-vs-t.

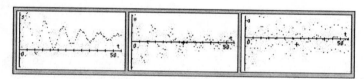

- Press [PPLOT] to get the phase portraits v-vs-x, a-vs-x, and a-vs-v.

Solutions to some specific second-order equations

In this section we present and solve specific types of ordinary differential equations whose solutions are defined in terms of some classical functions, e.g., Bessel's functions, Hermite polynomials, etc.

The Cauchy or Euler equation

An equation of the form

$$x^2 \cdot (d^2y/dx^2) + a \cdot x \cdot (dy/dx) + b \cdot y = 0,$$

where a and b are real constants, is known as the Cauchy or Euler equation. A solution to the Cauchy equation can be found by assuming that

$$y(x) = x^n.$$

In the HP 49 G calculator, type the equation as:

'x^2*d1d1y(x)+a*x*d1y(x)+b*y(x)=0' [ENTER]

Then, type and substitute the suggested solution:

'y(x) = x^n'[ENTER] [↵][ALG][SUBST]

The result is:

'x^2*(n*(x^(n-1-1)*(n-1)))+a*x*(n*x^(n-1))+b*x^n =0

which simplifies to

'n*(n-1)*x^n+a*n*x^n+b*x^n = 0'.

Dividing by x^n, results in an auxiliary algebraic equation:

'n*(n-1)+a*n+b = 0',

or

$$n^2 + (a-1) \cdot n + b = 0.$$

- If the equation has two different roots, say n_1 and n_2, then the general solution of this equation is

$$y(x) = K_1 \cdot x^{n_1} + K_2 \cdot x^{n_2}.$$

- If $b = (1-a)^2/4$, then the equation has a double root $n_1 = n_2 = n = (1-a)/2$, and the solution turns out to be

$$y(x) = (K_1 + K_2 \cdot \ln x)x^n.$$

237

Legendre's equation

An equation of the form

$$(1-x^2) \cdot (d^2y/dx^2) - 2 \cdot x \cdot (dy/dx) + n \cdot (n+1) \cdot y = 0,$$

where n is a real number, is known as the Legendre's differential equation. Any solution for this equation is known as a Legendre's function. When n is a nonnegative integer, the solutions are called Legendre's polynomials. Legendre's polynomial of order n is given by

$$P_n(x) = \sum_{m=0}^{M} (-1)^m \cdot \frac{(2n-2m)!}{2^n \cdot m! \cdot (n-m)! \cdot (n-2m)!} \cdot x^{n-2m}$$

$$= \frac{(2n)!}{2^n \cdot (n!)^2} \cdot x^n - \frac{(2n-2)!}{2^n \cdot 1! \cdot (n-1)!(n-2)!} \cdot x^{n-2} + \ldots - \ldots$$

where M = n/2 or (n-1)/2, whichever is an integer.

Legendre's polynomials are pre-programmed in the HP 49 G calculator and can be recalled by using the function LEGENDRE given the order of the polynomial, n. The function LEGENDRE can be obtained from the command catalog ([CAT]) or through the menu: [←][ARITH][POLY][NXT][NXT][LEGEN]. The first six Legendre polynomials are obtained as follows:

0 [ENTER][LEGEN], result: 1,   i.e, $P_0(x) = 1.0$.
1 [ENTER][LEGEN], result: 'X',   i.e, $P_1(x) = x$.
2 [ENTER][LEGEN], result: '(3*X^2-1)/2',   i.e, $P_2(x) = (3x^2-1)/2$.
3 [ENTER][LEGEN], result: '(5*X^3-3*X)/2',   i.e, $P_3(x) = (5x^3-3x)/2$.
4 [ENTER][LEGEN], result: '(35*X^4-30*X^2+3)/8',   i.e, $P_4(x) = (35x^4-30x^2+3)/8$.
5 [ENTER][LEGEN], result: '(63*X^5-70*X^3+15*X)/8',   i.e, $P_5(x) = (63x^5-70x^3+15x)/8$.

Plots of these five polynomials can be obtained by defining the functions:

'P0(X) = 1'	[ENTER][←][DEF]
'P1(X) = X'	[ENTER][←][DEF]
'P2(X) = (3*X^2-1)/2'	[ENTER][←][DEF]
'P3(X) = (5*X^3-3*X)/2'	[ENTER][←][DEF]
'P4(X) = (35*X^4-30*X^2+3)/8''	[ENTER][←][DEF]
'P5(X) = (63*X^5-70*X^3+15*X)/8'	[ENTER][←][DEF]

Store the list { 'P0(X)' 'P1(X)' 'P2(X)' 'P3(X)' 'P4(X)' 'P5(X)' }into variable EQ. Check that the independent variable is X, and set your X-range to (-1,1) and your Y-range to (-1.1,1.1). The resulting plot is:

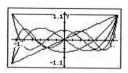

The ODE $$(1-x^2) \cdot (d^2y/dx^2) - 2 \cdot x \cdot (dy/dx) + [n \cdot (n+1) - m^2/(1-x^2)] \cdot y = 0,$$

has for solution the function $y(x) = P_n{}^m(x) = (1-x^2)^{m/2} \cdot (d^m Pn/dx^m)$.

This function is referred to as an associated Legendre function.

Bessel's equation

The ordinary differential equation

$$x^2 \cdot (d^2y/dx^2) + x \cdot (dy/dx) + (x^2 - v^2) \cdot y = 0,$$

where the parameter v is a nonnegative real number, is known as Bessel's differential equation.   Solutions to Bessel's equation are given in terms of *Bessel functions of the first kind of order v*:

$$J_v(x) = x^v \cdot \sum_{m=0}^{\infty} \frac{(-1)^m \cdot x^{2m}}{2^{2m+v} \cdot m! \, \Gamma(v+m+1)},$$

where v is not an integer, and the function Gamma $\Gamma(\alpha)$ is defined as

$$\Gamma(\alpha) = \int_0^{\infty} e^{-t} t^{\alpha-1} dt.$$

Gamma and di-gamma functions

The *Gamma function* was introduced in Chapter ... in relation to continuous probability distributions. It was shown in that Chapter that the Gamma function is related to the factorial function for $\alpha = n$ integer as:

$$\Gamma(n+1) = n!, \text{ or } \Gamma(n) = (n-1)!.$$

While this relationship applies to integer values, in the HP 49 G calculator it has been generalized to apply to any real number. Therefore, the Gamma function in the HP 49 G is calculated by using the factorial function, which is available in the menu: [↰][MTH][NXT][PROB].

Related to the Gamma function is the *di-gamma function*, defined as the derivative of the

$$\psi(z) = d[\ln \Gamma(z)]/dz = \Gamma'(z)/\Gamma(z),$$

which can be calculated in the HP 49 G calculator by using the calculator function Psi (available through the command catalog [CAT]). For example, to calculate $\psi(2)$ use:

2 [ENTER][CAT][ALPHA][P] (... find Psi...)[OK].

The result is 'Psi(2)', or with [↱][→NUM], 0.422784885098.

If $v = n$, an integer, the *Bessel functions of the first kind for n = integer* are defined by

239

$$J_n(x) = x^n \cdot \sum_{m=0}^{\infty} \frac{(-1)^m \cdot x^{2m}}{2^{2m+n} \cdot m! (n+m)!}.$$

Regardless of whether we use n (non-integer) or n (integer) in the HP 49 G calculator, we can define the Bessel functions of the first kind by using the following finite series:

$$J(x,n,k) = x^n \cdot \sum_{m=0}^{k} \frac{(-1)^m \cdot x^{(2 \cdot m)}}{2^{(2 \cdot m + n)} \cdot m! (n+m)!}$$

Thus, we have control over the function's order, n, and of the number of elements in the series, k. Once you have typed this function, you can press [ENTER] to get it in the stack, and use [←][DEF] to define the function. This will create the variable [J   ] in the soft-menu keys. For example, to evaluate $J_3(0.1)$ using 5 terms in the series, use:

0.1 [ENTER] 3 [ENTER] 5 [ENTER] [J   ].

The result is 2.08203157E-5.

If you want to obtain an expression for $J_0(x)$ with, say, 5 terms in the series, use:

'x' [ENTER] 0 [ENTER] 5 [ENTER] [J   ]

The result is

'1-0.25*x^3+0.015625*x^4-4.3403777E-4*x^6+6.782168E-6*x^8-6.78168*x^10'.

The following plot was obtained by using 10 terms in the series:

'x' [ENTER] 0 [ENTER] 10 [ENTER] [J   ]

You can define this expression as the function $J_0(x)$, by using:

'J0(x)' [ENTER] [▶] [↱][=] [←][DEF].

Plot this function using:

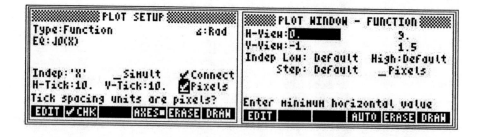

The result is:

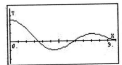

For non-integer values v, the solution to the Bessel equation is given by

$$y(x) = K_1 \cdot J_v(x) + K_2 \cdot J_{-v}(x).$$

For integer values, the functions $J_n(x)$ and $J_{-n}(x)$ are linearly dependent, since

$$J_n(x) = (-1)^n \cdot J_{-n}(x),$$

therefore, we cannot use them to obtain a general function to the equation. Instead, we introduce the *Bessel functions of the second kind* defined as

$$Y_v(x) = [J_v(x) \cos v\pi - J_{-v}(x)]/\sin v\pi,$$

for non-integer v, and for n integer, with n > 0, by

$$Y_n(x) = \frac{2}{\pi} \cdot J_n(x) \cdot (\ln\frac{x}{2} + \gamma) + \frac{x^n}{\pi} \cdot \sum_{m=0}^{\infty} \frac{(-1)^{m-1} \cdot (h_m + h_{m+n})}{2^{2m+n} \cdot m!(m+n)!} \cdot x^{2m}$$

$$- \frac{x^{-n}}{\pi} \cdot \sum_{m=0}^{n-1} \frac{(n-m-1)!}{2^{2m-n} \cdot m!} \cdot x^{2m}$$

where γ is the so-called *Euler constant*, defined by

$$\gamma = \lim_{r \to \infty}[1 + \frac{1}{2} + \frac{1}{3} + ... + \frac{1}{r} - \ln r] \approx 0.57721566490...,$$

and h_m represents the harmonic series

$$h_m = 1 + \frac{1}{2} + \frac{1}{3} + ... + \frac{1}{m}.$$

For the case n = 0, the Bessel function of the second kind is defined as

$$Y_0(x) = \frac{2}{\pi} \cdot \left[J_0(x) \cdot (\ln\frac{x}{2} + \gamma) + \sum_{m=0}^{\infty} \frac{(-1)^{m-1} \cdot h_m}{2^{2m} \cdot (m!)^2} \cdot x^{2m} \right].$$

With these definitions, a general solution of Bessel's equation for all values of v is given by

$$y(x) = K_1 \cdot J_v(x) + K_2 \cdot Y_v(x).$$

241

In some instances, it is necessary to provide complex solutions to Bessel's equations by defining *the Bessel functions of the third kind of order v* as

$$H_n^{(1)}(x) = J_v(x)+i \cdot Y_v(x), \text{ and } H_n^{(2)}(x) = J_v(x)-i \cdot Y_v(x),$$

These functions are also known as *the first and second Hankel functions of order v*.

In some applications you may also have to utilize the so-called *modified Bessel functions of the first kind of order v* defined as $I_v(x) = i^v \cdot J_v(i \cdot x)$, where i is the unit imaginary number. These functions are solutions to the differential equation

$$x^2 \cdot (d^2y/dx^2) + x \cdot (dy/dx) - (x^2+v^2) \cdot y = 0.$$

The modified Bessel functions of the second kind,

$$K_v(x) = (\pi/2) \cdot [I_{-v}(x) - I_v(x)]/\sin v\pi,$$

are also solutions of this ODE.

You can implement functions representing Bessel's functions in the HP 49 G calculator in a similar manner to that used to define Bessel's functions of the first kind, but keeping in mind that the infinite series in the calculator need to be translated into a finite series.

Chebyshev or Tchebycheff polynomials

The functions

$$T_n(x) = \cos(n \cdot \cos^{-1} x), \text{ and } U_n(x) = \sin[(n+1) \cos^{-1} x]/(1-x^2)^{1/2},$$

n = 0, 1, ... are called *Chebyshev or Tchebycheff polynomials of the first and second kind*, respectively. The polynomials Tn(x) are solutions of the differential equation

$$(1-x^2) \cdot (d^2y/dx^2) - x \cdot (dy/dx) + n^2 \cdot y = 0.$$

In the HP 49 G calculator the function TCHEBYCHEFF generates the Chebyshev or Tchebycheff polynomial of the first kind of order n, given a value of n > 0. If the integer n is negative (n < 0), the function TCHEBYCHEFF generates a Tchebycheff polynomial of the second kind of order n whose definition is

$$U_n(x) = \sin(n \cdot \arccos(x))/\sin(\arccos(x)).$$

You can access the function TCHEBYCHEFF through the command catalog ([CAT]).

The first four Chebyshev or Tchebycheff polynomials of the first and second kind are obtained as follows:

0 [ENTER] [CAT] (TCHEBYCHEFF) [OK], result: 1,	i.e,	$T_0(x) = 1.0$.
-0 [ENTER] [CAT] (TCHEBYCHEFF) [OK], result: 1,	i.e,	$U_1(x) = 1.0$.
1 [ENTER] [CAT] (TCHEBYCHEFF) [OK], result: 'X',	i.e,	$T_1(x) = x$.
-1 [ENTER] [CAT] (TCHEBYCHEFF) [OK], result: 1,	i.e,	$U_1(x) = 1.0$.
2 [ENTER] [CAT] (TCHEBYCHEFF) [OK], result: '2*X^2-1,	i.e,	$T_2(x) = 2x^2-1$.
-2 [ENTER] [CAT] (TCHEBYCHEFF) [OK], result: '2*X',	i.e,	$U_2(x) = 2x$.
3 [ENTER] [CAT] (TCHEBYCHEFF) [OK], result: '4*X^3-3*X',	i.e,	$T_3(x) = 4x^3-3x$.
-3 [ENTER] [CAT] (TCHEBYCHEFF) [OK], result: '4*X^2-1',	i.e,	$U_3(x) = 24x^2-1$.

242

Laguerre's equation

Laguerre's equation is the second-order, linear ODE of the form

$$x \cdot (d^2y/dx^2) + (1-x) \cdot (dy/dx) + n \cdot y = 0.$$

Laguerre polynomials, defined as

$$L_0(x) = 1, \quad L_n(x) = \frac{e^x}{n!} \cdot \frac{d^n(x^n \cdot e^{-x})}{dx^n}, \, n = 1,2,\ldots$$

are solutions to Laguerre's equation. Laguerre's polynomials can also be calculated with:

$$L_n(x) = \sum_{m=0}^{n} \frac{(-1)^m}{m!} \cdot \binom{n}{m} \cdot x^m = 1 - n \cdot x + \frac{n(n-1)}{4} \cdot x^2 - \ldots + \ldots + \frac{(-1)^n}{n!} \cdot x^n.$$

The term

$$\binom{n}{m} = \frac{n!}{m!(n-m)!} = C(n,m)$$

is the m-th coefficient of the binomial expansion $(x+y)^n$. It also represents the number of combinations of n elements taken m at a time. This function is available in the HP 49 G calculator by using:

[←][MTH][NXT][PROB][COMB]

You can define the following function to calculate Laguerre's polynomials:

$$L(x,n) = \sum_{m=0}^{n} \frac{(-1)^m}{m!} \cdot COMB(n,m) \cdot x^m$$

When done typing it in the equation writer press [ENTER] and [←][DEF]. This will create the variable
[L]. To generate the first four Laguerre polynomials use:

'x' [SPC] 0 [ENTER][L], result: 1,   i.e, $L_0(x) = 1.0$.
'x' [SPC] 1 [ENTER][L], result: '1-x',   i.e, $L_1(x) = 1-x$.
'x' [SPC] 2 [ENTER][L], result: '1-2*x+5*x^2',   i.e, $L_2(x) = 1-$
$2x+5x^2$.
'x' [SPC] 3 [ENTER][L], result: '1-3x+1.5x^2-0.1666*x^3',   i.e, $L_3(x) = 1-3x+(3/2)x^2-$
$x^3/6$.

Weber's equation and Hermite polynomials

Weber's equation is defined as

$$d^2y/dx^2 + (n+1/2 - x^2/4)y = 0,$$

For n = 0, 1, 2, ... A particular solution of this equation is given by the function

$$y(x) = \exp(-x^2/4)H^*(x/\sqrt{2}),$$

where the function $H^*(x)$ is the Hermite polynomial:

$$H_0^* = 1, \quad H_n^*(x) = (-1)^n e^{x^2} \frac{d^n}{dx^n}(e^{-x^2}), \quad n = 1,2,...$$

In the HP 49 G calculator, the function HERMITE, available through the menu

$$[\hookleftarrow][\text{ARITH}][\text{POLY}][\text{NXT}][\text{HERMI}],$$

as argument an integer number, n, and returns the Hermite polynomial of n-th degree. For example, the first four Hermite polynomials are obtained by using:

0 [ENTER][HERMI], result: 1,   i.e., $H_0^* = 1$.
1 [ENTER][HERMI], result: '2*X',   i.e., $H_1^* = 2x$.
2 [ENTER][HERMI], result: '4*X^2-2', i.e., $H_2^* = 4x^2-2$.
3 [ENTER][HERMI], result: '8*X^3-12*X', i.e., $H_3^* = 8x^3-12x$.

Orthogonal functions and series expansions

The concept of orthogonal functions apply to the case of functions of an independent variable x often defined in terms of an index n over a certain interval, for example, $g_n(x) = \sin(n\pi x)$ on the interval (0,1), with n = 1, 2, 3, ... The functions $g_n(x)$ and $g_m(x)$ are said to be orthogonal on an interval a < x < b, if

$$(g_n, g_m) = \int_a^b g_n(x) \cdot g_m(x) \cdot dx = 0,$$

for n ≠ m.

If n = m, then the resulting integral represents the square of a quantity, $||g_n||$, known as the

$$\| g_n \|^2 = (g_n, g_n) = \int_a^b [g_n(x)]^2 \cdot dx \neq 0.$$

norm of $g_n(x)$:

244

Example 1 -- For the functions $g_n(x) = \sin(n\pi x)$ on the interval (0,1), you can check in the calculator that the integral

$$\int_0^1 \text{SIN}(n \cdot \pi \cdot x) \cdot \text{SIN}(m \cdot \pi \cdot x) \, dx$$

EDIT CURS BIG ▪ EVAL FACTO TEXPA

evaluates to

$$\frac{(m-n) \cdot \text{SIN}((m+n) \cdot \pi) - (m+n) \cdot \text{SIN}((m-n) \cdot \pi)}{\left(2 \cdot m^2 - 2 \cdot n^2\right) \cdot \pi}$$

This latter expression is equal to zero for $n \neq m$ (n and m integers), and it is not defined if m = n. For the case m = n, we can calculate the value of the integral by using:

$$\int_0^1 \text{SIN}(x \cdot n \cdot \pi)^2 \, dx \blacktriangleleft$$

EDIT CURS BIG ▪ EVAL FACTO TEXPA

which evaluates to

$$\frac{\text{SIN}(2 \cdot n \cdot \pi) - 2 \cdot n \cdot \pi}{4 \cdot n \cdot \pi}$$

EDIT CURS BIG ▪ EVAL FACTO TEXPA

For n integer, $\sin(2n\pi) = 0$, and the result simplifies to ½.

If a function $f(x)$ can be written as a series expansion of orthogonal functions $g_n(x)$, i.e.,

$$f(x) = \sum_{n=1}^{\infty} C_n \cdot g_n(x),$$

over the interval a < x < b, then we can use the property of orthogonality to obtain the coefficients C_n of the series as follows:

- Multiply the function by $g_m(x)$, i.e.,

$$f(x) \cdot g_m(x) = \sum_{n=1}^{\infty} C_n \cdot g_n(x) \cdot g_m(x).$$

245

- Integrate the resulting expression over the interval a < x < b, i.e.,

$$\int_a^b f(x) \cdot g_m(x) \cdot dx = \sum_{n=1}^{\infty} C_n \cdot \int_a^b g_n(x) \cdot g_m(x) \cdot dx.$$

Because all integrals in the summation in the right-hand side of the expression above are zero, except for m = n, the expression simplifies to:

$$\int_a^b f(x) \cdot g_m(x) \cdot dx = C_m \cdot \int_a^b [g_m(x)]^2 \cdot dx$$

- The coefficient Cn is calculated from the expression above by replacing m with n, i.e.,

$$C_n = \frac{\int_a^b f(x) \cdot g_n(x) \cdot dx}{\int_a^b [g_n(x)]^2 \cdot dx} = \frac{(f, g_n)}{\|g_n\|}.$$

Example 2 -- For the orthogonal functions $g_n(x) = \sin(n\pi x)$, 0<x<1, the corresponding series is a Fourier sine series, i.e.,

$$f(x) = \sum_{n=1}^{\infty} C_n \cdot \sin(n\pi x),$$

and,

$$C_n = \frac{\int_0^1 f(x) \cdot \sin(n\pi x) \cdot dx}{\int_0^1 \sin^2(n\pi x) \cdot dx} = \frac{\int_0^1 f(x) \cdot \sin(n\pi x) \cdot dx}{1/2} = 2 \cdot \int_0^1 f(x) \cdot \sin(n\pi x) \cdot dx.$$

Orthonormal functions

A set of normal functions $\phi_n(x)$ on an interval a < x < b is said to be orthonormal if

$$(\phi_n, \phi_m) = \int_a^b g_n(x) \cdot g_m(x) \cdot dx = \begin{cases} 0, \text{ when } m \neq n \\ 1, \text{ when } m = n \end{cases}$$

Thus, the norm of an orthonormal function is $\|\phi_n\| = 1.0$.

Given a set of orthogonal functions $g_n(x)$ on an interval a<x<b, you can generate the corresponding orthonormal set as

$$\phi_n(x) = g_n(x)/||g_n||.$$

Example 1 -- Determine the orthonormal functions corresponding to the set of orthogonal functions

$$g_n(x) = \cos(n\pi x),$$

on the interval $0 < x < 1$.

First, to verify that the set of functions given is orthogonal, evaluate the integral

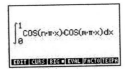

The result is

$$\frac{(m-n)\cdot\text{SIN}((m+n)\cdot\pi)+(m+n)\cdot\text{SIN}((m-n)\cdot\pi)}{(2\cdot m^2 - 2\cdot n^2)\cdot\pi}$$

For n and m integer, $\sin[(m+n)\pi] = \sin[(m-n)\pi] = 0$, therefore, $(g_n, g_m) = 0$. Thus, the functions $g_n(x)$ are orthogonal.

The norm of the function $g_n(x)$ is calculated as

which evaluates to

$$\frac{\text{SIN}(2\cdot n\cdot\pi)+2\cdot n\cdot\pi}{4\cdot n\cdot\pi}$$

For n = integer, $\sin(2n\pi) = 0$, thus $||g_n||^2 = \frac{1}{2}$, and $||g_n|| = 1/\sqrt{2}$. The orthonormal functions will be defined, therefore, as

$$\phi_n(x) = g_n(x)/||g_n|| = \sqrt{2}\cdot\cos(n\pi x).$$

247

Orthogonality with respect to a weight function

Some functions are _orthogonal with respect to a weight function p(x)_, so that

$$\int_a^b p(x) \cdot g_n(x) \cdot g_m(x) \cdot dx = 0.$$

In this case, the norm squared of $g_n(x)$ is given by

$$\| g_n \|^2 = \int_a^b p(x) \cdot [g_n(x)]^2 \cdot dx \neq 0.$$

If a function f(x) can be expanded in terms of the functions $g_n(x)$, i.e.,

$$f(x) = \sum_{n=1}^{\infty} C_n \cdot g_n(x),$$

the coefficients of the series are given, in this case, by

$$C_n = \frac{\int_a^b p(x) \cdot f(x) \cdot g_n(x) \cdot dx}{\int_a^b p(x) \cdot [g_n(x)]^2 \cdot dx} = \frac{1}{\| g_n \|} \cdot \int_a^b p(x) \cdot f(x) \cdot g_n(x) \cdot dx.$$

Example 1 -- The Chebyshev or Tchebycheff polynomials $T_1(x) = x$, $T_2(x) = 2x^2-1$, on the interval -1 < x < 1, are orthogonal with respect to the weight function $p(x) = (1-x^2)^{-1/2}$, which can be demonstrated by calculating the integral

Highlighting the integral in the equation writer and press [EVAL] to get the result '0'.

Sturm-Liouville problem

Although the details of the proof are not included in this book, you can verify that Bessel functions, Laguerre polynomials, Hermite polynomials, and Chebyshev or Tchebycheff

248

polynomials are all sets of orthogonal functions. In fact, all of these functions can be obtained from solving the so-called Sturm-Liouville problem defined by the differential equation

$$\frac{d}{dx}\left[r(x)\cdot\frac{dy}{dx}\right]+[q(x)+\lambda\cdot p(x)]y=0,$$

to be solved in the interval a < x < b, and subject to the boundary conditions

$$\alpha_1 \cdot y(a) + \beta_1 \cdot y'(a) = 0,$$

and

$$\alpha_2 \cdot y(b) + \beta_2 \cdot y'(b) = 0.$$

By selecting the values of the functions r(x), p(x), and q(x), as well as the constants α_1, α_2, β_1, and β_2, we can generate, out of the general ODE shown above, the Bessel equation, Laguerre's equation, etc. The solutions to the Sturm-Liouville ODE are given in terms of different values of the parameter λ, known as the eigenvalues of the problem, while the solutions themselves are known as the eigenfunctions. Examples for obtaining eigenvalues and eigenfunctions are presented when discussing partial differential equations.

Numerical solution to ordinary differential equations

To solve differential equations numerically we can replace the derivatives in the equation with finite difference approximations on a discretized domain. This results in a number of algebraic equations that can be solved one at a time (explicit methods) or simultaneously (implicit methods) to obtain values of the dependent function y_i corresponding to values of the independent function x_i in the discretized domain.

Finite differences

Finite differences is a technique by which derivatives of functions are approximated by function differences between a given value of the independent variable, say x_0, and a small increment (x_0+h). For example, from the definition of derivative,

$$df/dx = \lim_{h \to 0} (f(x+h)-f(x))/h,$$

we can approximate the value of df/dx by using the finite difference approximation

$$(f(x+h)-f(x))/h$$

with a small value of h. The following exercise shows approximations to the derivative of the function

$$f(x) = \exp(-x) \sin (x^2/2),$$

at x = 2, using finite differences:

'f(x) = EXP(-x)*SIN(x^2/2)' [ENTER] [⟶][DEF]   Define function f(x)
'df(x,h) = (f(x+h)-f(x))/h' [ENTER] [⟶][DEF]   Define   derivative
approximation

Estimates of the derivative for different values of h are calculated as follows:

2 [SPC] 0.1   [ENTER][df] [⟶][NUM],   Result: -0.244160077287
2 [SPC] 0.01   [ENTER][df] [⟶][NUM],   Result: -0.2366848292
2 [SPC] 0.001   [ENTER][df] [⟶][NUM],   Result: -0.235798687
2 [SPC] 0.0001   [ENTER][df] [⟶][NUM],   Result: -0.23570874
2 [SPC] 0.00001   [ENTER][df] [⟶][NUM],   Result: -0.2356997
2 [SPC] 0.000001   [ENTER][df] [⟶][NUM],   Result: -0.235699

The actual value of the derivative can be calculated by using:

'f(x)' [ENTER] 'x' [ENTER] [⟶][∂] 'x=2' [⟶][ALG][SUBST] [⟶][NUM],   Result: -0.23569874791.

This exercise illustrates the fact that, as h→0, the value of the finite difference approximation, $(f(x+h)-f(x))/h$, approaches that of the derivative, df/dx, at the point of interest.

250

Finite difference formulas based on Taylor series expansions

In chapter 13 we defined a Taylor series expansion of the function f(x) about the point x = x_0 as

$$f(x) = \sum_{n=0}^{\infty} \frac{f^{(n)}(x_0)}{n!} \cdot (x - x_0)^n.$$

Where $f^{(n)}(x_0) = (d^n f/dx^n)|_{x=x0}$, and $f^{(0)}(x_0) = f(x_0)$. If we let x = x0+h, then x-x0 = h, and the series can be written as

$$f(x_0 + h) = \sum_{n=0}^{\infty} \frac{f^{(n)}(x_0)}{n!} \cdot h^n = f(x_0) + \frac{f'(x_0)}{1!} \cdot h + \frac{f''(x_0)}{2!} \cdot h^2 + O(h^3),$$

Where the expression $O(h^3)$ represents the remaining terms of the series and indicates that the leading term is of order h^3. Because h is a small quantity, we can write 1 > h, and $h > h^2 > h^3 > h^4 > ...$ Therefore, the remaining of the series represented by $O(h^3)$ provides the order of the error incurred in neglecting this part of the series expansion when calculating f(x0+h).

From the Taylor series expansion shown above we can obtain an expression for the derivative f'(x_0) as

$$f'(x_0) = \frac{f(x_0 + h) - f(x_0)}{h} + \frac{f''(x_0)}{2!} \cdot h + O(h^2) = \frac{f(x_0 + h) - f(x_0)}{h} + O(h).$$

In practical applications of finite differences, we will replace the first-order derivative df/dx at x = x_0, with the expression (f(x0+h)-f(x0))/h, selecting an appropriate value for h, and indicating that the error introduced in the calculation is of order h, i.e., error = O(h).

Forward, backward and centered finite difference approximation to the first derivative

The approximation

$$df/dx = (f(x_0+h)-f(x_0))/h$$

is called a _forward difference formula_ because the derivative is based on the value x = x_0 and it involves the function f(x) evaluated at x = x_0+h, i.e., at a point located forward from x_0 by an increment h.

If we include the values of f(x) at x = x_0 - h, and x = x_0, the approximation is written as

$$df/dx = (f(x_0)-f(x_0-h))/h$$

and is called a _backward difference formula_. The order of the error is still O(h).

A centered difference formula for df/dx will include the points (x_0-h,f(x_0-h)) and (x_0+h,f(x_0+h)). To find the expression for the formula as well as the order of the error we use the Taylor series expansion of f(x) once more. First we write the equation corresponding to a forward expansion:

$$f(x_0+h) = f(x_0)+f'(x_0)\cdot h+1/2\cdot f''(x_0)\cdot h^2+1/6\cdot f^{(3)}(x_0)\cdot h^3 + O(h^4).$$

251

Next, we write the equation for a backward expansion:

$$f(x_0-h) = f(x_0)-f'(x_0)\cdot h+1/2\cdot f''(x_0)\cdot h^2-1/6\cdot f^{(3)}(x_0)\cdot h^3 + O(h^4).$$

Subtracting these two equations results in

$$f(x_0+h)- f(x_0-h) = 2\cdot f'(x_0)\cdot h+1/3\cdot f^{(3)}(x_0)\cdot h^3+O(h^5).$$

Notice that the even terms in h, i.e., h^2, h^4, ..., vanish. Therefore, the order of the remaining terms in this last expression is $O(h^5)$. Solving for $f'(x_0)$ from the last result produces the following _centered difference formula for the first derivative_:

$$\frac{df}{dx}\Big|_{x=x_0} = \frac{f(x_0+h)-f(x_0-h)}{2\cdot h}+\frac{1}{3}\cdot f^{(3)}(x)\cdot h^2+O(h^4),$$

or,

$$\frac{df}{dx} = \frac{f(x_0+h)-f(x_0-h)}{2\cdot h}+O(h^2).$$

This result indicates that the centered difference formula has an error of the order $O(h^2)$, while the forward and backward difference formulas had an error of the order $O(h)$. Since $h^2<h$, the error introduced in using the centered difference formula to approximate a first derivative will be smaller than if the forward or backward difference formulas are used.

Forward, backward and centered finite difference approximation to the second derivative

To obtain a _centered finite difference formula for the second derivative_, we'll start by using the equations for the forward and backward Taylor series expansions from the previous section but including terms up to $O(h^5)$, i.e.,

$$f(x_0+h) = f(x_0)+f'(x_0)\cdot h+1/2\cdot f''(x_0)\cdot h^2+1/6\cdot f^{(3)}(x_0)\cdot h^3 + 1/24\cdot f^{(4)}(x_0)\cdot h^4 + O(h^5).$$

and

$$f(x_0-h) = f(x_0)-f'(x_0)\cdot h+1/2\cdot f''(x_0)\cdot h^2-1/6\cdot f^{(3)}(x_0)\cdot h^3 + 1/24\cdot f^{(4)}(x_0)\cdot h^4 - O(h^4).$$

Next, add the two equations and solve for $f''(x_0)$:

$$d^2f/dx^2 = [f(x_0+h)-2\cdot f(x_0)+f(x_0-h)]/h^2 + O(h^2).$$

Forward and backward finite difference formulas for the second derivatives are given, respectively, by

$$d^2f/dx^2 = [f(x_0+2\cdot h)-2\cdot f(x_0+h)+f(x0)]/h^2 + O(h),$$

and

$$d^2f/dx^2 = [f(x_0) -2\cdot f(x_0-h)+f(x_0-2\cdot h)]/h^2 + O(h).$$

252

Solution of a first-order ODE using finite differences - Euler forward method

Consider the ordinary differential equation,

$$dy/dx = g(x,y),$$

subject to the boundary condition,

$$y(x_1) = y_1.$$

To solve this differential equation numerically, we need to use one of the formulas for finite differences presented earlier. Suppose that we use the forward difference approximation for dy/dx;, i.e.,

$$dy/dx = (y(x+h)-y(x))/h.$$

Then, the differential equation is transformed into the following difference equation:

$$(y(x+h)-y(x))/h = g(x,y),$$

from which,

$$y(x+h) = y(x)+h \cdot g(x,y).$$

This result is known as _Euler's forward method_ for numerical solution of first-order ODEs.

Since we know the boundary condition (x_1,y_1) we can start by solving for y at $x_2 = x_1+h$, then we solve for y at $x_3 = x_2+h$, and so on. In this way, we generate a series of points (x_1, y_1), (x_2, y_2), ..., (x_n, y_n), which will represent the numerical solution to the original ODE. The upper limit of the independent variable x_n is either given or selected arbitrarily during the solution.

The term _"discretizing the domain of the independent variable"_ refers to obtaining a series of values of the independent variable, namely, x_i, $i = 1,2;...,$ n, that will be used in the solution. Suppose that the range of the independent variable (a,b) is known, and that we use a constant value $h = \Delta x$ to divide the range into n equal intervals. By making $x_1 = a$, and $x_n = b$, then we find that the values of x_i, $i = 2,3, ...$ n, are given by

$$x_i = x_1 +(i-1) \cdot \Delta x = a+(i-1) \cdot \Delta x,$$

and that for $i = n$, $x_n = x_1 +(n-1) \cdot \Delta x$. This latter result can be used to find n given Δx,

$$n = (x_n -x_1)/ \Delta x + 1 = (b-a)/ \Delta x + 1,$$

or, to find Δx given n,

$$\Delta x = (x_n-x_1)/(n-1) = (b-a)/(n-1).$$

The recurrent equation for solving for y is given by

$$y_{i+1} = y_i + \Delta x \cdot g(x_i,y_i),$$

for $i = 1,2, ..., $ n-1. Because the method solves $y_{i+1} = f(x_i,y_i, \Delta x)$, i.e., one value of the dependent variable at a time, the method is said to be an _explicit method_.

253

Example 1 - Given the ODE,

$$dy/dx = y \cdot \sin(x),$$

and the boundary condition,

$$y(0) = 1,$$

use the Euler method to obtain a numerical solution to this ODE in the interval $0 < x < 2.5$. Use $\Delta x = 0.25$, 0.1, and 0.05.

Exact solution. The exact solution can be obtained by using the HP 49 G's DESOL function. Enter the differential equation and the function to solve for as shown in the screen below:

Press [DESOL] to obtain the result:

$$\{ \text{'y(x)=-(y*COS(x))+C0'} \}.$$

Press [→][EVAL] to remove the equation from the list. You notice that the solution involves the term y(x) as well as the term y. We need to replace y(x) with y, and then solve for y, as follows:

'y(x) = y' [ENTER] [→][ALG][SUBST] 'y' [ENTER] [←][S.SLV][ISOL]

The result is

$$\text{'y=C0/(COS(x)+ 1)'}.$$

To determine the value of C0, let's first press [ENTER] to keep an additional copy of this result, then use the following entries:

'x = 0' [ENTER] [→][ALG][SUBST]   Replace x = 0
'y=1'   [ENTER][SUBST]   Replace y = 1
'C0'   [ENTER] [←][S.SLV][ISOL] [→][EVAL]   Solve for C0

Next, the solution is obtained by using: [→][ALG][SUBST]. The final result is

$$\text{'y = 2/(COS(x)+1)'}.$$

To define this expression as a function, use:

'y = f(x)' [ENTER] [→][ALG][SUBST] [←][DEF].

To see a graph of the solution set up your plot screens to look like this:

254

The graph of the function is the following:

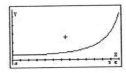

Numerical solution.

For the numerical solution we can create the following program

```
<< → a b Dx y0 << '(b-a)/Dx+1' EVAL → n << 1 n FOR i 'a+(i-1)*Dx' EVAL NEXT n
→ARRY DUP → x << y0 DUP DUP 1 'n-1' EVAL FOR i  'x(i)'  EVAL   SWAP   g   Dx
* + DUP DUP NEXT n →ARRY   2   COL→   STOΣ  "Solution ready"   MSGBOX  >>  >>
>>
```

Save it under the name NUMO1 (NUMerical solution to ODEs – program 1).

We also need to define the function

'g(x,y) = y*SIN(x)' [ENTER] [←][DEF].

To run the program type the values of a, b, Dx, and y(a) = y0, then press [NUMO1]:

0 [ENTER] 2.5 [ENTER] 0.25 [ENTER] 1 [ENTER] [NUMO1]

When the message Solution ready shows up in the screen, the variable SDAT, containing values of xi and yi in columns 1 and 2, respectively, will be ready for further operations. For example, you may want to plot the scatterplot resulting from the numerical solution and compare it with the plotting of the function f(x) = 2/(cos(x)+1), which represents the exact solution to the ODE. This comparison is shown in the figure below.

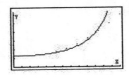

255

The dots represent the numerical solution. Notice that the agreement is excellent for small values of x but the discrepancies between the numerical and exact solutions increase with the value of x. Since we use a finite difference formula with order O(h), numerical errors accumulate at a relatively high rate, which results in the discrepancies shown in the figure.

The reader can try the solution of the ODE for other values of Dx, namely 0.1 and 0.05, using NUMODE1.

Finite difference formulas using indexed variables

In the presentation of the Euler forward method, above, we showed how you can get, from the general formula for the first derivative,

$$dy/dx = [y(x+h)-y(x)]/h,$$

the recurrence formula for the explicit solution, namely,

$$y_{i+1} = y_i + \Delta x \cdot g(x_i, y_i),$$

for i = 1,2;,..., n-1. This suggest re-writing the formula for the derivative as,

$$dy/dx = (y_{i+1}-y_i)/\Delta x + O(\Delta x).$$

Using this sub-index notation, we can summarize the forward, centered, and backward approximations for the first and second derivatives as shown below:

First Derivative
FORWARD: $dy/dx = (y_{i+1}-y_i)/\Delta x + O(\Delta x).$

CENTERED: $dy/dx = (y_{i+1}-y_{i-1})/(2\cdot\Delta x) + O(\Delta x^2).$

BACKWARD: $dy/dx = (y_i-y_{i-1})/\Delta x + O(\Delta x).$

Second Derivative
FORWARD: $d^2y/dx^2 = (y_{i+2}-2\cdot y_{i+1}+y_i)/(\Delta x^2) + O(\Delta x).$

CENTERED: $d^2y/dx^2 = (y_{i+1}-2\cdot y_i+y_{i-1})/(\Delta x^2) + O(\Delta x^2).$

BACKWARD: $d^2y/dx^2 = (y_i-2\cdot y_{i-1}+y_{i-2})/(\Delta x^2) + O(\Delta x).$

Solution of a first-order ODE using finite differences - an implicit method

Consider again the ordinary differential equation, $dy/dx = g(x,y)$, subject to the boundary condition, $y(x_1) = y_1$. This time, however, we use the centered difference approximation for dy/dx, i.e.

$$dy/dx = (y(x+h)-y(x-h))/(2*h).$$

With this approximation the ODE becomes,

$$(y(x+h)-y(x-h))/(2*h) = g(x,y).$$

256

In terms of sub-indexed variables, this latter equation can be written as:

$$y_{i-1}+2 \cdot \Delta x \cdot g(x_i,y_i)-y_{i+1} = 0, \ (\ i = 2,3, \ ..., \ n-1 \ )$$

where the substitutions $y(x) = y_i, y(x+h) = y_{i+1}, y(x-h) = y_{i-1}$, and $h = \Delta x$, have been used.

If the function $g(x,y)$ is linear in y, then the equations described above consist of a set of (n-2) equations. For example, if n = 5, we have 3 equations:

$$y_1+2 \cdot \Delta x \cdot g(x_2,y_2)-y_3 = 0$$

$$y_2+2 \cdot \Delta x \cdot g(x_3,y_3)-y_4 = 0$$

$$y_3+2 \cdot \Delta x \cdot g(x_4,y_4)-y_5 = 0$$

Since y_i is known (it is the initial condition), there are still 4 unknowns, y_2, y_3, y_4, and y_5. We need to find a fourth equation to obtain a solution. We could use, for example, the forward difference equation applied to i = 1, i.e.,

$$(y_2-y_1)/\Delta x = g(x_1,y_1),$$

or

$$y_2-\Delta x \cdot g(x_1,y_1)-y_1= 0.$$

The values of x_i, and n (or Δx), can be obtained as in the Euler forward (explicit) solution.

Example 1 --   Solve the ODE

$$dy/dx = -y/x,$$

with initial conditions y(1) = 1, in the interval 1 < x < 3.5. Use Dx = 0.25.

Exact solution: To obtain an exact solution use:

'd1y(x)=-y(x)/x' [ENTER] 'y(x)' [ENTER] [←][CALC][DIFF][DESOL]

The result is { 'y(x) = C0*(1/x)' }. Use [→][EVAL][ENTER] to make two copies of the expression. To obtain C0 use:

'x = 1' [ENTER] [→][ALG][SUBST] 'y(1) = 1' [SUBST] 'C0' [←][S.SLV][ISOL]

The result is 'C0 = 1'. Press [→][ALG][SUBST] [→][EVAL] to obtain the exact solution of the ODE:

'y(x) = 1/x'.

Numerical solution:

Using a centered difference formula for dy/dx, i.e.,

$$dy/dx = (y_{i+1}-y_{i-1})/(2 \cdot \Delta x),$$

into the ODE, we get $(y_{i+1}-y_{i-1})/(2 \cdot \Delta x) = -y_i/x_i,$ which results in the (n-2) implicit equations:

$$-x_i \cdot y_{i-1}+2 \cdot \Delta x \cdot y_i+x_i \cdot y_{i+1} = 0, \ (i = 2, 3, \ ..., \ n-1).$$

257

We already know that

$$y_1 = 1$$

(initial condition), thus we have (n-1) unknowns. We still need to come up with an additional equation, which could be obtained by using a forward difference formula for i = 1, i.e.,

$$dy/dx|_{x=1} = (y_2-y_1)/\Delta x = -y_1/x_1,$$

or

$$(-x_1+\Delta x)\cdot y_1 + x_1\cdot y_2 = 0.$$

These equations can be written in the form of matrices by using

$$
\begin{bmatrix}
1 & 0 & 0 & 0 & \cdots & 0 \\
-x_1+\Delta x & x_1 & 0 & 0 & \cdots & 0 \\
-x_3 & 2\cdot\Delta x & x_3 & 0 & \cdots & 0 \\
0 & -x_4 & 2\cdot\Delta x & x_4 & \cdots & 0 \\
\vdots & \vdots & \vdots & \vdots & \ddots & \vdots \\
0 & 0 & 0 & 0 & \cdots & x_n
\end{bmatrix}
\cdot
\begin{bmatrix}
y_1 \\ y_2 \\ y_3 \\ y_4 \\ \vdots \\ y_n
\end{bmatrix}
=
\begin{bmatrix}
1 \\ 0 \\ 0 \\ 0 \\ 0 \\ 0
\end{bmatrix}
$$

For the numerical solution we can create the following program

```
<< → a b Dx y1 << '(b-a)/Dx+1' EVAL → n << 1 n FOR i 'a+(i-1)*Dx' EVAL NEXT n
→ARRY → x << { n n } 0 CON 1 1 PUT {n n} 0 CON {1 1} 1 PUT {2 1} '-a+Dx' EVAL
PUT {2 2} 'x(2)' EVAL PUT 2 'n-1' FOR i {'i+1' 'i-1'} '-x(i)' EVAL PUT {'i+1'
'i+1'} 'x(i)'  EVAL PUT {'i+1' i} '2*Dx' EVAL PUT NEXT / 2   COL→   STOΣ
"Solution ready"  MSGBOX >>  >>  >>  >>
```

Save it under the name NUMO2 (NUMerical solution to ODEs - program 2).

To run the program type the values of a, b, Dx, and y(a) = y1, then press [NUMO2]:

1 [ENTER] 3.5 [ENTER] 0.25 [ENTER] 1 [ENTER] [NUMO2]

The following plot compares the exact solution with the numerical solution. As you can see the agreement is acceptable, however, it is obvious that the error increases with x, producing a certain oscillation of the numerical solution about the exact solution.

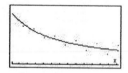

Explicit versus implicit methods

The idea behind the _explicit method_ is to be able to obtain values such as

$$y_{i+1} = f(x_i, y_i), \quad y_{i+2} = f(x_i, x_{i+1}, y_i, y_{i+1}), \text{ etc.}$$

In other words, your solution proceeds by solving explicitly for a new unknown value in the solution array, given all previous values in the array. On the other hand, _implicit methods_ imply the simultaneous solution of n linear algebraic equations that provide, at once, the elements of the solution array. With this distinction in mind between explicit and implicit methods, we outline explicit and implicit solutions for second-order, linear ODEs.

Outline of explicit solution for a second-order ODE

For example, to solve the ODE

$$d^2y/dx^2 + y = 0,$$

in the x-interval (0,20) subject to $y(0) = 1$, $dy/dx; = 1$ at $y = 0$. Use $\Delta x = 0.1$.

First, we discretize the differential equation using the finite difference approximation

$$d^2y/dx^2 = (y_{i+2} - 2 \cdot y_{i+1} + y_i)/(\Delta x^2) ,$$

which results in

$$(y_{i+2} - 2 \cdot y_{i+1} + y_i)/(\Delta x^2) + y_i = 0.$$

An explicit solution can be obtained from the recurrence equation:

$$y_{i+2} = 2 \cdot y_{i+1} - (1 + \Delta x^2) \cdot y_i, \quad i = 1, 2, \ldots, n-2;.$$

This equation is based on the two previous values of y_i, therefore, to get started we need the values $y = y_1$, and $y = y_2$. The value y_1 is provided in the initial condition, $y(0) = 1$, i.e.,

$$y_1 = 1.$$

The value of y_2 can be obtained from the second initial condition, $dy/dx = 1$, by replacing the derivative with the finite difference approximation:

$$dy/dx = (y_2 - y_1)/\Delta x,$$

which results in

$$(y_2 - y_1)/\Delta x = 1,$$

or

$$y_2 = y_1 + \Delta x.$$

The x-domain is discretized in a similar fashion as in the previous examples for first derivatives, i.e., by making $x_1 = a$, and $x_n = b$, and computing the values of x_i, $i = 2, 3, \ldots n$, with

$$x_i = x_1 + (i-1) \cdot \Delta x = a + (i-1) \cdot \Delta x,$$

where,

$$n = (x_n - x_1)/\Delta x + 1 = (b-a)/\Delta x + 1.$$

259

Outline of the implicit solution for a second-order ODE

We use the same problem from the previous section: solve the ODE

$$d^2y/dx^2+y = 0,$$

in the x-interval (0,20) subject to y(0) = 1, dy/dx; = 1 at y = 0. Use Δx = 0.1.

We discretize the differential equation using the finite difference approximation

$$d^2y/dx^2 = (y_{i+2}-2 \cdot y_{i+1}+y_i)/(\Delta x^2) ,$$

which results in

$$(y_{i+1}-2^*y_i+y_{i-1})/(\Delta x^2)+y_i = 0.$$

From this result we get the following implicit equations:

$$y_{i-1}-(2-\Delta x^2) \cdot y_i+y_{i+1} = 0,$$

for i = 2,3;, ..., n-1. There are a total of (n-2) equations. Since we have n unknowns, i.e., $y_1, y_2, ...,y_n$, we need two more equations to solve a system of linear equations. The remaining equations are provided by the two initial conditions:

From the initial condition, y(0) = 1, we can write y_1 = 1. For the second initial condition, dy/dx = 1, at x = 0, we will use a forward difference, i.e.,

$$dy/dx = (y_2 - y_1)/ \Delta x,$$

or

$$y_2 - y_1 = \Delta x.$$

The x-domain is discretized in a similar fashion as in the previous examples.

Numerical and graphical ODE solutions using the HP 49 G's own features

Through the use of the numerical solver ([→][NUM.SLV]), you can access an input form that lets you solve first-order, linear ordinary differential equations. The use of this feature is presented using the following example. The method used in the solution is a fourth-order Runge-Kutta algorithm.

Example 1 -- Suppose we want to solve the differential equation,

$$dv/dt = -1.5 \, v^{1/2},$$

with v = 4 at t = 0. We are asked to find v for t = 2.

First, create the expression defining the derivative and store it into variable EQ:

[→]['][1][.][5][+/-][×][√x][ALPHA][↰][V][ENTER]
[→]['][ALPHA][ALPHA][E][Q][ALPHA][STO]

Then, enter the NUMERICAL SOLVER environment:

[↵][NUM.SLV][▼][OK][▼][ALPHA][↤][T][OK][0][OK][2][OK][ALPHA][↤][V][OK][4][OK]

The SOLVE screen should look like this:

```
░░░░░SOLVE Y'(T)=F(T,Y)░░░░░
F:   t
INDEP: t  INIT: 0      FINAL:2
SOLN: v  INIT: 4      FINAL:█
TOL: .0001 STEP: Dflt  _STIFF
PRESS SOLVE FOR FINAL SOLN VALUE
 EDIT              INIT+ SOLVE
```

To solve, press: [SOLVE](wait)[EDIT].   The result is $0.2499 \approx 0.25$. Press [OK].

Solution presented as a table of values
Suppose we wanted to produce a table of values of v, for t = 0.00, 0.25, ..., 2.00, we will proceed as follows:

First, prepare a table to write down your results:

t	v
0.00	0.00
0.25	
...	...
2.00	

Next, within the SOLVE environment, change the final value of the independent variable to 0.25, use :

[▲][.][2][5][OK] [▶][▶] [SOLVE](wait)[EDIT]
Solves for v at t = 0.25, v = 3.285.
Write down values of x and x' in the table.

[OK][INIT+][▲][.][5][OK][▶][▶][SOLVE](wait)[EDIT]
Change initial value of t to 0.25, and final value of t to 0.5, solve again for v(0.5) = 2.640.

[OK][INIT+][▲][.][7][5][OK][▶][▶][SOLVE](wait)[EDIT]
Change initial value of t to 0.5, and final value of t to 0.75, solve again for v(0.75) = 2.066.

[OK][INIT+][▲][1][OK][▶][▶] [SOLVE](wait)[EDIT]
Change initial value of t to 0.75, and final value of t to 1, solve again for v(1) = 1.562

Repeat for t = 1.25, 1.50, 1.75, 2.00. To finish, press [OK], [ON]. The different solutions will be shown in the stack, with the latest result in level 1.

The final results look as follows:

t	v
0.00	4.000
0.25	3.285
0.50	2.640
0.75	2.066
1.00	1.562
1.25	1.129
1.50	0.766
1.75	0.473
2.00	0.249

261

Graphical solution to a differential equation

When we can not obtain a closed-form solution for the integral, we can always plot the integral by selecting `Diff Eq` in the `TYPE` field of the PLOT environment as follows: suppose that we want to plot the position x(t) for a velocity function

$$v(t) = \exp(-t^2),$$

with x = 0 at t = 0. We know there is no closed-form expression for the integral, however, we know that the definition of v(t) is

$$dx/dt = \exp(-t^2).$$

The HP48G series calculator allows for the plotting of the solution of differential equations of the form

$$Y'(T) = F(T,Y).$$

For our case, we let Y = x and T = t, therefore,

$$F(T,Y) = f(t, x) = \exp(-t^2).$$

Let's plot the solution, x(t), for t = 0 to 5, by using the following keystroke sequence:

[↵][2D/3D] (simultaneously)   To enter PLOT environment

Highlight the field in front of `TYPE`, using the [▲] [▼] keys.   Then, press [CHOOS], and highlight `Diff Eq`, using the [▲] [▼] keys. Press [OK].

Enter the function f(t,x) by using:

$$[▼] \; [↦][\; ' \;][↵][e^x][-][ALPHA][↵][T] \; [y^x][2] \; [OK].$$

Make sure that the following parameters are set: `H-VAR: 0`   `V-VAR: 1`

Change the independent variable to t by using.

[▼][↦]['][↵][ALPHA][↵][T][OK]	To define t (lowercase) as the independent variable (`INDEP`)
[NXT][OK]	Accept changes to PLOT SETUP
[↵][WIN] (simultaneously)	To enter PLOT WINDOW environment

Change the horizontal and vertical view window to the following settings:

`H-VIEW: -1  5;  V-VIEW: -1   1.5`

Move the cursor to the Init: field and change parameters as follows:

[0][OK][5][OK]	To set the range of values of t [0, 2.5].
[▼][0][OK]	To define the initial condition (or initial value) for x
[OPTS]	To define plot options.
[ERASE][DRAW]	To plot the graph.

When you observe the graph being plotted, you'll notice that the graph is not very smooth. That is because the plotter is using a time step that is too large. To refine the graph and make it smoother, use a step of 0.1. Try the following keystrokes:

[CANCL] [▼][▼][▼] [.][1][OK][OK][ERASE][DRAW]

The plot will take longer to be completed, but the shape is definitely smoother than before.

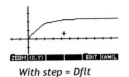
With step = Dflt

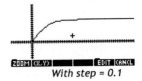
With step = 0.1

Try the following:

[EDIT][NXT][LABEL][MENU]   To see axes labels and range.

Notice that the labels for the axes are shown as 0.000 (horizontal) and 1.000 (vertical). These are the definitions for the axes as given in the OPTS screen (see above), i.e., H-VAR (t): 0, and V-VAR(x): 1.

[NXT][NXT][PICT]   To recover menu and return to PICT environment.
[(X,Y)]   To determine coordinates of any point on the graph.

Use [▶] and [◀] to move the cursor in the plot area. At the bottom of the screen you will see the coordinates of the cursor as (X,Y), i.e., the calculator uses X and Y as the default names for the horizontal and vertical axes, respectively.

[NXT][CANCL]   To recover the menu and return to the PLOT
environment
[ON]   To return to stack.

Solving second-order ODEs with the numerical solver

Problems involving the interaction of a harmonic force (e.g., a mass-spring system) and a damping force result in the equation of motion being a second-order ODE. Integration of such ODEs can be accomplished by defining the solution as a vector. As an example, suppose that a spring-mass system is subject to a damping force proportional to its speed. The resulting differential equation is:

$$\frac{d^2x}{dt^2} = -18.75 \cdot x - 1.962 \cdot \frac{dx}{dt}$$

or,

$$x'' = -18.75\ x - 1.962\ x',$$

subject to the initial conditions, v = x' = 6, x = 0, at t = 0. We want to find x, x' at t = 2. Re-write the ODE as:

$$\begin{bmatrix} x \\ x' \end{bmatrix}' = \begin{bmatrix} 0 & 1 \\ -18.75 & -1.962 \end{bmatrix} \cdot \begin{bmatrix} x \\ x' \end{bmatrix}$$

or,

$$w' = Aw,$$

263

where $w = [\ x\ \ x'\ ]^T$, and A is the 2 x 2 matrix shown above.

The initial conditions are now written as $w = [0\ \ 6]^T$, for t = 0. (Note: The symbol $[\ ]^T$ means the transpose of the vector or matrix).

To solve this problem, first, we'll create the matrix A, as follows:

[↵][MTRW][0][SPC][1][ENTER][▼] [◄][◄] [1][8][.][7][5][+/-][SPC][1][.][9][6][2][+/-]
[ENTER][ENTER][→]['][ALPHA][A][STO►]

Then, use the following keystroke sequence to solve for the differential equation for t = 2 s:

[→][NUM.SLV][▼][OK]	Invoke Numerical solver for ODEs
[→]['][ALPHA][ALPHA][A][×][W][ALPHA][OK]	Define F(T,Y), as A·w
[→]['][ALPHA][↵][T] [0][OK][2][OK]	Define independent variable and range.
[→]['][ALPHA][W][OK][↵][[ ]] [0][SPC][6] [OK]	Enter dependent variable and init. cond.
[SOLVE]	Solve for w(t=2). Wait.
[EDIT]	To see the solution vector.

The solution reads [.16716... -.6271...], i.e., x(2) = 0.16716, and x'(2) = v(2) = -0.6271. Press [CANCL] to return to SOLVE environment.

<u>Solution presented as a table of values</u>

In the previous example we were interested only in finding the values of the position and velocity at a given time t. If we wanted to produce a table of values of x and x', for t = 0.00, 0.25, ..., 2.00, we will proceed as follows: First, prepare a table to write down your results:

t	x	x'
0.00	0.00	6.00
0.25		
...	...	...
2.00		

Next, within the SOLVE environment, change the final value of the independent variable to 0.25, use:

[▲][.][2][5][OK] [►][►] [SOLVE](wait)[EDIT]	Solves for w at t = 0.25, w = [0.968 1.368]. Write down values of x and x' in the table.
[OK][INIT+][▲][.][5][OK][►][►][SOLVE](wait)[EDIT]	Change initial value of t to 0.25, and final value of t to 0.5, solve again for w(0.5) = [0.748 -2.616]
[OK][INIT+][▲][.][7][5][OK][►][►][SOLVE](wait)[EDIT]	Change initial value of t to 0.5, and final value of t to 0.75, solve again for w(0.75) = [0.0147 -2.859]
[OK][INIT+][▲][1][OK][►][►] [SOLVE](wait)[EDIT]	Change initial value of t to 0.75, and final value of t to 1, solve again for w(1) =

[-0.469 -0.607]

Repeat for t = 1.25, 1.50, 1.75, 2.00. To finish, press [OK], [ON]. The different solutions will be shown in the stack, with the latest result in level 1.
The final results look as follows:

t	x	x'	t	x	x'
0.00	0.000	6.000	1.25	-0.354	1.281
0.25	0.968	1.368	1.50	0.141	1.362
0.50	0.748	-2.616	1.75	0.227	0.268
0.75	-0.015	-2.859	2.00	0.167	-0.627
1.00	-0.469	-0.607			

Graphical solution for a second-order ODE

To plot x, x' vs. t, use the following:

Start by pressing [↦][NUM.SLV] (simultaneously), then, highlight the TYPE field and choose Diff Eq (Use [CHOOS]...[OK]). Change the initial and final values of t to 0 and 2, respectively, and the initial value of w to [0 6]. The screen should look like this:

```
TYPE:   Diff Eq        ∠: Rad
F:       'A*W'
INDEP: t   INIT: 0     FINAL: 2
SOLN:  W   INIT: [ -… _STIFF
```

Before plotting, make the following changes in the OPTS screen:

[OPTS] [▼][▶][1][+/-][OK][2][.][5][OK][▶] [5][+/-][OK] [5][OK] [.][5][OK] [5][OK]

Also, make sure that there is *not* a check mark, ✓, in front of PIXELS in the lower right corner of this screen. Now, press [◀][◀][▲][1][OK] (This indicates that we want to plot x, the first variable in the vector w). Press [ERASE][DRAW].

to plot the x' vs. t curve, press :

[CANCL][OPTS] [▼][▼][2][OK][DRAW]   *warning: do not press [ERASE]*

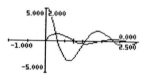

To see labels, press [EDIT][NXT][LABEL][MENU]. The x-axis is identified as 0.000, while the y-axis is identified as 2.000, since variable 2 (x') was the last plotted.

Press [NXT][NXT][PICT], to return to the PICT environment. Press [CANCL] to return to the PLOT environment, and press [ON] to return to the stack.

Numerical solution for stiff ordinary differential equations

Consider the ODE:

$$dy/dt = -100y+100t+101,$$

subject to the initial condition y(0) = 1.

Exact solution. This equation can be also written as

$$dy/dt + 100\, y = 100\, t + 101,$$

and solved using an integrating factor, IF(t) = exp(100t), as follows:

'(100*t+101)*EXP(100*t)' [ENTER] 't' [ENTER] [↩][CALC][DIFF][NXT][RISCH]

The result is   '(t+1)*EXP(100*t)'.

Next, we add an integration constant, by using:

'C' [ENTER] [+]

Then, we divide by FI(x), by using:

'EXP(100*t)' [ENTER] [÷][↩][EVAL].

The result is: '((t+1)*EXP(100*t)+C)/EXP(100*t)', i.e.,

$y(t) = 1 + t + C \cdot e^{100t}$.

Use of the initial condition y(0) = 1, results in $1 = 1 + 0 + C \cdot e^0$, or C = 0, the particular solution being

$$y(t) = 1+t.$$

Numerical solution. If we attempt a direct numerical solution of the original equation

$$dy/dt = -100y+100t+101$$

266

using the HP 49 G's own numerical solver, we will find that the solver will seem to take an inordinate amount of time in solving the equation. To check this out, set your differential equation numerical solver ([➝][NUM.SLV] [▼][OK]) to:

Here we are trying to obtain the value of y(2) given y(0) = 1. With the Soln: Final field highlighted, press [SOLVE]. You can check that there will be no solution after 2 minutes. Press [ON] to cancel the calculation.

This is an example of a _stiff ordinary differential equation_. A stiff ODE is one whose general solution contains components that vary at widely different rates under the same increment in the independent variable. In this particular case, the general solution,

$$y(t) = 1 + t + C \cdot e^{100t},$$

contains the components 't' and '$C \cdot e^{100t}$', which vary at very different rates, except for the cases C=0 or C≈0 (e.g., for C = 1, t =0.1, $C \cdot e^{100t}$ =22026).

The HP 49 G calculator's ODE numerical solver allows for the solution of stiff ODEs by selecting the option _Stiff in the SOLVE Y'(T) = F(T,Y) screen. With this option selected you need to provide the values of ∂f/∂y and ∂f/∂t. For the case under consideration ∂f/∂y =-100 and ∂f/∂t = 100.

Enter those values in the corresponding fields of the SOLVE Y'(T) = F(T,Y) screen:

When done, move the cursor to the Final field and press [SOLVE]. Press [EDIT] to see the solution: 2.9999999999, i.e., 3.0.

Note: The option Stiff is also available for graphical solutions of differential equations.

16 Partial Differential Equations and Fourier transforms

Basic concepts and definitions for partial differential equations were introduced in Chapter 15. Some definitions related to partial differential equations (PDE) are reviewed following. Solutions to a variety of PDEs are presented in this chapter. The basic idea is to demonstrate some advanced applications of the HP 49 G calculator, rather than being a comprehensive presentation on partial differential equations.

Definitions

- Equations involving one or more partial derivatives of a function of two or more independent variables are called *partial differential equations (PDEs).*

- Well known examples of PDEs are the following equations of mathematical physics in which the notation: $u = \partial u / \partial x$, $u_{xy} = \partial u / \partial y \partial x$, $u_{xx} = \partial^2 u / \partial x^2$, etc., is used:

  [1] One-dimensional wave equation: $\quad u_{tt} = c^2\, u_{xx}$

  [2] One-dimensional heat equation: $\quad u_t = c^2\, u_{xx}$

  [3] Laplace equation: $\quad u_{xx} + u_{yy} = 0$, (2-D), or $u_{xx} + u_{yy} + u_{zz} = 0$ (3-D)

  [4] Poisson equation: $\quad u_{xx} + u_{yy} = f(x,y)$, (2-D), or $u_{xx} + u_{yy} + u_{zz} = f(x,y,z)$ (3-D)

- The order of the highest derivative is the *order* of the equation. For example, all of the PDEs in the examples shown above are of the second order.

- A PDE is *linear* if the dependent variable and its functions are all of first order. All of the PDEs shown above are also linear.

- A PDE is *homogeneous* if each term in the equation contains either the dependent variable or one of its derivatives. Otherwise, the equation is said to be *non-homogeneous*. Equations [1], [2], and [3] above are homogeneous equations. Equation [4] is non-homogeneous.

- A *solution* of a PDE in some region R of the space of independent variables is a function, which has all the derivatives that appear on the equation, and satisfies the equation everywhere in R. For example, $u = x^2 - y^2$, $u = e^x \cos(y)$, and $u = \ln(x^2 + y^2)$, are all solutions to the two-dimensional Laplace equation (equation [3] above).

Example 1 -- Verify that u = sin wct sin wx satisfies the wave equation.

In the calculator type:

'd2d2u(x,t) = c^2*d1d1u(x,t)' [ENTER] 'u(x,t) = SIN(w*c*t)*SIN(w*x)' [ENTER]

[↦][ALG][SUBST] [↦][EVAL]

The result is: '-(w^2*c^2* SIN(w*c*t)*SIN(w*x)) = -(w^2*c^2* SIN(w*c*t)*SIN(w*x))'. Thus, the wave equation is satisfied by the proposed solution.

Example 2 -- Determine the value of *c* so that the function u = e^{-t} sin 3x   satisfies the heat equation.

In the calculator type:

'd2u(x,t) = c^2*d1d1u(x,t)' [ENTER] 'u(x,t) = EXP(-t)*SIN(3*x)' [ENTER]

[↦][ALG][SUBST] [↦][EVAL]

The result is:
'-(SIN(3*x)/EXP(t)) = -(9*c^2* SIN(3*x)/EXP(t))'.

Dividing this equation by SIN(3*x)/EXP(t)), result in

'1=9*c^2'

From which,   c = ± 1/3.

Example 3 -- Verify that the function u = tan^{-1}(y/x)   are solutions of Laplace's equation in two dimensions.

In the calculator type:

'd1d1u(x,y) + d2d3u(x,y)' [ENTER] 'u(x,t) = ATAN(y/x)' [ENTER]

[↦][ALG][SUBST] [↦][EVAL]

The result is 0. Thus, the Laplace equation is satisfied by the proposed solution.

- A unique solution to a PDE is obtained by using an appropriate number of *initial conditions* (conditions dependent on time given typically at t = 0), and/or *boundary conditions* (conditions at specific points of the solution domain known as boundaries of the domain).

Example 4 -- Verify that $u(x,y) = a \ln(x^2+y^2)+b$ satisfies Laplace's equation in two dimensions, and determine *a* and *b* so that *u* satisfies the boundary condition *u* = *0* on the circle $x^2+y^2= 1$ and *u* = *5* on the circle $x^2+y^2=9$.

In the calculator type:

'd1d1u(x,y) + d2d3u(x,y)' [ENTER] 'u(x,t) = a*LN(x^2+y^2)+b' [ENTER]

269

[↦][ALG][SUBST] [↦][EVAL]

The result is '0=0'. Thus, the Laplace equation is satisfied by the proposed solution. To determine the constants a and b we use the boundary conditions, u = 0 on $x^2+y^2=1$, and u = 5 on $x^2+y^2 = 9$, thus:

$$1 = a \ln(1) + b \rightarrow b = 1,$$

and

$$5 = a \ln(9) + 1 \rightarrow a = 4/\ln(9) = 8.788898...$$

- In general there should be as many boundary or initial conditions as the highest order of the corresponding partial derivative. For example, the one dimensional heat equation (equation [2]) applied to a insulated bar of length L, will require an initial condition, say

$$u(x,t=0) = f(x), \ 0 < x < L,$$

as well as two boundary conditions, e.g., $u(x=0,t) = u_0$ and $u(x=L,t) = u_L$, or, $u_x(x=0,t) = u_{x0}$ and $u_x(x=L) = u_{xL}$, or some combination of these, for $t > 0$.

Classification of linear, second-order PDEs

Linear, second-order PDEs, as the examples shown above as equations [1] through [4], are commonly encountered in science and engineering. For that reason special attention is paid in this section to this type of equations. First, we learn how to classify linear, second-order PDEs as follows:

An equation of the form:

$$Au_{xx} + 2Bu_x + Cu_{yy} = F(x,y,u,u_x,u_y),$$

is said to be:

- <u>elliptic</u>, if $AC - B^2 > 0$, e.g., heat flow and diffusion-type problems.

- <u>parabolic</u>, if $AC - B^2 = 0$, e.g., vibrating systems and wave motion problems.

- <u>hyperbolic</u>, if $AC - B^2 < 0$, e.g., steady-state, potential-type problems.

Analytical solutions of PDEs

There are a variety of methods for obtaining symbolic, or closed-form, solutions to differential equations. In this section we will present two of those techniques:

1. Separation of variables
2. Integral transforms (Laplace transforms, Fourier transforms)

The method of separation of variables can be used to obtain analytical solutions for some simple PDEs. The method consists in writing the general solution as the product of functions of a single variable, then replacing the resulting function into the PDE, and separating the PDE into ODEs of a single variable each. The ODEs are solved separately and their solutions combined into the solution of the PDE.

270

In many cases, the ODEs resulting from the separation of variables produce solutions that depend on a parameter known as an *eigenvalue* (if the eigenvalue appears in a sine or cosine function that depends on time, it is referred to as an *eigenfrequency*). The solutions involving eigenvalues are known as *eigenfunctions*.

The use of integral transforms reduces a PDE in n independent variables into one that has only (n-1) independent variables, thus a PDE with two variables can be easily changed into an ODE.

Integral Transforms

In Chapter 14 we introduced Laplace transforms for the solution of ordinary differential equations. In this section we introduce other integral transforms that we will use in the solution of partial differential equations. In general, an _integral transform_ is a transformation that relates a function f(t) to a new function F(s) by an integration of the form

$$F(s) = \int_a^b \kappa(s,t) \cdot f(t) \cdot dt.$$

The function $\kappa(s,t)$ is known as the _kernel of the transformation_.

The use of an integral transform allows us to resolve a function into a given _spectrum of components_. To understand the concept of a spectrum, consider the Fourier series

$$f(t) = a_0 + \sum_{n=1}^{\infty} (a_n \cdot \cos \omega_n x + b_n \cdot \sin \omega_n x),$$

representing a periodic function with a period T. This Fourier series can be re-written as

$$f(x) = a_0 + \sum_{n=1}^{\infty} A_n \cdot \cos(\frac{n\pi x}{T} + \phi_n),$$

where

$$A_n = \sqrt{a_n^2 + b_n^2}, \quad \tan^{-1}\left(\frac{b_n}{a_n}\right)$$

for n =1,2, ...

The amplitudes A_n will be referred to as the spectrum of the function and will be a measure of the magnitude of the component of f(x) with frequency

$f_n = n/T.$

The basic or fundamental frequency in the Fourier series is $f_0 = 1/T$, thus, all other frequencies are multiples of this basic frequency, i.e., $f_n = n \cdot f_0$. Also, we can define an angular frequency,

$\omega_n = 2n\pi/T = 2\pi f_n = 2\pi \cdot n \cdot f_0 = n \cdot \omega_0,$

where ω_0 is the basic or fundamental angular frequency of the Fourier series.

Using the angular frequency notation, the Fourier series expansion is written as

$$f(x) = a_0 + \sum_{n=1}^{\infty} A_n \cdot \cos(\omega_n x + \phi_n) = a_0 + \sum_{n=1}^{\infty} \left(a_n \cdot \cos \omega_n x + b_n \cdot \sin \omega_n x \right).$$

A plot of the values A_n vs. ω_n is the typical representation of a discrete spectrum for a function. The discrete spectrum will show that the function has components at angular frequencies ω_n which are integer multiples of the fundamental angular frequency ω_0.

Suppose that we are faced with the need to expand a non-periodic function into sine and cosine components. A non-periodic function can be thought of as having an infinitely large period. Thus, for a very large value of T, the fundamental angular frequency, $\omega_0 = 2\pi/T$, becomes a very small quantity, say $\Delta\omega$. Also, the angular frequencies corresponding to $\omega_n = n \cdot \omega_0 = n \cdot \Delta\omega$, (n = 1, 2, ..., ∞), now take values closer and closer to each other, suggesting the need for a continuous spectrum of values.

The non-periodic function can be written, therefore, as

$$f(x) = \int_0^{\infty} [C(\omega) \cdot \cos(\omega \cdot x) + S(\omega) \cdot \sin(\omega \cdot x)] d\omega,$$

where

$$C(\omega) = \frac{1}{2\pi} \cdot \int_{-\infty}^{\infty} f(x) \cdot \cos(\omega \cdot x) \cdot dx,$$

and

$$S(\omega) = \frac{1}{2\pi} \cdot \int_{-\infty}^{\infty} f(x) \cdot \sin(\omega \cdot x) \cdot dx.$$

The continuous spectrum is given by

$$A(\omega) = \sqrt{[C(\omega)]^2 + [S(\omega)]^2}$$

The functions $C(\omega)$, $S(\omega)$, and $A(\omega)$ are continuous functions of a variable ω, which becomes the transform variable for the Fourier transforms defined below.

Example 1 - Determine the coefficients $C(\omega)$, $S(\omega)$, and the continuous spectrum $A(\omega)$, for the function $f(x) = \exp(-x)$, for x > 0, and $f(x) = 0$, x < 0.

In the calculator, set up and evaluate the following integrals to calculate $C(\omega)$ and $S(\omega)$, respectively:

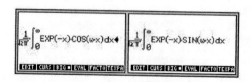

272

Their results are, respectively:

The continuous spectrum, A(ω) is calculated as:

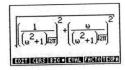

which simplifies to

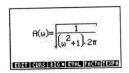

Define this expression as a function by using [ENTER][⌐][DEF]. Then, plot the continuous spectrum as:

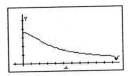

Fourier transforms

In Chapter 14 we introduced the Laplace transforms indicating that the transform will take a function, f(t), in t-space, and transform it into a function, F(s), in s-space. Thus, F(s) = L{f(t)} represents the Laplace transform of f(t), and f(t) = L⁻¹{F(s)} represents the inverse Laplace transform of F(s). In this section we introduce three types of transform and their inverses as follows:

Fourier sine transform:

$$Fs\{f(t)\} = F(\omega) = \frac{2}{\pi} \cdot \int_0^\infty f(t) \cdot \sin(\omega \cdot t) \cdot dt$$

273

Inverse sine transform:

$$F_s^{-1}\{F(\omega)\} = f(t) = \int_0^\infty F(\omega) \cdot \sin(\omega \cdot t) \cdot dt$$

Fourier cosine transform:

$$Fc\{f(t)\} = F(\omega) = \frac{2}{\pi} \cdot \int_0^\infty f(t) \cdot \cos(\omega \cdot t) \cdot dt$$

Inverse cosine transform:

$$F_c^{-1}\{F(\omega)\} = f(t) = \int_0^\infty F(\omega) \cdot \cos(\omega \cdot t) \cdot dt$$

Fourier transform (proper):

$$F\{f(t)\} = F(\omega) = \frac{1}{\sqrt{2\pi}} \cdot \int_{-\infty}^\infty f(t) \cdot e^{-i\omega t} \cdot dt$$

Inverse Fourier transform

$$F^{-1}\{F(\omega)\} = f(t) = \frac{1}{\sqrt{2\pi}} \cdot \int_{-\infty}^\infty F(\omega) \cdot e^{-i\omega t} \cdot dt$$

Example 1 - Determine the Fourier transform of the function f(t) = exp(-t), for t >0, and f(t) = 0, for t<0.

The continuous spectrum, $F(\omega)$, is calculated with the integral:

$$\frac{1}{\sqrt{2\pi}} \int_0^\infty e^{-(1+i\omega)t} dt = \lim_{\varepsilon \to \infty} \frac{1}{\sqrt{2\pi}} \int_0^\varepsilon e^{-(1+i\omega)t} dt = \lim_{\varepsilon \to \infty} \frac{1}{\sqrt{2\pi}} \left[\frac{1 - \exp(-(1+i\omega)t)}{1+i\omega} \right] = \frac{1}{\sqrt{2\pi}} \cdot \frac{1}{1+i\omega}.$$

This result can be rationalized by multiplying numerator and denominator by the conjugate of the denominator, namely, 1-iω. The result is now:

$$F(\omega) = \frac{1}{\sqrt{2\pi}} \cdot \frac{1}{1+i\omega} = \frac{1}{\sqrt{2\pi}} \cdot \left(\frac{1}{1+i\omega}\right)\left(\frac{1-i\omega}{1-i\omega}\right) = \frac{1}{\sqrt{2\pi}} \left(\frac{1}{1+\omega^2} - i \cdot \frac{\omega}{1+\omega^2}\right)$$

which is a complex function.

The real and imaginary parts of the function can be plotted as shown below

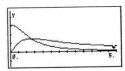

Notes:

The absolute value of the Fourier transform, $|F(\omega)|$, is the frequency spectrum of the original function $f(t)$. For the example shown above, $|F(\omega)| = 1/[2\pi(1+\omega^2)]^{1/2}$. The plot of $|F(\omega)|$ vs. ω was shown earlier.

Some functions, such as constant values, sin x, exp(x), x2, etc., do not have Fourier transform. Functions that go to zero sufficiently fast as x goes to infinity do have Fourier transforms.

Properties of the Fourier transform

Linearity: If a and b are constants, and f and g functions, then $F\{a\cdot f + b\cdot g\} = a\,F\{f\} + b\,F\{g\}$.

Transformation of partial derivatives. Let $u = u(x,t)$. If the Fourier transform transforms the variable x, then

$$F\{\partial u/\partial x\} = i\omega\,F\{u\}$$
$$F\{\partial^2 u/\partial x^2\} = -\omega^2\,F\{u\}$$
$$F\{\partial u/\partial t\} = \partial F\{u\}/\partial t$$
$$F\{\partial^2 u/\partial t^2\} = \partial^2 F\{u\}/\partial t^2$$

Convolution: For Fourier transform applications, the operation of convolution is defined as

$$(f * g)(x) = \frac{1}{\sqrt{2\pi}} \cdot \int f(x-\xi) \cdot g(\xi) \cdot d\xi.$$

The following property holds for convolution:

$$F\{f*g\} = F\{f\} \cdot F\{g\}.$$

275

Analytical solutions to parabolic equations

Case I -- One-dimensional solution of the heat equation

The flow of heat in a thin, laterally insulated homogeneous rod is modeled by

$$\partial u/\partial t = k \cdot (\partial^2 u/\partial x^2),$$

where u = temperature, k = a parameter resulting from combining thermal conductivity and density, together with an initial condition

$$u(x,0) = f(x)$$

and constant-value boundary conditions

$$u(0,t) = u_0, \text{ and } u(L,t) = u_L.$$

The physical phenomenon described by this PDE and its initial and boundary conditions is illustrated in the figure below.

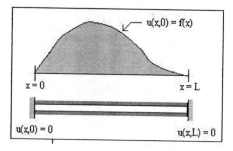

In the calculator the governing PDE is entered as:

'd2u(x,t) = k*d1d1u(x,t)' [ENTER].

We will try to find a solution to the PDE by the method of _separation of variables_. This method assumes that the solution, u(x,t), can be expressed as the product of two functions, X(x) and T(t), as follows:

'X(x)*T(t)' [ENTER][ENTER] [ENTER]

This will make 3 copies of u(x,t) available in stack.

Let's calculate the derivative d2u(x,t) first:
't' [ENTER] [↦][∂]
Then, calculate d1d1u(x,t) as follows:

[▶]'x' [ENTER] [↦][∂] 'x' [ENTER] [↦][∂]

Multiply this result by k and set up the equation by using:

'k' [ENTER] [×] [↦][=]

276

Now, divide by X(x)*T(t) by using:

$$[\blacktriangleright]\ [\text{ENTER}]\ [\rightarrow][=]\ [\div]$$

To simplify this equation use the equation writer:

[▼]	Trigger the equation writer
[▼][FACTO]	Select left-hand side of equation and factor terms out
[▶][FACTO]	Select right-hand side of equation, factor terms out

The result is now:

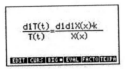

Since the left-hand side of the simplified equation is a function of t only, while the right-hand side is a function of x only, the only possibility is that both sides of the equation are equal to a constant value, say s −α. This substitution produces two differential equations:

$$dT/dt + \alpha T = 0, \ [A]$$

and

$$d^2X/dx^2 + (\alpha/k)X = 0. \ [B]$$

The solution to equation [A] can be easily found by using:

$$0\ [\text{ENTER}]\ \text{'X}+\alpha\text{'}\ [\text{ENTER}]\ [\hookleftarrow][\text{CALC}][\text{DIFF}][\text{LDEC}].$$

The result is: 'C0*EXP(-(α*X))', or $\quad$ $T(t) = C_0 \cdot \exp(-\alpha \cdot t)$.

For equation [B], the solution is found by using:

$$0\ [\text{ENTER}]\ \text{'X^2}+\alpha/k\text{'}\ [\text{ENTER}]\ [\hookleftarrow][\text{CALC}][\text{DIFF}][\text{LDEC}].$$

The result produced by the calculator (after about a minute of processing) is a complicated expression in terms of 'EXP(i·(α/k)^½·X)'. Assuming that a > 0, then this solution can be written simply as:

$$X(x) = C_1 \sin((\alpha/k)^{\frac{1}{2}} \cdot x) + C_2 \cos((\alpha/k)^{\frac{1}{2}} \cdot x).$$

Suppose that the boundary conditions are u(0,t) = 0, and u(L,t) = 0. Replacing these conditions in the equation for X(x) results in the equations:

$$0 = C_1 \cdot 0 + C_2 \cdot 1 \ \blacktriangleright \ C_2 = 0,$$

and

$$0 = C_1 \cdot \sin((\alpha/k)^{\frac{1}{2}} \cdot L) + 0 \cdot \cos((\alpha/k)^{\frac{1}{2}} \cdot x) \ \blacktriangleright \ C_1 \cdot \sin((\alpha/k)^{\frac{1}{2}} \cdot L) = 0.$$

The latter result produces $C_1 \neq 0$ only if $\quad$ $\sin((\alpha/k)^{\frac{1}{2}} \cdot L) = 0$.

This equation is satisfied as long as $(\alpha/k)^{\frac{1}{2}} \cdot L = n\pi$, where n = ...-3, -2, -1, 0 , 1, 2, 3, ... Because there is a different value of α for every value of n, we will identify those values as α_n (eigenvalues) and write:

$$\alpha_n = n^2\pi^2 k/L^2, \quad n = 0, 1, 2, \ldots$$

Thus, $(\alpha/k)^{1/2} = n\pi/L$, and the solution corresponding to a particular value of n (eigenfunctions) can be written as

$$X_n(x) = b_n \cdot \sin(n\pi x/L).$$

where C_1 has been replaced by bn to emphasize the dependency of the solution on the value of n.

The solution for the time-dependent component, T(t), in terms of n, can be written now as:

$$T(t) = C_0 \cdot \exp(-n^2\pi^2 kt/L^2).$$

Combining the results for $X_n(x)$ and T(t) into a single solution, and letting C_0 be absorbed by b_n, we get as the general solution for a particular value of n:

$$u_n(x,t) = b_n \cdot \exp(-n^2\pi^2 kt/L^2) \cdot \sin(n\pi x/L).$$

The most general solution is, of course, an infinite series representing the linear combination of all possible solutions $u_n(x,t)$, i.e.,

$$u(x,t) = \sum_{n=1}^{\infty} b_n \cdot \exp\left(-\frac{n^2\pi^2 kt}{L}\right) \cdot \sin\left(\frac{n\pi x}{L}\right).$$

restricting the solution to only positive values of n.

The initial condition u(x,0) = f(x), when replaced into this general equation produces a Fourier sine series, i.e.,

$$f(x) = \sum_{n=1}^{\infty} b_n \cdot \sin\left(\frac{n\pi x}{L}\right) = u(x, t = 0).$$

The coefficients b_n are therefore found as in a Fourier series:

$$b_n = \frac{2}{L}\int_0^L f(x) \cdot \sin\left(\frac{n\pi x}{L}\right) \cdot dx, \quad n \neq 0.$$

Recall that $b_0 = 0$.

Example 1 - Determine the solution for the one-dimensional heat equation subjected to u(0,t) = u(L,t) = 0, if the initial conditions are given by u(x,0) = f(x) = $4 \cdot (x/L)^3 \cdot (1-x/L)^2$.

Without loss of generality we can take L = 1, and define the function:

'f(X) = 4*X^3*(1-X)^2' [ENTER][¬][DEF]

We will store in separate variables the values of the constants k and L, and of the number of components to be included in the series solution, m. For example, for k = 1, L = 1, and m = 3, we will use:

1 [ENTER] [↱]['] [ALPHA][↰][K] [STO▶]
1 [ENTER] [↱]['] [ALPHA][L] [STO▶]
3 [ENTER] [↱]['] [ALPHA][↰][M] [STO▶]

To calculate the coefficient bn, we define the function bb(n) using the following program:

```
<< →n <<-105 CF n 'π' * 'X' * L / SIN 'f(X)' EVAL * 0 SWAP L SWAP 'X'∫2 L / * EVAL
>>
```

The program will be stored in variable [bb] by using:

[ALPHA][ALPHA][↰][B][↰][B][ENTER][STO▶].

The following program, GETb, is used to obtain a vector with the values of the coefficients b_n:

```
<< → m << 1 m FOR n 'bb(n)' EVAL NEXT m →ARRY 'b' STO >> >>
```

The coefficients will be stored in variable b.   Press

3 [ENTER][GETb]

and allow the calculator about a minute to calculate array b for m = 3.   Press [↱][b] to see the contents of the array:

['-((16*π^2-192)/π^5)' '(2*π^2-30)/π^5' '-((48*π^2-64)/(81*π^5)'].

Press [↱][NUM] to obtain floating-point results for b:

[0.11138606854   -3.35298404164E-2   -1.65300837009E-2].

Store this version of the vector in variable b, by using: [↰][b]

To calculate the function F(x,t), defined as:

$$F(x,t) = \sum_{n=1}^{m} b(n) \cdot EXP\left(-\frac{n^2 \cdot \pi^2 \cdot k \cdot t}{L}\right) \cdot SIN\left(\frac{n \cdot \pi \cdot x}{L}\right)$$

use the following program:

```
<< → x t << 0  1 m  FOR n 'b(n)' EVAL 'EXP(-n^2*π^2*k*t/L)' EVAL
* 'SIN(n*π*x/L)' EVAL * + NEXT >> >>
```

Store the program in variable F, as   [↱]['] [ALPHA][F] [STO▶].

Check the proper operation of F(x,t) by using the following values:

0.1 [ENTER] 0.1 [ENTER] [F], the result is 1.2448375716E-2

0.5 [ENTER] 0.05 [ENTER] [F], the result is 6.81957051351E-2

0.8 [ENTER] 0.01 [ENTER] [F], the result is 0.074338303467

A three dimensional picture of the solution F(x,t) can be obtained by using the following:

Press [↩][2D/3D] (simultaneously) to get the PLOT SETUP screen. The screen should be modified to look like this:

When done with the setting up of this screen, press [NXT][OK]. Next, press [↩][WIN] (simultaneously) to get the PLOT WINDOW screen. The screen should be modified to look like this:

When done with the changes in X-, Y-, and Z-ranges, press [ERASE][DRAW]. In the following graph Y represents time t. A view of the three-dimensional depiction of F(x,t) is shown below:

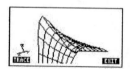

Press [EXIT], and then [CANCEL], to return to the PLOT WINDOW screen. Press [ON] to return to normal calculator display.

To see an animation of the function F(x,t), which will show F vs. x for different values of t, press [↩][2D/3D] (simultaneously) to get the PLOT SETUP screen. Change the type of function to Y-Slice, then press [ERASE][DRAW]. After a couple of minutes the calculator will show an animation of the temperature vs. x for different values of t. Notice that the animation in the calculator is actually run backwards. The temperature should be decreasing with time, rather than increasing with time as suggested by the animation. Press [ON] to stop the animation. Press [CANCL] to return to the PLOT SETUP screen. Finally, press [ON] to return to normal calculator display.

To see a particular temperature distribution for a fixed value of t, say for t = 0.01, first generate the expression corresponding to this value of t by using:

'X' [ENTER] 0.01 [ENTER][F]

The result is an expression involving SIN functions of X. Define this expression as a function h(X) by using:

280

'h(X)' [ENTER] [▶] [↵][=] [↵][DEF].

The plot of h(X) vs. X can be generated as follows:

Press [↵][2D/3D] (simultaneously) to get the PLOT SETUP screen. The screen should be modified to look like this:

When done with the setting up of this screen, press [NXT][OK]. Next, press [↵][WIN] (simultaneously) to get the PLOT WINDOW screen. The screen should be modified to look like this:

When done with the changes in X-, and Y-ranges, press [ERASE][DRAW]. The figure should look like this:

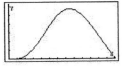

Check that the temperature distribution for t = 0.1 corresponds to the lower curve in the following figure:

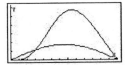

Case II - Solving the heat equation with non-zero boundary conditions

The heat equation solved in the previous section corresponds to an insulated rod subjected to zero temperature in both ends of the rod.   If the boundary conditions turn out to be different non-zero values of temperature on both ends, say $u(0,t) = u_0$, and $u(L,t) = u_L$, the solution can still be obtained by separation of variables, but a change of variable must be introduced.   The set up for initial and boundary conditions, as well as the general behavior of $u(x,t)$, for $t > 0$, is depicted in the figure below.

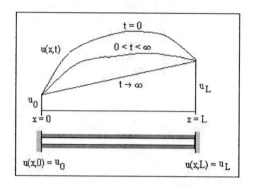

As time goes to infinity, the solution $u(x,t)$ will tend towards a steady state $S(x)$ which will be a linear function of x as illustrated in the figure, i.e.,

$$S(x) = u_0 + (u_L - u_0)(x/L).$$

Notice that $\qquad \partial S/\partial x = (u_L - u_0)/L., \partial^2 S/\partial x^2 = 0,$ and $\partial S/\partial t = 0.$

The solution $u(x,t)$ can be written as the sum of the steady-state component, $S(x)$, and a unsteady component, $U(x,t)$, i.e.,

$$u(x,t) = S(x) + U(x,t).$$

Replacing this result in the governing PDE, $u_t = k\,u_{xx}$, with $u_t = U_t$, and $u_{xx} = U_{xx}$, we obtain a governing PDE for $U(x)$, i.e.,

$$\partial U/\partial t = k \cdot (\partial^2 U/\partial x^2).$$

Also, the boundary condition at $x = 0$ becomes $u(0,t) = u_0 = S(0) + U(0,t)$, i.e., $u_0 = u_0 + U(0,t)$, or

$$U(0,t) = 0.$$

Similarly, the boundary condition at $x = L$ is transformed into

$$U(L,t) = 0.$$

The initial condition, $u(x,0) = f(x) = S(x) + U(x,0)$, or,

$$U(x,0) = f(x) - S(x) = g(x).$$

Thus, the original problem with non-zero, constant boundary conditions has been transformed into a problem of zero-valued boundary conditions for the transient component of the solution, $U(x,t)$. In terms of $U(x,t)$, the solution to this problem is exactly the same as for $u(x,t)$ in the previous section, except that the initial condition is now $g(x) = f(x) - S(x)$, rather than simply $f(x)$. With that difference in mind we can write as the solution for $U(x,t)$:

$$U(x,t) = \sum_{n=1}^{\infty} b_n \cdot \exp(-\frac{n^2 \pi^2 kt}{L}) \cdot \sin(\frac{n\pi x}{L}),$$

with

$$b_n = \frac{2}{L}\int_0^L (f(x) - S(x)) \cdot \sin(\frac{n\pi x}{L}) \cdot dx.$$

The solution of the original PDE is, therefore, written as:

$$u(x,t) = u_0 + (u_L - u_0) \cdot (\frac{x}{L}) + \sum_{n=1}^{\infty} b_n \cdot \exp(-\frac{n^2 \pi^2 kt}{L}) \cdot \sin(\frac{n\pi x}{L}).$$

Example 1 - Determine the solution to the heat equation with k = 1, L = 1, if the boundary conditions are $u(0,t) = u_0 = 2$, $u(L,t) = u_L = 1$.

Before using the program, store the values of u0, uL, and L in the calculator, i.e.,

2 [ENTER] 'u0' [ENTER][STO▶]   1 [ENTER] 'u0' [ENTER][STO▶]   1 [ENTER] 'L' [ENTER][STO▶]

To calculate the coefficient b_n, we define the function bb(n) using the following program:

```
<< →n <<-105 CF n 'π' * 'X' * L / SIN 'f(X)-S(X)' EVAL EVAL * 0 SWAP L SWAP 'X' ∫2 L
/ * EVAL >>
```

The program will be stored in variable [bb] by using:

[ALPHA][ALPHA][↩][B][↩][B][ENTER][STO▶].

We can now use the program GETb to obtain a vector with the values of the coefficients b_n. Press

3 [ENTER][GETb]

and allow the calculator about a minute or two to calculate array b for m = 3. The coefficients will be stored in variable b.   Press [→][b] to see the contents of the array:

[0.891088   -6.9035E-12   -0.13224].

Next, modify program F, from the previous section, to read:

```
<< → x t << 0  1 m  FOR n 'b(n)' EVAL 'EXP(-n^2*π^2*k*t/L)' EVAL
   * 'SIN(n*π*x/L)' EVAL * 'S(x)' EVAL + + NEXT >> >>
```

Store this program under the name 'G'.

283

To see an animation of the function G(x,t), which will show G vs. x for different values of t, first press [←][2D/3D], and change the ranges in X, Y, and Z, respectively to (0,1), (0,1), and (0, 3). Then, press [NXT][OK]. The next step is to press [←][WIN] (simultaneously) to get the PLOT SETUP screen. Change the type of function to Y-Slice, then press [ERASE][DRAW]. After a couple of minutes the calculator will show an animation of the temperature vs. x for different values of t. Press [ON] to stop the animation. Press [CANCL] to return to the PLOT SETUP screen. Finally, press [ON] to return to normal calculator display.

A three-dimensional depiction of the solution G(x,t) can be obtained by selecting Fast3D for the Type in the PLOT SETUP window. Also, change the Y-range to (0, 0.2) in the PLOT WINDOW screen.

A view of the surface z = G(x,t) is shown below:

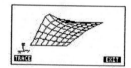

Press [EXIT][CANCL][ON] to return to normal calculator display.

Other forms of the heat equation and of its boundary conditions

The heat equation solved in the two previous sections, namely,

$$\partial u/\partial t = k \cdot (\partial^2 u/\partial x^2),$$

corresponds to an insulated rod subjected to zero temperature in both ends of the rod. Other versions of the equation are:

Lateral heat loss due to convection:

$$\partial u/\partial t = k \cdot (\partial^2 u/\partial x^2) - \kappa \cdot (u-u_A),$$

where u_A = average ambient temperature in the fluid (air, water) that surrounds the rod. The term

$$\kappa \cdot (u-u_A),$$

represents the flux of heat loss due to convection, i.e., temperature difference between the rod's temperature u(x,t), and the ambient temperature u_A. The physical phenomenon described by this ODE is sketched below.

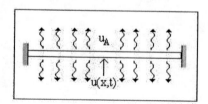

284

Existence of an *internal heat source* (or sink)

$$\partial u / \partial t = k \cdot (\partial^2 u / \partial x^2) + \phi(x,t),$$

where $\phi(x,t)$ is a function describing the heat flux along the rod and as a function of time due to a source of heat (hot spot) within the rod.

We distinguish three *basic types of boundary conditions* for heat transfer/diffusion type problems:

Temperature defined as a function of time, i.e., $u(0,t) = g_1(t)$, or $u(L,t) = g_2(t)$.

Temperature gradient normal to the boundary defined as a function of time, i.e., $\partial u / \partial n |_{x=0} = g_1(t)$, or $\partial u / \partial n |_{x=L} = g_2(t)$.

A linear combination of the gradient and the temperature given as a function of time, i.e., $(\partial u / \partial n + u)|_{x=0} = g_1(t)$, or $(\partial u / \partial n + u)|_{x=L} = g_2(t)$.

These three basic types of boundary conditions are also commonly used for elliptic and hyperbolic PDE problems. The last two examples of solutions for PDEs (sections Parabolic Equations (I) and (II)) use the first type of boundary conditions, i.e., temperature defined as a function of time (actually constant values). In the next section, we show how to solve the heat equation with one derivative boundary condition.

Case III - Solving the heat equation with a derivative boundary condition

In this section we solve the PDE:

$$\partial u / \partial t = k \cdot (\partial^2 u / \partial x^2),$$

subjected to the homogeneous boundary conditions:

$$u(0,t) = 0$$
$$u_x(L,t) + \beta \cdot u(L,t) = 0$$

and the initial condition:

$$u(x,0) = f(x).$$

Using separation of variables we can write:
$$u(x,t) = X(x)T(t).$$

This generates the following ODEs (see Case I for parabolic equations):

$$dT/dt + \alpha T = 0,$$

whose solution is

$$T(t) = C_0 \cdot \exp(-\alpha \cdot t),$$

and

$$d^2X/dx^2 + (\alpha/k)X = 0,$$

whose solution is

$$X(x) = C_1 \cdot \sin((\alpha/k)^{\frac{1}{2}} \cdot x) + C_2 \cdot \cos((\alpha/k)^{\frac{1}{2}} \cdot x),$$

where α is an arbitrary constant. The general solution of the PDE is, therefore,

$$u(x,t) = X(x) \cdot T(t) = \exp(-\alpha \cdot t) \cdot [C_1 \cdot \sin((\alpha/k)^{\frac{1}{2}} \cdot x) + C_2 \cdot \cos((\alpha/k)^{\frac{1}{2}} \cdot x)],$$

where the constant C_0 has been absorbed into constants C_1 and C_2.

To find the value(s) of the constant a that satisfy the boundary conditions we now replace this general solution into the expressions for the first boundary condition:

$$u(0,t) = C_2 \cdot \exp(-\alpha \cdot t) = 0, \rightarrow C_2 = 0,$$

which makes

$$u(x,t) = X(x) \cdot T(t) = C_1 \cdot \exp(-\alpha \cdot t) \cdot \sin((\alpha/k)^{\frac{1}{2}} \cdot x).$$

The second boundary condition produces the equation:

$$u_x(L,t) + \beta \cdot u(L,t) = C_1 \cdot (\alpha/k)^{\frac{1}{2}} \cdot \exp(-\alpha \cdot t) \cdot \cos((\alpha/k)^{\frac{1}{2}} \cdot L) + \beta \cdot C_1 \cdot \exp(-\alpha \cdot t) \cdot \sin((\alpha/k)^{\frac{1}{2}} \cdot L) = 0$$

The term $\exp(-\alpha \cdot t) \neq 0$ for $\alpha > 0$ and $t > 0$. Under these conditions and for $C_1 \neq 0$, the equation above reduces to:

$$\tan((\alpha/k)^{\frac{1}{2}} \cdot L) = -(\alpha/k)^{\frac{1}{2}}/\beta.$$

The solution(s) of this equation depend on the values of β, k, and L, and can, in general, be obtained through graphical or numerical methods.

Example 1 – Determine the solutions for α from the equation above if $k = 1$, $L = 1$, and $\beta = 1$.

The equation to solve is $\tan(\alpha^{1/2}) = -\alpha^{1/2}$, or, using $\lambda = \alpha^{1/2}$, $\tan \lambda = -\lambda$.

To solve

$$tan(\lambda) = -\lambda,$$

you could plot the functions $f_1(X) = TAN(X)$, and $f_2(X) = -X$, and find their intersections as shown below:

- Press [↩][2D/3D], simultaneously to access to the PLOT SETUP window.

➢ Change TYPE to FUNCTION, if needed, by using [CHOOS].

➢ Press [▼] and type in the equation list { 'TAN(X)' '–X' }.

➢ Make sure the independent variable is set to 'X'.

➢ Press [NXT][OK] to return to normal calculator display.

- Press [↩][WIN], simultaneously, to access the PLOT window.

➢ Change the H-VIEW range to 0 to 12, and the V-VIEW range to -6 to 0.

➢ Press [ERASE][DRAW] to plot the function in polar coordinates. The resulting plot looks as follows:

➢ Notice the vertical asymptotes. These are not part of the graph, but show up because TAN(X) goes to ± ∞ at certain values of X. There are three roots of the equation tan(λ) = -λ in this interval. One of the roots, although not obvious from the figure, is λ = 0. To find the next one to the right, move the cursor near the intersection of the two lines, and press [FCN][ISECT]. The result is I-sect: (2.028757, -2.028757). Thus, the first positive solution of tan(λ) = -λ is

$$\lambda = 2.028757.$$

The second solution can also be obtained from the graph by moving the cursor closer to the second intersection shown and using ISECT again. This time the result is:

$$\lambda = 4.91318.$$

➢ Press [NXT][NXT][PICT][CANCL][ON] to return to normal calculator display.

To determine more solutions you can re-draw the graph using a more appropriate range for both X and Y, or use the HP 49 G's numerical solver as follows (angular measures in radians):

[↱][NUM.SLV][OK]   Start equation solver
[↱]['][TAN][X] [▶] [↱][=] [+/-][X] [OK]   Enter equation 'TAN(X)=–X'

Since we want to obtain solutions larger than the values already found (2.028757 and 4.91318), we enter next a value of 6 in the field labeled X:, i.e.

[6][OK]   Enter initial value of 6 for X
[▼] [SOLVE]   Move cursor back to X and solve equation

Interestingly enough, this starting value of X (X=6) returns a solution of X = 0, which we already know. Let's try changing the starting value to 7, i.e.,

[7][OK]   Enter initial value of 7 for X
[▼] [SOLVE]   Move cursor back to X and solve equation

The starting value of X = 7 produces a solution X = -2.028757. Since we are interested only in positive solutions we change the initial value once more to 8, i.e.,

[8][OK]   Enter initial value of 8 for X
[▼] [SOLVE]   Move cursor back to X and solve equation

The solution is now X = 7.97867, which is larger than the last value found graphically, i.e., λ = 4.91318. Continue changing the initial value of X to 9, 10, 11, etc. and check that you get the following solutions:

Initial X	Solution	Initial X	Solution
6	0.0000	14	0.0000
7	-2.0875	15	14.2074
8	7.9787	16	0.0000
9	0.0000	17	11.2709
10	4.9132	18	17.3363
11	11.0855	19	0.0000
12	11.0855	20	0.0000
13	0.0000	21	20.4692

The solution that results when using 17 as an initial value is not correct. You can check with the calculator all other solutions and all satisfy the equation 'TAN(X) = -X', except for the value of 11.2709. This is obviously a fluke in the algorithm used for the numerical solution of the equation, and should be dropped form the list of solutions. In summary, thus, the first six positive solutions to the equation $\tan \lambda = -\lambda$, and the corresponding values of α, are:

n	λ_n	$\alpha_n = \lambda_n^2$
1	2.0875	4.3577
2	4.9132	24.1395
3	7.9787	63.6597
4	11.0855	122.8883
5	14.2074	201.8502
6	20.4692	418.9881

The sub-index n is used to indicate the different solutions. The values of α_n in this case are eigenvalues of the solution

$u_n(x,t) = C_n \cdot \exp(-\alpha_n \cdot t) \cdot \sin((\alpha_n/k)^{1/2} \cdot x) = C_n \cdot \exp(-\alpha_n \cdot t) \cdot \sin(\alpha_n^{1/2} \cdot x)$, with k = 1.

The most general solution for the PDE subjected to the boundary conditions under consideration is the linear combination of an infinite number of these solutions $u_n(x,t)$, i.e.,

$$u(x,t) = \sum_{n=1}^{\infty} C_n \cdot \exp(-\alpha_n \cdot t) \cdot \sin(\sqrt{\alpha_n} \cdot x),$$

or,

$$u(x,t) = \sum_{n=1}^{\infty} C_n \cdot \exp(-\lambda_n^2 \cdot t) \cdot \sin(\lambda_n \cdot x).$$

To find the coefficients C_n we use the initial condition u(x,0) = f(x), or

$$f(x) = \sum_{n=1}^{\infty} C_n \cdot \sin(\lambda_n \cdot x),$$

which is a series expansion similar to a Fourier sine series. To obtain the values of the coefficients C_n, n = 1, 2, 3, ..., we use the concept of orthogonal functions which were presented earlier in Chapter 15.

288

First, define the functions

$$g_n(x) = \sin(\lambda_n \cdot x), \quad n = 1, 2, 3, \ldots$$

To check whether these functions are orthogonal we calculate the integral

$$\int_0^1 \mathrm{SIN}(\lambda_n \cdot x) \cdot \mathrm{SIN}(\lambda_m \cdot x) \, dx \blacktriangleleft$$

EDIT	CURS	BIG ▪	EVAL	FACTO	TEXPA

which evaluates to

$$\frac{(\lambda_m - \lambda_n) \cdot \mathrm{SIN}(\lambda_m + \lambda_n) - (\lambda_m + \lambda_n) \cdot \mathrm{SIN}(\lambda_m - \lambda_n)}{2\lambda_m^2 - 2\lambda_n^2}$$

To check whether this expression evaluates to zero, first press [ENTER] to get back to stack display. Then press [↱][TRIG][NXT][TEXPA] [↱][EVAL] to expand and simplify the expression

$$\frac{\lambda_n \cdot \mathrm{COS}(\lambda_n) \cdot \mathrm{SIN}(\lambda_m) - \lambda_m \cdot \mathrm{COS}(\lambda_m) \cdot \mathrm{SIN}(\lambda_n)}{\lambda_m^2 - \lambda_n^2}$$

to:

Now, recalling that λ_n and λ_m are roots of the equation

$$\tan \lambda = -\lambda,$$

then

$$\sin \lambda / \cos \lambda = -\lambda,$$

or

$$\sin \lambda = -\lambda \cdot \cos \lambda.$$

Thus, replacing $\sin \lambda_m = -\lambda_m \cdot \cos \lambda_m$, and $\sin \lambda_n = -\lambda_n \cdot \cos \lambda_n$, in the numerator of the expression framed above, we have:

$$(\lambda_n \cdot \cos \lambda_n \cdot (-\lambda_m \cdot \cos \lambda_m) - \lambda_m \cdot \cos \lambda_m \cdot (-\lambda_n \cdot \cos \lambda_n)) = -\lambda_n \cdot \lambda_m \cdot \cos \lambda_n \cdot \cos \lambda_m + \lambda_n \cdot \lambda_m \cdot \cos \lambda_n \cdot \cos \lambda_m = 0.$$

Thus, the functions $g_n(x) = \sin(\lambda_n \cdot x)$, $n = 1, 2, 3, \ldots$, where λ_n are roots of the equation $\tan \lambda = -\lambda$, are orthogonal functions.

The value of the integral when $n = m$ can be obtained using the calculator by setting up the integral

289

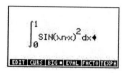

This value is

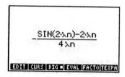

Using $\sin(2\lambda_n) = 2 \sin \lambda_n \cdot \cos \lambda_n$, this expression simplifies to

$$\int_0^1 \sin^2 \lambda_n x \cdot dx = \frac{\lambda_n - \sin \lambda_n \cdot \cos \lambda_n}{2 \cdot \lambda_n}.$$

The coefficients of the expansion, C_n, are calculated as

$$C_n = \frac{\int_0^1 f(x) \cdot \sin \lambda_n x \cdot dx}{\int_0^1 \sin^2 \lambda_n x \cdot dx} = \frac{2 \cdot \lambda_n}{\lambda_n - \sin \lambda_n \cdot \cos \lambda_n} \cdot \int_0^1 f(x) \cdot \sin \lambda_n x.$$

Example 2 -- If the initial condition for the problem under consideration is given by f(x) = x, determine the solution for the heat equation.

We will need to calculate a few coefficients C_n, say for n = 1, 2, 3, by using the equation obtained above. I propose we use a function

‘C(n)=2*λ(n)/(λ(n)-SIN(λ(n))*COS(λ(n)))*∫(0,1,f(x)*SIN(l(n)*x),x)’

Use [↵][DEF] to create the function. Also, define the function

‘f(x) = x’

by using [↵][DEF] once more.

We also create a vector containing the values of ln, i.e.,

[2.0875   4.9132   7.9787] [ENTER] ‘λ’ [ENTER][STO]

To obtain the three coefficients use:

290

1 [C], Result: $C_1 = 0.723490$
2 [C], Result: $C_2 = -0.156169$
3 [C], Result: $C_3 = 0.061405$

We can create a vector with these three values in the stack by using

$$3 \text{ [ENTER] } [\neg][\text{PRG}][\text{TYPE}][\rightarrow\text{ARRY}],$$

and save it under the name cc:

$$\text{'cc'[STO▶]}$$

The solution, with three components, can now be written as

$$u(x,t) = \sum_{n=1}^{3} cc(n) \cdot \exp(-\lambda(n)^2 \cdot t) \cdot \sin(\lambda(n) \cdot x).$$

In the stack this is entered as

$$\text{'u(x,t)=}\Sigma\text{(n=1,3,cc(n)*EXP(-(}\lambda\text{(n)\textasciicircum 2*t)*SIN(}\lambda\text{(n)*x))'}$$

Use $[\neg][\text{DEF}]$ to define the function u.

To see an animation of the function u(x,t), which will show u vs. x for different values of t, first press $[\neg][\text{2D/3D}]$, and change the ranges in X, Y, and Z, respectively to (0,1), (0,1), and (0, 1). Then, press [NXT][OK]. The next step is to press $[\neg][\text{WIN}]$ (simultaneously) to get the PLOT SETUP screen. Change the type of function to Y-Slice, then press [ERASE][DRAW]. After a couple of minutes the calculator will show an animation of the temperature vs. x for different values of t. Press [ON] to stop the animation. Press [CANCL] to return to the PLOT SETUP screen. Finally, press [ON] to return to normal calculator display.

A three-dimensional depiction of the solution G(x,t) can be obtained by selecting Fast3D for the Type in the PLOT SETUP window. Change the Z-scale to (-0.5,1). Then, use [ERASE][DRAW].

A view of the surface z = u(x,t) is shown below:

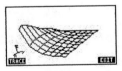

Press [EXIT][CANCL][ON] to return to normal calculator display.

Case IV - Solving the heat equation with heat convection loss

In this section we solve the PDE:

$$\partial u / \partial t = k \cdot (\partial^2 u / \partial x^2) - \beta u,$$

subjected to the homogeneous boundary conditions:

$$u(0,t) = 0$$
$$u(L,t) = 0$$

and the initial condition:

$$u(x,0) = f(x).$$

A simple approach to the solution is to replace the temperature function $u(x,t)$ with

$$u(x,t) = \exp(-\beta \cdot t) \cdot w(x,t).$$

You can easily check that

$$u_t(x,t) = -\beta \cdot \exp(-\beta \cdot t) \cdot w(x,t) + \exp(-\beta \cdot t) \cdot w_t(x,t),$$
$$u_x(x,t) = \exp(-\beta \cdot t) \cdot w_x(x,t),$$

and

$$u_{xx}(x,t) = \exp(-\beta \cdot t) \cdot w_{xx}(x,t),$$

which reduces the PDE to

$$\partial w / \partial t = k \cdot (\partial^2 w / \partial x^2),$$

and the corresponding boundary and initial conditions to

$$w(0,t) = 0, \ w(L,t) = 0, \text{ and } w(x,0) = f(x).$$

This is basically as the problem solved in Case I. Once the solution $w(x,t)$ for the latter system is found, the solution to the original system, is simply $u(x,t) = e^{-\beta t} \cdot w(x,t)$.

Case V - Solving the diffusion-convection equation with constant flow velocity

Many equations related to diffusion in moving fluids include a term involving the flow velocity v (in the x-direction)

$$\partial u / \partial t + v \cdot (\partial u / \partial x) = k \cdot (\partial^2 u / \partial x^2).$$

If v is a constant, this equation can also be reduced to

$$\partial w / \partial t = k \cdot (\partial^2 w / \partial x^2),$$

by using the transformation

$$u(x,t) = \exp[\frac{v}{2 \cdot k} \cdot (x - \frac{1}{2} \cdot v \cdot t)] \cdot w(x,t).$$

The reduced equation is the same as the original heat equation without heat sources or sinks and can be solved by separation of variables with an appropriate set of boundary conditions.

292

Case VI - Solving the non-homogeneous heat equation by eigenfunction expansion

In this section we solve the PDE:

$$\partial u / \partial t = k \cdot (\partial^2 u / \partial x^2) + h(x,t),$$

subjected to the homogeneous boundary conditions:

$$u(0,t) = 0$$
$$u(L,t) = 0$$

and the initial condition:

$$u(x,0) = f(x).$$

The eigenfunction expansion method consists in writing the heat source term, $h(x,t)$, as the series expansion

$$h(x,t) = \sum_{n=1}^{\infty} g_n(t) \cdot \sin(n\pi x),$$

and the solution to the PDE as

$$u(x,t) = \sum_{n=1}^{\infty} T_n(t) \cdot \sin(n\pi x).$$

This method is called eigenfunction expansion is because the orthogonal functions $\{\sin(n\pi x)\}$, used in the expansions for both $h(x,t)$ and $u(x,t)$, are the eigenfunctions of the Sturm-Liouville problem (see Chapter 14) that results from the homogeneous PDE solution using separation of variables.

Replacing the expression for $u(x,t)$ in the PDE system

$$\frac{\partial u}{\partial t} = k \cdot \frac{\partial^2 u}{\partial x^2} + \sum_{n=1}^{\infty} g_n(t) \cdot \sin(n\pi x),$$

$$u(0,t) = 0$$
$$u(L,t) = 0$$
$$u(x,0) = f(x).$$

Results in the simplified problem

$$\sum_{n=1}^{\infty} \left[\frac{dT_n}{dt} + n^2 \cdot \pi^2 \cdot k \cdot T_n(t) - g_n(t) \right] \cdot \sin(n\pi x) = 0,$$

$$\sum_{n=1}^{\infty} T_n(0) \cdot \sin(n\pi x) = f(x).$$

The first equation is satisfied if

293

$$\frac{dT_n}{dt} + n^2 \cdot \pi^2 \cdot k \cdot T_n(t) = g_n(t).$$

The second equation represents a Fourier sine series with

$$T_n(t) = b_n \cdot \exp(-n^2 \cdot \pi^2 \cdot k \cdot t) + \int_0^t \exp[(-n^2 \cdot \pi^2 \cdot k) \cdot (t-\tau)] \cdot g_n(\tau) \cdot d\tau.$$

The solution for $T_n(t)$, using an integrating factor in the last linear, first-order ODE, and the initial condition $T_n(0) = b_n$, is

$$b_n = T_n(0) = 2 \cdot \int_0^1 f(\xi) \cdot \sin(n\pi\xi) \cdot d\xi.$$

Replacing these results in the expression for u(x,t) produces the following solution for the original PDE:

$$u(x,t) = U(x,t) + S(x,t) = \sum_{n=1}^{\infty} b_n e^{-n^2 \pi^2 kt} \sin(n\pi x) + \sum_{n=1}^{\infty} \sin(n\pi x) \cdot \int_0^t e^{-n^2 \pi^2 k(t-\tau)} g_n(\tau) d\tau,$$

where U(x,t), equal to the first summation in the solution, represents a transient component consequence of the initial condition, and S(x,t), equal to the second summation, represents a steady-state component generated by the heat source h(x,t).

Example 1 -- To solve the non-homogeneous problem

$$\partial u/\partial t = \partial^2 u/\partial x^2 + \sin(\pi x),$$

subject to the boundary conditions

$$u(0,t) = 0, \ u(1,t) = 0,$$

and to the initial condition,

$$u(x,0) = 1,$$

by eigenfunction expansion, we identify the following parameters:

$$k = 1, \text{ and, } h(x,t) = \sin(\pi x).$$

Thus, the heat source term has only one term, n = 1, and $g_1(x) = \sin(\pi x)$.

The coefficient b_1 is calculated using:

Which results in

$$b_1 = 4/\pi.$$

294

Also, the integral in the steady-state term, for n = 1, can be calculated using

$$\int_0^t EXP\left\{-\left(\pi^2 \cdot (t-\tau)\right)\right\} \cdot 1 \, d\tau \blacktriangleleft$$

The result being

$$\frac{EXP\left(t \cdot \pi^2\right) - 1}{\pi^2 \cdot EXP\left(t \cdot \pi^2\right)}$$

or, $(1/\pi^2) \cdot [1 - exp(-\pi^2 t)]$.

The solution to the PDE is, therefore, written as

$$u(x,t) = (4/\pi) \cdot exp(-\pi^2 t) \cdot sin(\pi x) + (1/\pi^2) \cdot [1 - exp(-\pi^2 t)] \cdot sin(\pi x),$$

or

$$u(x,t) = (sin(\pi x)/\pi) \cdot [4 \cdot exp(-\pi^2 t) + [1 - exp(-\pi^2 t)] \, / \pi \,].$$

In the stack this is entered as

'u(x,t) = (SIN(π*x) / π)*(4*EXP(-π^2*t)+(1- EXP(-π^2*t))/π)'

Use [←][DEF] to define the function u.

To see an animation of the function u(x,t), which will show u vs. x for different values of t, first press [←][2D/3D], and change the ranges in X, Y, and Z, respectively to (0,1), (0,1), and (0, 1.5). Then, press [NXT][OK]. The next step is to press [←][WIN] (simultaneously) to get the PLOT SETUP screen. Change the type of function to Y-Slice, then press [ERASE][DRAW]. After a couple of minutes the calculator will show an animation of the temperature vs. x for different values of t. Press [ON] to stop the animation. Press [CANCL] to return to the PLOT SETUP screen. Finally, press [ON] to return to normal calculator display.

A three-dimensional depiction of the solution u(x,t) can be obtained by selecting Fast3D for the Type in the PLOT SETUP window. Change the Z-scale to (-0.5,1). Then, use [ERASE][DRAW].

A view of the surface z = u(x,t) is shown below:

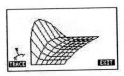

Press [EXIT][CANCL][ON] to return to normal calculator display.

295

Case VII: Solving the heat equation in a semi-infinite domain using Fourier sine transforms

To solve partial differential equations using integral transforms we take advantage of the fact that you can reduce the order of a derivative by one by introducing the transforms into the equation. In Chapter 14, when using Laplace transforms to solve ordinary differential equations, we managed to convert the ODEs to algebraic equations. A similar approach can be used to solve PDEs with Fourier sine and cosine transforms, which obey the following rules for derivatives:

$$F_s\{df/dt\} = -\omega F_c\{f(t)\}$$
$$F_s\{d^2f/dt^2\} = (2/\pi)\cdot\omega\cdot f(0) -\omega^2\cdot F_s\{f(t)\}$$
$$F_c\{df/dt\} = -(2/\pi)\cdot f(0) +\omega F_s\{f(t)\}$$
$$F_c\{d^2f/dt^2\} = -(2/\pi)\cdot f(0) -\omega^2\cdot F_s\{f(t)\}$$

We will use these rules to obtain the solution to the one-dimensional heat equation in a semi-infinite domain ($0<x<\infty$):

$$\partial u/\partial t = k\cdot(\partial^2 u/\partial x^2),$$

subject to the boundary condition $u(0,t) = u_0$, and to the initial condition $u(x,0) = 0$. Applying the Fourier sine transforms to both sides of the PDE we can write

$$F_s\,[\partial u/\partial t] = k\cdot F_s\,[\partial^2 u/\partial x^2].$$

The term in the left-hand side of the equation is written as $F_s\{\partial u/\partial t\} = \partial\Phi_s\{u\}/\partial t = dU(t)/dt$, where $U(t) = F_s\{u(x,t)\}$. The integral to calculate this transform uses the variable x, therefore, the resulting transform is only a function of t.

The term in the right-hand side of the equation is transformed by using the rule:

$$\Phi_s\{\partial^2 u/\partial x^2\} = (2/\pi)\cdot\omega\cdot u(0,t) -\omega^2\cdot\Phi_s\{u(x,t)\} = (2/\pi)\cdot\omega\cdot u(0,t) -\omega^2\cdot U(t) = 2\cdot\omega u_0/\pi -\omega^2\cdot U(t).$$

The original PDE is transformed into the ODE:

$$dU/dt = k[-\omega^2\cdot U(t).\ 2\cdot\omega\ u_0/\pi\,],$$

Subject to the transformed boundary condition $\Phi_s\{u(x,0)\} = U(0) = 0$.

The resulting ODE can be re-cast as: $dU/dt+k\omega^2 U(t) = 2k\omega u_0/\pi$, subject to $U(0) = 0$, which can be solved using the calculator as:

['d1U(t)+k*ω^2*U(t)=2*k*ω*t0/π' 'U(0)=u0'][ENTER] 'U(t)' [ENTER] [↰][CALC][DIFF][DESOL]

The solution is
$$U(t) = 2\cdot u_0\cdot[1 - \exp(-k\cdot\omega^2\cdot t^2)]/(\pi\cdot\omega).$$

The inverse Fourier sine transform will provide the solution to the PDE, i.e., $u(x,t) = \Phi_s^{-1}\{U(t)\}$. Using a table of transforms [such as that given in Table B, Appendix 1 of Farlow, Stanley J., 1982, "Partial Differential Equations for Scientists and Engineers," Dover Publications Inc., New York], we find that the inverse Sine Fourier transform of the function U(t) above is

$$u(x,t) = u_0\cdot erfc(x/2\sqrt{(kt)}),$$

296

where erfc(ξ), defined as

$$erfc(x) = \frac{2}{\pi} \cdot \int_x^\infty e^{-t^2}\, dt,$$

is the complementary-error function. Also, if erf(x) is the error function of x, then erf(x) + erfc(x) = 1.

The error function

Although the calculator does not provide the error function, nor its complement, as a pre-programmed functions, we can obtain an expression for erfc(x) in terms of the Upper-Tail Probability Normal (UTPN) function. The UTPN(μ,σ^2,x) is defined in the menu [←][MTH][NXT][PROB][NXT][UTPN]. Specifically, we want to use the standard normal distribution,

Φ(z) = UTPN(0,1,z),

which has mean μ = 0 and variance σ^2 = 1 (See Chapters 4 and 12 for more information on the UTPN function).

The function Φ(z) is defined by

$$\Phi(z) = \frac{1}{\sqrt{2\pi}} \cdot \int_{-\infty}^z e^{-t^2/2}\, dt,.$$

The value of Φ(z) at z = 0 is Φ (0) = ½, thus, we can write

$$\Phi(z) = \Phi(0) + \frac{1}{\sqrt{2\pi}} \cdot \int_0^z e^{-t^2/2}\, dt = \frac{1}{2} + \frac{1}{\sqrt{\pi}} \cdot \int_0^{z/\sqrt{2}} e^{-\xi^2}\, d\xi = \frac{1}{2} \cdot [1 + erf(z/\sqrt{2})].$$

Replacing z = x·$\sqrt{2}$, and solving for erf(x), we find the following expression for the error function:

$$erf(x) = 1 - 2 \cdot \Phi(x \cdot \sqrt{2}) = 1 - 2 \cdot UTPN(0,1, x \cdot \sqrt{2}).$$

The complementary error function, thus, can be written in the calculator as

$$erfc(x) = 1 - erf(x) = 2 \cdot UTPN(0,1, x \cdot \sqrt{2}).$$

For u_0 = 1, and k = 1, the function u(x,t), which solves the PDE under consideration, can be defined in the calculator as the following program: << → x t << 0 1 'x/ (2*t)' EVAL UTPN 2 * >> >>, which is to be stored in the variable u: [→]['][ALPHA][←][U][STO▶].

To see an animation of the function u(x,t), which will show u vs. x for different values of t, first press [←][2D/3D], and change the ranges in X, Y, and Z, respectively to (0,1), (0,1), and (0, 1). Then, press [NXT][OK]. The next step is to press [←][WIN] (simultaneously) to get the

297

PLOT SETUP screen. Change the type of function to Y-Slice, then press [ERASE][DRAW]. Because the erfc(x) function requires the evaluation of an infinite integral, it will take a few minutes to come up with the animation. Press [ON] to stop the animation. Press [CANCL] to return to the PLOT SETUP screen. Finally, press [ON] to return to normal calculator display.

A three-dimensional depiction of the solution u(x,t) can be obtained by selecting Fast3D for the Type in the PLOT SETUP window. Then, use [ERASE][DRAW].

A view of the surface z = u(x,t) is shown below:

Press [EXIT][CANCL][ON] to return to normal calculator display.

Case VIII – Solution to the Cauchy problem (initial value problem)

The Cauchy problem consists of solving the heat equation

$$\partial u/\partial t = k \cdot (\partial^2 u/\partial x^2),$$

in an infinitely long rod subjected to an initial condition u(x,0) = f(x).

The solution to the Cauchy problem can be tackled by using Fourier transforms, so that the equation is transformed to

$$dU/dt = -k\omega^2 U,$$

subject to

$$U(0) = F(\omega),$$

where F(ω) = Φ\{f(x)\}.

The problem, having been transformed into an ODE, is easily solved with the calculator:

['d1U(t)+k*ω^2*U(t)=0' 'U(0)=F(ω)'][ENTER] 'U(t)' [ENTER] [↰][CALC][DIFF][DESOL]

The solution is: $U(t) = F(\omega)\exp(-kw^2 t).$

The inverse Fourier transform of this result can be found by using the convolution property:

$$u(x,t) = F^{-1}\{F(\omega)\cdot\exp(-kw^2 t)\} = F^{-1}\{F(\omega)\}*F^{-1}\{\exp(-k\omega^2 t)\} = f(x)*[(2kt)^{-1/2}\cdot\exp(-x^2/4kt)],$$

thus, the solution is

$$u(x,t) = \frac{1}{2\sqrt{\pi kt}}\int_{-\infty}^{+\infty} f(x)\exp[-\frac{(x-\omega)^2}{4kt}]d\omega.$$

298

Fast Fourier Transform (FFT) applications

The Fast Fourier Transform is a computer algorithm by which one can calculate very efficiently a discrete Fourier transform (DFT). This algorithm has applications in the analysis of different types of time-dependent signals, from turbulence measurements to communication signals.

The discrete Fourier transform of a sequence of data values $\{x_j\}$, $j = 0, 1, 2, ..., n-1$, is a new finite sequence $\{X_k\}$, defined as

$$X_k = \frac{1}{n}\sum_{j=0}^{n-1} x_j \cdot \exp(-i \cdot 2\pi kj / n), \qquad k = 0,1,2,...,n-1.$$

The direct calculation of the sequence X_k involves n^2 products, which would involve enormous amounts of computer (or calculator) time particularly for large values of n. The Fast Fourier Transform reduces the number of operations to the order of $n \cdot log_2 n$.   For example, for n = 100, the FFT requires about 664 operations, while the direct calculation would require 10,000 operations. Thus, the number of operations using the FFT is reduced by a factor of 10000/664 $\approx$ 15.

The FFT operates on the sequence $\{x_j\}$ by partitioning it into a number of shorter sequences. The DFT's of the shorter sequences are calculated and later combined together in a highly efficient manner.   For details on the algorithm refer, for example, to Newland, D.E., 1993, "An Introduction to Random Vibrations, Spectral & Wavelet Analysis - Third Edition," Longman Scientific and Technical, New York (Chapter 12).
The only requirement for the application of the FFT is that the number n be a power of 2, i.e., select your data so that it contains 2, 4, 8, 16, 32, 62, etc., points.

Examples of FFT applications

FFT applications usually involve data discretized from a time-dependent signal. The calculator can be fed that data, say from a computer or a data logger, for processing. Or, you can generate your own data by programming a function and adding a few random numbers to it.

Example 1 - Define the function f(x) = 2 sin (3x) + 5 cos(5x) + 0.5*RAND, where RAND is the uniform random number generator provided by the calculator. Generate 128 data points by using values of x in the interval (0,12.8). Store those values in an array, and perform a FFT on the array.

First, we define the function f(x) as a program:

$$<< \rightarrow x \ \text{'2*SIN(3*x) + 5*COS(5*x)' EVAL RAND 5 * + } \rightarrow \text{NUM} >>$$

and store this program in variable [f]. Next, type the following program to generate 2^m data values between a and b. The program will take the values of m, a, and b:

$$<< \rightarrow \text{m a b} << \text{'2\^m' EVAL} \rightarrow \text{n} << \text{'(b-a)/(n+1)' EVAL} \rightarrow \text{Dx} << \text{1 n FOR j 'a+(j-1)*Dx' EVAL f}$$
$$\text{NEXT n} \rightarrow \text{ARRY} >> \ >> \ >> \ >>$$

Store this program under the name GDATA (Generate DATA). Then, run the program for the values:

5 [SPC] 0 [SPC] 100 [SPC] [GDATA]

The figure below is a box plot of the data produced. To obtain the graph, first copy the array just created, then transform it into a column vector, and store it in ΣDAT by using:

[ENTER] [←][PRG][TYPE][OBJ→] [1] [+] [→ARRY] 'ΣDAT' [STO►]

Select Bar in the TYPE for graphs, change the view window to H-VIEW: 0 32, V-VIEW: -10 10, and BarWidth to 1.

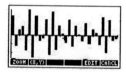

Press [CANCL][ON] to return to normal calculator display.

To perform the FFT on the array in stack level 1 use

[←][MTH][NXT][FFT][FFT]

The FFT returns an array of complex numbers that are the arrays of coefficients X_k of the DFT. The magnitude of the coefficients X_k represents a frequency spectrum of the original data. To obtain the magnitude of the coefficients proceed as follows:

[ENTER][←][MATRICES][OPER][AXL][←][ABS][AXL]

To plot a bar plot of these results convert the resulting array into a column vector and store it in ΣDAT before producing the bar plot (see procedure for the bar plot above). The spectrum of frequencies is the following:

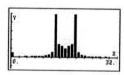

The spectrum shows two large components for two frequencies (these are the sinusoidal components, sin (3x) and cos(5x)), and a number of smaller components for other frequencies.

Example 2 - To produce the signal given the spectrum, we modify the program GDATA to include an absolute value, so that it reads:

```
<< → m a b << '2^m' EVAL → n << '(b-a)/(n+1)' EVAL → Dx << 1 n FOR j 'a+(j-1)*Dx' EVAL f
                ABS NEXT  n →ARRY >>  >>  >>  >>
```

Store this version of the program under GSPEC (Generate SPECtrum). Run the program with:

6 [SPC] 0 [SPC] 100 [GSPEC]

Press [ENTER] when done, to keep an additional copy of the spectrum array.

300

Using a bar plot, the spectrum generated in my calculator looks like this:

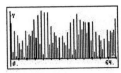

To reproduce the signal whose spectrum is shown , use

[↰][MTH][NXT][FFT][FFT]

The signal is shown as an array with complex numbers. We are interested only in the real part of the elements, use:

[↰][MTH][NXT][CMPLX][RE]

A bar plot of the signal is shown below:

Except for a large peak at t = 0, the signal is mostly noise. A smaller vertical scale shows the signal as follows:

301

17 Statistical applications

The subject of statistics (the analysis and inference of information from data) is closely related to the subject of probability (the analysis of random events). Throughout this book we have presented probability-related subject as illustrative examples of the applications of some mathematical techniques. Some of those applications are listed below:

- In Chapter 4 review the following sections:

    PROB menu
    Combinatorics, random numbers, and probability functions
    Factorials, permutations, and combinations
    The Gamma function
    Generating random numbers
    Examples of probability calculations for continuous random variables
    Normal distribution pdf
    Normal distribution cdf
    The Student-t distribution
    The Chi-squared (χ^2) distribution
    The F distribution

- In Chapter 5 review the following sections:

    Applications of list operations
    Mean, variance, and standard deviation of a sample
    Calculating statistics from grouped data
    Mean, variance, and standard deviation from a discrete probability distribution
    Applications of programs for list generation
    Generating tables of mass and cumulative distribution functions
    Binomial distribution
    Poisson distribution
    Geometric distribution

- In Chapter 10, under the heading *Matrix applications*, review the following sections which use least-square methods:

    Multiple linear fitting
    Polynomial fitting
    Selecting the best fitting

- In Chapter 11, review the sections on:

    Plotting histograms, bar plots, and scatter plots
    Bar plots
    Scatter plots

- Also, in Chapter 11, under the heading *Programming examples using drawing functions*, review the following section which uses least-square methods:

302

Example 3 - A program to visualize a polynomial fitting

- In <u>Chapter 12</u>, under the heading *Solving equations with one unknown through NUM.SLV*, review

    Example 3 - Upper tail probabilities for Normal, Student-t, χ^2, and F distributions

- In <u>Chapter 13</u>, under the heading *Univariate calculus applications*, review the section on

    Probability: Calculations with continuous random variables

Pre-programmed statistical features in the HP 49 G

The HP 49 G provides pre-programmed statistical features that accessible through the keystroke combination [→][STAT] (same key as the number 5 key). These are the same available in the HP 48 G, except that the HP 49 G includes *hypothesis testing* and *confidence interval* applications that are not accessible in the HP 48 G. The applications available in the HP 49 G are:

1. Single-var..
2. Frequencies..
3. Fit data..
4. Summary stats..
5. Hypoth. Tests..
6. Conf. Interval..

Entering data

For the analysis of a single set of data we can use applications number 1, 2, and 4 from the list above. All of these applications require that the data be available as columns of the matrix ΣDAT. This can be accomplished by entering the data in columns using the matrix writer, [←][MTRW].

This operation may become tedious for large number of data points. You may want to enter the data as a list, by using [←][{}], and separating the elements of the list by spaces (using the [SPC] key). When you finish entering the data in a given list, press [ENTER]. The list will be in level 1 of the stack.

The next step is to transform this list into a column vector. Here is a program that will accomplish this task. Type the following:

   [→][<<>>] [←][PRG] [TYPE] [OBJ→] [1] [SPC] [2] [→LIST] [→ARRY] [ENTER]

This program will be stored in a variable called LXC (meaning List transformed to Column vector), by using:

   [→]['][ALPHA][ALPHA][L][X][C][ENTER][STO▶].

It is preferable that you keep this program in your HOME directory so they will be accessible to all your directories.

The next step is to store the column vector into the variable ΣDAT. One way to do it is to simply type that name in stack level 1 and store the data by using:

[→]['] [→][Σ][▶][⇦][⇦][ALPHA][ALPHA][D][A][T] [ENTER] [STO▶].

Example 1 – Using the program LXC, defined above, create a column vector using the following data:

$$2.1 \quad 1.2 \quad 3.1 \quad 4.5 \quad 2.3 \quad 1.1 \quad 2.3 \quad 1.5 \quad 1.6 \quad 2.2 \quad 1.2 \quad 2.5.$$

Type in the data in a list:

{2.1 1.2 3.1 4.5 2.3 1.1 2.3 1.5 1.6 2.2 1.2 2.5 } [ENTER][LXC][VAR].

Next, store the resulting column vector in variable ΣDAT, as shown above.

Calculating single-variable statistics

I assume that at this point you have your data stored as a column vector in variable ΣDAT. To access the different STAT programs, press [→][STAT]. Press [OK] to select **1. Single-var..** There will be available to you an input form labeled **SINGLE-VARIABLE STATISTICS**, with the data currently in your ΣDAT variable listed in the form as a vector. Since you only have one column, the field **Col:** should have the value 1 in front of it. The **Type** field determines whether you are working with a sample or a population, the default setting is Sample. Move the cursor to the horizontal line preceding the fields **Mean, Std Dev, Variance, Total, Maximum, Minimum**, pressing the [✓CHK] key to select those measures that you want as output of this program. When ready, press [OK]. The selected values will be listed, appropriately labeled, in the screen of your calculator.

Example 1 -- For the data stored in the previous example, the single-variable statistics results are the following:

Mean: 2.13333333333,   Std Dev: .964207949406,   Variance: .929696969697
          Total: 25.6,   Maximum: 4.5,   Minimum: 1.1

The *definitions* used for these quantities are the following:

Suppose that you have a number data points x_1, x_2, x_3, ..., representing different measurements of the same discrete or continuous variable x. The set of all possible values of the quantity x is referred to as the *population* of x. A *finite population* will have only a fixed number of elements x_i. If the quantity x represents the measurement of a continuous quantity, and since, in theory, such a quantity can take an infinite number of values, the population of x in this case is *infinite*. If you select a sub-set of a population, represented by the n data values {x_1, x_2, ..., x_n}, we say you have selected a *sample* of values of x.

Samples are characterized by a number of measures or *statistics*. There are *measures of central tendency*, such as the mean, median, and mode, and *measures of spreading*, such as the the range, variance, and standard deviation.

Measures of central tendency

The *mean (or arithmetic mean)* of the sample, $\bar{x}$, is defined as the average value of the sample elements,

$$\bar{x} = \frac{1}{n} \cdot \sum_{i=1}^{n} x_i.$$

The value labeled Total obtained above represents the summation of the values of x, or $\Sigma x_i = n \cdot \bar{x}$.

This is the value provided by the calculator under the heading Mean. Other mean values used in certain applications are the _geometric mean_, x_g, or the _harmonic mean_, x_h, defined as:

$$x_g = \sqrt[n]{x_1 \cdot x_2 \cdots x_n}, \qquad \frac{1}{x_h} = \sum_{i=1}^{n} \frac{1}{x_i}.$$

Example 2 - To calculate the geometric and harmonic mean of the following data (entered into the calculator in the form of a list), use:

{ 1.2 1.1 1.3   1.5   1.0 } [ENTER][ENTER]   Make two copies of the list
[←] [MTH][LIST][ΠLIST] 5 [→] [ˣ√y]   Calculates the geometric mean
[▶][1/x][ΣLIST] 5 [÷] [1/x]   Calculates the harmonic mean

The _median_ is the value that splits the data set in the middle when the elements are placed in increasing order. If you have an _odd_ number, n, of ordered elements, the median of this sample is the value located in position $(n+1)/2$. If you have an _even_ number, n, of elements, the median is the average of the elements located in positions $n/2$ and $(n+1)/2$. Although the pre-programmed statistical features of the HP 49 G calculator do not include the calculation of the median, it is very easily to write a program to calculate such quantity by working with lists. For example, if you want to use the data in ΣDAT to find the median, type the following program:

<< → nC << RCLΣ DUP SIZE 2 GET IF 1 > THEN nC COL− SWAP DROP OBJ→ 1 + →ARRY END

OBJ→ OBJ→ DROP DROP DUP → n << →LIST SORT IF 'n mod 2 == 0' THEN DUP 'n/2' EVAL

GET SWAP '(n+1)/2' EVAL GET + 2 / ELSE '(n+1)/2' EVAL GET END "Median" →TAG>>

|Store this program under the name MED. To run the program, first you need to prepare your ΣDAT matrix. Then, enter the column in ΣDAT whose median you want to find, and press [MED].

Example 3 - For the data currently in ΣDAT (entered in an earlier example), use:

1 [ENTER][VAR][MED].

The result is   Median: 2.15.

The _mode_ of a sample is better determined from histograms, therefore, we leave its definition for a later section.

305

The *variance* (Var) of the sample is defined as

$$s_x^2 = \frac{1}{n-1} \cdot \sum_{i=1}^{n} (x_i - \bar{x})^2.$$

The *standard deviation* (St Dev) of the sample is just the square root of the variance, i.e., s_x.

The *range* of the sample is the difference between the maximum and minimum values of the sample. Since the calculator, through the pre-programmed statistical functions provides the maximum and minimum values of the sample, you can easily calculate the range.

The coefficient of variation of a sample combines the mean, a measure of central tendency, with the standard deviation, a measure of spreading, and is defined, as a percentage, by:

$$V_x = (s_x / \bar{x})100.$$

The pre-programmed functions for single-variable statistics used above can be applied to a finite population by selecting the Type: Population in the SINGLE-VARIABLE STATISTICS screen. The main difference is in the values of the variance and standard deviation which are calculated using n in the denominator of the variance, rather than (n-1).

Example 4 -- If you were to repeat the exercise in Example 1 of this section, using Population rather than Sample as the Type, you will get the same values for the mean, total, maximum, and minimum. The variance and standard deviation, however, will be given by:

Variance: 0.85222222222, Std Dev: 0.923158828275.

Obtaining frequency distributions

The program **2. Frequencies..** can be used to obtain frequency distributions for a set of data. Again, the data must be present in the form of a column vector stored in variable ΣDAT. To get started, press [⊢][STAT][▼][OK]. The resulting input form contains the following fields:

ΣDAT: the matrix containing the data of interest.
Col: the column of ΣDAT that is under scrutiny.
X-Min: the minimum class boundary to be used in the frequency distribution (default = -6.5).
Bin Count: the number of classes used in the frequency distribution (default = 13).
Bin Width: the uniform width of each class in the frequency distribution (default = 1).

To understand the meaning of these parameters we present the following *definitions*:

Given a set of n data values: $\{x_1, x_2, ..., x_n\}$ listed in no particular order, it is often required to group this data into a series of _classes_ by counting the _frequency_ or number of values corresponding to each class. (Note: the HP 49 G refers to classes as *bins*).

Suppose that the classes, or bins, will be selected by dividing the interval (x_{bot}, x_{top}), into $k =$ Bin Count classes by selecting a number of _class boundaries_, i.e., $\{xB_1, xB_2, ..., xB_{k+1}\}$, so that class number 1 is limited by xB_1-xB_2, class number 2 by xB_2-xB_3, and so on. The last class, class number k, will be limited by xB_k - xB_{k+1}.

The value of x corresponding to the middle of each class is known as the _class mark_, and is defined as

$$xM_i = (xB_i + xB_{i+1})/2, \text{ for } i = 1, 2, ..., k.$$

If the classes are chosen such that the class size is the same, then we can define the _class size_ as the value

$$\text{Bin Width} = \Delta x = (x_{max} - x_{min}) / k,$$

and the class boundaries can be calculated as

$$xB_i = x_{bot} + (i - 1) * \Delta x.$$

Any data point, x_j, $j = 1, 2, ..., n$, belongs to the i-th class, if $xB_i \leq x_j < xB_{i+1}$

The program **2. Frequencies..** will perform this frequency count, and will keep track of those values that may be below the minimum and above the maximum class boundaries (i.e., the _outliers_).

Example 1 -- In order to better illustrate obtaining frequency distributions, we want to generate a relatively large data set, say 200 points, by using the following:

- First, seed the random number generator using: 25 [↰][MTH][NXT][PROB]

- Type in the following program:

      << → n << 1 n FOR j RAND 100 * 2 RND NEXT n →LIST >> >>

  and save it under the name RDLIST (RanDom number LIST generator).

- Generate the list of 200 number by entering: 200 [ENTER][VAR][RDLIST]

- With the list generated in stack level 1, press [LXC] to convert it into a column vector.

- Store the column vector into SDAT, by using: [CAT][ALPHA][S] (... find STOΣ...)[OK].

- Obtain single-variable information using: [↱][STAT][OK]. Use Sample for the Type of data set, and select all options as results. The results are:

  Mean: 51.63715,   Std Dev: .29.8571984431,   Variance: .891.452298872

  Total: 10327.43,   Maximum: 99.35,   Minimum: 0.09

307

This information indicates that our data ranges from values close to zero to values close to 100. Working with whole numbers, we can select the range of variation of the data as (0,100). To produce a frequency distribution we will use the interval (10,90) dividing it into 8 bins of width 10 each.

- Select the program **2. Frequencies..** by using [↪][STAT][▼][OK]. The data is already loaded in ΣDAT, and the option Col should hold the value 1 since we have only one column in ΣDAT.

- Change X-Min to 10, Bin Count to 8, and Bin Width to 10, then press [OK].

The results are shown in the stack as a column vector in stack level 2, and a row vector of two components in stack level 1. The vector in stack level 1 is the number of outliers outside of the interval where the frequency count was performed. For this case, I get the values [24. 25.] indicating that there are, in my ΣDAT vector, 24 values smaller than 10 and 25 larger than 90.

- Press [⇦] to drop the vector of outliers from the stack. The remaining result is the frequency count of data. This can be translated into a table as follows:

Class No.	Class	Boundaries	Class Mark	Frequency	Cumulativ
i	XB_i	XB_{i+1}	Xm_i	f_i	frequency
< XB_1	outliers	below range		24	
1	10	20	15	18	18
2	20	30	25	15	33
3	30	40	35	16	49
4	40	50	45	17	66
5	50	60	55	23	89
6	60	70	65	22	111
7	70	80	75	19	130
k = 8	80	90	85	21	151
>XB_k	outliers	above range		25	

This table was prepared from the information we provided to generate the frequency distribution, although, the only column returned by the calculator is the Frequency, f_i, column. The class numbers, and class boundaries are easy to calculate for uniform-size classes (or bins), and the class mark is just the average of the class boundaries for each class. Finally, the _cumulative frequency_ is obtained by adding to each value in the last column, except the first, the frequency in the next row, and replacing the result in the last column of the next row. Thus, for the second class, the cumulative frequency is 18+15 = 33, while for class number 3, the cumulative frequency is 33 + 16 = 49, and so on. The cumulative frequency represents the frequency of those numbers that are smaller than or equal to the upper boundary of any given class.

Given the vector of frequencies generated by the calculator, you can obtain a cumulative frequency vector by using the following program:

<< DUP SIZE 1 GET → freq k << {k 1} 0 CON → cfreq << 'freq(1)' EVAL 'cfreq(1)' STO 2 n FOR j 'cfreq(j-1) +freq(j)' EVAL 'cfreq (j)' STO NEXT cfreq >> >> >>

Save it under the name CFREQ. With the vector frequency in stack level 1, press [VAR][CFREQ]. The result, for this example, is a column vector representing the last column of the table above.

Histograms

A *histogram* is a bar plot showing the frequency count as the height of the bars while the class boundaries shown the base of the bars. If you have your raw data (i.e., the original data before the frequency count is made) in the variable ΣDAT, you can select Histogram as your graph type and provide information regarding the initial value of x, the number of bins, and the bin width, to generate the histogram. Alternatively, you can generate the column vector containing the frequency count, as performed in the example above, store this vector into ΣDAT, and select Barplot as your graph type. In the example above, we show you how to use the first method to generate a histogram.

Example 1 – Using the 200 data points generated in the example above (stored as a column vector in ΣDAT), generate a histogram plot of the data using X-Min = 10, Bin Count = 16, and Bin Width = 5.

- First, press [↰][2D/3D] (simultaneously) to enter the PLOT SETUP screen. Within this screen, change Type: to Histogram, and check that the option Col: 1 is selected. Then, press [NXT][OK].

- Next, press [↰][WIN] (simultaneously) to enter the PLOT WINDOW – HISTOGRAM screen. Within that screen modify the information to H-View: 10   90, V-View: 0   15, Bar Width: 5.

- Press [ERASE][DRAW] to generate the following histogram:

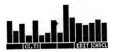

- Press [CANCEL] to return to the previous screen. Change the V-view and Bar Width once more, now to read V-View: 0   30, Bar Width: 10. The new histogram, based on the same data set, now looks like this:

A plot of frequency count, f_i, vs. class marks, xM_i, is known as a *frequency polygon*. A plot of the cumulative frequency vs. the upper boundaries is known as a cumulative frequency ogive. You can produce scatterplots that simulate these two plots by entering the proper data in

309

columns 1 and 2 of a new SDAT matrix and changing the Type: to SCATTER in the PLOT SETUP window.

Fitting data to a function y = f(x)

The program **3. Fit data..**, available as option number 3 in the pre-programmed statistical features of the HP 49 G calculator, can be used to fit linear, logarithmic, exponential, and power functions to data sets (x,y), stored in columns of the ΣDAT matrix. In order for this program to be effective, you need to have at least two columns in your ΣDAT variable.

Example 1 – Fit a linear relationship to the data shown in the table below:

x	y
0	0.5
1	2.3
2	3.6
3	6.7
4	7.2
5	11

- First, enter the two columns of data into variable ΣDAT by using the matrix writer.

- To access the program **3. Fit data..**, use the following keystrokes: [→][STAT][▼][▼][OK]. The input form will show the current ΣDAT, already loaded. If needed, change your set up screen to the following parameters for a linear fitting:

```
X-COL: 1    Y-COL: 2
    MODEL: Linear Fit
```

- To obtain the data fitting press [OK]. The output from this program, shown below for our particular data set, consists of the following three lines:

```
3: '0.195238095238 + 2.00857242857*X'
2: Correlation: 0.983781424465
1: Covariance: 7.03
```

Level 3 shows the form of the equation. In this case, y = 0.06924 + 0.00383 x. Level 2 shows the sample correlation coefficient, and level 1 shows the covariance of x-y.

Definitions for these two terms are provided below.

For a sample of data points (x,y), we define the sample *covariance* as

$$s_{xy} = \frac{1}{n-1}\sum_{i=1}^{n}(x_i - \bar{x})(y_i - \bar{y})$$

The *sample correlation coefficient* for x,y is defined as

$$r_{xy} = \frac{s_{xy}}{s_x \cdot s_y}$$

310

Where s_x, s_y are the standard deviations of x and y, respectively, i.e.

$$s_x^2 = \frac{1}{n-1} \sum_{i=1}^{n} (x_i - \overline{x})^2 \qquad s_y^2 = \frac{1}{n-1} \sum_{i=1}^{n} (y_i - \overline{y})^2$$

The values s_{xy} and r_{xy} are the "Covariance" and "Correlation," respectively, obtained by using the "Fit data" feature of the HP48G calculator.

Linearized relationships

Many curvilinear relationships "straighten out" to a linear form. For example, the different models for data fitting provided by the HP48G calculator can be linearized as described below:

Type of Fitting	Actual Model	Linearized Model	Independent variable ξ	Dependent Variable η	Covariance $s_{\xi\eta}$
Linear	$y = a + bx$	$y = a + bx$ [same]	x	y	s_{xy}
Logarithmic	$y = a + b \ln(x)$	$y = a + b \ln(x)$ [same]	$\ln(x)$	y	$s_{\ln(x),y}$
Exponential	$y = a\, e^{bx}$	$\ln(y) = \ln(a) + bx$	x	$\ln(y)$	$s_{x,\ln(y)}$
Power	$y = a\, x^b$	$\ln(y) = \ln(a) + b \ln(x)$	$\ln(x)$	$\ln(y)$	$s_{\ln(x),\ln(y)}$

The sample *covariance* of ξ,η is given by

$$s_{\xi\eta} = \frac{1}{n-1} \sum (\xi_i - \overline{\xi})(\eta_i - \overline{\eta})$$

Also, we define the sample *variances* of ξ and η, respectively, as

$$s_\xi^2 = \frac{1}{n-1} \sum_{i=1}^{n} (\xi_i - \overline{\xi})^2 \qquad s_\eta^2 = \frac{1}{n-1} \sum_{i=1}^{n} (\eta_i - \overline{\eta})^2$$

The sample *correlation coefficient* $r_{\xi\eta}$ is

$$r_{\xi\eta} = \frac{s_{\xi\eta}}{s_\xi \cdot s_\eta}$$

The general form of the *regression equation* is $\eta = A + B\xi$.

311

© 2000 Gilberto E. Urroz

Best data fitting

The HP48G/GX can determine which one of its linear or linearized relationship offers the best fitting for a set of (x,y) data points. We will illustrate the use of this feature with an example. Suppose you want to find which one of the data fitting functions provides the best fit for the following data:

x	y
0.20	3.16
0.50	2.73
1.00	2.12
1.50	1.65
2.00	1.29
4.00	0.47
5.00	0.29
10.00	0.01

First, enter the data as a matrix, either by using the matrix editor and entering the data, or by entering two lists of data corresponding to x and y and using the program CRMT (see frame below). To use the latter approach use the following keystrokes:

[←][8] [.][2][SPC] [.][5][SPC] [1][SPC] [1][.][5][SPC] [2][SPC] [4][SPC] [5][SPC] [1][0] [ENTER]

[←][8] [3][.][1][6][SPC] [2][.][7][3][SPC] [2][.][1][2][SPC] [1][.][6][5][SPC] [1][.][2][9][SPC] [.][4][7][SPC] [.][2][9][SPC] [.][0][1][ENTER]

[2][ENTER] [CRMT]

Next, save this matrix into the statistical matrix ΣDAT, by using: [←][STAT][DATA][←][ΣDAT]

Finally, the following instructions will allow you to find the best fit for your data: [→][STAT][▼][▼][OK]

The display shows the current ΣDAT, already loaded. Change your set up screen to the following parameters if needed:

```
X-COL: 1   Y-COL: 2
MODEL: Best Fit
```

Press [OK], to get:

```
1: '3.99504833324*EXP(-.579206831203*X)'
2: Correlation: -0.996624999526
3: Covariance: -6.23350666124
```

The best fit for the data is, therefore, $y = 3.995\ e^{-0.58 \cdot x}$.

The program [CRMT], introduced in Chapter 10, in the section entitled *"A program to build a matrix out of a number of lists -- Lists represent columns of the matrix,"* allows you to put together a *p×n* matrix (i.e., *p* rows, *n* columns) out of *n* lists of *p* elements each. To use this program, enter the *n* lists in the order that you want them as columns of the matrix, enter the value of *n*, and press [CRMT]. A listing of the program was presented in Chapter 10.

Obtaining additional summary statistics

The program **4. Summary stats..** can be useful in some calculations of measures for a sample. To get started, press [→][STAT] once more, move to the fourth option using the down-arrow key, and press [OK]. The resulting input form contains the following fields:

ΣDAT: the matrix containing the data of interest.

X-Col, Y-Col: these options apply only when you have more than two columns in the matrix ΣDAT. By default, the x column is column 1, and the y column is column 2. If you have only one column, then the only setting that makes sense is to have **X-Col: 1**.

_ΣX _ ΣY...: summary statistics that you can choose as results of this program by checking the appropriate field using [✓CHK] when that field is selected.

Many of these summary statistics are used to calculate statistics of two variables (x,y) that may be related by a function y = f(x). Therefore, this program can be thought off as a companion to program **3. Fit data..**

Example 1 - For the x-y data currently in ΣDAT, obtain all the summary statistics.

- To access the **summary stats...** option, use: [→][STAT][▼][▼][▼][OK].

- Select the column numbers corresponding to the x- and y-data, i.e., X-Col: 1, and Y-Col: 2.

- Using the [✓CHK] key select all the options for outputs, i.e., _ΣX, _ΣY, etc.

- Press [OK] to obtain the following results:

ΣX: 15, ΣY: 31.3, ΣX2: 55, ΣY2: 236.23, ΣXY: 113.4, NΣ:6

These results represent the following values:

$$\Sigma X = \sum_{i=1}^{n} x_i = 15, \quad \Sigma Y = \sum_{i=1}^{n} y_i = 31.3, \quad \Sigma X2 = \sum_{i=1}^{n} x_i^2 = 55,$$

$$\Sigma Y2 = \sum_{i=1}^{n} y_i^2 = 236.23, \quad \Sigma XY = \sum_{i=1}^{n} x_i \cdot y_i = 113.4, \quad N\Sigma = n = 6.$$

313

There two other programs under the menu [→][STAT], namely, **5. Hypth. tests..** and **6. Conf. Interval..** These two programs correspond to more advanced subjects and will be discussed later in the chapter.

Calculation of percentiles

The basic procedure to calculate the 100 pth Percentile $(0 < p < 1)$ in a sample of size n is as follows:

1. Order the n observations from smallest to largest.
2. Determine the product np
    A. If np is not an integer, round it up to the next integer and find the corresponding ordered value.
    B. If np is an integer, say k, calculate the mean of the kth and $(k-1)$th ordered observations.

[Note: Integer rounding rule, for a non-integer x.yz..., if $y \geq 5$, round up to x+1; if $y < 5$, round up to x.]

For example, in variable DT4 we have the data entered the same data as in array DT1, but this time as a list. If we want to calculate the 37th percentile ($p = 0.37$) of that data set, we proceed as follows (assuming you are in the appropriate subdirectory):

[VAR][DT4]	Places contents of DT4 in display level 1.
[MTH][LIST][SORT]	Orders list from smallest to largest.
[ENTER] [ENTER]	Creates two more copies of the list for later use.
[PRG][LIST][ELEM][SIZE]	Gives n as 60 ($n = 60$)
[0][.][3][7][×]	Enter p in level 1 and multiply n times p, to give 22.2. Round that number up to 22.
[◁]	Drop 22.2 from level 1.
[2][2][GET]	Indicates that element number 22 of the ordered list in display level 2 is to be extracted. GET produces a value of 26.4 for the percentile.

We write the result as $P_{0.37} = 26.4$ for the data in DT4.

If we wanted to obtain the third quartile of the data in DT4, i.e., $Q_3 = P_{0.75}$, with n = 60 and p = 0.75, we find that $np = 45 = k$ is indeed an integer. Therefore, to determine Q_3 we extract from the ordered list elements number 44 (= $k-1$) and 45 (=k) and calculate their average. The procedure is as follows:

[VAR][DT4]	Places contents of DT4 in display level 1.
[MTH][LIST][SORT]	Orders list from smallest to largest.
[ENTER] [ENTER]	Creates two more copies of the list for later use.
[PRG][LIST][ELEM]	Displays programs that operate on elements of lists.
[4][4][GET]	Gets element number 44 of the ordered list. Display level 1 shows a value of 31, i.e., $x_{44} = 31$, where x_i represents the ith element of the ordered list.
[↰][SWAP]	Swaps objects in levels 1 and 2 of the display, placing the ordered list in level 1.
[4][5][GET]	Gets element number 45 of the ordered list. Display level 1shows that $x_{45} = 31.3$.

314

[+][2][÷]   Calculates $Q_3 = (x_{44} + x_{45})/2$. Display level 1 shows that $Q_3 =$ 31.15

Please notice that there is a variety of ways to calculate percentiles, and that the way presented above may not be the same utilized in your class or other books.

The STAT soft menu

The STAT soft menu key, that in the HP 48 G is obtained by pressing [→][STAT], is not readily available in the HP 49 G. However, you can create your own program to access it by typing the following:

[→][<<>>] [9][6][.][0][1] [←][PRG] [NXT] [MODES] [MENU] [MENU] [ENTER]

Next, store the program in a variable called [STATm], by entering:

[→]['][ALPHA][ALPHA] [S][T][A][T] [←][M] [ENTER] [STO>].

To recover your list of variables, press [VAR]. There should now be a program called [STATm] in your menu. Press the corresponding button to obtain the STAT soft key menu.

At this point you should be able to use the operations outlined in the handout provided during the first lecture for the [→][STAT] in the HP 48 G. However, I suggest you change the settings of the calculator from choose box to soft menu as indicated below.

Use of STAT soft menu for data analysis, plots, and data fitting

The keystroke combination [←][STAT], in the HP 48 G, or the program [STATm], in the HP 49 G, provides direct access to several of the statistical functions in the calculator, namely:

[DATA][ΣPAR][1VAR][PLOT][FIT][SUMS]

Pressing the key corresponding to any of these menus provides access to different functions as described below.

[DATA]: Commands under this menu are used to manipulate the statistics matrix ΣDATA.

[Σ+]: add row in level 1 to bottom of ΣDATA matrix.
[Σ-]: removes last row in ΣDATA matrix and places it in level of 1 of the stack. The modified
        ΣDATA matrix remains in memory.
[CLΣ]: erases current ΣDATA matrix.
[ΣDAT]: places contents of current ΣDATA matrix in level 1 of the stack.
[←][ΣDAT]: stores matrix in level 1 of stack into ΣDATA matrix.
[STAT]: returns to STAT menu.

[ΣPAR]: <u>Commands under this menu are used to modify statistical parameters</u>. The parameters shown in
the display are:

        Xcol: indicates column of ΣDATA representing x (Default: 1)
        Ycol: indicates column of ΣDATA representing y (Default: 2)
        Intercept: shows intercept of most recent data fitting ((Default: 0)
        Slope: shows slope of most recent data fitting (Default: 0)
        Model: shows current data fit model (Default: LINFIT)

n [XCOL]: changes Xcol to n.
n [YCOL]: changes Xcol to n.
[MODL]: lets you change model to LINFIT, LOGFIT, EXPFIT, PWRFIT or BESTFIT by
        pressing the appropriate button, or press [ΣPAR] to return to the ΣPAR menu.
[ΣPAR]: shows statistical parameters.
[RESET]: reset parameters to default values
[INFO]: shows statistical parameters
[NXT][STAT]: returns to [STAT] menu.

[1VAR] : <u>Commands under this menu are used to calculate statistics of columns in ΣDATA matrix</u>.

[TOT]: show sum of each column in ΣDATA matrix.
[MEAN]: shows average of each column in ΣDATA matrix.
[SDEV]: shows standard deviation of each column in ΣDATA matrix.
[MAXΣ]: shows maximum value of each column in ΣDATA matrix.
[MINΣ]: shows average of each column in ΣDATA matrix.
x_s, Δx, n [BINS]: provides frequency distribution for data in *Xcol* column in ΣDATA
        matrix with the frequency bins defined as $[x_s, x_s+\Delta x]$, $[x_s, x_s+2\Delta x]$,..., $[x_s, x_s+n\Delta x]$.

[NXT]: to access the second menu. Within this menu you will find the following commands:
[VAR]: shows variance of each column in ΣDATA matrix.
[PSDEV]: shows population standard deviation (based on *n* rather than on (*n-1*)) of each
        column in ΣDATA matrix.
[PVAR]: shows population variance of each column in ΣDATA matrix.
[MINΣ]: shows average of each column in ΣDATA matrix.
[STAT]: returns to [STAT] menu.

[PLOT]: <u>Commands under this menu are used to produce plots with the data in the ΣDATA matrix</u>.

[BARPL]: produces a bar plot with data in *Xcol* column of the ΣDATA matrix.
[HISTP]: produces histogram of the data in *Xcol* column in the ΣDATA matrix, using the
        default width corresponding to 13 bins unless the bin size is modified using
        [←][STAT][1BAR][BINS]. Press [CANCL] to return to normal display.
[SCATR]: produces a scatterplot of the data in Ycol column of the ΣDATA matrix vs.
        the data in Xcol column of the ΣDATA matrix. Press [CANCL] to return to
        normal display. Equation fitted will be stored in the variable EQ.
[STAT]: returns to [STAT] menu.

[FIT]: Commands under this menu are used to fit equations to the data in columns *Xcol* and *Ycol* of the

ΣDATA matrix.

[ΣLINE]: provides the equation corresponding to the most recent fitting.

[LR]: provides intercept and slope of most recent fitting.

y [PREDX]: given y find x for the fitting y = f(x).

x [PREDY]: given x find y for the fitting y = f(x).

[CORR]: provides the correlation coefficient for the most recent fitting.

[COV]: provides sample co-variance for the most recent fitting

[NXT]: to access the second menu. Within this menu you will find the following commands:

[PCOV]: shows population co-variance for the most recent fitting.

[STAT]: returns to [STAT] menu.

[SUMS]: Commands under this menu are used to obtain summary statistics of the data in columns *Xcol* and

Ycol of the ΣDATA matrix.

[ΣX]: provides the sum of values in *Xcol* column.

[ΣY]: provides the sum of values in *Ycol* column.

[ΣX^2]: provides the sum of squares of values in *Xcol* column.

[ΣY^2]: provides the sum of squares of values in *Ycol* column.

[ΣX*Y]: provides the sum of x·y, i.e., the products of data in columns *Xcol* and *Ycol*.

[NΣ]: provides the number of columns in the ΣDATA matrix.

Example1 -- Let ΣDATA be the matrix:

$$\begin{bmatrix} 1.1 & 3.7 & 7.8 \\ 3.7 & 8.9 & 101 \\ 2.2 & 5.9 & 25 \\ 5.5 & 12.5 & 612 \\ 6.8 & 15.1 & 2245 \\ 9.2 & 19.9 & 24743 \\ 10.0 & 21.5 & 55066 \end{bmatrix}$$

• Type the matrix in level 1 of the stack by using the matrix editor.

• To store the matrix into ΣDATA, use: [STATm] [DATA] [←][ΣDAT]

• Calculate statistics of each column: [STAT][1VAR]:

[TOT]	produces [38.5 87.5 82799.8]
[MEAN]	produces [5.5. 12.5 11828.54...]
[SDEV]	produces [3.39... 6.78... 21097.01...]
[MAXΣ]	produces [10 21.5 55066]
[MINΣ]	produces [1.1 3.7 7.8]
[NXT][VAR]	produces [11.52 46.08 445084146.33]
[PSDEV]	produces [3.142... 6.284... 19532.04...]
[PVAR]	produces [9.87... 39.49... 381500696.85...]

317

- Generate a scatterplot of the data in columns 1 and 2 and fit a straight line to it:

  [STAT][ΣPAR][RESET]   resets statistical parameters
  [NXT][STAT][PLOT][SCATR] produces scatterplot
  [STATL]   draws data fit as a straight line
  [CANCL]   returns to main display

- Determine the fitting equation and some of its statistics:

  [STAT][FIT][ΣLINE]   produces '1.5+2*X'
  [LR]   produces Intercept: 1.5, Slope: 2
  3 [PREDX]   produces 0.75
  1 [PREDY]   produces 3. 50
  [CORR]   produces 1.0
  [COV]   produces 23.04
  [NXT][PCOV]   produces 19.74

- Obtain summary statistics for data in columns 1 and 2: [STAT][SUMS]:

  [ΣX]   produces 38.5
  [ΣY]   produces 87.5
  [ΣX^2]   produces 280.87
  [ΣY^2]   produces 1370.23
  [ΣX*Y]   produces 619.49
  [NΣ]   produces 7

- Fit data using columns 1 (x) and 3 (y) using a logarithmic fitting:

  [NXT][STAT][ΣPAR][3][YCOL]   select Ycol = 3, and
  [MODL][LOGFI]   select Model = Logfit
  [NXT][STAT][PLOT][SCATR]   produce scattergram of y vs. x
  [STATL]   show line for log fitting

  Obviously, the log-fit is not a good choice.

  [CANCL]   returns to normal display.

- Select the best fitting by using:

  [STAT][ΣPAR][MODL][BESTF]   shows EXPFIT as the best fit for these data
  [NXT][STAT][FIT][ΣLINE]   produces '2.6545*EXP(0.9927*X)'
  [CORR]   produces 0.99995... (good correlation)
  2300[PREDX]   produces 6.8139
  5.2 [PREDY]   produces 463.37

- To return to STAT menu use: [NXT][STATS]

- To get your variable menu back use: [VAR].

Next, we will introduce some advanced concepts in statistics relevant to the generation of confidence intervals, and to the testing of hypotheses using statistics from samples.

318

Confidence intervals

Statistical inference is the process of making conclusions about a population based on information from sample data. In order for the sample data to be meaningful, the sample must be random, i.e., the selection of a particular sample must have the same probability as that of any other possible sample out of a given population. The following are some terms relevant to the concept of random sampling:

- *Population*: collection of all conceivable observations of a process or attribute of a component.
- *Sample*: sub-set of a population.
- *Random sample*: a sample representative of the population.
- *Random variable*: real-valued function defined on a sample space. Could be discrete or continuous.

If the population follows a certain probability distribution that depends on a parameter θ, a random sample of observations $(X_1, X_2, X_3, \dots, X_n)$, of size n, can be used to estimate θ.

- *Sampling distribution*: the joint probability distribution of $X_1, X_2, X_3, \dots, X_n$.
- *A statistic*: any function of the observations that is quantifiable and does not contain any unknown parameters. A statistic is a random variable that provides a means of estimation.
- *Point estimation*: when a single value of the parameter θ is provided.
- *Confidence interval*: a numerical interval that contains the parameter θ at a given level of probability.
- *Estimator*: rule or method of estimation of the parameter θ.
- *Estimate*: value that the estimator yields in a particular application.

Example 1 -- Let X represent the time (hours) required by a specific manufacturing process to be completed. Given the following *sample* of values of X:

$$2.2 \quad 2.5 \quad 2.1 \quad 2.3 \quad 2.2$$

The *population* from where this sample is taken is the collection of all possible values of the process time, therefore, it is an infinite population. Suppose that the population *parameter* we are trying to estimate is its mean value, μ. We will use as an *estimator* the mean value of the sample, $\bar{X}$, defined by (a rule):

$$\bar{X} = \frac{1}{n} \cdot \sum_{i=1}^{n} X_i.$$

For the sample under consideration, the *estimate* of μ is the sample *statistic*

$$\bar{x} = (2.2+2.5+2.1+2.3+2.2)/5 = 2.36.$$

This single value of $\bar{X}$, namely $\bar{x} = 2.36$, constitutes a *point estimation* of the population parameter μ.

A note on random variables

319

Typically the name of a random variable is referred to by using an upper case letter (as in $\bar{X}$ in the example above), while a specific value taken by the variable is referred to with the corresponding lower case letter (as in $\bar{x}$ in the example above).

When calculating probabilities of _discrete random variables_, for example, you would write "_the probability that the random variable X takes the value x is 025_" using the notation: $Pr[X = x] = 0.25$.   If a random variable X can only take the discrete values x_1, x_2, x_3, ..., then we can write:

$$Pr[X \leq x_k] = Pr[X=x_1] + Pr[X=x_2]+...+ Pr[X=x_k]$$
$$Pr[X < x_k] = Pr[X \leq x_{k-1}] = Pr[X=x_1] + Pr[X=x_2]+...+ Pr[X=x_{k-1}]$$
$$Pr[X > x_k] = 1 - Pr[X \leq x_k]$$
$$Pr[X \geq x_k] = 1 - Pr[X < x_k] = 1 - Pr[X \leq x_{k-1}]$$

For _continuous random variables_ it does not make sense to talk about the random variable X being equal to a specific value (in fact, for any continuous random variable X and any value x, $Pr[X=x] = 0$). Instead, we talk about the random variable X belonging to the interval limited by the values x_1 and x_2, or $x_1 < X < x_2$. If this probability is p, the following expression can be written:

$$Pr[x_1 < X < x_2] = Pr[x_1 < X \leq x_2] = Pr[x_1 \leq X < x_2] = Pr[x_1 \leq X \leq x_2] = p.$$

Refer to Chapters 3 and 4 for some examples on calculations using well-known continuous and discrete probability distributions.

Estimation of Confidence Intervals

The next level of inference from point estimation is _interval estimation_, i.e., instead of obtaining a single value of an estimator we provide two statistics, a and b, which define an interval containing the parameter θ with a certain level of probability. The end points of the interval are known as _confidence limits_, and the interval (a,b) is known as the _confidence interval_.

Definitions

Let (C_l, C_u) be a confidence interval containing an unknown parameter θ.

- _Confidence level_ or confidence coefficient is the quantity $(1-\alpha)$, where $0 < \alpha < 1$, such that

$$Pr[C_l < \theta < C_u] = 1 - \alpha.$$

This defines the so-called _two-sided confidence limits_.

- A _lower one-sided confidence interval_ is defined by $Pr[C_l < \theta] = 1 - \alpha.$

- An _upper one-sided confidence interval_ is defined by $Pr[\theta < C_u] = 1 - \alpha.$

- The parameter α is known as the _significance level_. Typical values of α are 0.01, 0.05, 0.1, corresponding to confidence levels of 0.99, 0.95, and 0.90, respectively.

320

Let $\bar{X}$ be the mean of a random sample of size n, drawn from an infinite population with known standard deviation σ. The 100(1-α) % [i.e., 99%, 95%, 90%, etc.], *central, two-sided confidence interval for the population mean* μ is ($\bar{X}-z_{\alpha/2}\cdot\sigma/\sqrt{n}$, $\bar{X}+z_{\alpha/2}\cdot\sigma/\sqrt{n}$), where $z_{\alpha/2}$ is a standard normal variate that is exceeded with a probability of α /2. The standard error of the sample mean, $\bar{X}$, is $\sigma/\sqrt{n}$.

The one-sided upper and lower 100(1-α) % confidence limits for the population mean μ are, respectively,
$X+z_{\alpha}\cdot\sigma/\sqrt{n}$, and $\bar{X}-z_{\alpha}\cdot\sigma/\sqrt{n}$. Thus, a *lower, one-sided, confidence interval* is defined as (-∞ , $X+z_{\alpha}\cdot\sigma/\sqrt{n}$), and an *upper, one-sided, confidence interval* as (X-$z_{\alpha}\cdot\sigma/\sqrt{n}$,+$\infty$). Notice that in these last two intervals we use the value z_{α}, rather than $z_{\alpha/2}$.

To indicate that the continuous random variable X follows the normal probability distribution we use the notation X ~ N(μ,σ^2), read as "N is normal with mean μ and variance σ^2." A continuous random variable Z that follows the *standard normal distribution* is described as Z ~ N(0,1), i.e., a normal distribution with μ = 0, and σ^2 = 1.

The definition of the value $z_{\alpha/2}$, used earlier to define the two-sided confidence interval for the mean, is presented in the figure below. The curve represents the probability density function of the standard normal distribution.

In general, the value z_k in the standard normal distribution is defined as that value of z whose probability of exceedence is k, i.e., Pr[Z>z_k] = k, or Pr[Z<z_k] = 1 - k. The normal distribution was described in Chapter 4.

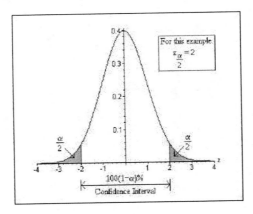

Confidence intervals for the population mean when the population variance is unknown

Let $\bar{X}$ and S, respectively, be the mean and standard deviation of a random sample of size n, drawn from an infinite population that follows the normal distribution with unknown standard deviation σ. The $100 \cdot (1-\alpha)$ % [i.e., 99%, 95%, 90%, etc.] central two-sided confidence interval for the population mean μ, is ($\bar{X} - t_{n-1,\alpha/2} \cdot S/\sqrt{n}$, $\bar{X} + t_{n-1,\alpha/2} \cdot S/\sqrt{n}$), where $t_{n-1,\alpha/2}$ is Student's t variate with $\nu = n-1$ degrees of freedom and probability $\alpha/2$ of exceedence.

The one-sided upper and lower $100 \cdot (1-\alpha)$ % confidence limits for the population mean μ are, respectively,

$X + t_{n-1,\alpha/2} \cdot S/\sqrt{n}$, and $\bar{X} - t_{n-1,\alpha/2} \cdot S/\sqrt{n}$.

Small samples and large samples

The behavior of the Student's t distribution is such that for n>30, the distribution is indistinguishable from the standard normal distribution. Thus, for samples larger than 30 elements when the population variance is unknown, you can use the same confidence interval as when the population variance is known, but replacing σ with S. Samples for which n>30 are typically referred to as *large samples*, otherwise they are *small samples*.

Confidence Interval for a Proportion

A discrete random variable X follows a Bernoulli distribution if X can take only two values, X = 0 (failure), and X = 1 (success). Let X ~ Bernoulli(p), where p is the probability of success, then the mean value, or expectation, of X is E[X] = p, and its variance is Var[X] = p(1-p).

If an experiment involving X is repeated n times, and k successful outcomes are recorded, then an estimate of p is given by p'= k/n, while the standard error of p' is $\sigma_{p'} = \sqrt{(p \cdot (1-p)/n)}$. In practice, the sample estimate for p, i.e., p'replaces p in the standard error formula.

For a *large sample* size, n>30, and np > 5 and n(1-p)>5, the sampling distribution is very nearly normal. Therefore, the $100(1-\alpha)$ % central two-sided confidence interval for the population mean p is (p'+$z_{\alpha/2} \cdot \sigma_{p'}$, p'+$z_{\alpha/2} \cdot \sigma_{p'}$). For a *small sample* (n<30), the interval can be estimated as (p'-$t_{n-1,\alpha/2} \cdot \sigma_{p'}$,p'+$t_{n-1,\alpha/2} \cdot \sigma_{p'}$).

Sampling distribution of differences and sums of statistics

Let S_1 and S_2 be independent statistics from two populations based on samples of sizes n_1 and n_2, respectively. Also, let the respective means and standard errors of the sampling distributions of those statistics be μ_{S1} and μ_{S2}, and σ_{S1} and σ_{S2}, respectively. The differences between the statistics from the two populations, S_1-S_2, have a sampling distribution with mean

$$\mu_{S1-S2} = \mu_{S1} - \mu_{S2},$$

and standard error

$$\sigma_{S1-S2} = (\sigma_{S1}^2 + \sigma_{S2}^2)^{1/2}.$$

Also, the sum of the statistics T_1+T_2 has a mean

322

$$\mu_{S1+S2} = \mu_{S1} + \mu_{S2},$$

and standard error

$$\sigma_{S1+S2} = (\sigma_{S1}^2 + \sigma_{S2}^2)^{1/2}.$$

Estimators for the mean and standard deviation of the difference and sum of the statistics S_1 and S_2 are given by:

$$\hat{\mu}_{S_1 \pm S_2} = \overline{X}_1 \pm \overline{X}_2, \qquad \hat{\sigma}_{S_1 \pm S_2} = \sqrt{\frac{\sigma_{S1}^2}{n_1} + \frac{\sigma_{S2}^2}{n_2}}.$$

In these expressions, $\overline{X}_1$ and $\overline{X}_2$ are the values of the statistics S_1 and S_2 from samples taken from the two populations, and σ_{S1}^2 and σ_{S2}^2 are the variances of the populations of the statistics S_1 and S_2 from which the samples were taken.

Confidence intervals for sums and differences of mean values

If the population variances σ_1^2 and σ_2^2 are known, the confidence intervals for the difference and sum of the mean values of the populations, i.e., $\mu_1 \pm \mu_2$, are given by:

$$\left((\overline{X}_1 \pm X_2) - z_{\alpha/2} \cdot \sqrt{\frac{\sigma_1^2}{n_1} + \frac{\sigma_2^2}{n_2}}, (\overline{X}_1 \pm X_2) + z_{\alpha/2} \cdot \sqrt{\frac{\sigma_1^2}{n_1} + \frac{\sigma_2^2}{n_2}} \right)$$

For large samples, i.e., $n_1 > 30$ and $n_2 > 30$, and unknown, but equal, population variances $\sigma_1^2 = \sigma_2^2$, the confidence intervals for the difference and sum of the mean values of the populations, i.e., $\mu_1 \pm \mu_2$, are given by:

$$\left((\overline{X}_1 \pm X_2) - z_{\alpha/2} \cdot \sqrt{\frac{S_1^2}{n_1} + \frac{S_2^2}{n_2}}, (\overline{X}_1 \pm X_2) + z_{\alpha/2} \cdot \sqrt{\frac{S_1^2}{n_1} + \frac{S_2^2}{n_2}} \right)$$

If one of the samples is small, i.e., $n_1 < 30$ or $n_2 < 30$, and with unknown, but equal, population variances $\sigma_1^2 = \sigma_2^2$, we can obtain a "pooled" estimate of the variance of $\mu_1 \pm \mu_2$, as

$$s_p^2 = [(n_1-1) \cdot s_1^2 + (n_2-1) \cdot s_2^2] / (n_1 + n_2 - 2).$$

In this case, the centered confidence intervals for the sum and difference of the mean values of the populations, i.e., $\mu_1 \pm \mu_2$, are given by:

$$\left((\overline{X}_1 \pm X_2) - t_{v,\alpha/2} \cdot s_p^2, (\overline{X}_1 \pm X_2) + t_{v,\alpha/2} \cdot s_p^2 \right),$$

where $v = n_1 + n_2 - 2$ is the number of degrees of freedom in the Student's t distribution.

In the last two options we specify that the population variances, although unknown, must be equal. This will be the case in which the two samples are taken from the same population, or from two populations about which we suspect that they have the same population variance.

323

However, if we have reason to believe that the two unknown population variances are different, we can use the following confidence interval

$$\left((\overline{X}_1 \pm X_2) - t_{v,\alpha/2} \cdot s^2_{\overline{X}_1 \pm \overline{X}_2}, (\overline{X}_1 \pm X_2) + t_{v,\alpha/2} \cdot s^2_{\overline{X}_1 \pm \overline{X}_2}\right)$$

where the estimated standard deviation for the sum or difference is

$$s_{\overline{X}_1 \pm \overline{X}_2} = \sqrt{\frac{s_1^2}{n_1} + \frac{s_2^2}{n_2}},$$

and n, the degrees of freedom of the t variate, are calculated using the integer value closest to

$$v = \frac{[(S_1^2/n_1) + (S_2^2/n_2)]^2}{[(S_1^2/n_1)/(n_1-1)] + [(S_2^2/n_2)/(n_2-1)]}.$$

Determining confidence intervals using the HP 49 G's own features

The program **6. Conf Interval** can be accessed by using [→][STAT][▲][OK]. The program offers the following options:

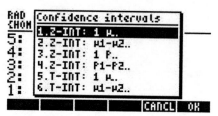

These options are to be interpreted as follows:

1. Z-INT: 1 μ.: Single sample confidence interval for the population mean, μ, with known population variance, or for large samples with unknown population variance.
2. Z-INT: μ1–μ2.: Confidence interval for the difference of the population means, μ_1- μ_2, with either known population variances, or for large samples with unknown population variances.
3. Z-INT: 1 p.: Single sample confidence interval for the proportion, p, for large samples with unknown population variance.
4. Z-INT: p1– p2.: Confidence interval for the difference of two proportions, p_1-p_2, for large samples with unknown population variances.
5. T-INT: 1 μ.: Single sample confidence interval for the population mean, μ, for small samples with unknown population variance.
6. T-INT: μ1–μ2.: Confidence interval for the difference of the population means, μ_1- μ_2, for small samples with unknown population variances.

324

Example 1 - Determine the centered confidence interval for the mean of a population if a sample of 60 elements indicate that the mean value of the sample is x̄ = 23.2, and its standard deviation is s = 5.2. Use $\alpha = 0.05$. The confidence level is C = $1-\alpha$ = 0.95.

Select case 1 from the menu shown above by pressing [OK]. Enter the values required in the input form as shown:

Press [HELP] to obtain a screen explaining the meaning of the confidence interval in terms of random numbers generated by a calculator. To scroll down the resulting screen use the down-arrow key [▼]. Most pre-programmed random number generators produce uniform random numbers in the interval (0,1). Therefore, the population mean and standard deviation are 0.5 and 0.2887, respectively. The explanation presented when you press [HELP] emphasizes the fact that the value of $\mu = 0.5$ must be contained in the resulting confidence interval. Press [OK] when done with the help screen. This will return you to the screen shown above.

To calculate the confidence interval, press [OK]. The result shown in the calculator is:

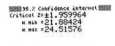

The result indicates that a 95% confidence interval has been calculated. The Critical z value shown in the screen above corresponds to the values $\pm z_{\alpha/2}$ in the confidence interval formula ($\bar{X} - z_{\alpha/2} \cdot \sigma / \sqrt{n}$, $\bar{X} + z_{\alpha/2} \cdot \sigma / \sqrt{n}$). The values μ Min and μ Max are the lower and upper limits of this interval, i.e., μ Min = $\bar{X} - z_{\alpha/2} \cdot \sigma / \sqrt{n}$, and μ Max = $\bar{X} + z_{\alpha/2} \cdot \sigma / \sqrt{n}$.

Press [GRAPH] to see a graphical display of the confidence interval information:

The graph shows the standard normal distribution pdf (probability density function), the location of the critical points $\pm z_{\alpha/2}$, the mean value (23.2) and the corresponding interval limits (21.88424 and 24.51576). Press [TEXT] to return to the previous results screen, and/or press [OK] to exit the confidence interval environment. The results will be listed in the calculator's stack as follows:

Example 2 -- Data from two samples (samples 1 and 2) indicate that x̄$_1$ = 57.8 and x̄$_2$ = 60.0. The sample sizes are n$_1$ = 45 and n$_2$ = 75. If it is known that the populations' standard

deviations are $\sigma_1 = 3.2$, and $\sigma_2 = 4.5$, determine the 90% confidence interval for the difference of the population means, i.e., $\mu_1 - \mu_2$.

Press [⇨][STAT][▲][OK] to access the confidence interval feature in the calculator. Press [▼][OK] to select option 2. Z-INT: $\mu 1 - \mu 2$.. Enter the following values:

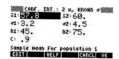

When done, press [OK]. The results, as text and graph, are shown below:

The variable $\Delta\mu$ represents $\mu 1 - \mu 2$.

Example 3 – A survey of public opinion indicates that in a sample of 150 people 60 favor increasing property taxes to finance some public projects. Determine the 99% confidence interval for the population proportion that would favor incresing taxes.

Press [⇨][STAT][▲][OK] to access the confidence interval feature in the calculator. Press [▼][▼][OK] to select option 3. Z-INT: $\mu 1 - \mu 2$.. Enter the following values:

When done, press [OK]. The results, as text and graph, are shown below:

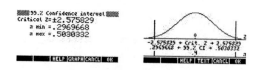

Example 4 -- Determine a 90% confidence interval for the difference between two proportions if sample 1 shows 20 successes out of 120 trials, and sample 2 shows 15 successes out of 100 trials.

Press [⇨][STAT][▲][OK] to access the confidence interval feature in the calculator. Press [▼][▼][▼][OK] to select option 4. Z-INT: p1 – p2.. Enter the following values:

326

When done, press [OK]. The results, as text and graph, are shown below:

Example 5 - Determine a 95% confidence interval for the mean of the population if a sample of 50 elements has a mean of 15.5 and a standard deviation of 5. The population's standard deviation is unknown.

Press [→][STAT][▲][OK] to access the confidence interval feature in the calculator. Press [▲][▲][OK] to select option 5. T-INT: μ. Enter the following values:

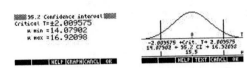

When done, press [OK]. The results, as text and graph, are shown below:

The figure showns the Student's t *pdf* for ν = 50 - 1 = 49 degrees of freedom.

Example 6 -- Determine the 99% confidence interval for the difference in means of two populations given the sample data: $\bar{x}_1$ = 157.8 , $\bar{x}_2$ = 160.0, n_1 = 50, n_2 = 55.   The populations standard deviations are s_1 = 13.2, s_2 = 24.5.

Press [→][STAT][▲][OK] to access the confidence interval feature in the calculator. Press [▲][OK] to select option 6. T-INT: μ1–μ2.. Enter the following values:

When done, press [OK]. The results, as text and graph, are shown below:

These results assume that the values s_1 and s_2 are the population standard deviations. If these values actually represent the samples' standard deviations, you should enter the same values as before, but with the option _pooled selected. The results now become:

327

Confidence intervals for the variance

To develop a formula for the confidence interval for the variance, first we introduce the _sampling distribution of the variance_: Consider a random sample X_1, X_2 ..., X_n of independent normally-distributed variables with mean μ, variance σ^2, and sample mean $\overline{X}$. The statistic

$$\hat{S}^2 = \frac{1}{n-1} \cdot \sum_{i=1}^{n} (X_i - \overline{X})^2,$$

is an unbiased estimator of the variance σ^2.

The quantity,

$$(n-1) \cdot \frac{\hat{S}^2}{\sigma^2} = \sum_{i=1}^{n} (X_i - \overline{X})^2,$$

has a χ_{n-1}^2 (chi-square) distribution with $\nu = n-1$ degrees of freedom.

The $(1-\alpha) \cdot 100$ % two-sided confidence interval is found from

$$\Pr[\chi^2_{n-1,1-\alpha/2} < (n-1) \cdot S^2/\sigma^2 < \chi^2_{n-1,\alpha/2}] = 1 - \alpha.$$

as illustrated in the figure below.

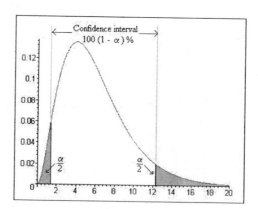

The confidence interval for the population variance σ^2 is therefore,

328

$$[(n-1)\cdot S^2 / \chi^2_{n-1,\alpha/2} \,; \, (n-1)\cdot S^2 / \chi^2_{n-1,1-\alpha/2}].$$

where $\chi^2_{n-1,\alpha/2}$, and $\chi^2_{n-1,1-\alpha/2}$ are the values that a χ^2 variable, with ν = n-1 degrees of freedom, exceeds with probabilities $\alpha/2$ and 1- α /2, respectively.

The one-sided upper confidence limit for σ^2 is defined as $(n-1)\cdot S^2 / \chi^2_{n-1,1-\alpha}$.

Example 1 - Determine the 95% confidence interval for the population variance σ^2 based on the results from a sample of size n = 25 that indicates that the sample variance is s^2 = 12.5.

In Chapter 12 we defined a variable EQC containing the program $\ll \gamma$ x UTPC α - $\gg$. In this program, γ represents the degrees of freedom (n-1), and α represents the probability of exceeding a certain value of x (χ^2), i.e.,
$$Pr[\chi^2 > \chi_\alpha^2] = 1 - \alpha.$$

The contents of EQC can be copied into variable EQ , and the HP 49 G numerical solver used to solve for x (χ^2) given the probability of exceedence, α. For the present example, the value of α = 0.05. To obtain the value $\chi^2_{n-1,\alpha/2} = \chi^2_{24,0.025}$, we use the following:

[VAR][EQC] 'EQ' [STO] [↵][NUM.SLV][OK]

Enter the values γ = 24 and α = 0.025 in the input form. Highlight the field for x, and press [SOLVE]. The result is shown in the screen below:

Thus,
$$\chi^2_{n-1,\alpha/2} = \chi^2_{24,0.025} = 39.3640770266.$$

On the other hand, the value $\chi^2_{n-1,\alpha/2} = \chi^2_{24,0.975}$ is calculated by using the values γ = 24 and α = 0.975. The input screen for the numerical solver will look like this:

Thus,
$$\chi^2_{n-1,1-\alpha/2} = \chi^2_{24,0.975} = 12.4011502175.$$

The lower and upper limits of the interval will be:

$$(n-1)\cdot S^2 / \chi^2_{n-1,\alpha/2} = (25-1)\cdot 12.5/39.3640770266 = 7.62116179676$$
and,
$$(n-1)\cdot S^2 / \chi^2_{n-1,1-\alpha/2} = (25-1)\cdot 12.5/12.4011502175 = 24.1913044144$$

Thus, the 95% confidence interval for this example is: $7.62116179676 < \sigma^2 < 24.1913044144$.

329

Hypothesis testing

A *hypothesis* is a declaration made about a population (for instance, with respect to its mean). Acceptance of the hypothesis is based on a statistical test on a sample taken from the population. The consequent action and decision making are called *hypothesis testing*.

The process of hypothesis testing consists on taking a random sample from the population and making a statistical hypothesis about the population. If the observations do not support the model or theory postulated, the hypothesis is rejected. However, if the observations are in agreement, then hypothesis is not rejected, but it is not necessarily accepted. Associated with the decision is a level of significance α.

Procedure for testing hypotheses

The procedure for hypothesis testing involves the following six steps:

1. Declare a null hypothesis, H_0. This is the hypothesis to be tested. For example, $H_0: \mu_1 - \mu_2 = 0$, i.e., we hypothesize that the mean value of population 1 and the mean value of population 2 are the same. If H_0 is true, any observed difference in means is attributed to errors in random sampling.
2. Declare an alternate hypothesis, H_1. For the example under consideration, it could be $H_1: \mu_1 - \mu_2 \neq 0$ [Note: this is what we really want to test.]
3. Determine or specify a test statistic, T. In the example under consideration, T will be based on the difference of observed means, $\bar{X}_1 - \bar{X}_2$.
4. Use the known (or assumed) distribution of the test statistic, T.
5. Define a rejection region (the critical region, R) for the test statistic based on a pre-assigned significance level α.
6. Use observed data to determine whether the computed value of the test statistic is within or outside the critical region. If the test statistic is within the critical region, then we say that the quantity we are testing is significant at the 100α percent level.

Notes:

1. For the example under consideration, the alternate hypothesis $H_1: \mu_1 - \mu_2 \neq 0$ produces what is called a *two-tailed test*. If the alternate hypothesis is $H_1: \mu_1 - \mu_2 > 0$ or $H_1: \mu_1 - \mu_2 < 0$, then we have a *one-tailed test*.

2. The probability of rejecting the null hypothesis is equal to the level of significance, i.e., $Pr[T \in R | H_0] = \alpha$. The notation $Pr[A|B]$ represents the *conditional probability of event A given that event B occurs*.

Errors in hypothesis testing

In hypothesis testing we use the terms errors of Type I and Type II to define the cases in which a true hypothesis is rejected or a false hypothesis is accepted (not rejected), respectively. Let T = value of test statistic, R = rejection region, A = acceptance region, thus, $R \cap A = \varnothing$, and $R \cup A = \Omega$, where Ω = the parameter space for T, and $\varnothing$ = the empty set. The probabilities of making an error of Type I or of Type II are as follows:

Rejecting a true hypothesis, $\quad\quad\quad$ $Pr[\text{Type I error}] = Pr[T \in R | H_0] = \alpha$
Not rejecting a false hypothesis, $\quad\quad$ $Pr[\text{Type II error}] = Pr[T \in A | H_1] = \beta$

Now, let's consider the cases in which we make the correct decision:

Not rejecting a true hypothesis, $\quad$ Pr[Not(Type I error)] = Pr[T∈A|H$_0$] = 1 - α
Rejecting a false hypothesis, $\quad$ Pr[Not(Type II error)] = Pr [T∈R|H$_1$] = 1 - β

The complement of β is called the *power of the test of the null hypothesis H$_0$ vs. the alternative H$_1$*. The power of a test is used, for example, to determine a minimum sample size to restrict errors.

Selecting values of α and β

A typical value of the level of significance (or probability of Type I error) is α = 0.05, (i.e., incorrect rejection once in 20 times on the average). If the consequences of a Type I error are more serious, choose smaller values of α, say 0.01 or even 0.001.

The value of β, i.e., the probability of making an error of Type II, depends on α, the sample size n, and on the true value of the parameter tested. Thus, the value of β is determined after the hypothesis testing is performed. It is customary to draw graphs showing β, or the power of the test (1- β), as a function of the true value of the parameter tested. These graphs are called *operating characteristic curves* or *power function curves*, respectively.

Inferences concerning one mean

Two-sided hypothesis

The problem consists in testing the null hypothesis H$_0$: μ = μ$_o$, against the alternative hypothesis, H$_1$: μ≠μ$_o$ at a level of confidence (1-α)100%, or significance level α, using a sample of size n with a mean $\bar{x}$ and a standard deviation s. This test is referred to as a *two-sided or two-tailed* test. The procedure for the test is as follows:

First, we calculate the appropriate statistic for the test (t$_o$ or z$_o$) as follows:

- If n < 30 and the standard deviation of the population, σ, is known, use

$$z_o = \frac{\bar{x} - \mu_o}{\sigma / \sqrt{n}}$$

- If n > 30, and σ is known, use z$_o$ as above. If σ is not known, replace s for σ in z$_o$, i.e., use

$$z_o = \frac{\bar{x} - \mu_o}{s / \sqrt{n}}$$

- If n < 30, and s is unknown, use the t-statistic

$$t_o = \frac{\bar{x} - \mu_o}{s / \sqrt{n}}$$

with ν = n - 1 degrees of freedom.

Then, calculate the P-value (a probability) associated with either z_o or t_o, and compare it to α to decide whether or not to reject the null hypothesis. The P-value for a two-sided test is defined as either

$$\text{P-value} = P(|z| > |z_o|), \text{ or, } \text{P-value} = P(|t| > |t_o|).$$

The criteria to use for hypothesis testing is:

- Reject H_o if P-value $< \alpha$
- Do not reject H_o if P-value $> \alpha$.

The P-value for a two-sided test can be calculated using the probability functions in the HP48G/GX as follows:

- If using z, $\quad$ P-value = $2 \cdot \text{UTPN}(0,1,|z_o|)$
- If using t, $\quad$ P-value = $2 \cdot \text{UTPT}(v,|t_o|)$

Example 1 -- Test the null hypothesis H_o: $\mu = 22.5$ ($= \mu_o$), against the alternative hypothesis, H_1: $\mu \neq 22.5$, at a level of confidence of 95% i.e., $\alpha = 0.05$, using a sample of size n = 25 with a mean $\bar{x} = 22.0$ and a standard deviation s = 3.5. We assume that we don't know the value of the population standard deviation, therefore, we calculate a t statistic as follows:

$$t_o = \frac{\bar{x} - \mu_o}{s / \sqrt{n}} = \frac{22.0 - 22.5}{3.5 / \sqrt{25}} = -0.7142$$

The corresponding P-value, for n = 25 - 1 = 24 degrees of freedom is

$$\text{P-value} = 2 \cdot \text{UTPT}(24, -0.7142) = 2 \cdot 0.7590 = 1.5169,$$

since 1.5169 > 0.05, i.e., P-value > α, we cannot reject the null hypothesis H_o: $\mu = 22.0$.

One-sided hypothesis

The problem consists in testing the null hypothesis H_o: $\mu = \mu_o$, against the alternative hypothesis, H_1: $\mu > \mu_o$ or H_1: $\mu < \mu_o$ at a level of confidence $(1-\alpha)100\%$, or significance level α, using a sample of size n with a mean $\bar{x}$ and a standard deviation s. This test is referred to as a *one-sided* or *one-tailed* test. The procedure for performing a one-side test starts as in the two-tailed test by calculating the appropriate statistic for the test (t_o or z_o) as indicated above.

Next, we use the P-value associated with either z_o or t_o, and compare it to α to decide whether or not to reject the null hypothesis. The P-value for a two-sided test is defined as either

$$\text{P-value} = P(z > |z_o|), \text{ or, } \text{P-value} = P(t > |t_o|).$$

The criteria to use for hypothesis testing is:

- Reject H_o if P-value $< \alpha$
- Do not reject H_o if P-value $> \alpha$.

332

Notice that the criteria are exactly the same as in the two-sided test. The main difference is the way that the P-value is calculated. The P-value for a one-sided test can be calculated using the probability functions in the HP48G/GX as follows:

- If using z,   P-value = UTPN(0,1,z_o)
- If using t,   P-value = UTPT(v,t_o)

Example 2 -- Test the null hypothesis H_o: μ = 22.0 (= μ_o), against the alternative hypothesis, H_1: μ >22.5 at a level of confidence of 95% i.e., α = 0.05, using a sample of size n = 25 with a mean $\bar{x}$ = 22.0 and a standard deviation s = 3.5. Again, we assume that we don't know the value of the population standard deviation, therefore, the value of the t statistic is the same as in the two-sided test case shown above, i.e., t_o = -0.7142, and P-value, for v = 25 - 1 = 24 degrees of freedom is

$$\text{P-value} = \text{UTPT}(24, |-0.7142|) = \text{UTPT}(24, 0.7124) = 0.2409,$$

since 0.2409 > 0.05, i.e., P-value > α, we cannot reject the null hypothesis H_o: μ = 22.0.

Inferences concerning two means

The null hypothesis to be tested is H_o: μ_1-μ_2 = δ, at a level of confidence (1-α)100%, or significance level α, using two samples of sizes, n_1 and n_2, mean values $\bar{x}_1$ and $\bar{x}_2$, and standard deviations s_1 and s_2. If the populations standard deviations corresponding to the samples, σ_1 and σ_2, are known, or if n_1 > 30 and n_2 > 30 (large samples), the test statistic to be used is

$$z_o = \frac{(\bar{x}_1 - \bar{x}_2) - \delta}{\sqrt{\dfrac{\sigma_1^2}{n_1} + \dfrac{\sigma_2^2}{n_2}}}$$

If n_1 < 30 or n_2 < 30 (at least one small sample), use the following test statistic:

$$t = \frac{(\bar{x}_1 - \bar{x}_2) - \delta}{\sqrt{(n_1 -1)s_1^2 + (n_2 -1)s_2^2}} \sqrt{\frac{n_1 n_2 (n_1 + n_2 - 2)}{n_1 + n_2}}$$

Two-sided hypothesis

If the alternative hypothesis is a two-sided hypothesis, i.e., H_1: μ_1-μ_2 ≠ δ, The P-value for this test is calculated as

- If using z,   P-value = 2·UTPN(0,1, $|z_o|$)
- If using t,   P-value = 2·UTPT($v, |t_o|$)

with the degrees of freedom for the t-distribution given by v = n_1 + n_2 - 2.
The test criteria are

333

- Reject H_o if P-value $< \alpha$
- Do not reject H_o if P-value $> \alpha$.

One-sided hypothesis

If the alternative hypothesis is a two-sided hypothesis, i.e., H_1: $\mu_1 - \mu_2 < \delta$, or, H_1: $\mu_1 - \mu_2 < \delta$,, the P-value for this test is calculated as:

- If using z, P-value = UTPN(0,1, $|z_o|$)
- If using t, P-value = UTPT(v, $|t_o|$)

The criteria to use for hypothesis testing is:

- Reject H_o if P-value $< \alpha$
- Do not reject H_o if P-value $> \alpha$.

Paired sample tests

When we deal with two samples of size n with paired data points, instead of testing the null hypothesis, H_o: $\mu_1 - \mu_2 = \delta$, using the mean values and standard deviations of the two samples, we need to treat the problem as a single sample of the differences of the paired values. In other words, generate a new random variable $X = X_1 - X_2$, and test H_o: $\mu = \delta$, where μ represents the mean of the population for X. Therefore, you will need to obtain $\bar{x}$ and s for the sample of values of x. The test should then proceed as a one-sample test using the methods described earlier.

Inferences concerning one proportion

Suppose that we want to test the null hypothesis, H_o: $p = p_0$, where p represents the probability of obtaining a successful outcome in any given repetition of a Bernoulli trial. To test the hypothesis, we perform n repetitions of the experiment, and find that k successful outcomes are recorded. Thus, an estimate of p is given by
$$p' = k/n.$$

The variance for the sample will be estimated as

$$s_p^2 = p'(1-p')/n = k \cdot (n-k)/n^3.$$

Assume that the Z score, $Z = (p - p_0)/s_p$, follows the standard normal distribution, i.e., $Z \sim N(0,1)$. The particular value of the statistic to test is $z_0 = (p' - p_0)/s_p$.

Instead of using the P-value as a criterion to accept or not accept the hypothesis, we will use the comparison between the critical value of z0 and the value of z corresponding to α or $\alpha/2$.

Two-tailed test

If using a two-tailed test we will find the value of $z_{\alpha/2}$, from

$$Pr[Z > z_{\alpha/2}] = 1 - \Phi(z_{\alpha/2}) = \alpha/2, \text{ or } \Phi(z_{\alpha/2}) = 1 - \alpha/2,$$

334

where $\Phi(z)$ is the cumulative distribution function (CDF) of the standard normal distribution.

Reject the null hypothesis, H_0, if $z_0 > z_{\alpha/2}$, or if $z_0 < -z_{\alpha/2}$.

In other words, the rejection region is R = { $|z_0| > z_{\alpha/2}$ }, while the acceptance region is A = { $|z_0| < z_{\alpha/2}$ }.

One-tailed test

If using a one-tailed test we will find the value of S , from

$$Pr[Z > z_\alpha] = 1 - \Phi(z_\alpha) = \alpha, \text{ or } \Phi(z_\alpha) = 1 - \alpha,$$

Reject the null hypothesis, H_0, if $z_0 > z_\alpha$, and H_1: $p > p_0$, or if $z_0 < -z_\alpha$, and H_1: $p < p_0$.

Testing the difference between two proportions

Suppose that we want to test the null hypothesis, H_0: $p_1 - p_2 = p_0$, where the p's represents the probability of obtaining a successful outcome in any given repetition of a Bernoulli trial for two populations 1 and 2. To test the hypothesis, we perform n_1 repetitions of the experiment from population 1, and find that k_1 successful outcomes are recorded. Also, we find k_2 successful outcomes out of n_2 trials in sample 2. Thus, estimates of p_1 and p_2 are given, respectively, by

$$p_1' = k_1/n_1, \text{ and } p_2' = k_2/n_2.$$

The variances for the samples will be estimated, respectively, as

$$s_1^2 = p_1'(1-p_1')/n_1 = k_1 \cdot (n_1-k_1)/n_1^3, \text{ and } s_2^2 = p_2'(1-p_2')/n_2 = k_2 \cdot (n_2-k_2)/n_2^3.$$

And the variance of the difference of proportions is estimated from:

$$s_p^2 = s_1^2 + s_2^2.$$

Assume that the Z score, $Z = (p_1-p_2-p_0)/s_p$, follows the standard normal distribution, i.e., $Z \sim N(0,1)$. The particular value of the statistic to test is $z_0 = (p_1'-p_2'-p_0)/s_p$.

Two-tailed test

If using a two-tailed test we will find the value of $z_{\alpha/2}$, from

$$Pr[Z > z_{\alpha/2}] = 1 - \Phi(z_{\alpha/2}) = \alpha/2, \text{ or } \Phi(z_{\alpha/2}) = 1 - \alpha/2,$$

where $\Phi(z)$ is the cumulative distribution function (CDF) of the standard normal distribution.

Reject the null hypothesis, H_0, if $z_0 > z_{\alpha/2}$, or if $z_0 < -z_{\alpha/2}$.

In other words, the rejection region is R = { $|z_0| > z_{\alpha/2}$ }, while the acceptance region is A = { $|z_0| < z_{\alpha/2}$ }.

<u>One-tailed test</u>

If using a one-tailed test we will find the value of z_a, from

$$\Pr[Z > z_\alpha] = 1 - \Phi(z_\alpha) = \alpha, \quad \text{or } \Phi(z_\alpha) = 1 - \alpha,$$

Reject the null hypothesis, H_0, if $z_0 > z_\alpha$, and H_1: $p_1\text{-}p_2 > p_0$, or if $z_0 < -z_\alpha$, and H_1: $p_1\text{-}p_2 < p_0$.

Hypothesis testing using pre-programmed features

The HP 49 G calculator provides with hypothesis testing procedures under program **6. Conf Interval** can be accessed by using [→][STAT][▲][▲][OK].

As with the calculation of confidence intervals, discussed earlier, this program offers the following 6 options:

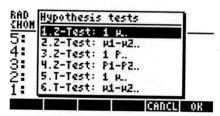

These options are interpreted as in the confidence interval applications:

1. Z-Test: 1 μ.: Single sample hypothesis testing for the population mean, μ, with known population variance, or for large samples with unknown population variance.
2. Z-Test: $\mu 1\text{-}\mu 2$.: Hypothesis testing for the difference of the population means, $\mu_1\text{-}\mu_2$, with either known population variances, or for large samples with unknown population variances.
3. Z-Test: 1 p.: Single sample hypothesis testing for the proportion, p, for large samples with unknown population variance.
4. Z-Test: p1– p2.: Hypothesis testing for the difference of two proportions, $p_1\text{-}p_2$, for large samples with unknown population variances.
5. T-Test: 1 μ.: Single sample hypothesis testing for the population mean, μ, for small samples with unknown population variance.
6. T-Test: $\mu 1\text{-}\mu 2$.: Hypothesis testing for the difference of the population means, $\mu_1\text{-}\mu_2$, for small samples with unknown population variances.

Try the following exercises:

<u>*Example 1*</u> - For $\mu_0 = 150$, $\sigma = 10$, $\bar{x} = 158$, n = 50, for $\alpha = 0.05$, test the hypothesis H_0: $\mu = \mu_0$, against the alternative hypothesis, H_1: $\mu \neq \mu_0$.

Press [→][STAT][▲][▲][OK] to access the confidence interval feature in the calculator. Press [OK] to select option 1. Z-Test: 1 μ.

Enter the following data and press [OK]:

You are then asked to select the alternative hypothesis:

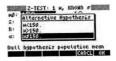

Select $\mu \neq 150$. Then, press [OK]. The result is:

Then, we reject H_0: $\mu = 150$, against H_1: $\mu \neq 150$. The test z value is $z_0 = 5.656854$. The P-value is 1.54×10^{-8}. The critical values of $\pm z_{\alpha/2} = \pm 1.959964$, corresponding to critical $\bar{x}$ range of $\{147.2 \ 152.8\}$.

This information can be observed graphically by pressing the soft-menu key [GRAPH]:

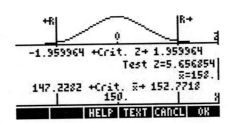

Example 2 -- For $\mu_0 = 150$, $\bar{x} = 158$, $s = 10$, $n = 50$, for $\alpha = 0.05$, test the hypothesis H_0: $\mu = \mu_0$, against the alternative hypothesis, H_1: $\mu > \mu_0$. The population standard deviation, σ, is not known.

Press [→][STAT][▲][▲][OK] to access the confidence interval feature in the calculator. Press [OK] [▲][▲] to select option 5. T-Test: 1 μ.:

337

Enter the following data and press [OK]:

Select the alternative hypothesis, H_1: $\mu > 150$, and press [OK]. The result is:

We reject the null hypothesis, H_0: $\mu_0 = 150$, against the alternative hypothesis, H_1: $\mu > 150$. The test t value is $t_0 = 5.656854$, with a P-value = 0.000000393525. The critical value of t is t_α = 1.676551, corresponding to a critical $\bar{x} = 152.371$.

Press [GRAPH] to see the results graphically as follows:

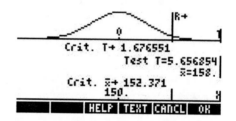

Example 3 – Data from two samples show that $\bar{x}_1 = 158$, $\bar{x}_1 = 160$, $s_1 = 10$, $s_2 = 4.5$, $n1 = 50$, and $n_2 = 55$. For $\alpha = 0.05$, and a "pooled" variance, test the hypothesis H_0: $\mu_1 - \mu_2 = 0$, against the alternative hypothesis, H_1: $\mu_1 - \mu_2 < 0$.

Press [→][STAT][▲][▲][OK] to access the confidence interval feature in the calculator. Press [OK] [▲] to select option 5. T-Test: $\mu_1 - \mu_2$.: Enter the following data and press [OK]:

Select the alternative hypothesis $\mu_1 < \mu_2$, and press [OK]. The result is:

338

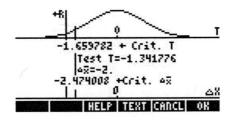

Thus, we accept (more accurately, we do not reject) the hypothesis: H_0: $\mu_1-\mu_2 = 0$, or H_0: $\mu_1=\mu_2$, against the alternative hypothesis H_1: $\mu_1-\mu_2 < 0$, or H_1: $\mu_1\neq\mu_2$. The test t value is $t_0 = -1.341776$, with a P-value = 0.09130961, and critical t is $-t_\alpha = -.1659782$.

The graphical results are:

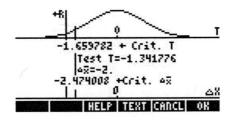

These three examples should be enough to understand the operation of the hypothesis testing pre-programmed feature in the calculator.

Inferences concerning one variance

The null hypothesis to be tested is , H_0: $\sigma^2 = \sigma_0^2$, at a level of confidence $(1-\alpha)100\%$, or significance level α, using a sample of size n, and variance s^2. The test statistic to be used is a chi-squared test statistic defined as

$$\chi_o^2 = \frac{(n-1)s^2}{\sigma_0^2}$$

Depending on the alternative hypothesis chosen, the P-value is calculated as follows:

- H_1: $\sigma^2 < \sigma_0^2$,   P-value = $P(\chi^2<\chi_o^2)$ = 1-UTPC(v,χ_o^2)
- H_1: $\sigma^2 > \sigma_0^2$,   P-value = $P(\chi^2>\chi_o^2)$ = UTPC(v,χ_o^2)
- H_1: $\sigma^2 \neq \sigma_0^2$,   P-value =2·min[$P(\chi^2<\chi_o^2)$, $P(\chi^2>\chi_o^2)$] = 2·min[1-UTPC(v,χ_o^2), UTPC(v,χ_o^2)]

where the function min[x,y] produces the minimum value of x or y (similarly, max[x,y] produces the maximum value of x or y). UTPC(v,x) represents the HP48G/GX upper-tail probabilities for v = n - 1 degrees of freedom.
The test criteria are the same as in hypothesis testing of means, namely,

- Reject H_0 if P-value < α
- Do not reject H_0 if P-value > α.

339

Please notice that this procedure is valid only if the population from which the sample was taken is a Normal population. In order to check for normality of data, you can use the procedure outlined in section 5.11 in your Textbook, or use the CHKN sub-directory described in section 12 of Part II of this guide.

Example 1 -- Consider the case in which $\sigma_0^2 = 25$, $\alpha=0.05$, n = 25, and $s^2 = 20$, and the sample was drawn from a normal population. To test the hypothesis, H_0: $\sigma^2 = \sigma_0^2$, against H_1: $\sigma^2 < \sigma_0^2$, we first calculate

$$\chi_o^2 = \frac{(n-1)s^2}{\sigma_0^2} = \frac{(25-1)\cdot 20}{25} = 189.2$$

With $v = n - 1 = 25 - 1 = 24$ degrees of freedom, we calculate the P-value as,

$$\text{P-value} = P(\chi^2 < 19.2) = 1 - \text{UTPC}(24, 19.2) = 0.2587...$$

Since, 0.2587... > 0.05, i.e., P-value > α, we cannot reject the null hypothesis, H_0: $\sigma^2 = 25 (= \sigma_0^2)$.

Inferences concerning two variances

The null hypothesis to be tested is , H_0: $\sigma_1^2 = \sigma_2^2$, at a level of confidence $(1-\alpha)100\%$, or significance level α, using two samples of sizes, n_1 and n_2, and variances s_1^2 and s_2^2. The test statistic to be used is an F test statistic defined as

$$F_o = \frac{s_N^2}{s_D^2}$$

where s_N^2 and s_D^2 represent the numerator and denominator of the F statistic, respectively. Selection of the numerator and denominator depends on the alternative hypothesis being tested, as shown below. The corresponding F distribution has degrees of freedom, $v_N = n_N-1$, and $v_D = n_D-1$, where n_N and n_D, are the sample sizes corresponding to the variances s_N^2 and s_D^2, respectively.

The following table shows how to select the numerator and denominator for F_o depending on the alternative hypothesis chosen:

Alternative hypothesis	Test statistic	Degrees of freedom
H_1: $\sigma_1^2 < \sigma_2^2$ (one-sided)	$F_o = s_2^2/s_1^2$	$v_N = n_2-1$, $v_D = n_1-1$
H_1: $\sigma_1^2 > \sigma_2^2$ (one-sided)	$F_o = s_1^2/s_2^2$	$v_N = n_1-1$, $v_D = n_2-1$
H_1: $\sigma_1^2 \neq \sigma_2^2$ (two-sided)	$F_o = s_M^2/s_m^2$	$v_N = n_M-1, v_D = n_m-1$ (*)
	$s_M^2 = \max(s_1^2, s_2^2)$, $s_m^2 = \min(s_1^2, s_2^2)$	

(*) n_M is the value of n corresponding to the s_M, and n_m is the value of n corresponding to s_m.

The P-value is calculated, in all cases, as: $\quad\quad$ P-value = $P(F > F_o) = \text{UTPF}(v_N, v_D, F_o)$

The test criteria are:

- Reject H_o if P-value $< \alpha$
- Do not reject H_o if P-value $> \alpha$.

Example1 -- Consider two samples drawn from normal populations such that $n_1 = 21$, $n_2 = 31$, s_1^2 = 0.36, and s_2^2 = 0.25. We test the null hypothesis, H_o: $\sigma_1^2 = \sigma_2^2$, at a significance level α = 0.05, against the alternative hypothesis, H_1: $\sigma_1^2 \neq \sigma_2^2$. For a two-sided hypothesis, we need to identify s_M and s_m, as follows:

$$s_M^2 = \max(s_1^2, s_2^2) = \max(0.36, 0.25) = 0.36 = s_1^2$$

$$s_m^2 = \min(s_1^2, s_2^2) = \max(0.36, 0.25) = 0.25 = s_2^2$$

Also,

$$n_M = n_1 = 21,$$

$$n_m = n_2 = 31,$$

$$\nu_N = n_M - 1 = 21-1 = 20,$$

$$\nu_D = n_m - 1 = 31-1 = 30.$$

Therefore, the F test statistics is

$$F_o = s_M^2 / s_m^2 = 0.36/0.25 = 1.44$$

The P-value is

$$\text{P-value} = P(F > F_o) = P(F > 1.44) = UTPF(\nu_N, \nu_D, F_o) = UTPF(20, 30, 1.44) = 0.1788\ldots$$

Since $0.1788\ldots > 0.05$, i.e., P-value $> \alpha$, therefore, we cannot reject the null hypothesis that H_o: $\sigma_1^2 = \sigma_2^2$.

Additional notes on linear regression

The method of least squares

Let x = independent, non-random variable, and Y = dependent, random variable. The **regression curve** of Y on x is defined *as the relationship between x and the mean of the corresponding distribution of the Y's*.

Assume that the regression curve of Y on x is linear, i.e., mean distribution of Y's is given by A + Bx.

Y differs from the mean (A + B·x) by a value ε, thus

$$Y = A + B \cdot x + \varepsilon,$$

where ε is a random variable.

To visually check whether the data follows a linear trend, draw a *scattergram* or *scatter plot*.

Suppose that we have *n* paired observations (x_i, y_i); we predict y by means of

$$\hat{y} = a + b \cdot x,$$

where a and b are constant.

Define the *prediction error* as,

$$e_i = y_i - \hat{y}_i = y_i - (a + b \cdot x_i).$$

The method of least squares requires us to choose a, b so as to minimize the *sum of squared errors* (SSE)

$$SSE = \sum_{i=1}^{n} e_i^2 = \sum_{i=1}^{n} [y_i - (a + bx_i)]^2$$

the conditions

$$\frac{\partial}{\partial a}(SSE) = 0 \qquad \frac{\partial}{\partial b}(SSE) = 0$$

We get the, so-called, *normal equations*:

$$\sum_{i=1}^{n} y_i = a \cdot n + b \cdot \sum_{i=1}^{n} x_i$$

$$\sum_{i=1}^{n} x_i \cdot y_i = a \cdot \sum_{i=1}^{n} x_i + b \cdot \sum_{i=1}^{n} x_i^2$$

This is a system of linear equations with a and b as the unknowns, which can be solved using the linear equation features of the calculator. There is, however, no need to bother with these calculations because you can use the **3. Fit Data ...** option in the [→][STAT] menu as presented earlier.

342

Notes:

- a,b are unbiased estimators of A, B.
- The Gauss-Markov theorem indicates that among all unbiased estimators for A and B, the least-square estimators (a,b) are the most efficient.

Additional equations for linear regression

The summary statistics such as Σx, Σx^2, etc., can be used to define the following quantities:

$$S_{xx} = \sum_{i=1}^{n}(x_i - \overline{x})^2 = (n-1)\cdot s_x^2 = \sum_{i=1}^{n}x_i^2 - \frac{1}{n}\left(\sum_{i=1}^{n}x_i\right)^2$$

$$S_y = \sum_{i=1}^{n}(y_i - \overline{y})^2 = (n-1)\cdot s_y^2 = \sum_{i=1}^{n}y_i^2 - \frac{1}{n}\left(\sum_{i=1}^{n}y_i\right)^2$$

$$S_{xy} = \sum_{i=1}^{n}(x_i - \overline{x})(y_i - \overline{y})^2 = (n-1)\cdot s_{xy} = \sum_{i=1}^{n}x_i y_i - \frac{1}{n}\left(\sum_{i=1}^{n}x_i\right)\left(\sum_{i=1}^{n}y_i\right)$$

From which it follows that the *standard deviations* of x and y, and the *covariance* of x,y are given, respectively, by

$$s_x = \sqrt{\frac{S_{xx}}{n-1}} \qquad s_y = \sqrt{\frac{S_{yy}}{n-1}} \qquad s_{xy} = \frac{S_{yx}}{n-1}$$

Also, the *sample correlation coefficient* is

$$r_{xy} = \frac{S_{xy}}{\sqrt{S_{xx}\cdot S_{yy}}}.$$

In terms of $\overline{x}$, $\overline{y}$, S_{xx}, S_{yy}, and S_{xy}, the solution to the normal equations is:

$$a = \overline{y} - b\overline{x} \qquad\qquad b = \frac{S_{xy}}{S_{xx}} = \frac{s_{xy}}{s_x^2}$$

343

Prediction error

The regression curve of Y on x is defined as $Y = A + B \cdot x + \varepsilon$. If we have a set of n data points (x_i, y_i), then we can write

$$Y_i = A + B \cdot x_i + \varepsilon_i. \qquad (i = 1, 2, ..., n)$$

Where Y_i = independent, normally distributed random variables with mean $(A + B \cdot x_i)$ and the common variance σ^2; ε_i = independent, normally distributed random variables with mean zero and the common variance σ^2.

Let y_i = actual data value, $\hat{y}_i = a + bx_i$ = least-square prediction of the data. Then, the *prediction error* is:

$$e_i = y_i - \hat{y}_i = y_i - (a + b \cdot x_i).$$

An estimate of σ^2 is the, so-called, *standard error of the estimate*,

$$s_e^2 = \frac{1}{n-2}\sum[y_i - (a + bx_i)]^2 = \frac{S_{yy} - (S_{xy})^2/S_{xx}}{n-2} = \frac{n-1}{n-2}\cdot s_y^2 \cdot (1 - r_{xy}^2)$$

Confidence intervals and hypothesis testing in linear regression

Here are some concepts and equations related to statistical inference for linear regression:

- *Confidence limits for regression coefficients*:

    For the slope (B):
    $$b - (t_{n-2,\alpha/2}) \cdot s_e / \sqrt{S_{xx}} < B < b + (t_{n-2,\alpha/2}) \cdot s_e / \sqrt{S_{xx}},$$

    For the intercept (A):
    $$a - (t_{n-2,\alpha/2}) \cdot s_e \cdot [(1/n) + \bar{x}^2/S_{xx}]^{1/2} < A < a + (t_{n-2,\alpha/2}) \cdot s_e \cdot [(1/n) + \bar{x}^2/S_{xx}]^{1/2},$$

    where t follows the Student's t distribution with $v = n - 2$, degrees of freedom, and n represents the number of points in the sample.

- *Hypothesis testing on the slope, B*:

    Null hypothesis, H_0: $B = B_0$, tested against the alternative hypothesis, H_1: $B \neq B_0$. The test statistic is

    $$t_0 = (b - B_0)/(s_e/\sqrt{S_{xx}}),$$

    where t follows the Student's t distribution with $v = n - 2$, degrees of freedom, and n represents the number of points in the sample. The test is carried out as that of a mean value hypothesis testing, i.e., given the level of significance, α, determine the critical value of t, $t_{\alpha/2}$, then, reject H_0 if $t_0 > t_{\alpha/2}$ or if $t_0 < - t_{\alpha/2}$.

344

If you test for the value $B_0 = 0$, and it turns out that the test suggests that you do not reject the null hypothesis, H_0: B = 0, then, the validity of a linear regression is in doubt. In other words, the sample data does not support the assertion that B ≠ 0. Therefore, this is a test of the *significance of the regression model.*

- *Hypothesis testing on the intercept , A:*

  Null hypothesis, H_0: A = A_0, tested against the alternative hypothesis, H_1: A ≠ A_0. The test statistic is

  $$t_0 = (a-A_0)/[(1/n)+ \bar{x}^2/S_{xx}]^{1/2},$$

  where t follows the Student's t distribution with ν = n − 2, degrees of freedom, and n represents the number of points in the sample. The test is carried out as that of a mean value hypothesis testing, i.e., given the level of significance, α, determine the critical value of t, $t_{\alpha/2}$, then, reject H_0 if $t_0 > t_{\alpha/2}$ or if $t_0 < - t_{\alpha/2}$.

- *Confidence interval for the mean value of Y at x = x_0, i.e., $\alpha + \beta x_0$:*

  $$a+b \cdot x-(t_{n-2,\alpha/2}) \cdot s_e \cdot [(1/n)+(x_0- \bar{x})^2/S_{xx}]^{1/2} < \alpha+\beta x_0 < a+b \cdot x+(t_{n-2,\alpha/2}) \cdot s_e \cdot [(1/n)+(x_0- \bar{x})^2/S_{xx}]^{1/2}.$$

- *Limits of prediction: confidence interval for the predicted value $Y_0 = Y(x_0)$:*

  $$a+b \cdot x-(t_{n-2,\alpha/2}) \cdot s_e \cdot [1+(1/n)+(x_0- \bar{x})^2/S_{xx}]^{1/2} < Y_0 < a+b \cdot x+(t_{n-2,\alpha/2}) \cdot s_e \cdot [1+(1/n)+(x_0- \bar{x})^2/S_{xx}]^{1/2}.$$

Procedure for inference statistics for linear regression using the calculator

1) Enter (x,y) as columns of data in the statistical matrix ΣDAT.

2) Produce a scatterplot for the appropriate columns of ΣDAT, and use appropriate H- and V-VIEWS to check linear trend. Press [CANCL][ENTER] to return to normal display.

3) [↱][STAT][▼][▼][OK], to fit straight line, and get a, b, s_{xy} (Covariance), and r_{xy} (Correlation).

4) [↰][STAT][1VAR][MEAN][SDEV] to obtain $\bar{x}$, $\bar{y}$, s_x, s_y.

5) Calculate

   $$S_{xx} = (n-1) \cdot s_x^2 \qquad\qquad s_e^2 = \frac{n-1}{n-2} \cdot s_y^2 \cdot (1-r_{xy}^2)$$

6) For either confidence intervals or two-tailed tests, obtain $t_{\alpha/2}$, with (1- α)100% confidence, from t-distribution with ν = n -2.

345

7) For one- or two-tailed tests, find the value of t using the appropriate equation for either A or B. Reject the null hypothesis if P-value < α.

8) For confidence intervals use the appropriate formulas as shown above.

Example 1 -- For the following (x,y) data, determine the 95% confidence interval for the slope B and the intercept A

x	2.0	2.5	3.0	3.5	4.0
y	5.5	7.2	9.4	10.0	12.2

Enter the (x,y) data in columns 1 and 2 of ΣDAT, respectively. A scatterplot of the data shows a good linear trend:

Use the Fit Data.. option in the [→][STAT] menu, to get:

```
3: '-.86 + 3.24*X'
2: Correlation: 0.989720229749
1: Covariance: 2.025
```

These results are interpreted as a = -0.86, b = 3.24, r_{xy} = 0.989720229749, and s_{xy} = 2.025. The correlation coefficient is close enough to 1.0 to confirm the linear trend observed in the graph.

From the Single-var… option of the [→][STAT] menu we find: $\bar{x}$ = 3, s_x = 0.790569415042, $\bar{y}$ = 8.86, s_y = 2.58804945857.

Next, with n = 5, calculate

$$S_{xx} = (n-1) \cdot s_x^2 = (5-1) \cdot 0.790569415042^2 = 2.5$$

$$s_e^2 = \frac{n-1}{n-2} \cdot s_y^2 \cdot (1 - r_{xy}^2) = \frac{5-1}{5-2} \cdot 2.5880494585 \; 7^2 \cdot (1 - 0.9897202297 \; 49^2) = 0.1826666666 \; 67.$$

Confidence intervals for the slope (B) and intercept (A):

- First, we obtain $t_{n-2,\alpha/2} = t_{3,0.025} = 3.18244630528$ (See chapter 12 for a program to solve for $t_{v,a}$):

- Next, we calculate the terms

    $(t_{n-2,\alpha/2}) \cdot s_e / \sqrt{S_{xx}}$ = 3.18244630528·(0.18266666667/2.5)$^{1/2}$ = 0.860242178182

    $(t_{n-2,\alpha/2}) \cdot s_e \cdot [(1/n) + \bar{x}^2/S_{xx}]^{1/2}$ = 3.18244630528·$\sqrt{0.18266666667}$·[(1/5)+3^2/2.5]$^{1/2}$ = 2.65

- Finally, for the slope B, the 95% confidence interval is

346

(-0.86-0.860242, -0.86+0.860242) = (-1.72, -0.00024217)

For the intercept A, the 95% confidence interval is (3.24-2.6514, 3.24+2.6514) = (0.58855,5.8914).

Example 2 -- Suppose that the y-data used in Example 1 represent the elongation (in hundredths of an inch) of a metal wire when subjected to a force x (in tens of pounds). The physical phenomenon is such that we expect the intercept, A, to be zero. To check if that should be the case, we test the null hypothesis, H_0: A = 0, against the alternative hypothesis, H_1: A ≠ 0, at the level of significance α = 0.05.

The test statistic is

$$t_0 = (a-0)/[(1/n)+ \bar{x}^2/S_{xx}]^{1/2} = (-0.86)/ [(1/5)+3^2/2.5]^{1/2} = -0.44117$$

The critical value of t, for ν = n – 2 = 3, and α/2 = 0.025, can be calculated using the numerical solver for the program EQT, whose contents are: << γ t UTPT α - >>. In this program, γ represents the degrees of freedom (n-2), and α represents the probability of exceeding a certain value of t, i.e.,

$$Pr[t>t_\alpha] = 1 - \alpha.$$

The contents of EQT can be copied into variable EQ , and the HP 49 G numerical solver used to solve for t given the probability of exceedence, α. For the present example, the value of the level of significance is α = 0.05. To obtain the value $t_{n-2,\alpha/2} = t_{3,0.025}$, we use the following:

[VAR][EQT] 'EQ' [STO] [→][NUM.SLV][OK]

Enter the values γ = 3 and α = 0.025 in the input form. Highlight the field for x, and press [SOLVE]. The result is shown in the screen below:

Thus,

$$t_{n-2,\alpha/2} = t_{3,0.025} = 3.18244630528.$$

Because $t_0 > - t_{n-2,\alpha/2}$, we cannot reject the null hypothesis, H_0: A = 0, against the alternative hypothesis, H_1: A ≠ 0, at the level of significance α = 0.05.

This result suggests that taking A = 0 for this linear regression should be acceptable. After all, the value we found for a, was -0.86, which is relatively close to zero.

Example 3 - Test of significance for the linear regression. Test the null hypothesis for the slope H_0: B = 0, against the alternative hypothesis, H_1: B ≠ 0, at the level of significance α = 0.05, for the linear fitting of Example 1.

The test statistic is

$$t_0 = (b - B_0)/(s_e/\sqrt{S_{xx}}) = (3.24-0)/(\sqrt{0.18266666667/2.5}) = 18.95$$

The critical value of t, for $v = n - 2 = 3$, and $\alpha/2 = 0.025$, was obtained in Example 2, as $t_{n-2,\alpha/2}$ = $t_{3,0.025}$ = 3.18244630528.

Because, $t_0 > t_{\alpha/2}$, we must reject the null hypothesis H_1: $B \neq 0$, at the level of significance $\alpha = 0.05$, for the linear fitting of Example 1.

Note: The exercises presented in this chapter are a few of the statistical operations that can be performed in the HP 49 G calculator. I have included here only those operations that relate to those already programmed in the calculator. The number of statistical applications that can be developed for the HP 49 G is larger than presented here, but it would require a separate volume to present them all. Many of the calculations presented in this chapter can be programmed in User RPL language for high-volume calculations.

348

REFERENCES – Vol. I only

Devlin, Keith, 1998, "The Language of Mathematics," W.H. Freeman and Company, New York.

Heath, M. T., 1997, "Scientific Computing: An Introductory Survey," WCB McGraw-Hill, Boston, Mass.

Newland, D.E., 1993, "An Introduction to Random Vibrations, Spectral & Wavelet Analysis – Third Edition," Longman Scientific and Technical, New York.

Tinker, M. and R. Lambourne, 2000, "Further Mathematics for the Physical Sciences," John Wiley & Sons, LTD., Chichester, U.K.

REFERENCES – Vol. II only

Farlow, Stanley J., 1982, "Partial Differential Equations for Scientists and Engineers," Dover Publications Inc., New York.

Friedman, B., 1956, "Principles and Techniques of Applied Mathematics," (reissued 1990), Dover Publications Inc., New York.

Kottegoda, N. T., and R. Rosso, 1997, "Probability, Statistics, and Reliability for Civil and Environmental Engineers," The Mc-Graw Hill Companies, Inc., New York.

Kreysig, E., 1983, "Advanced Engineering Mathematics – Fifth Edition," John Wiley & Sons, New York.

REFERENCES – For both Vols. I and II

Gullberg, J., 1997, "Mathematics – From the Birth of Numbers," W. W. Norton & Company, New York.

Harris, J.W., and H. Stocker, 1998, "Handbook of Mathematics and Computational Science," Springer, New York.

Hewlett Packard Co., 1999, HP 49 G GRAPHING CALCULATOR USER'S GUIDE.

Hewlett Packard Co., 2000, HP 49 G GRAPHING CALCULATOR ADVANCED USER'S GUIDE

Index

No index available for this volume.   The Table of Contents, at the beginning of the book, contains enough information to facilitate finding any subject to interest.

ABOUT THE AUTHOR

Gilberto E. Urroz is an Associate Professor of Civil and Environmental Engineering and a researcher at the Utah Water Research Laboratory, both at Utah State University, in Logan, Utah. He has been a teacher of engineering disciplines for more than 15 years both in his native Nicaragua and in the United States.

His teaching experience includes courses on introductory physics, engineering mechanics, probability and statistics for engineers, computer programming, fluid mechanics, hydraulics, and numerical methods. His research interests include mathematical and numerical modeling of fluid systems, hydraulic structures, and erosion control applications.

Dr. Urroz is an expert on the HP 48 G and HP 49 G series calculator and has written several books on applications of these computing devices to disciplines such as engineering mechanics, hydraulics, and science and engineering mathematics. His personal interests include reading, music, opera, theater, and taijiquan.

ABOUT GREATUNPUBLISHED.COM